GDI+ Programming
in C# and VB .NET

NICK SYMMONDS

D1599661

Apress™

GDI+ Programming in C# and VB .NET
Copyright © 2002 by Nick Symmonds

ISBN (pbk): 1-59059-035-X

Printed and bound in the United States of America 12345678910

Trademarked names may appear in this book. Rather than use a trademark symbol with every occurrence of a trademarked name, we use the names only in an editorial fashion and to the benefit of the trademark owner, with no intention of infringement of the trademark.

Technical Reviewer: Adriano Baglioni

Editorial Directors: Dan Appleman, Peter Blackburn, Gary Cornell, Jason Gilmore, Karen Watterson, John Zukowski

Managing Editor: Grace Wong

Project Manager and Development Editor: Tracy Brown Collins

Copy Editor: Nicole LeClerc

Production Editor and Proofreader: Kari Brooks

Compositor: Susan Glinert Stevens

Artist and Cover Designer: Kurt Krames

Indexer: Valerie Perry

Manufacturing Manager: Tom Debolski

Marketing Manager: Stephanie Rodriguez

Distributed to the book trade in the United States by Springer-Verlag New York, Inc., 175 Fifth Avenue, New York, NY, 10010 and outside the United States by Springer-Verlag GmbH & Co. KG, Tiergartenstr. 17, 69112 Heidelberg, Germany.

In the United States, phone 1-800-SPRINGER, email orders@springer-ny.com, or visit http://www.springer-ny.com.

Outside the United States, fax +49 6221 345229, email orders@springer.de, or visit http://www.springer.de.

For information on translations, please contact Apress directly at 2560 9th Street, Suite 219, Berkeley, CA 94710. Phone 510-549-5930, fax: 510-549-5939, email info@apress.com, or visit http://www.apress.com.

The information in this book is distributed on an "as is" basis, without warranty. Although every precaution has been taken in the preparation of this work, neither the author nor Apress shall have any liability to any person or entity with respect to any loss or damage caused or alleged to be caused directly or indirectly by the information contained in this work.

The source code for this book is available to readers at http://www.apress.com in the Downloads section.

This book is dedicated to my parents, Ann and Barry Symmonds. Without their guidance and support, I could not have achieved the goals I have reached today. I want you both to know that all your efforts on my behalf are very much appreciated.

Contents at a Glance

Contents

About the Author

NICK SYMMONDS started out his professional life as an electronics technician. While getting his bachelor's degree in electrical engineering from the University of Hartford, he started to gravitate toward programming. Nick has spent quite a few years programming in assembly, C, C++, and VB. Recently, he has latched onto .NET like a lamprey and loves digging into the .NET core. Nick has written several articles on programming and has another book currently out called *Internationalization and Localization Using Microsoft .NET* (Apress, 2002). He works for the Security and Safety Solutions division of Ingersoll-Rand, developing and integrating security software. Nick lives with his family in the northwest hills of Connecticut and enjoys woodworking, biking, and exploring the hills on his motorcycle.

About the
Technical Reviewer

ADRIANO BAGLIONI got his first taste of computers as a freshman in high school, using BASIC on a PDP-11/70. He pursued his interest in computers at Rensselaer Polytechnic Institute (RPI), where he graduated with a bachelor's degree in computer and systems engineering. He followed that up with a master's degree in computer science, also from RPI. He has worked in the computer industry for 19 years, programming mostly in C and C++. His experience runs the gamut from embedded programming on 8051s to scientific programming on mainframes. He currently works at Veeder-Root Co., developing environmental monitoring equipment software. When it's time to take a break from the computer, he enjoys hiking, biking, and camping with his wife, Carol.

Acknowledgments

THIS IS MY SECOND BOOK on Visual Studio .NET. I would like to thank Tracy Brown Collins for being the project manager for this book as well as my last one. Her insights and patience with me over the course of writing this book have helped make the whole process enjoyable.

I want to thank Nicole LeClerc for her deft copyediting touch and for catching so many technical as well as grammatical errors. She has definitely improved my technical writing ability.

All technical books from Apress require a technical reviewer: a sort of test engineer, if you will. I want to thank Adriano Baglioni for agreeing to tackle that role for this book. Without his thoughtful and thorough reviews, this book would have contained some terrible hacks. Thanks for saving me from myself.

At the beginning of each chapter, I use quotes from the Bulwer-Lytton Fiction Contest. I want to thank Professor Scott Rice from San Jose State University for allowing me this pleasure.

I would like to thank Mary and Jerry Leblanc for giving me that first college course in electronics so long ago. There are many triggers in life that force a change in direction. This was one that helped *give* me a direction.

I started this book pretty much on the heels of finishing my last book for Apress. Without the support of my family, I could not have done that and still have kept my sanity. I'd like my wife, Celeste, and my kids, Kate, Ashley, Jared, and Alec, to know how just how much I appreciate their support and how much they all mean to me.

Introduction

*"It was a dark and stormy night and the rain fell in torrents—
except at occasional intervals, when it was checked by a violent
gust of wind which swept up the streets (for it is in London that our
scene lies), rattling along the housetops, and fiercely agitating the
scanty flame of the lamps that struggled against the darkness."*

—Edward George Bulwer-Lytton,
opening line to his 1830 novel, *Paul Clifford*[1]

WHAT IS GDI+? GDI is the *graphics device interface.* The plus sign in GDI+ means that it has been improved for the first release of .NET.

Traditionally, GDI programming was more like straight application programming interface (API) programming—not very object oriented. .NET was designed from the ground up to be fully object oriented. Graphics programming is such a big part of Windows programming in general that it needed to become object oriented. This is the plus in GDI+.

What Does This Book Cover?

Programming in GDI means that you will be programming graphics. Graphics can encompass such things as

- Drawing lines, curves, and so on

- Drawing shapes of all kinds

- Filling in shapes with colors, bitmaps, or hatching

- Working with bitmaps and other graphic images

- Drawing text

---

1. In 1982 the English department at San Jose State University started sponsoring the Bulwer-Lytton Fiction Contest, a literary competition that challenges entrants to compose the worst opening sentence to a novel that they can think of. You will find my favorites (some winners, some not) at the start of each chapter.

- Working with fonts

- Working with colors, gradients, blending, and brushes

- Manipulating images and text

- Working with Windows Forms

These topics and more are explained in this book. I go over the namespaces and the classes in those namespaces that pertain to GDI+ programming. I show you how GDI programming was done in C++ and also how graphics programming was done in Visual Basic (VB) 6.0. These examples are contrasted with the same examples in GDI+ using C# and VB .NET. The object-oriented aspects of GDI+ will then become clear.

Throughout this book, you will be exposed to all the classes and methods that encompass GDI+ programming. You will work with simple lines and graduate to creating more complex shapes and rendering text. You will also get comfortable with handling images in .NET. The Graphics object will become very important, as in the final chapters you will make a custom window control and a graphical compiler.

What Makes This Book Unique?

Traditionally, computer books on programming tend toward a particular language. This book differs from that tradition. The .NET Framework allows any Common Language Specification (CLS)–compliant language to run against the common language runtime (CLR). This is evident in the fact that Visual Studio .NET ships with four languages right out of the box: C#, VB .NET, JScript, and Managed Extensions for C++.

All the examples in this book are written in the two most popular .NET languages: C# and VB .NET. These two languages are fully CLS-compliant and were designed to take full advantage of the CLR. There are a few examples of C++ in this book as well. The C++ examples are necessary to illustrate the differences between GDI and GDI+.

This book is written in two parts: Theory and Application Notes. The first part is, as the name implies, all about the theory. Part One consists of the first eight chapters. Part Two is about applying the theory. While I have included numerous examples throughout the first eight chapters, Chapters 9 and 10 really bring everything together in a nice way.

Why Read This Book?

Microsoft has released a new programming paradigm called Visual Studio (VS) .NET. VS .NET has some major improvements for developing robust programs. Some of these improvements are as follows:

- Code is *managed,* which basically means garbage collection takes care of freeing any resources—including memory—that you forgot to free.

- Software created with .NET can be written in any language that complies with the CLS. This means that you can write a method in VB .NET that calls a property in a C# class.

- Remoting is no longer dependent upon COM. While COM is great in theory, there are a lot of problems with it. Objects are managed through garbage collection instead of reference counting.

- Localization capability is built in instead of an afterthought.

- Graphics programming has been greatly improved.

It is the last point that I address in this book. On your journey through the book's examples, you will also touch on some of the other points in the list. You will not only learn GDI+ programming, but you will also learn programming in .NET. Because the examples are presented in both C# and VB, you will get to see firsthand what some of the true differences between the languages are when you compare the C# code to the VB code.

Who Should Read This Book?

When I browse through the computer book aisles in my local bookstore, I often see many books on the same subject. They all seem to be about 2 feet thick and weigh about 20 pounds. The first thing I look at, of course, is the cover (I can tell a lot about a book by its cover). I then look at the back cover to see the level of complexity of the book. This is where I identify for whom the book is intended. I look for books that I can use, not just read. I look for books that I would dog-ear. You know the kinds of books that have the pages that say, "This page intentionally left blank"? I like to write notes all over those pages. This, I hope, is one of those books.

While this book is about .NET, it is not a primer. I will not explain loops, keywords, syntax, or how to program. This stuff is easy and you will remember it right away. No need to keep that kind of book around. In order for this book to be any kind of reference, it needs to have lots of examples, and not just silly ones either.

This book assumes a basic level of competence in VS .NET. To get the most out of this book, you need to feel comfortable with the following aspects of programming:

- Some C++, C#, VB .NET, or VB 6.0 programming experience

- Familiarity with object-oriented programming

- Familiarity with .NET namespaces and how they are used

- Familiarity with the VS .NET IDE

VS .NET has been out in various forms for some time now (how else do you explain the many VS .NET books in the bookstore only days after its release?). I am sure that you have received one of the ubiquitous .NET Beta 2 CDs. Perhaps you have even played with the release version. Whatever the case, if you are reading this book, you have probably already played around with .NET. If so, this book is for you.

As you turn to Chapter 1, you will enter into the world of a truly rich programming environment using the most universal of all languages: graphics.

A Note About the Examples

All the examples in this book are available for download from the Downloads section of the Apress Web site (http://www.apress.com). I encourage you to download the examples and run them as you need. Some examples use specific cursors or icons. If you download the code you will get these items as well.

Although I think it is best to type in as many of the examples as you can yourself, I realize that some of the examples are rather long. Typing them in can sometimes be tedious and lead to errors.

By the way, although this book and all the examples were reviewed extensively, I realize that some errors may get through. Because I am the original source for everything in this book, I take responsibility for any errors you may find and I would like to know about them. I welcome any comments and corrections. Please e-mail me at NickSymmonds@attbi.com.

Part One
Theory

HERE STARTS the first part of the book. First part, you say?

The book is essentially divided into two sections, the first part being theory and the second part being application.

You will get quite a bit of classroom time in Part One, which consists of Chapters 1 through 8. I lead you through all aspects of GDI+, from the simple drawing of lines to complex 2D graphics to image handling and beyond. These first eight chapters are laid out in order from easiest to most complex. Each succeeding chapter builds upon what you learned in previous chapters. By the time you have finished Part One, you should know how to work with all the constituent parts of the GDI+ library.

You will see a lot of code in Part One. Many examples are small, some as small as a few lines. Other examples, however, are longer. As the book progresses, the examples become more and more interactive and, I think, they represent some of the things you will do in the "real world."

Unlike some books, though, I don't end this book suddenly without telling you how everything you have learned fits together. This is where Part Two comes in.

The second part of this book consists of Chapters 9 and 10. These two chapters contain rather complex projects that make use of just about everything you have learned about GDI+. These real applications will solidify your understanding of GDI+ and give you some ideas about how to do real graphics programming using either C# or Visual Basic .NET.

CHAPTER 1

.NET Primer

*The bone-chilling scream split the warm summer night in two, the first half
being before the scream when it was fairly balmy and calm and pleasant for
those who hadn't heard the scream at all, but not calm or balmy or even very
nice for those who did hear the scream, discounting the little period of time
during the actual scream itself when your ears might have been hearing it but
your brain wasn't reacting yet to let you know.*

—Patricia E. Presutti, Lewiston, New York (1986 Winner)

BEFORE I GET INTO the details of programming with VS. NET GDI+, I think it is a
good time for a short refresher on .NET programming itself. Those of you who are
familiar with object-oriented programming can probably skip this section. That
does not include Visual Basic (VB) 6.0 programmers, though. You have to stay for a
little remedial programming help.

VB .NET is not the next version of VB 6.0. If that is what you think, you are in
for a big surprise. VB 6.0 allows you to do some object-oriented programming, but
quite a bit is left out. Now that .NET is here, and all .NET languages must adhere to
the Common Language Specification (CLS), VB was brought up to the level of
object-oriented capability that C++ users enjoy. For a VB 6.0 programmer this can
be exhilarating and scary at the same time.

This chapter serves as a light primer, and I introduce you to some of the terms
you will see and use throughout the book. For a soup-to-nuts, how-to-program-
in-.NET book, I suggest you get one of the Apress books geared toward beginners.

Constructing Your Class

In VB 6.0 a class has a load event. This function is called whenever your class is
instantiated. If you wanted to set any properties, you would first instantiate your
class, set the properties, and then call any methods in your class. This is always a
three-step process in VB. There is no way to pass any arguments to a load event in
VB 6.0.

All .NET classes have what is called a *constructor*. This constructor has the
same use as the load event in VB but with some important differences. First of all,

the constructor in VB .NET is called **New**(). When you instantiate a class in VB .NET, the **New**() method gets called. In VB .NET the **New**() constructor can also take arguments. This allows you to bypass the properties-setting step that is necessary in VB 6.0. Listing 1-1 shows a small sample of instantiating a class from a form and the class constructor itself.

Listing 1-1. Instantiating a VB .NET Class

```
Private Sub Form1_Load(ByVal sender As System.Object, _
            ByVal e As System.EventArgs) Handles MyBase.Load

  Dim x As SampleClass = New SampleClass( 2 )

End Sub
```

Class Constructor

```
Public Class SampleClass
  Public Sub New( x as Integer )

  End Sub
End Class
```

C# has a constructor mechanism that is closer to C++. A constructor in C# uses the same name as the class. If you have a class called MyClass, the constructor would be called **MyClass**(). Listing 1-2 shows a C# example.

Listing 1-2. Instantiating a C# Class

```
private void Form1_Load(object sender, System.EventArgs e)
{
  SampleClass1 y = new SampleClass1(2);
}
```

Class Constructor

```
public class SampleClass1
  {
  public SampleClass1(int x)
  {
  }
}
```

One other very important aspect of constructors in .NET also applies to all methods in .NET. This feature has always been available to C++ programmers and has been a much-desired feature of mine for VB: the ability to overload.

Overloading Functions

An *overloaded function* is one that has the same name but with different arguments. What does this mean for you? Suppose you wanted a function to multiply two numbers and give the integer part as a result. The numbers could be either two integers or two doubles. In VB you would have two separate functions. One would multiply the two integers and return the result. The other would multiply the two doubles and return the truncated result.

.NET allows you to overload this function. You would instead have two functions with the same name but different arguments. Here's an example:

- Multiply (*x* as integer, *y* as integer)

- Multiply (x as double, y as double)

When you call the multiply function, the compiler will direct the call to the correct function by looking at the arguments. Your calling function would look like this:

- Multiply (1, 2)

- Multiply (1.3, 2.6)

Overload can also apply to constructors. You will see this all over .NET. Some of the constructors for the drawing functions have eight or more overloaded versions. Listing 1-3 shows an example of overloaded constructors.

Listing 1-3a. Overloaded Constructors in C#

```
public class SampleClass1
{
    public SampleClass1()
    {
    }
    public SampleClass1(int x)
    {
    }
}
```

Listing 1-3b. Overloaded Constructors in VB

```
Public Class SampleClass

  Public Sub New()
  End Sub

  Public Sub New(ByVal x As Int32)
  End Sub

End Class
```

Overloading is a very important and frequently used part of .NET. Once you get used to overloading constructors, you will not want to program in VB 6.0 again.

 NOTE *How does the compiler know which method you are calling? Through a mechanism called name mangling. What happens is that the compiler makes a separate function for each overloaded version. The name consists of a combination of the function name and the arguments. This name is normally hidden from the user. The debugger translates the name back to the original name, so the user never knows this name mangling is going on. This provides a unique name for all overloaded functions.*

Collecting the Garbage

Garbage collection in .NET is a topic worthy of a few hundred pages in itself. I will give you the *Reader's Digest* version here.

VB 6.0 has automatic destruction of classes and objects when they go out of scope. If you created and instantiated a form in VB 6.0 within a function, that form would automatically get destroyed when the function ended.

VB 6.0's automatic destruction is a good thing, as forgetting to release memory is a big problem in programming—it is a major source of bugs. C++ has no mechanism for automatically destroying a class. You need to explicitly call the class' destructor by calling the class' delete operator.

While VB 6.0 does some garbage collection, it does not go far enough. All VB 6.0 objects are COM objects. COM objects have a life span defined by reference counting. If you have a COM-based component in VB 6.0, it keeps a count of how many processes are using it. When that count goes to zero, the component destroys itself. Well, this does not always happen. In fact, circumstances can occur where objects can keep references to other objects and none of those objects are being used by anyone. In this case, the reference counts never go to zero and the objects just hang around. This is nasty.

.NET does not use reference counting to keep track of objects. If an object is not being used by anyone and it is hanging around, .NET detects this and destroys it, reclaiming memory. When does this happen? Who knows? This is the drawback to a garbage collector. There is no deterministic finalization. At least with VB you know that your class got destroyed as soon as it went out of scope.

In .NET if you create a pen and forget to destroy it, .NET will get around to it eventually, but this is not a good way to program. You may need the memory that the object is taking up. So how can you destroy objects in .NET deterministically? I cover this subject next.

Cleaning Up After Yourself

VB 6.0 has the unload event for forms and the terminate event for classes. C++ has a destructor. .NET has the **Dispose** and **Finalize** methods.

The garbage collector (GC) calls the **Finalize** method when it determines that the object is no longer in use. After calling the **Finalize** method, the GC marks the object as ready for destruction and then destroys the object in the next collection cycle. The **Finalize** method is your last chance to clean up after yourself.

The **Dispose** method is a method that all objects should have. This method is similar to the unload event in VB 6.0, except that you must call this method explicitly.[1]

The **Dispose** method is where you release all memory and any other resources such as file handles and COM ports taken up by your class, including any extraneous objects it may have created.

Exception Handling

By a show of hands, who thinks that using the GoTo command in VB 6.0 is a good thing? How many of you use GoTo other than during error handling? If you raised your hand, it is time for a new career.

Unfortunately, you must use GoTo when designing error handling in VB 6.0. While this is not the only place you can use the GoTo command, it definitely should be. The typical way of handling errors in VB 6.0 is shown here:

---

1. C# has a way to automatically call the **Dispose** method with an unusual use of the Using keyword.

```
Private Sub foo()

On Error GoTo ErrHandle

  'Some code

  Exit Sub
ErrHandle:
  MsgBox "Failed!  Ha Ha"
End Sub
```

There is an error object in VB 6.0 that you can query as to the exact nature of the error and there is also a way to percolate errors up the calling chain by raising errors or events.

If you like, you can write completely crash-proof code using the following VB construct:

```
On Error Resume Next
```

You can just ignore all errors. I have actually seen this, and it is scary!

Well, as you know, error handling in VB 6.0 is terrible. .NET handles things differently—more like traditional C++, as a matter of fact. .NET uses a very good exception-handling mechanism.

Exception handling consists of putting code inside of Try-Catch blocks. What are Try-Catch blocks? They are a way of sectioning off some code so you can trap any errors that may occur in the Try-Catch section. The Catch block gets invoked when something bad happens, such as when an exception occurs. It is within this Catch block that you write exception-handling code. Try a small example. Make a new console project in either C# or VB.

 NOTE   *Yes, folks, you can make a console app using VB code. It is actually easier than making a Windows app. It is also very handy, as your C++ buddies will tell you.*

Enter the code in Listing 1-4, which shows a simple program that divides two integers.

Listing 1-4a. Exception-Handling Program in VB

```
Module Module1

  Sub Main()
    Dim x As Int32 = 100
    Dim y As Int32 = 0
    Dim k As Int32

    Try
      k = x / y
    Catch e As Exception
      Console.WriteLine(e.Message)
    End Try

    Console.ReadLine()
  End Sub

End Module
```

Listing 1-4b. Exception-Handling Program in C#

```
using System;

namespace CatchMe_c
{
    /// <summary>
    /// Summary description for Class1.
    /// </summary>
    class Class1
    {
      /// <summary>
      /// The main entry point for the application.
      /// </summary>
      [STAThread]
      static void Main(string[] args)
      {
       int x = 100;
       int y = 0;
       int k;
```

```
      try
      {
        k = x/y;
      }
      catch ( Exception e )
      {
        Console.WriteLine(e.Message);
      }

      Console.ReadLine();
    }
  }
}
```

Run the program and you will get a message on the screen telling you that you tried to divide by zero. The C# message tells you that you tried to divide by zero. The VB message tells you that you have an overflow condition. In this case, C# is a lot clearer about what happened.

So, is this it? Not hardly. This code catches any exception that happens. You can also use multiple Catch blocks after a Try block to catch specific errors. Catching a specific error results in much cleaner code than catching everything and then trying to figure out what happened. Catching specific errors also allows your Try block to ignore some errors, which then get handled by the calling function. You can be very specific in this case.

Well, this is fine for system errors, but what about other types of errors? There is an exception class that lets you define your own exceptions that can be handled in the normal manner. An example of this would be a call to a function you made that is supposed to draw a shape in a clipping region. If the clipping region were invalid, your function would throw an exception that could be handled in a Try-Catch block. For a more detailed explanation of exception handling, I suggest you read the MSDN help for .NET.

Special Case Try Blocks

There is a special case of the Try-Catch block: You can extend the Try-Catch block to a Try-Catch-Finally block. As you can probably guess, the Finally block gets run after all other code in the function has been run. What's the point of this? One of the major uses of the Finally block is to reclaim memory before you exit the function. You reclaim memory by calling an object's **Dispose** method. The next small example illustrates this.

Make a new C# or VB Windows Forms project. Go into the code pane and enter the following method just below the Form_Load event:

VB

```
Protected Overrides Sub OnPaint(ByVal e As PaintEventArgs)
  Dim P As Pen = New Pen(Color.Azure)

  Try
    e.Graphics.DrawLine(P, 10, 10, 100, 100)
  Finally
    P.Dispose()
  End Try
End Sub
```

C#

```
protected override void OnPaint ( PaintEventArgs e )
{
  Pen P = new Pen(Color.Azure);

  try
  {
    e.Graphics.DrawLine(P, 10, 10, 100, 100 );
  }
  finally
  {
    P.Dispose();
  }
}
```

You will see the OnPaint event handler a few more times in this book.[2] The Try-Finally method of calling the **Dispose** methods works well, but it is a little clunky. C# has another way to automatically call a **Dispose** method. You do not need to remember to make the call and you do not need the clunky Try-Finally construct.

C# has the Using keyword, which contains an object in a block and automatically calls the **Dispose** method when the object is out of scope. Consider the following code snippet:

```
using (Pen P2 = new Pen(Color.Black))
{
  e.Graphics.DrawLine(P2, 100, 100, 200, 200 );
}
```

---

2. In fact, it will become ingrained in your mind.

What happens is that Pen P2 is created and used within the *using* block to draw a line on the screen. When P2 goes out of scope, the Pen's **Dispose** method is automatically called. Cool, huh?

Sorry, you VBers. This construct does not exist for you. You will still need to explicitly call the **Dispose** method.

 NOTE   *The .NET IDE is itself written in C#. The programmers at Microsoft invented the Using construct during coding to clean up their own code.*

Delegating Events

VB 6.0 has an event capture mechanism where the name of the event sink is derived from the name of the source object and the name of the event itself. For instance, suppose you had a class called MyClass that raised an event called MyEvent. If you created a form and declared the class as "WithEvents," you would have the opportunity to sink the MyEvent from the MyClass class. The name of the event would be myclass_myevent().

In VB 6.0 you have no choice in this matter. Event handlers are created for you by VB 6.0. .NET has a different method for handling events.

In .NET, event handlers are called *delegates*. These delegates are assigned by you to take care of a particular event. If you had a button on a form and you double-clicked that button, you would be taken to the code pane and VB .NET would have made an event delegate for you called Button1_Click. This is where the similarity between VB 6.0 event handlers and VB .NET event handlers ends.

Try this:

1. Make a blank VB .NET Windows Forms project.

2. Add a button to the form.

3. Double-click the button.

The code you see should look like this:

```
Private Sub Button1_Click(ByVal sender As System.Object, _
                    ByVal e As System.EventArgs) Handles Button1.Click

End Sub
```

Notice that there are arguments that tell you who fired the event as well as arguments about the event. At the end of the method you see the words "Handles Button1.Cick". This is important.

In VB 6.0 each event must have a corresponding event handler. There is no way for a single event handler to handle multiple events. .NET changes that with the Handles keyword.

Add another button to your form and go back to the button click event handler. Add a comma at the very end of the click event line. You should see a drop-down box with a listing of objects that have events you can capture. Choose Button2.Click. Your code should look like this:

```
Private Sub Button1_Click(ByVal sender As System.Object, _
                    ByVal e As System.EventArgs) _
                    Handles Button1.Click, Button2.Click


End Sub
```

Put a breakpoint at the End Sub line of the event handler (delegate) and run the program. Click the two buttons and you will see that this delegate gets called for both buttons.

This is really neat. If you are thinking hard about this method, you will see that the name of the delegate has nothing to do with the event that it handles. If you want, you can rename this delegate to anything else.

C# does delegates a little differently. Open a new C# Windows form and add two buttons. Double-click the first one to bring you to the delegate assigned to this button. You should see the following method:

```
private void button1_Click(object sender, System.EventArgs e)
{
}
```

So, where is the Handles keyword? How would you allow this delegate to handle multiple events? This is where you will need to dig into C# a little. The easy stuff was just done for you by the C# wizard, but you will need to change some of the code that the wizard made to allow your delegate to handle multiple events.

NOTE *C# has a nice feature in the properties window that allows you to specify common delegates for a particular control. It's easy and fast. It also insulates you from what's going on. If you don't want to know what's going on, that's fine . . . but you won't become a .NET guru like that.*

There is a section in your code called "Windows Form Designer generated code." If you open up this section of code you will see the standard Visual Studio Wizard admonishment:

```
Required method for Designer support - do not modify the contents of this method
with the code editor.
```

Well, you have been suitably warned. Now you need to go modify this code. Scroll down to the section for Button1 and Button2. Your code should look like this:

```
//
// button1
//
this.button1.Location = new System.Drawing.Point(152, 72);
this.button1.Name = "button1";
this.button1.Size = new System.Drawing.Size(64, 24);
this.button1.TabIndex = 0;
this.button1.Text = "button1";
this.button1.Click += new System.EventHandler(this.button1_Click);
//
// button2
//
this.button2.Location = new System.Drawing.Point(152, 112);
this.button2.Name = "button2";
this.button2.Size = new System.Drawing.Size(64, 24);
this.button2.TabIndex = 1;
this.button2.Text = "button2";
```

The last line for Button1 is the delegate declaration. It says that the event handler for Button1.Click is button1_Click. Remember that this is only a declaration. The actual handler is at the bottom of your code. Okay, back to the question at hand. How do you change the handler and how would you have one handler for multiple events?

The answer is simple. Clone the button1 event handler declaration and make it the handler for Button2. The code is as follows:

```
this.button1.Click += new System.EventHandler(this.button1_Click);
this.button2.Click += new System.EventHandler(this.button1_Click);
```

I am now using the button1_click delegate to handle the click event from both buttons.

Try renaming the delegate to something different. The code in Listing 1-5 is for a form that has two buttons and a delegate named clicker that handles the events from both.

Listing 1-5. Complete C# Listing for Creating a Delegate on a Simple Form

```csharp
using System;
using System.Drawing;
using System.Collections;
using System.ComponentModel;
using System.Windows.Forms;
using System.Data;

namespace RSI_c
{
  /// <summary>
  /// Summary description for Form1.
  /// </summary>
  public class Form1 : System.Windows.Forms.Form
    {
    private System.Windows.Forms.Button button1;
    private System.Windows.Forms.Button button2;
    /// <summary>
    // Required designer variable.
    /// </summary>
    private System.ComponentModel.Container components = null;

        public Form1()
          {
           //
           // Required for Windows Form Designer support
           //
           InitializeComponent();

           //
           // TODO: Add any constructor code after InitializeComponent call
           //
          }
```

```
        /// <summary>
    /// Clean up any resources being used.
    /// </summary>
    protected override void Dispose( bool disposing )
     {
     if( disposing )
      {
      if (components != null)
        {
         components.Dispose();
        }
      }
      base.Dispose( disposing );
      }


#region Windows Form Designer generated code
/// <summary>
/// Required method for Designer support - do not modify
/// the contents of this method with the code editor.
/// </summary>
private void InitializeComponent()
{
    this.button1 = new System.Windows.Forms.Button();
     this.button2 = new System.Windows.Forms.Button();
     this.SuspendLayout();
     //
     // button1
     //
     this.button1.Location = new System.Drawing.Point(152, 72);
     this.button1.Name = "button1";
     this.button1.Size = new System.Drawing.Size(64, 24);
     this.button1.TabIndex = 0;
     this.button1.Text = "button1";
     this.button1.Click += new System.EventHandler(this.Clicker);
     //
     // button2
     //
     this.button2.Location = new System.Drawing.Point(152, 112);
     this.button2.Name = "button2";
     this.button2.Size = new System.Drawing.Size(64, 24);
     this.button2.TabIndex = 1;
     this.button2.Text = "button2";
     this.button2.Click += new System.EventHandler(this.Clicker);
```

```
        //
        // Form1
        //
        this.AutoScaleBaseSize = new System.Drawing.Size(5, 13);
        this.ClientSize = new System.Drawing.Size(292, 273);
        this.Controls.AddRange(new System.Windows.Forms.Control[] {
                                                    this.button2,
                                                    this.button1});
        this.Name = "Form1";
        this.Text = "Form1";
        this.Load += new System.EventHandler(this.Form1_Load);
        this.ResumeLayout(false);

    }
#endregion
/// <summary>
/// The main entry point for the application.
/// </summary>
[STAThread]
static void Main()
{
            Application.Run(new Form1());
}

private void Form1_Load(object sender, System.EventArgs e)
    {
      SampleClass1 x = new SampleClass1();
      SampleClass1 y = new SampleClass1(2);
    }

    private void Clicker(object sender, System.EventArgs e)
    {
    }
  }
}
```

This completes your introduction to delegates in VB and C#. By the way, you should note that all delegates need to have the same signature. This is to say that they need these two arguments: *object sender* and *System.EventArgs e.*

> **NOTE** *Obviously, the **InitializeComponent** method is not the only place you can declare delegates. You can declare them in the constructor where it says TODO. The reason I chose to edit the **InitializeComponent** method is because this is where .NET always puts its delegate declarations. Just double-click a control in design mode and this is where the wizard places the delegate declaration for you.*

The Proper Delegate Calling Chain

Remember when I told you about the **OnPaint** method? I said you would be seeing it quite often in this book. In fact, you will see it in almost every example I present. Here is something else you will see: In every **OnPaint** method that you override, you will need to call the base class' **OnPaint** method as well.

> **NOTE** *You should already be familiar with the practice of declaring methods as private, protected, and public. You should also be familiar with overriding a base class' protected methods and all that implies. Beyond this short discussion, I will not cover the basics of inheritance.*

First of all, let me clarify something. Technically speaking, the base class OnPaint does not really do any painting. What it does do, though, is call any registered delegates that need to see the OnPaint event.

Now, I know that you are going to forget this step in quite a few situations. After all, the OnPaint event is not the only event that you can override. You can override several events from the form's base class. Some of these events you may want to override and some you may want to extend. One other event, or set of events, that comes to mind is/are the mouse events.

Handling mouse events is such a basic part of Windows programming that it is just as important that you know how to handle them as how to handle the paint event. Let's consider the MouseMove event, for instance.

There are actually two ways to handle this event. One way is to override the form's base event handler and the other is to register a new delegate with the form. I will show you both methods and what you need to be careful of.

Let's start with a small demonstration program. Open up a new project in either VB or C#. Put a label on the form somewhere. Now double-click the form to take you into the code pane. Here you will enter a very simple delegate. The VB code for this is as follows:

```
Public Sub MyMouseMove(ByVal sender As Object, _
                      ByVal e As System.Windows.Forms.MouseEventArgs) _
                      Handles MyBase.MouseMove

  Label1.Text = "X= " + e.X.ToString() + ", Y= " + e.Y.ToString()
End Sub
```

The C# code for the same delegate is slightly different. First, you will need to define the delegate. Do this in the form's constructor just after the InitializeComponent() call.

```
this.MouseMove += new
               System.Windows.Forms.MouseEventHandler(this.MyMouseHandler);
```

It is important that you look at this line of code closely. Notice that I am *adding* this delegate to the OnMouseMove delegate chain.

Now you can add the delegate code itself. Do this below the form's load event.

```
private void MyMouseHandler(object sender,
                           System.Windows.Forms.MouseEventArgs e)
{
   label1.Text = "X= " + e.X.ToString() + ", Y= " + e.Y.ToString();
}
```

Compile and run the form. You should see the *X* and *Y* coordinates of the mouse appear in the label you placed on the screen. Big deal, right? Let's add a little wrinkle to this. Enter the following function below the mouse delegate code:

VB

```
Protected Overrides Sub OnMouseMove(ByVal e As MouseEventArgs)

End Sub
```

C#

```
protected override void OnMouseMove( MouseEventArgs e )
{
}
```

They are both empty functions. Now compile and run the code. What happens when you move your mouse over the screen now? What's that? Nothing? Why?

Add the following line inside the overridden event. Your code should look like this:

VB

```
Protected Overrides Sub OnMouseMove(ByVal e As MouseEventArgs)
  MyBase.OnMouseMove(e)
End Sub
```

C#

```csharp
protected override void OnMouseMove( MouseEventArgs e )
{
  base.OnMouseMove(e);
}
```

Now run the code and you should see your mouse's *X* and *Y* coordinates appear back on the screen.

So, what happened here? Overriding a base class method means that the base class method does not get called. Only your overridden method gets called. You *must* call the base class method after you are finished processing your own method. You will get unpredictable results otherwise. In this case you got no results.

Obviously, you realize that you could dispense with the MyMouseHandler delegate and show the mouse coordinates from within the overridden event handler. In fact, this is a choice you will need to make quite often. Do you override a base class or do you add a new delegate? If you want my opinion, I would say add a new delegate. Here's why.

First of all, overriding a base class means that you will have to call the base class method. Personally, I know I will at some point forget to do this and I will end up spending debugging time trying to track down some obscure problem.

The second reason is more interesting programmatically. Suppose you had some complicated code in an event delegate that you wanted to turn off at some point. You could do it logically with a switch at the top of the delegate code telling it to bail out if true. The better way is to not ever enter that piece of code again. This is ever-so-briefly mentioned in the MSDN help: You can remove a delegate by using the "-=" command. Let's modify the C# example a little.

Add two buttons to the screen. Call one "On" and the other "Off." Now double-click each button to get the click event handlers. Enter code in the click events to detach and attach the MyMouseHandler delegate. Here's the code:

```csharp
private void Off_Click(object sender, System.EventArgs e)
{
  this.MouseMove -= new
    System.Windows.Forms.MouseEventHandler(this.MyMouseHandler);
}
```

```
private void On_Click(object sender, System.EventArgs e)
{
  this.MouseMove += new
    System.Windows.Forms.MouseEventHandler(this.MyMouseHandler);
}
```

Run the program and alternately click the Off and On buttons. Be sure to click the Off button first. You will see that clicking the Off button detaches the MyMouseHandler delegate, and the mouse coordinates are no longer shown on the screen. This means that the MyMouseHandler delegate is officially dead code . . . until you revive it, that is.

Okay, I know you clicked the On button a few times in succession before clicking the Off button. The mouse coordinates were still being written to the screen. This is because each time you clicked the On button, you added another call to this same delegate in the chain. Click it 100 times and you will call the MyMouseHandler delegate 100 times. Click Off once and you will call the MyMouseHandler delegate 99 times. You get it.

Now, suppose you overrode a delegate and wrote code that had several points of exit. This is not uncommon at all. Consider the following piece of VB code. This is the OnMouseMove delegate you used earlier:

```
Protected Overrides Sub OnMouseMove(ByVal e As MouseEventArgs)
  Dim x As Boolean = True
  Dim y As Boolean = False

  If x Then
    'Do some complicated stuff
    MyBase.OnMouseMove(e)
    Exit Sub
  End If

  If y Then
    'Do some complicated stuff
    MyBase.OnMouseMove(e)
    Exit Sub
  End If

  'Do some really complicated stuff here.

  MyBase.OnMouseMove(e)
End Sub
```

As you can see, I need to make sure that I call the base class event before I exit any of the code blocks within this method. I guarantee you that in a really complicated method with many exit points, you will miss one of the base class calls. It will probably happen after the quality assurance (QA) group has been through it with a fine-tooth comb and you are just about to go on vacation. Suddenly a strange bug appears intermittently in the field. . . .

There is a better way to handle this type of situation: Use a Try-Finally block. Change your VB code to look like this:

```
Protected Overrides Sub OnMouseMove(ByVal e As MouseEventArgs)
  Dim x As Boolean = True
  Dim y As Boolean = False

  Try
    If x Then
      'Do some complicated stuff
      Exit Sub
    End If

    If y Then
      'Do some complicated stuff
      Exit Sub
    End If

    'Do some really complicated stuff here.
  Finally
    MyBase.OnMouseMove(e)
  End Try
End Sub
```

As you can see, I still have multiple points of exit but only one call to the base class method. The code in the Finally block runs as the last thing that happens before the method exits.

This is good programming practice, as you can add any amount of complicated code or any number of exit points in this method and you never have to worry about calling the base class. You can feel confident that the Finally block will do it automatically. It also makes your code cleaner.

Everything Is an Object

This section's heading is a rather all-encompassing statement. Can it really be true?

.NET was designed from the ground up to be object oriented. To this end, Microsoft also wanted to have every object in .NET be able to describe itself to anyone who queried it.

All classes in .NET derive from the base object, Object. This is the Adam and Eve of all classes in .NET, and it is the root of the complete type hierarchy. This base class has the following members:

- Equals

- GetHashCode

- ToString

- GetType

- Finalize

Many of these methods are overridden along the way to becoming other objects, but all derived classes have these methods in common. Scan through the MSDN help for some of the classes. You will see these methods in every class.

So, I said that everything is an object. You cannot let that statement go by without trying to refute it! Here is the first thing I thought of when I was playing around with this concept: *What about numbers?* If everything is truly an object, I should be able to call, say, the **ToString** method of the base object.

Try this. Open up a new console project in C# or VB. The code will be almost identical. My projects are called IsObject-vb and IsObject-c. I will show you the code for both. Your code should end up looking like Listing 1-6.

Listing 1-6a. Simple VB Console Application Showing That All Things Are Objects

```
Module Module1

  Sub Main()
    Dim a As Double = 5.678
    Dim b As Int32 = 123

    Console.WriteLine(a)
    Console.WriteLine(b)

    Console.ReadLine()
  End Sub

End Module
```

Listing 1-6b. Simple C# Console Application Showing That All Things Are Objects

```csharp
using System;
namespace IsObject_c
{
/// <summary>
/// Summary description for Class1.
/// </summary>
class Class1
{
/// <summary>
/// The main entry point for the application.
/// </summary>
[STAThread]
static void Main(string[] args)
  {
      double a = 5.678;
      int b = 123;

      Console.WriteLine(a);
      Console.WriteLine(b);

      Console.ReadLine();
    }
}
}
```

The main thing to note is that I declare and initialize two variables and write them to the screen. Console.ReadLine is there so the DOS screen does not disappear until you press a key.

Not a very exciting program. Change the console output lines to the following:

VB

```
Console.WriteLine(a.ToString)
Console.WriteLine(b.ToString)
```

C#

```
Console.WriteLine(a.ToString());
Console.WriteLine(b.ToString());
```

I called the **ToString**() method for each of the declared variables. This tells you that data types are objects. After doing this type of thing, I tried something else that blew me away. What if you don't declare a variable? Is it still an object? Add the following line of code below the last WriteLine:

VB

```
Console.WriteLine(456.987.ToString)
```

C#

```
Console.WriteLine(456.987.ToString());
```

Press F5 and run the program. You will see all three numbers appear on the screen. The last line prints a number that was never declared and calls its **ToString** method. Very neat if you ask me.

I guess that I should note here that .NET is playing some games behind the scenes when you manipulate numerical data types like this. In simple terms, what happens is this: The number is declared on the stack as a simple data type called a *value type*. .NET assumes that you only want to do something simple with this number. However, as soon as you manipulate the value type as an object, .NET performs a task called *boxing*. Boxing is the method whereby .NET makes a reference type out of a value type by "boxing" it in an object. Once you have finished using the number as an object, .NET unboxes it.

Calling a **ToString** method on a value type such as a number forces a boxing operation. This is as far as I will go with boxing, but I will say this, however: It pays to know when .NET performs boxing automatically. In programs that depend on speed, boxing can be time consuming.

Integer vs. Long

This applies to you VBers out there. You may think you know what an integer and a long is, but you have been working under a misconception. An integer in VB 6.0 is 2 bytes and a long in VB 6.0 is 4 bytes. In C++ an integer and a long are not any particular size but are compiler defined.

You've been deceived! For those of you who have worked with the Windows API calls extensively, you already know this. Most of the Windows API calls need integers for arguments. However, VB 6.0 always requires you to provide a long. This is a kind of data type thunking.[3]

An integer from VB 6.0, as described by VB .NET, is now a Short. An integer defined in .NET is an Int32. A long in .NET is defined as an Int64.

Again, this is an example of the upgrade from VB 6.0 to .NET-compatible language.

Using Reflection

Reflection is a method whereby you can get description information about an object. You can also use reflection to get information about a program. For instance, you can use reflection to get a list of all the methods and properties and how they are used from a .NET DLL. This is powerful stuff. It is also pretty insecure if you think about it.

Reflection is worth a few chapters in itself, but I will concentrate on just one aspect of it here. When I described how everything in .NET is an object, I listed five methods common to all objects. One of those methods is **GetType**. This is a reflection method that allows you to get type information for any class. Because an object is basically an instantiated class, perhaps you can extract information about that object by using the **GetType** function.

Just a few paragraphs ago I told you that an integer in .NET resolves to an Int32. Did you believe me? Why not find out for yourself? Try adding the following three lines of code in your C# or VB console program and running it. See what the output would be.

VB

```
Dim c As Integer
Console.WriteLine(c.GetType())
Console.WriteLine(c.GetType().ToString)
```

C#

```
int c=1;
Console.WriteLine(c.GetType());
Console.WriteLine(c.GetType().ToString());
```

I ran my program and this is what I got:

---

3. Not really, but it is a cool term. Those of you who have been programming for fewer than 7 years may not even know what the word means. Look it up. You will be using thunking again when we all go to 64-bit processors.

```
5.678
123
456.987
System.Int32
System.Int32
```

The last two lines are the result of the last two Console.WriteLine commands. As you can see, an integer is actually an Int32. Proof!

Why did I bother with showing **GetType** and **GetType.ToString**? **GetType** returns a value of type "Type". **ToString** returns a value of type "String". Because there is no format specifier in my arguments for WriteLine, this must mean that Console.WriteLine is overloaded. Sure enough, it is. As at matter of fact, it has 19 overloaded versions.

Turn On Strict Type Checking

In the preceding piece of example code I showed the VB code with a variable called c that was not initialized. The C# code showed the same code, but in this case the variable c was initialized to 1.

The C# compiler throws an error if you try to use a variable that has not been initialized. This is a good error. You should always initialize your variables before you use them.

VB initializes your variables for you to zero or null or an empty string, whatever the case may be for a particular type. VB did not throw an error because the variable c was initialized to zero by the compiler before it was used.

Personally, I prefer the C# way. You as a programmer should know exactly what your variables are and how they are being changed at all times. There should be no uninitialized variables, and you should not depend upon the compiler to do it for you. What happens in VB version 8.0 if Microsoft decides to turn off autoinitialization? All your legacy apps that depended on VB for initializing variables will crash or act really funny.[4]

There is one other thing that VB .NET has carried over from VB 6.0 that in my opinion is really bad: evil type coercion. This is not an actual approved term, but it is very common in the programming world.

So, what is *evil type coercion?* It is where you try to use one type as another type and VB makes a guess as to what you are trying to do. It then changes the type of the variable for you and performs the operation, all without your intervention or knowledge.[5]

---

4. If this happens, I am sure Microsoft will make an upgrade wizard to fix the problem, but still. . . .

5. As an experienced VB 6.0 programmer, you definitely should know by now that this is going on.

Why is this bad? Suppose you had a value that was defined as a long. This variable has a value of, say, 50. You then passed this variable to a function that takes an argument of type Integer. In this case, all would be well. VB 6.0 would see this and happily convert the number from a long to an integer and your function would perform as planned. Now suppose your long value has a value of 33,000. Passing this to a function that takes an integer would lose precision because an integer cannot go this high. The maximum value an integer can hold is 32,767. Internally, your function may see a value of (–233). This is the evil part.

How do you stop this from happening in VB .NET? You can set a directive called Option Strict to on or off. Unfortunately, Microsoft set this value to off as a default. It is possible to set it on project-wide, but not for VB .NET as a whole.

The first thing you should do in any project is set strict type checking, a staple of object-oriented programming. It may mean that you need to type some more code, but being explicit at design time can save some serious type-checking problems later on.

Go into your VB console project and type the following code at the top of the page, under the Module declaration:

```
Const x = "This is a string"
```

Run the program and you will see nothing wrong. VB .NET has assumed you meant that *x* is a type String. Type in the following line of code as the first line in the program:

```
Option Strict On
```

Now run the program. You will get a compile error saying that you need to be explicit in defining your constant. Change the const declaration to this:

```
  Const x As String = "This is a string"
```

Compile the program and you will get no errors. VB will no longer assume what you meant to do. You will need to be explicit.

Summary

This chapter reviewed some of the programming aspects of .NET. While this chapter was by no means comprehensive, a firm grasp of the concepts covered will bring you a long way toward understanding the examples presented in the rest of the book.

After reading this chapter you should understand the following concepts:

- Constructors

- Method overloading

- The **Dispose** method

- Garbage collection

- Event handling in the form of delegates

- Everything is an object

- How some data types have changed between VB 6.0 and VB .NET

- Reflection

- Strict type checking in VB .NET

Chapter 2 introduces you to GDI+ and explains how it is different from existing GDI.

CHAPTER 2
GDI Explained

Just beyond the Narrows the river widens.

—Warren Tupper Way, Wayzata, Wisconsin

SOME OF YOU may have previous experience programming in the graphics device interface (GDI) and want to know what's new. Some of you may have picked up this book because you know that .NET has made graphics programming less arcane and you now want to learn the ins and outs of graphics programming.

Newcomers and experienced programmers alike will find that Microsoft has made some changes that affect them. GDI has indeed changed, and it has been enhanced to give experienced programmers a better model to program against. These changes to GDI have also made the interface clearer, which gives new programmers an easier interface to learn.

GDI is, at its lowest level, a set of API calls that let you manipulate the properties of individual pixels on a screen. GDI+ even includes some methods to manipulate the screen on the subpixel level. This is how Microsoft's ClearType technology works. You will be introduced to this in Chapter 7, which covers GDI+ and text.

So, you may ask, what is the plus sign in GDI+ for? Is it just another marketing addition? Well, no, it isn't. The plus sign denotes enough changes to write a whole book about. GDI+ has changed dramatically from the GDI you used in Visual Studio 6.0.

You should know that GDI+ is actually a set of wrapper classes around GDI. Before things get drawn on the screen, the GDI API calls are actually being used to render the drawings. This brings up an interesting point. There may actually be some drawing functions that are not realized in the GDI+ library. Because GDI is still around, it is possible to call GDI directly from inside C# or VB .NET by using the PInvoke functions. One function that comes to mind is GDI's **BitBlt** function. I will demonstrate how to use some of the GDI API functions in a later chapter.

Some Cool New Features

Before I get into the real meat of this chapter, I want to introduce you to some really cool new features of GDI+. The following list is by no means comprehensive, but it will give you a sense of the power of GDI+ and what you can do with it.

- *Path objects:* A *path* is sequence of lines and curves that is maintained in the GraphicsPath object. Paths can be extremely complex.

- *Path gradient brush:* This brush allows you to start filling a path with one color and gradually end it with another.

- *Cardinal splines:* Drawing a cardinal spline is like using a French curve. The sequence of curves is joined seamlessly, with no abrupt changes.

- *Scalable regions:* A region can be stored in world coordinates and then transformed by scale, rotation, or translation. You can perform complex copy/paste functions with scalable regions.

- *Alpha blending:* This feature allows you to set the transparency of pixels so the union of one shape drawn on top of another gives a combined color.

- *Matrix operations:* A 3×3 matrix allows easy transformation and translation of shapes.

- *Antialiasing:* This feature allows you to smooth the edges of lines and curves. This technology is extended to fonts as well in the form of Microsoft's ClearType technology.

Unmanaged Code

Visual Studio .NET comes in basically two flavors: managed code and unmanaged code. In its simplest form, *unmanaged* code is what you have been writing all along.[1] This is code that has no garbage collection, relies on pointer math, uses reference counting to keep track of object lifetime, and also happens to be very fast in the hands of the right programmer. Unmanaged code in .NET is written using C++.

Because it is possible to write unmanaged code in .NET, it should be possible to write to GDI as well using unmanaged code. Well, GDI as you know it is still around.

---

1. I like to refer to VB as *semimanaged* code. It has automatic object destruction, but that's about it.

NOTE *In the beta version of .NET, the GDI for unmanaged code was called GDI+ for C++. There were actually three ways to write to the GDI in Beta 2: normal GDI, GDI+ for the C++ class interface, and GDI+ for managed classes. The final release version got rid of GDI+ for the C++ class interface. Microsoft now calls it the GDI+ SDK.*

Listing 2-1 is an example of drawing a simple line on the screen using C++ and GDI. I will contrast this with the same example in GDI+.

Listing 2-1. Drawing a Line Using GDI in C++

```
HDC          hdc;
PAINTSTRUCT  ps;
HPEN         hPen;
...
hdc = BeginPaint(hWnd, &ps);
   hPen = CreatePen(PS_SOLID, 3, RGB(255, 0, 0));
   SelectObject(hdc, hPen);
   MoveToEx(hdc, 20, 10, NULL);
   LineTo(hdc, 200, 100);
EndPaint(hWnd, &ps);
```

Quite a few separate tasks are involved just to draw a simple line. Here are the steps in plain English:

1. Get a device context. This is where you will draw the line.

2. Create a Pen object. The Pen object is selected according to the line type, the line weight, and the line color.

3. Use the SelectObject command to tie the pen to the device context. If the device context were a particular window, the pen would draw only in that window.

4. Move the cursor to a particular spot in the device context where the line will start.

5. Draw the line using the LineTo command.

6. End the drawing process.

This is quite a bit of work for just one simple line. Can you imagine the code necessary to create a modern-looking video game using GDI?

By the way, you C++ veterans will notice something missing after the line has been drawn. Any time you create a pen or some other GDI object, you take up memory. This memory must be released or you will soon run out. How many of you have seen the dreaded "GDI Resources Low" Windows error? This, folks, is called a *memory leak.* It is the most nefarious of C++ bugs.

 TIP *Whenever you are programming with GDI or GDI+, test your drawing routines in a tight loop while the Windows Task Manager is on the screen. Monitor the performance of the memory and see if the amount of free memory goes down while your program is running. If it does, you have a memory leak—probably in the GDI code.*

Listing 2-1 showed you a tiny fraction of what GDI can do. This tiny code fraction should tell you that there is a lot to learn.

Is There an Unmanaged GDI+?

Perhaps you are thinking that while Microsoft made this new GDI+ and was concentrating so much on .NET, C++ got left behind. Well, it so happens that this is not true. There is an SDK that comes with your .NET installation disk called, funnily enough, the GDI+ SDK. The GDI+ SDK contains all the same classes, structures, and enumerations as GDI+ for .NET does. The GDI+ SDK is located in the file called gdiplus.dll. This DLL is included in the Windows XP and Windows .NET Server operating systems. If you are using a previous version of Windows and do not have .NET installed, you will need to download the distributable from the MSDN site.

The .NET GDI+ code is located in two different DLLs:

- System.drawing.dll

- System.drawing.design.dll

GDI+ for .NET is like any other set of programming interfaces for .NET. The classes are all organized in separate namespaces. The namespaces make it easy to organize classes by function. The GDI+ SDK for C++ is not broken up into namespaces. Instead, everything is organized according to the following topics:

- Classes

- Functions

- Constants

- Enumerations

- Structures

Managed Code

.NET consists mainly of *managed* code, which is code that uses methods and classes from the common language runtime (CLR) library, uses sophisticated garbage collection, and does away with pointers. Essentially, managed code has far fewer opportunities for the programmer to introduce those nasty memory leak bugs and circular reference bugs that can plague COM programmers. Managed code is written in C#, VB .NET, J#, and now a whole host of other languages that use the CLR. Managed code can also be written using C++. Along with writing unmanaged code in C#, I will not cover writing managed code using C++ in this book.

Because .NET has managed code, it also has a GDI that you can use in the managed world: GDI+. Listing 2-2 shows the same line drawing example as Listing 2-1, except it uses the GDI+ classes and C#.

Listing 2-2. Drawing a Line with C# and GDI+

```
protected override void OnPaint(PaintEventArgs e)
{
   Pen myPen = new Pen(Color.Red, 3);
   Graphics myGraphics = e.Graphics;
   myGraphics.DrawLine(myPen, 20, 10, 200, 100);
}
```

Let's take apart this method and see what's going on:

1. Get a reference to the Graphics object. Using the **OnPaint** method is a convenient way to do this.

2. Create a Pen object similar to what is shown in Listing 2-1.

3. Use the **DrawLine** method of the Graphics object using the pen you created.

As you can see, this method of drawing a line is easier to understand and also more flexible than using GDI in C++. There is no need to select the Pen object into the device context. There is also no need to move the cursor to the starting point before you start drawing.

The other nice thing about GDI+ is that there is no longer any such thing as a device context or a handle; there is only the Graphics object. This makes life so much easier.

The Device Context vs. the Graphics Object

One of the main differences between GDI and GDI+ is the shift from using a device context to using a Graphics object. While the end result of the drawing operation is the same, the way you use a device context is very different from the way you use a Graphics object.

Using a Device Context

A *device context* is an internal structure that contains information about the capabilities of a particular device, such as a video screen or a printer. The device context also contains attributes that determine how items such as lines, circles, and so forth are drawn on that device.

A device context need not be limited to the whole video screen. A device context for a display is often a particular window on the display. In order to draw on a particular window, you first need to get the handle to that window, known as the *handle to the device context* (HDC). This handle is then passed as an argument to any of the generic GDI functions that draw, get the HDC attributes, or set the HDC attributes.

Before you can draw in a device context, you must first make a call to the **SelectObject** function to associate the Pen object with the device context. All subsequent calls to any drawing function using that HDC will be drawn using the pen you selected into that device context. What does this mean? Suppose you want to draw a box using the **LineTo** function. Suppose you also want each side of the box to be a different color. Here is what you need to do:

1. Create a Pen object whose color is red.

2. Use the **SelectObject** function to tie the pen to the window you are drawing in.

3. Use the **LineTo** function to draw the first line.

4. Create a Pen object whose color is green.

5. Use the **SelectObject** function to tie the pen to the window you are drawing in.

6. Use the **LineTo** function to draw the second line.

7. Create a Pen object whose color is blue.

8. Use the **SelectObject** function to tie the pen to the window you are drawing in.

9. Use the **LineTo** function to draw the third line.

10. Create a Pen object whose color is yellow.

11. Use the **SelectObject** function to tie the pen to the window you are drawing in.

12. Use the **LineTo** function to draw the last line.

As you can see, you need to create a different Pen object for each line and you also need to select the pen into the device context each time you draw a line. What a pain![2] So you say, "Just write a wrapper class that does all this." You could do that, and countless programmers have done it countless times over the years. In fact, Microsoft did this themselves with the Microsoft Foundation Class (MFC) Library. The MFC Library does a great job of hiding API details from the programmer. Why bother with this, though, when .NET now has the Graphics object?

Using the Graphics Object

GDI+ has done away with device contexts and handles. The HDC has always been a conceptual sticking point with new programmers. The Graphics object makes things so much easier. In a similar fashion to the HDC in the GDI world, the Graphics object is the center of the GDI+ world. The Graphics object is where everything happens as far as drawing is concerned.

All you need to do is create a Graphics object and call its methods and properties as you would any other class-based object. The Graphics object is associated with a window just as a device context would be. However, whereas a device

---

2. There is, of course, a rectangle function to draw a box, but it is not nearly as instructive in this case.

context needs to be associated with a particular pen or brush, the Graphics object does not—there is no need to tie a pen to a Graphics object before you draw. Instead, you pass the Pen object as an argument to the drawing method of the Graphics object. In the previous box-drawing example, this would allow you to use a different pen to draw each side of the box without first associating the pen with the Graphics object.

Parameters for Drawing Functions

Keeping the drawing tools, such as pens, brushes, paths, images, and fonts, separate from the Graphics object opens up some interesting possibilities. Just as an artist has a box with different brushes and pens that is totally separate from any canvas he or she works on, so can you create your own box that includes a collection of different pens, brushes, images, and so forth. Your set of drawing tools is totally separate from your canvas, which is the Graphics object. As a matter of fact, .NET includes a rich set of collection classes that allow you to do just that. I will take you through an example of creating and using a drawing toolbox in Chapter 10.

GDI has several drawing functions that take as a parameter the HDC. As stated earlier, this means that in order to change from one drawing tool to another, you must first associate the drawing tool with a device context using the **SetObject** function before passing the device context to a drawing function.

GDI+ does things differently. The Graphics object has many drawing functions, each of which takes a drawing tool, such as a pen or brush, as a parameter directly. Because of this, many of the drawing functions are overloaded functions.

No More Moving the Cursor

GDI has a concept called *current cursor position.* Remember in Listing 2-1 where you had to first move the cursor to the start position before calling the **LineTo** function? Any time you want to draw an object at a different starting point from where you are, you need to call the **MoveToEx** function first to make sure your cursor is in the right spot.

GDI+ does away with this process. Each of the drawing methods for the graphics class makes use of a starting point and an ending point as arguments. A simple line draw would be like this:

```
myGraphics.DrawLine(myPen, 20, 10, 200, 100);
```

This is much easier and more intuitive to use than having to call two functions. It avoids the scribble error, where you draw an object without first setting its starting point.

Filled Objects vs. Unfilled Objects

Here is another difference between GDI and GDI+. If you want to draw an ellipse using GDI, you do the following:

```
…
Ellipse ( hdc, left, top, right, bottom );
…
```

If the arguments for left, right, top, and bottom defined a square, you would get a circle. Anyway, my point here is that you would not just get a circle, you would get a *filled* circle. The **Ellipse** function draws the circle with the current pen and, at the same time, it fills the circle with the current brush. There is no function in GDI to draw an ellipse without filling it at the same time. For that matter, this applies to all the GDI drawing methods listed here:

- Chord

- Ellipse

- Pie

- Polygon

- PolyPolygon

- Rectangle

- RoundRect

These are called *filled shape functions.* GDI+ is a little different. Drawing a circle in GDI+ is like so:

```
…
Graphics.DrawEllipse(Pen, x, y, width, height)
…
```

What you get here is the outline of the circle. If you want the circle filled, call another function called **FillEllipse**(). This is much more flexible than the GDI method.

Notice one other thing about the GDI **Ellipse** function compared to the GDI+ **DrawEllipse** method: The GDI+ method takes arguments that specify the starting point and a width and height. The GDI function takes a left edge, right edge, top edge, and bottom edge. Again, the GDI+ way of doing things wins the prize for simplicity.

GDI Region vs. GDI+ Region

The last major difference between the GDI programming model and the GDI+ model concerns regions.

In GDI you have the device context, which could be a particular window on your screen. The GDI+ analog to this is the Graphics object. Any drawing you do within the device context or Graphics object is constrained to the borders of the window you are working in.

Suppose you want to draw within a smaller space within that window. There is no handle you can get from such an undefined space. What could you do? You could make a region. A region can be any user-defined border within either a device context for GDI or a Graphics object for GDI+. Often, a region is used for clipping some drawing you are creating.

For instance, you will often find code that builds one type of object by using other types of objects and a clipping region. Consider the case of slowly filling a globe from bottom to top. A 2D circle on your screen represents the globe. There is no easy way to fill only some of a circle. One way around this is to slowly create a stack of rectangles, filling each one as you go. These rectangles, however, are clipped by a circle. Figures 2-1 through 2-4 illustrate this process.

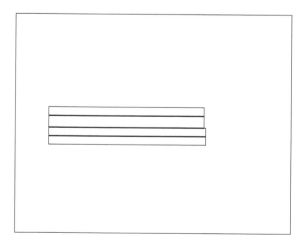

Figure 2-1. Stacked rectangles within a Graphics object or device context

Once you have the stacked rectangles, you fill them with the same color. This way, to the user it looks as though there is only one rectangle.

Figure 2-2 shows what happens when you create a circular clipping region that overlays the rectangles.

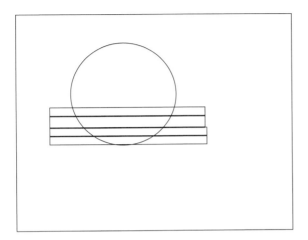

Figure 2-2. A circular clipping region overlays stacked rectangles

Figure 2-3 shows how the circular clipping region cuts off the display of the rectangles that are outside the clipping region.

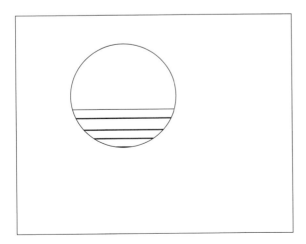

Figure 2-3. Behind-the-scenes construction of what the user sees on the screen

When all is said and done, the user sees only the circle that is partially filled. Figure 2-4 shows the result of clipping a set of rectangles with a circle. As a programmer, all you need to do to raise or lower the level in the circle is to add or delete small rectangles.

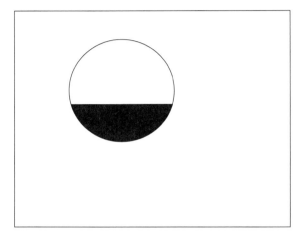

Figure 2-4. The final result of a partially filled circle. This is what the user really sees.

Now that you know what a region is and what it can be used for, what is the difference between how GDI deals with a region and how GDI+ deals with a region?

GDI has several functions you can use to create a region:

- CreateRectRgn

- CreateEllipticRgn

- CreateRoundRectRgn

- CreatePolygonRgn

- CreatePolyPolygonRgn

As you can see, there is a different function for each kind of region you can make. Not very polymorphic, is it?

GDI+ does things a little differently. The region constructor takes a Rectangle object and another constructor that takes a GraphicsPath object. While this may seem limiting, it is easy enough to create a graphics path in the form of a circle and then pass this to the region constructor. This method is very flexible and is also polymorphic.[3]

It is very easy to combine regions in GDI+ into more complex regions. A **Union** method and an **Intersect** method in the region class allow you to combine other regions. Creating a complex region within a rectangle allows you to fill that region really fast just by filling the rectangle.

One last thing about the differences between GDI and GDI+ with regard to regions. It is possible to make a region out of a path in GDI. However, the path is destroyed in the process. You would need to construct the path again if you needed to use it again. Passing a graphics path to a GDI+ region constructor will not destroy that path. This allows you to construct the path once and use it many times.

The Main Features of GDI+

The GDI+ classes consist of three main features:

- 2D vector graphics

- Imaging

- Text rendering

2D Vector Graphics

First of all, what is a *vector*? The mathematical description involves a starting point, a direction, and a magnitude. In physics, a vector is represented by an initial point in a rectangular coordinate system with an arrow leading from that point in a particular direction. The magnitude of that vector is the endpoint of the arrow. Well, that's all very nice, but what does this have to do with GDI+?

In GDI+ a vector is the same representation as a vector in physics but in two dimensions. A vector in GDI+ consists of a set of endpoints with a line drawn between them. A vector is a very compact way to describe a drawing. Not only that, vector drawing in GDI+ can be very complex. For instance, a Bézier spline is a sophisticated curve specified by four control points. Here are some basic 2D vector primitives:

---

3. Constructor overloading is so pervasive in .NET that you will soon find it to be second nature. You should use it in your own classes if you need to make them polymorphic.

- Lines

- Rectangles

- Curves

- Figures

Why use vectors? As I mentioned, a vector is a very compact and efficient method of describing a drawing. Contrast this to a bitmap image. A rectangle in vector graphics is described by a point giving the location of its upper-left corner and a pair of numbers giving its width and height. Vector math requires only four numbers to represent any rectangle of any size. A bitmap, on the other hand, explicitly describes the state of a set of pixels on the screen. A bitmap of a rectangle could consist of thousands of points (and their attributes), where a vector only consists of four.

GDI+ provides structures and classes that store information about the vector primitives themselves. There are also classes that provide information on how the vectors are to be drawn, and there are classes that do the drawing itself. The classes that store vector information and classes that describe how vectors are to be drawn are separate from each other. It is the classes that do the drawing that bring all this information together. For instance, a rectangle structure stores information about the location and size of the rectangle. The Pen class stores information about the line weight, color, and so forth. The **DrawRectangle** method uses the information in the rectangle structure and the information in the pen class to actually draw the rectangle on the screen.

It is also possible to store a sequence of vector commands, such as drawing several rectangles, lines, curves, in a sort of command set. This command set is referred to as a *metafile*. You can use a metafile to store animation sequences.

 NOTE   *Chapter 4 describes vector graphics in detail.*

GDI+ Imaging

You can see that vector graphics are superior to bitmaps for displaying gross forms of line art. However, in some instances vector graphics fall short, mainly in the area of pictures.

While a vector is compact and efficient, it is not very flexible. There is no easy way to draw a line where each pixel is a different color, for instance. You could do this with a metafile that contains a line vector for each pixel, but the amount of code and computation starts to get ridiculous with even a small line.

The way to display pictures and highly complex graphics is with a bitmap. While there are many graphics formats out there, displaying a picture comes down to turning on or off certain pixels with certain colors. This is essentially a bitmap.

GDI+ provides many classes and methods for working with bitmaps. There are also a few containers that you can use to do quite a bit of the bitmap display work for you. The Image and PictureBox controls come to mind.

 NOTE   *Chapter 6 explains imaging in detail.*

Displaying Text

The last major part of GDI+ is typography. Everyone is familiar with this to some degree. You write a Word processing document and choose the font you need. This is typography. To the user it is this easy.

GDI+ contains a rich set of classes that help in displaying text. Some of the things you can do with the typography classes are as follows:

- Enumerate all the fonts on your system.

- Create your own font sets.

- Install a private version of an existing font.

- Manipulate fonts on the subpixel level.

 NOTE   *Displaying text correctly can be quite a daunting task. Chapter 7 takes an in-depth look into the world of fonts.*

Important Objects in GDI+ Drawing

Drawing on the screen in GDI almost always involves these three main objects:

- Graphics object

- Pen object

- Brush object

I have already mentioned these objects in passing, and I expand on them in the sections that follow.

The Pen Object

This is one of the objects that both GDI and GDI+ use extensively. Just like drawing with pen and paper, you cannot get anything done without something to draw with. In the world of GDI, this "something" is the Pen object.

The Pen object has more than a dozen attributes you can use to change its behavior. Some of the properties of the Pen object are as follows:

- Color

- StartCap

- EndCap

- Width

Pens can be very versatile and they can also be personalized to the user. What do I mean by personalizing a pen? I am certainly old enough to remember taking drafting courses before the advent of AutoCAD and the widespread acceptance of computers in the workplace. Quite often, people had certain styles in drawing lines on paper. The style of the arrows and such could often indicate to you who made the drawing even before you looked at the title block.

The **StartCap** and **CustomStartCap** methods of the Pen object allow you to define how the line starts. For instance, you could have a shaped start to your line, such as a diamond or a circle, or perhaps something completely different and unique to you.

The **EndCap** and **CustomEndCap** methods for the pen are the same as the start methods, but these determine the end cap style.

Creating a pen with custom start and end caps could be a small way to differentiate your graphics programs from others around you. I discuss pens in much greater detail in Chapter 4.

The Brush Object

A brush is just a fat pen, right? Not quite. You use a pen to draw the outline of a drawing. In the GDI+ world, you use a brush to fill that drawing in. Brushes come in several types:

- SolidBrush

- HatchBrush

- TextureBrush

- LinearGradientBrush

- PathGradientBrush

As I mentioned before, in GDI a shape such as a rectangle or a circle is drawn and filled in at the same time. GDI+ requires that you create the pen, draw the shape, and then fill that shape in with a brush.

Two exciting changes to GDI+ are the LinearGradientBrush and the PathGradientBrush. These two brushes allow you to fill in a shape that changes color from the start of the shape to the end of the shape. For instance, you could define that a fill start out as blue and change slowly to end as green. This is cool!

 NOTE *Chapter 4 explains brushes in detail.*

The Graphics Object

All artists need something to paint on. You as the graphics programmer will paint your creations on the Graphics object. The Graphics object is your canvas.

The Graphics object is arguably the most important part of drawing. You can paint without a pen and draw without a brush, but you can do neither without a Graphics object. The Graphics object contains the following general types of methods:

- Drawing methods

- Shape-filling methods

- Clipping methods

- Text-rendering methods

 NOTE   *I explain the Graphics object in greater detail in Chapter 4.*

Summary

This chapter introduced you to GDI+ as an overall concept. I explained why GDI+ is better than GDI, and I also contrasted GDI+ to GDI, which is still used in the unmanaged C++ world.

GDI+ differs from GDI in many respects, and I provided some small examples to illustrate those differences. While explaining some of the more important aspects of GDI+, I provided some hints as to the power of graphics programming with GDI+.

In order to full appreciate GDI+, it is best to go back and take a brief look at GDI programming. Chapter 3 shows you how basic graphics operations were performed in C++ and Visual Basic.

CHAPTER 3

GDI and VB 6.0 Drawing Example

With a curvaceous figure that Venus would have envied, a tanned, unblemished oval face framed with lustrous thick brown hair, deep azure-blue eyes fringed with long black lashes, perfect teeth that vied for competition, and a small straight nose, Marilee had a beauty that defied description.

—Alice A. Hall, Fort Wayne, Indiana

BEFORE I GET INTO the inner workings of GDI+, I want to spend some time in the existing world of GDI. This chapter will give you an appreciation of the complexities of the GDI and VB 6.0 drawing tools.

Visual Studio 6.0 includes both C++ and Visual Basic 6.0. The philosophies behind these two programming platforms are about as different as you can get. One of the major differences, of course, relates to drawing capability.

This chapter will take you through an example that illustrates how graphical drawing is done using both the GDI and the VB 6.0 drawing tools. The same example will be written in VB 6.0 using the VB 6.0 drawing commands, VB 6.0 using the GDI API calls, and C++ using GDI.

Constructing a Fishbowl

The example I use in this chapter involves constructing a fishbowl and slowly filling it with sand and water. While the end result of each program will look the same to the user, the code will need to be very different based on the programming tools at hand. The graphical objects you will work with are as follows:

- PictureBox

- Lines

- Rectangles

- Circles

- Points

- Clipping regions

- Device context

So, why did I decide to use a fishbowl as the first project? It uses quite a few of the features of GDI without being too difficult. The methods used to program this type of object can also be readily used in the real world.

Using the VB 6.0 Drawing Tools

I mentioned in Chapter 1 that you could use a clipping region and rectangles to simulate filling a globe. Using stacking rectangles and showing only the part of the rectangle that is in the clipping circle is a very fast way to accomplish this task.

I also mentioned that this task is very difficult without using a clipping region. The VB 6.0 native graphics capability does not include any clipping region tool. This is unfortunate because as you will see, your programming life becomes really hard without it.

In VB 6.0, drawing is done on a particular object. Only those objects that allow you to draw on them have the methods necessary to allow this. Okay, what do I mean by this?

Open up a new VB 6.0 project and look at the properties of the default form. You have the following properties:

- DrawMode

- DrawStyle

- DrawWidth

- FillColor

- FillStyle

Now drop a button on the form and click it to view the properties. You will notice that these five properties do not exist for the button. There is also no provision to draw a circle or a line on the button. You cannot draw on quite a few VB 6.0 objects.

Let's look that these properties in a little more detail and try to equate them to GDI objects.

The **DrawMode** property allows you to determine how colors are blended the next time you draw something on the object. This would be equivalent to the color mask argument in the GDI **CreatePen** method.

The **DrawStyle** property sets the style of the line you want to draw, such as solid, dashed, and so forth. This property is equivalent to the pen style argument to the GDI **CreatePen** method.

The **DrawWidth** property sets the width of the line that will be drawn. This property is equivalent to the width argument to the GDI **CreatePen** method.

The **FillColor** property sets the color that the rectangle or circle will be filled with. This property is equivalent to setting the color argument of the GDI **CreateSolidBrush** method.

The **FillStyle** property determines how a shape is filled in. GDI has several types of brushes—for example, **CreateSolidBrush**, **CreatePatternBrush**, **CreateDIBPatternBrush**, and **CreateDIBPatternBrushPt**. Each of these brushes creates a different type of pattern inside a shape. The **FillStyle** property equates to choosing the type of brush you want.

GDI requires that you perform the following steps before you draw and fill a shape:

1. Create a pen and select its color and width.

2. Select the pen into the device context.

3. Create a brush and select its color and fill style.

4. Select the brush into the device context.

5. Draw the shape using one of the drawing tools, such as the rectangle tool.

VB 6.0 preselects the pen and brush into each object that allows drawing. The VB 6.0 properties mentioned previously are equivalent to setting up the arguments for the pen and brush when using the GDI methods.

Along with these properties you have four drawing methods available to you in VB 6.0:

- Circle

- Cls

- Pset

- Line

Yup, that's it. No explicit rectangle, ellipse, or any other type of shape. Not much to really work with here, but with judicious use of arguments you can get a few more shapes out of them.

Let's look at two of these four drawing methods in detail and try to equate them to GDI drawing methods.

The **Circle** drawing method has several arguments that allow you to change the shape into an arc, an ellipse, or a circle. However, you need to set up the width, fill color, and so forth beforehand using the properties from the object you want to draw on. Here is the basic circle command to draw on an object:

```
object.Circle (x,y), radius
```

If you leave out the object, VB assumes you want to create a shape on the form that the object is on. This is so different from the normal VB object methods as to be rather bizarre. The **Line** method is even stranger.

The **Line** drawing method has arguments that allow you to change the shape into a rectangle. Like the **Circle** method, however, you need to set up the width, fill color, and so forth beforehand using the properties from the object you want to draw on. The basic **Line** command is as follows:

```
object.Line (x1,y1) - (x2,y2), color, B, F
```

Again, if you leave out the object, VB assumes you want to create a shape on the form that the object is on.

Making the VB 6.0 Project

Now that I have given you a little background on drawing in VB, it is time to draw your fishbowl.

Open up a new VB 6.0 project and call it FishBowl_vb6. You will need a form and several controls. Here is a list of the objects you need for this project:

- *Form:* Call it FishBowl. Set the **BorderStyle** property to Fixed Single.

- *PictureBox:* Call it PicBowl. Make sure to set the PictureBox to AutoRedraw.

- *Label:* The caption should read "Elapsed Time".

- *Label:* Call this label lblTime, with no caption. Set the **BorderStyle** property to Fixed Single.

- *Button:* Call it cmdAPI. The caption should read "API Paint".

- *Button:* Call it cmdNative. The caption should read "Native Paint".

- *Button:* Call it cmdQuit. The caption should read "Quit".

- *BAS module:* Call it General.bas.

You will notice one extra button here called cmdAPI. For now it has no use, but later in the chapter you will write code to draw the same fishbowl using API calls. Figure 3-1 shows the layout of the form and its constituent controls.

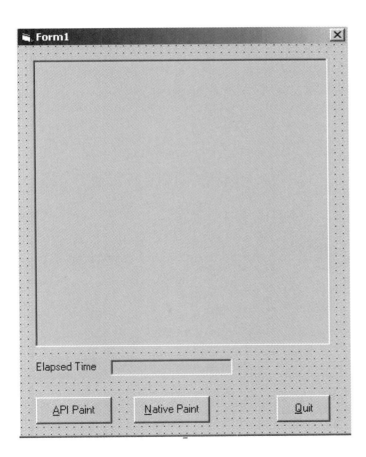

Figure 3-1. Layout of the VB 6.0 FishBowl form

As you can probably guess, the picture box is where the bowl will be drawn. The Elapsed Time box will give you an idea of how long it takes to fill the bowl from the bottom on up. Make the width and height of the picture box the same. If they are not the same, the circle, which represents the fishbowl, will become an ellipse.

> **TIP**   *Make sure that when you draw in a picture box, the aspect ratio is correct. A PictureBox can also host a bitmap picture. If the PictureBox is set to stretch the image to fit, it may not look right if the aspect ratio is wrong.*

Those of you who have never used the API to draw in VB 6.0 will be amazed at the speed increase. If you use VB 6.0 in the future or for legacy applications, you should become an API convert after this chapter.

It is time to enter some code to make this program work. You need some global constants and declarations for this program, so before you enter in code for the form, create a new module and call it General.bas. Listing 3-1 shows the initial code needed in this module. Later in the chapter, you will add quite a bit more to it.

Listing 3-1. General.bas Global Code

```
Option Explicit

Public Const PS_SOLID = 0
Public Const PIXEL_MODE = 3
```

Listing 3-2 shows the complete code to draw the fishbowl using native VB 6.0 commands. Let's get it working, and then I will dissect the code.

Listing 3-2. Code for the FishBowl Form

```
Option Explicit

Private tm As Single

Private Sub cmdNative_Click()
  Dim k As Single

  lblTime.Caption = ""
  cmdQuit.Enabled = False
```

```
    tm = Timer
    For k = 0.1 To 0.8 Step 0.01
      Call FillBowlNoAPI(k, 0.1)
      DoEvents
    Next

    lblTime.Caption = Format(Timer - tm, "0.###")
    cmdQuit.Enabled = True

End Sub

Private Sub cmdQuit_Click()
  End
End Sub

Private Sub FillBowlNoAPI(ht As Single, Sandht As Single)
    'The vb6 circle command draws either a circle, ellipse, or an arc.
    'The vb6 line command draws a line or a rectangle
    Dim x          As Integer
    Dim y          As Integer
    Dim r          As Integer
    Dim k          As Single
    Dim MaxY       As Integer
    Dim SandY      As Integer
    Dim SandColor  As Long
    Dim WaterColor As Long
    Dim Clr        As Long

    'Setup the object parameters
    picBowl.ScaleMode = PIXEL_MODE
    picBowl.Cls
    picBowl.DrawMode = 13              'blackness
    picBowl.DrawWidth = 1

    'Normalizing the circle parameters to the limits of the control
    x = picBowl.ScaleWidth / 2
    y = picBowl.ScaleHeight / 2
    r = (picBowl.ScaleHeight - 5) / 2

    'Draw the circle
    picBowl.FillColor = vbWhite
    picBowl.FillStyle = 0
    picBowl.Circle (x, y), r, vbBlack
```

55

```
    'This is so the water will not overflow the bowl :)
    If ht > 1# Then ht = 1#
    If Sandht > 1# Then Sandht = 1#

    'Normalize the heights to the limits of the control
    MaxY = picBowl.ScaleHeight - (ht * picBowl.ScaleHeight)
    SandY = picBowl.ScaleHeight - (Sandht * picBowl.ScaleHeight)

    SandColor = vbBlack
    WaterColor = vbBlue

'---------- Fill in using points ---------------------------------------------
    'This is how you would do it by setting each point individually
    For y = picBowl.ScaleHeight To MaxY Step -1
      If y > SandY Then
        Clr = SandColor
      Else
        Clr = WaterColor
      End If
      For k = 0 To picBowl.ScaleWidth
        If picBowl.Point(k, y) = vbWhite Then
          picBowl.PSet (k, y), Clr
        End If
      Next
    Next

    picBowl.Refresh

End Sub
```

Press F5 to run your program and look at the results. No errors should pop up. If errors do pop up, track them down and fix them.

Click the Native Paint button. What you should see (if you don't get too bored waiting) is the bowl first filling with black sand and then filling with blue water. Notice that the Quit button is disabled while the bowl is filling. I do this to keep you from killing the program before you see the results. Notice also that the bowl only fills to 80 percent of its volume. It would not be good to let the water spill onto the carpet. Figure 3-2 shows my screen after the program has run.

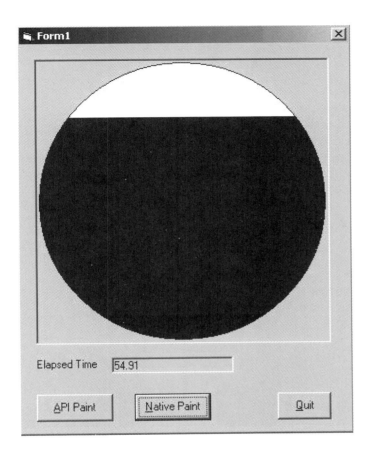

Figure 3-2. Filling the fishbowl using native VB 6.0 commands

My computer is no speed demon, but it's no slouch either. As you can see, it took almost 55 seconds to completely draw the image. Don't worry—things will speed up from here.

Filling by Using Individual Pixels

Open the code window for this form and I will explain what is going on. First of all, look at the **FillBowlNoAPI** function shown in Listing 3-3.

Listing 3-3. The FillBowlNoAPI Function

```vb
Private Sub FillBowlNoAPI(ht As Single, Sandht As Single)

    'The vb6 circle command draws either a circle, ellipse, or an arc.
    'The vb6 line command draws a line or a rectangle
    Dim x           As Integer
    Dim y           As Integer
    Dim r           As Integer
    Dim k           As Single
    Dim MaxY        As Integer
    Dim SandY       As Integer
    Dim SandColor   As Long
    Dim WaterColor  As Long
    Dim Clr         As Long

    'Setup the object parameters
    picBowl.ScaleMode = PIXEL_MODE
    picBowl.Cls
    picBowl.DrawMode = 13           'blackness
    picBowl.DrawWidth = 1

    'Normalizing the circle parameters to the limits of the control
    x = picBowl.ScaleWidth / 2
    y = picBowl.ScaleHeight / 2
    r = (picBowl.ScaleHeight - 5) / 2

    'Draw the circle
    picBowl.FillColor = vbWhite
    picBowl.FillStyle = 0
    picBowl.Circle (x, y), r, vbBlack

    'This is so the water will not overflow the bowl :)
    If ht > 1# Then ht = 1#
    If Sandht > 1# Then Sandht = 1#

    'Normalize the heights to the limits of the control
    MaxY = picBowl.ScaleHeight - (ht * picBowl.ScaleHeight)
    SandY = picBowl.ScaleHeight - (Sandht * picBowl.ScaleHeight)

    SandColor = vbBlack
    WaterColor = vbBlue
```

```
'---------- Fill in using points --------------------------------------------
  'This is how you would do it by setting each point individually
  For y = picBowl.ScaleHeight To MaxY Step -1
    If y > SandY Then
      Clr = SandColor
    Else
      Clr = WaterColor
    End If
    For k = 0 To picBowl.ScaleWidth
      If picBowl.Point(k, y) = vbWhite Then
        picBowl.PSet (k, y), Clr
      End If
    Next
  Next

  picBowl.Refresh

End Sub
```

The first thing I do in this function is set up the variables necessary to draw the circle. I said previously that the circle is defined by the aspect ratio of the picture box. You can see that I define the x, y, and r parameters of the circle according to the width and height of the picture box.

The arguments to this function are the height of the water and the height of the sand. I clamp these values to the maximum height of the bowl. This way, the water will not spill out onto the floor.

The algorithm for actually filling the space in the circle is as follows:

```
'---------- Fill in using points --------------------------------------------
  'This is how you would do it by setting each point individually
  For y = picBowl.ScaleHeight To MaxY Step -1
    If y > SandY Then
      Clr = SandColor
    Else
      Clr = WaterColor
    End If
    For k = 0 To picBowl.ScaleWidth
      If picBowl.Point(k, y) = vbWhite Then
        picBowl.PSet (k, y), Clr
      End If
    Next
  Next
```

This is a brute-force method of filling the bowl. What happens here is that I scan each line from left to right looking for a white pixel. If I find a white pixel, I know I am inside the circle (bowl). At this point (no pun intended) I set the pixel to either the color of the sand or the color of the water.

Now, is this efficient? No. Is it thorough? Yes. Does it take a long time to run? Yes, it does—a very long time, as shown by the 55 seconds it took to run on my computer. You can speed this up by fiddling with the algorithm a little to detect the last white point. When this happens, end the inside loop because you know there are no points left in the line that need to have their color changed. I tried this and it took about 3 seconds off the total time. Not worth it, really, considering that it took almost a minute to complete.

The next function to look at is the one that calls the **FillBowlNoAPI** function:

```
Private Sub cmdNative_Click()
  Dim k As Single

  lblTime.Caption = ""
  cmdQuit.Enabled = False

  tm = Timer
  For k = 0.1 To 0.8 Step 0.01
    Call FillBowlNoAPI(k, 0.1)
    DoEvents
  Next

  lblTime.Caption = Format(Timer - tm, "0.###")
  cmdQuit.Enabled = True

End Sub
```

The loop calls the **FillBowl** function 800 times. Each time, the bowl is filled a little more. This is supposed to simulate a smooth fill of the fishbowl. The DoEvents call allows the mouse to move smoothly on the screen.

Filling by Using Lines

It is time to speed things up a little. While the point method is very thorough, it is also very time consuming. Comment out the following code in the **FillBowlNoAPI** method:

```
'---------- Fill in using points -------------------------------------------
  'This is how you would do it by setting each point individually
  For y = picBowl.ScaleHeight To MaxY Step -1
    If y > SandY Then
      Clr = SandColor
    Else
      Clr = WaterColor
    End If
    For k = 0 To picBowl.ScaleWidth
      If picBowl.Point(k, y) = vbWhite Then
        picBowl.PSet (k, y), Clr
      End If
    Next
  Next
```

Add the following code right below the commented code:

```
'---------- Fill in by using line -------------------------------------------
  'Start at the left end and search till you get a white point.  This is StartX
  'Keep searching till you get a NOT white point.  This is EndX
  Dim StartX  As Integer
  Dim EndX    As Integer
  For y = picBowl.ScaleHeight To MaxY Step -1
    If y > SandY Then
      Clr = SandColor
    Else
      Clr = WaterColor
    End If

    For k = 0 To picBowl.ScaleWidth
      If picBowl.Point(k, y) = vbWhite Then
        StartX = k
        Exit For
      End If
    Next
    For k = StartX To picBowl.ScaleWidth
      If picBowl.Point(k, y) <> vbWhite Then
        EndX = k
        Exit For
      End If
    Next
    picBowl.Line (StartX, y)-(EndX, y), Clr
  Next
```

You can see that this code replaces the algorithm for filling the fishbowl from using individual pixels to using lines. Press F5 and run the program again.

Filling up the bowl with this algorithm took a little more than half the time at 31 seconds. I enhanced this algorithm a little by ending the For loop when the last white point was detected. Using the line method is a big improvement over using the point method.

So, what would a really big improvement be? I mentioned using stacking rectangles and a clipping region in the form of a circle. Unfortunately, VB 6.0 does not have any region capability built in. The **Line** method is able to create a rectangle, but that does not help you in this case.

Filling by Using the GDI API Calls

The best way to make this program work fast is to use the GDI API calls.

GDI has been around a long time. You will find the GDI library in the GDI32.DLL file in your Windows System directory. Since the GDI library is a DLL, its functions can be called from within VB 6.0. As with all Windows system calls, you will need to declare the functions first. In this program, the declarations are defined in the General.bas module file.

Declaring Your API Intentions

Open up the General.bas module and enter the code shown in Listing 3-4.

Listing 3-4. GDI Declarations

```
Option Explicit

Public Const PS_SOLID = 0
Public Const PIXEL_MODE = 3

'============ Windows API functions ========================
Declare Function CreatePen Lib "gdi32" (ByVal nPenStyle As Long, _
                                        ByVal nWidth As Long, _
                                        ByVal crColor As Long) As Long

Declare Function CreateEllipticRgn Lib "gdi32" (ByVal X1 As Long, _
                                                ByVal Y1 As Long, _
                                                ByVal X2 As Long, _
                                                ByVal Y2 As Long) As Long
```

```
Declare Function CreateSolidBrush Lib "gdi32" (ByVal crColor As Long) As Long

Declare Function DeleteObject Lib "gdi32" (ByVal hObject As Long) As Long

Declare Function Ellipse Lib "gdi32" (ByVal hdc As Long, _
                                      ByVal X1 As Long, _
                                      ByVal Y1 As Long, _
                                      ByVal X2 As Long, _
                                      ByVal Y2 As Long) As Long

Declare Function Rectangle Lib "gdi32" (ByVal hdc As Long, _
                                        ByVal X1 As Long, _
                                        ByVal Y1 As Long, _
                                        ByVal X2 As Long, _
                                        ByVal Y2 As Long) As Long

Declare Function RestoreDC Lib "gdi32" (ByVal hdc As Long, _
                                        ByVal nSavedDC As Long) As Long

Declare Function SaveDC Lib "gdi32" (ByVal hdc As Long) As Long

Declare Function SelectClipRgn Lib "gdi32" (ByVal hdc As Long, _
                                            ByVal hRgn As Long) As Long

Declare Function SelectObject Lib "gdi32" (ByVal hdc As Long, _
                                           ByVal hObject As Long) As Long

Declare Sub Sleep Lib "Kernel32" (ByVal dwMilliseconds As Long)
'=====================================================================
```

I include several GDI API functions:

- *CreatePen:* This function defines the pen that draws the shapes.

- *CreateSolidBrush:* This function defines the brush that fills in the shapes.

- *CreateEllipticRgn:* This function defines the clipping region (in your case, the circle).

- *DeleteObject:* This function deletes an object, thereby reclaiming its memory.

- *Ellipse:* This function creates the circle.

- *Rectangle:* This function creates the rectangles.

- *RestoreDC:* This function restores the device context to what it was before.

- *SaveDC:* This function saves the device context before you play around with it.

- *SelectClipRgn:* This function selects the clipping region into the device context.

- *SelectObject:* This function selects a drawing tool into the device context.

- *Sleep:* This function is not GDI related, but it allows the current thread to sleep.

Adding GDI Calls to the Main Program

Now it is time to make use of these GDI API functions and fill the fishbowl a little faster. Remember the extra button that invokes the API calls? You will be using that as well. Add the code in Listing 3-5 to the FishBowl form code.

Listing 3-5. GDI API Calls to Fill the Fishbowl

```
Private Sub FillBowlAPI(BK1ht As Single, BK3ht As Single)
  Dim Brush     As Long
  Dim Pen       As Long
  Dim OldPen    As Long
  Dim OldBrush  As Long
  Dim OldDc     As Long
  Dim hRegion   As Long

  Dim ScaleDiameter  As Integer
  Dim MidRect        As Integer
  Dim BottomRect     As Integer

  'Make sure that the mode is in pixels because that is what the WIN API
  'functions need
  picBowl.ScaleMode = PIXEL_MODE
  picBowl.Cls

  ScaleDiameter = picBowl.ScaleHeight
  If BK1ht > 1 Then BK1ht = 1
  If BK3ht > 1 Then BK3ht = 1
  MidRect = BK1ht * ScaleDiameter
  BottomRect = BK3ht * ScaleDiameter
```

```
'save the device context
OldDc = SaveDC(picBowl.hdc)

'The circle and clipping region only needs to be done once for the
'tank as a whole
'Create a series of stacking rectangles within the circle to
'represent the levels

' Create the clipping region for the circle
hRegion = CreateEllipticRgn(2, 2, picBowl.ScaleWidth - 2, ScaleDiameter - 2)
Call SelectClipRgn(picBowl.hdc, hRegion)

'Draw the main rectangle
'This draws a rectangle that starts above the bottom and ends at the bottom
Pen = CreatePen(PS_SOLID, 1, vbBlue)
OldPen = SelectObject(picBowl.hdc, Pen)
Brush = CreateSolidBrush(vbBlue)
OldBrush = SelectObject(picBowl.hdc, Brush)
Call Rectangle(picBowl.hdc, 0, ScaleDiameter - MidRect, _
                picBowl.ScaleWidth, ScaleDiameter)
'First restore original objects into the device context
Call SelectObject(picBowl.hdc, OldPen)
Call SelectObject(picBowl.hdc, OldBrush)
'Destroy objects to prevent memory leaks
Call DeleteObject(Pen)
Call DeleteObject(Brush)

'Draw the top rectangle
'This draws a rectangle that starts at the top and ends at the
'top of the previous rectangle
Pen = CreatePen(PS_SOLID, 1, vbWhite)
OldPen = SelectObject(picBowl.hdc, Pen)
Brush = CreateSolidBrush(vbWhite)
OldBrush = SelectObject(picBowl.hdc, Brush)
Call Rectangle(picBowl.hdc, 0, 0, picBowl.ScaleWidth, ScaleDiameter - MidRect)
'First restore original objects into the device context
Call SelectObject(picBowl.hdc, OldPen)
Call SelectObject(picBowl.hdc, OldBrush)
'Destroy objects to prevent memory leaks
Call DeleteObject(Pen)
Call DeleteObject(Brush)
```

```
'Draw the bottom rectangle
'This draws a rectangle that starts above the bottom and ends at the bottom
'It overwrites a portion of the first rectangle
Pen = CreatePen(PS_SOLID, 1, vbBlack)
OldPen = SelectObject(picBowl.hdc, Pen)
Brush = CreateSolidBrush(vbBlack)
OldBrush = SelectObject(picBowl.hdc, Brush)
Call Rectangle(picBowl.hdc, 0, ScaleDiameter - BottomRect, _
                picBowl.ScaleWidth, ScaleDiameter)
'First restore original objects into the device context
Call SelectObject(picBowl.hdc, OldPen)
Call SelectObject(picBowl.hdc, OldBrush)
'Destroy objects to prevent memory leaks
Call DeleteObject(Pen)
Call DeleteObject(Brush)

'Destroy the region to avoid memory leaks
Call DeleteObject(hRegion)
Call RestoreDC(picBowl.hdc, OldDc)

picBowl.Refresh
Me.Refresh

End Sub
```

Now that you have added the new code to fill the fishbowl using GDI functions, you will need to add code to the cmdAPI button to invoke this code. Listing 3-6 shows the code to invoke the GDI functions.

Listing 3-6. Button Code to Invoke GDI API Functions

```
'This piece of code creates a stack of 3 blocks that fills the
'whole picture control
'There is a clipping region that is made in the form of a circle
'It is the clipping region that make it appear to the user
'that the circle is being filled.
Private Sub cmdapi_Click()
  Dim k As Single

  lblTime.Caption = ""
  cmdQuit.Enabled = False
```

```
  tm = Timer
  For k = 0.1 To 0.8 Step 0.01
    Call FillBowlAPI(k, 0.1)
    DoEvents
  Next

  lblTime.Caption = Format(Timer - tm, "0.###")
  cmdQuit.Enabled = True

End Sub
```

This button code is identical to the button code that invokes the VB 6.0 drawing function. The loop runs the same number of times. After you enter in the code, press F5 to run the program. Click the API Paint button and see what happens.

On my machine, the result was that the painting was done in 0.18 seconds. That is less than 1 second to fill the fishbowl, which is over 300 times faster on my machine than using the native VB 6.0 commands. *Wow!*

If you want to see the bowl fill a little slower, add the **Sleep** function just after the DoEvents call in the button code. If the thread sleeps for about 30 milliseconds during every loop iteration, you will see a smooth filling of the circle.

Examining the GDI Code

It is very instructive to look at the GDI code in some detail. You will see what looks like a lot of repetitive code. It is, however, necessary.

Similar to the VB 6.0 drawing code, the first thing I do in this function is set up the picture box and the diameters of the rectangle and the circle clipping region. This is shown in the code that follows. You have probably noticed that I am fond of the pixel mode. Not to mention that the GDI API only works in pixels. The native graphics mode for any object in VB 6.0 is the twips mode. Microsoft has dispensed with twips in .NET. All graphics are done in pixels, as they should be.

```
…
  'Make sure that the mode is in pixels because that is what the
  'WIN API functions need
  picBowl.ScaleMode = PIXEL_MODE
  picBowl.Cls

  ScaleDiameter = picBowl.ScaleHeight
  If BK1ht > 1 Then BK1ht = 1
  If BK3ht > 1 Then BK3ht = 1
  MidRect = BK1ht * ScaleDiameter
  BottomRect = BK3ht * ScaleDiameter
…
```

The GDI API allows me to create a clipping region in the form of a circle. Doing this allows me to form the filled bowl with only three rectangles instead of thousands of pixels or hundreds of lines. It makes for a much faster draw.

The first thing I do as far as drawing is concerned is save the current device handle and draw the clipping region in the form of a circle.

```
...
'save the device context
OldDc = SaveDC(picBowl.hdc)

'The circle and clipping region only needs to be done once for the
'tank as a whole
'Create a series of stacking rectangles within the circle to represent the levels
' Create the clipping region for the circle
hRegion = CreateEllipticRgn(2, 2, picBowl.ScaleWidth - 2, ScaleDiameter - 2)
Call SelectClipRgn(picBowl.hdc, hRegion)
...
```

In this code I create the elliptical clipping region with identical height and width. This makes a circle. I also leave 2 pixels on either side of the circle to simulate a reveal. The next thing I do is to draw the three rectangles. The first one is the water, the second one is the ullage or empty space, and the third one is the sand. The code is shown in Listing 3-7.

Listing 3-7. Code to Draw Rectangles Using GDI API Calls

```
...
'Draw the main rectangle
'This draws a rectangle that starts above the bottom and ends at the bottom
Pen = CreatePen(PS_SOLID, 1, vbBlue)
OldPen = SelectObject(picBowl.hdc, Pen)
Brush = CreateSolidBrush(vbBlue)
OldBrush = SelectObject(picBowl.hdc, Brush)
Call Rectangle(picBowl.hdc, 0, ScaleDiameter - MidRect, picBowl.ScaleWidth, _
                         ScaleDiameter)
'First restore original objects into the device context
Call SelectObject(picBowl.hdc, OldPen)
Call SelectObject(picBowl.hdc, OldBrush)
'Destroy objects to prevent memory leaks
Call DeleteObject(Pen)
Call DeleteObject(Brush)
```

```
'Draw the top rectangle
'This draws a rectangle that starts at the top and ends at the top of the
' previous rectangle
Pen = CreatePen(PS_SOLID, 1, vbWhite)
OldPen = SelectObject(picBowl.hdc, Pen)
Brush = CreateSolidBrush(vbWhite)
OldBrush = SelectObject(picBowl.hdc, Brush)
Call Rectangle(picBowl.hdc, 0, 0, picBowl.ScaleWidth, ScaleDiameter - MidRect)
'First restore original objects into the device context
Call SelectObject(picBowl.hdc, OldPen)
Call SelectObject(picBowl.hdc, OldBrush)
'Destroy objects to prevent memory leaks
Call DeleteObject(Pen)
Call DeleteObject(Brush)

'Draw the bottom rectangle
'This draws a rectangle that starts above the bottom and ends at the bottom
'It overwrites a portion of the first rectangle
Pen = CreatePen(PS_SOLID, 1, vbBlack)
OldPen = SelectObject(picBowl.hdc, Pen)
Brush = CreateSolidBrush(vbBlack)
OldBrush = SelectObject(picBowl.hdc, Brush)
Call Rectangle(picBowl.hdc, 0, ScaleDiameter - BottomRect, picBowl.ScaleWidth, _
                     ScaleDiameter)
'First restore original objects into the device context
Call SelectObject(picBowl.hdc, OldPen)
Call SelectObject(picBowl.hdc, OldBrush)
'Destroy objects to prevent memory leaks
Call DeleteObject(Pen)
Call DeleteObject(Brush)
...
```

All three rectangles are drawn the same way. The only difference is where the rectangles are drawn, their color, and their height. Here are the steps involved:

1. Create the Pen.

2. Select the Pen into the picture box and save the old Pen.

3. Create a solid Brush.

4. Select the Brush into the picture box and save the old Brush.

5. Draw the rectangle in the picture box.

6. Select the old Pen back into the picture box.

7. Select the old Brush back into the picture box.

8. Delete the Pen and the Brush objects.

It is time to run a little experiment. You need to be warned, though: This experiment will at worst crash your computer, but most likely it will just cause funny things to happen. As the saying goes, save and close all other programs first.

Creating a Memory Leak

Comment out the code just after each call to the rectangle function. Your code should look like Listing 3-8.

Listing 3-8. Code to Draw Rectangles with Some Code Commented Out

```
...
'Draw the main rectangle
'This draws a rectangle that starts above the bottom and ends at the bottom
Pen = CreatePen(PS_SOLID, 1, vbBlue)
OldPen = SelectObject(picBowl.hdc, Pen)
Brush = CreateSolidBrush(vbBlue)
OldBrush = SelectObject(picBowl.hdc, Brush)
Call Rectangle(picBowl.hdc, 0, ScaleDiameter - MidRect, picBowl.ScaleWidth, _
                ScaleDiameter)
'First restore original objects into the device context
'Call SelectObject(picBowl.hdc, OldPen)
'Call SelectObject(picBowl.hdc, OldBrush)
'Destroy objects to prevent memory leaks
'Call DeleteObject(Pen)
'Call DeleteObject(Brush)

'Draw the top rectangle
'This draws a rectangle that starts at the top and ends at the
'top of the previous rectangle
Pen = CreatePen(PS_SOLID, 1, vbWhite)
OldPen = SelectObject(picBowl.hdc, Pen)
Brush = CreateSolidBrush(vbWhite)
OldBrush = SelectObject(picBowl.hdc, Brush)
Call Rectangle(picBowl.hdc, 0, 0, picBowl.ScaleWidth, ScaleDiameter - MidRect)
'First restore original objects into the device context
```

```
'Call SelectObject(picBowl.hdc, OldPen)
'Call SelectObject(picBowl.hdc, OldBrush)
'Destroy objects to prevent memory leaks
'Call DeleteObject(Pen)
'Call DeleteObject(Brush)

'Draw the bottom rectangle
'This draws a rectangle that starts above the bottom and ends at the bottom
'It overwrites a portion of the first rectangle
Pen = CreatePen(PS_SOLID, 1, vbBlack)
OldPen = SelectObject(picBowl.hdc, Pen)
Brush = CreateSolidBrush(vbBlack)
OldBrush = SelectObject(picBowl.hdc, Brush)
Call Rectangle(picBowl.hdc, 0, ScaleDiameter - BottomRect, _
                       picBowl.ScaleWidth,  ScaleDiameter)
'First restore original objects into the device context
' Call SelectObject(picBowl.hdc, OldPen)
'Call SelectObject(picBowl.hdc, OldBrush)
'Destroy objects to prevent memory leaks
'Call DeleteObject(Pen)
'Call DeleteObject(Brush)
…
```

Now change the code in the cmdAPI button click event. What you will do is add another loop to fill the fishbowl ten times. The code is shown in Listing 3-9.

Listing 3-9. New Code to Fill the Bowl Ten Times

```
…
Private Sub cmdapi_Click()
  Dim k As Single
  Dim j As Integer

  lblTime.Caption = ""
  cmdQuit.Enabled = False

  tm = Timer
  For j = 0 To 10
    For k = 0.1 To 0.8 Step 0.01
      Call FillBowlAPI(k, 0.1)
      DoEvents
    Next
  Next
```

```
        lblTime.Caption = Format(Timer - tm, "0.###")
        cmdQuit.Enabled = True

    End Sub
    ...
```

Now it is time to run the program again. Press F5 and see what happens.

NOTE   *This example is sure to cause a memory fault. You may see strange things happen or your computer may lock up. If you see strange things happen on your screen, just kill VB 6.0. This should release all GDI memory involved.*

Depending on the amount of memory your computer has, you should see your computer degrade after about the second or third time filling the fishbowl.

What you have just experienced is a very accelerated version of the GDI memory leak. This can be very insidious and may not show up for days or even weeks of running a normal program. This is one of the most common types of memory leaks you will come across. Fortunately, the .NET garbage collector will clean up these undeleted objects for you. When you work with GDI+, it is still best that you clean up after yourself, but if you forget to do so, the garbage collection will save you.

TIP   *Relying on the .NET garbage collector to clean up your messes is not good programming practice. This is why there is a **Dispose** method in the .NET GDI+ classes.*

Every time you create a GDI object such as a Pen or a Brush, you will need to free the object after you are done with it.

Graphics in C++

I have taken you through the fishbowl example in VB 6.0. There are few ways to accomplish the same drawing task, but as you saw, the GDI API is the best way. What about C++? How do C++ programmers do graphics in MFC or ATL?

The answer is that the graphics programming is done in C++ using the GDI32 API calls. There is no nice, neat, but limiting graphics capability in C++ as there is in VB 6.0. C++ programmers would use the exact same method I used in the GDI API algorithm for this project. The API calls would be identical and in the same order. Listing 3-10 shows the VB 6.0 **FillBowlAPI** function written in C++. I used this function some time ago to make an OCX in ATL. It is very fast indeed. I should note that some of the variables shown in this code snippet are global.

Listing 3-10. C++ Function to Fill a Circle Using GDI Calls

```cpp
void CBigTank::DrawTank()
{
  long ScaleDiam;
  long ScaleWater;
  long ScaleSand;
  COLORREF ColFill;

  HWND hFrame = GetDlgItem(IDC_BIGTANK);
  HDC  hdc    = ::GetDC(hFrame);
  RECT rect   = {0,0,0,0};
  ::GetClientRect (hFrame, &rect);

  ScaleDiam = rect.bottom - INNERBOUND;
  if (m_Diam == 0 )
  {
      ScaleWater  = 0;
      ScaleSand = 0;
  }
  else
  {
          ScaleWater  = (long)(( m_WaterHeight  / m_Diam) * ScaleDiam);
          ScaleSand = (long)(( m_SandHeight / m_Diam) * ScaleDiam);
  }


  // ********************* Draw the circle outline   *********************
  OleTranslateColor ( X_BLACK, NULL, &ColFill );
  HPEN hPen  = CreatePen( PS_SOLID,2, ColFill );
  HGDIOBJ hOldPen  = SelectObject( hdc, hPen );
  OleTranslateColor ( X_WHITE, NULL, &ColFill );
  HBRUSH hBrush  = CreateSolidBrush( ColFill );
  HGDIOBJ hOldBrush  = SelectObject( hdc, hBrush );
  Ellipse( hdc, rect.left+INNERBOUND, rect.top+INNERBOUND,
              rect.right-INNERBOUND, rect.bottom-INNERBOUND );
```

```
//Reselect old objects and destroy objects to prevent memory leaks
SelectObject( hdc, hOldPen );
SelectObject( hdc, hOldBrush );
DeleteObject( hPen );
DeleteObject( hBrush );


//Create the eliptical clipping region.  put stacked rectangles inside
HRGN hRegion = CreateEllipticRgn(INNERBOUND, INNERBOUND,
                 rect.right-INNERBOUND, rect.bottom-INNERBOUND);
SelectClipRgn (hdc, hRegion);

// ********************** Draw the Water rectangle  **********************
OleTranslateColor ( m_WaterColor, NULL, &ColFill );
hPen             = CreatePen( PS_SOLID,1, ColFill );
hOldPen = SelectObject( hdc, hPen );
hBrush  = CreateSolidBrush( ColFill );
hOldBrush  = SelectObject( hdc, hBrush );
Rectangle( hdc, rect.left+INNERBOUND, ScaleDiam-ScaleWater,
                 rect.right-INNERBOUND, rect.bottom-INNERBOUND );

//Reselect old objects and destroy objects to prevent memory leaks
SelectObject( hdc, hOldPen );
SelectObject( hdc, hOldBrush );
DeleteObject( hPen );
DeleteObject( hBrush );


// ********************** Draw the Ullage Rectangle **********************
OleTranslateColor ( m_UllageColor, NULL, &ColFill );
hPen             = CreatePen( PS_SOLID,1, ColFill );
hOldPen  = SelectObject( hdc, hPen );
hBrush   = CreateSolidBrush( ColFill );
hOldBrush  = SelectObject( hdc, hBrush );
Rectangle( hdc, rect.left+INNERBOUND, rect.top+INNERBOUND,
                 rect.right-INNERBOUND, rect.bottom-ScaleWater );

//Reselect old objects and destroy objects to prevent memory leaks
SelectObject( hdc, hOldPen );
SelectObject( hdc, hOldBrush );
DeleteObject( hPen );
DeleteObject( hBrush );
```

```
// ********************* Draw the Sand Rectangle *********************
OleTranslateColor ( m_SandColor, NULL, &ColFill );
hPen            = CreatePen( PS_SOLID,1, ColFill );
hOldPen  = SelectObject( hdc, hPen );
hBrush  = CreateSolidBrush( ColFill );
hOldBrush  = SelectObject( hdc, hBrush );
Rectangle( hdc, rect.left+INNERBOUND, ScaleDiam-ScaleSand,
                rect.right-INNERBOUND, rect.bottom-INNERBOUND );

//Reselect old objects and destroy objects to prevent memory leaks
SelectObject( hdc, hOldPen );
SelectObject( hdc, hOldBrush );
DeleteObject( hPen );
DeleteObject( hBrush );

DeleteObject( hRegion );
}
```

I will explain what is going on in this function for the benefit of those unfamiliar with GDI programming in C++. Let's look at the function in small chunks. The first part sets up the function for drawing:

```
...
HWND hFrame = GetDlgItem(IDC_BIGTANK);
HDC   hdc    = ::GetDC(hFrame);
RECT rect   = {0,0,0,0};
::GetClientRect (hFrame, &rect);

ScaleDiam = rect.bottom - INNERBOUND;
if (m_Diam == 0 )
{
    ScaleWater  = 0;
  ScaleSand = 0;
}
else
{
    ScaleWater  = (long)(( m_WaterHeight  / m_Diam ) * ScaleDiam);
    ScaleSand = (long)(( m_SandHeight / m_Diam ) * ScaleDiam);
}
...
```

First of all, I need to get a handle to the dialog window that will contain the drawing. In this case the object I am drawing on is a picture box whose identifier is

IDC_BIGTANK. Once I have the window handle, I use it to get the handle to the HDC or the device context.

Next, I set up the rectangle structure and fill this structure with the coordinates from the client frame. This is what the **GetClientRect** function does.

This function has a few more parameters to look at, such as the diameter of the tank. If the diameter is not zero, I set the water and sand height properties to the correct normalized values.

Next, I draw the circle and define the clipping region. The code that does this is as follows:

```
...
// ********************* Draw the circle outline    *********************
OleTranslateColor ( TLS_BLACK, NULL, &ColFill );
HPEN hPen  = CreatePen( PS_SOLID,2, ColFill );
HGDIOBJ hOldPe = SelectObject( hdc, hPen );
OleTranslateColor ( TLS_WHITE, NULL, &ColFill );
HBRUSH hBrush  = CreateSolidBrush( ColFill );
HGDIOBJ hOldBrush  = SelectObject( hdc, hBrush );
Ellipse( hdc, rect.left+INNERBOUND, rect.top+INNERBOUND,
            rect.right-INNERBOUND, rect.bottom-INNERBOUND );

//Reselect old objects and destroy objects to prevent memory leaks
SelectObject( hdc, hOldPen );
SelectObject( hdc, hOldBrush );
DeleteObject( hPen );
DeleteObject( hBrush );

//Create the eliptical clipping region.  put stacked rectangles inside
HRGN hRegion = CreateEllipticRgn(INNERBOUND, INNERBOUND,
                rect.right-INNERBOUND, rect.bottom-INNERBOUND);
SelectClipRgn (hdc, hRegion);
...
```

What happens here is that I draw a circle that has a black outline and a white filling (sounds like an Oreo cookie). I then create an elliptical clipping region that has the exact same outline as the circle. When I create the rectangle, the only part of what I draw that will show up will be inside the circle.

Notice that after I am done with a piece of the drawing, I select back the old pen and brush and then destroy the pen and brush that I created. This is the exact code I used in the VB 6.0 API function to free memory.

The next chunk of code creates the three rectangles that define the look of the filled bowl. The code for one of these rectangles is as follows:

```
...
// ********************* Draw the Water rectangle  *********************
OleTranslateColor ( m_FuelColor, NULL, &ColFill );
hPen           = CreatePen( PS_SOLID,1, ColFill );
hOldPen  = SelectObject( hdc, hPen );
hBrush = CreateSolidBrush( ColFill );
hOldBrush  = SelectObject( hdc, hBrush );
Rectangle( hdc, rect.left+INNERBOUND, ScaleDiam-ScaleWater,
               rect.right-INNERBOUND, rect.bottom-INNERBOUND );


//Reselect old objects and destroy objects to prevent memory leaks
SelectObject( hdc, hOldPen );
SelectObject( hdc, hOldBrush );
DeleteObject( hPen );
DeleteObject( hBrush );
...
```

This is pretty much the same code as for the circle. The other two rectangles use the same piece of code as well.

The last thing I do before I leave this function is delete the region I created. I cannot state it strongly enough: *Always clean up after yourself!* You will avoid so many bugs. The cost of carefully written software is so much less than that of buggy software.

Summary

This chapter took you through a tour of some graphics programming in VB 6.0 using both native functions and API calls. I also showed you the main routine for this project, as it would be written in C++.

It is important to go through this kind of chapter to give you some perspective on how much better GDI+ is. It is also important to note that VB 6.0 and C++ will be around for some time to come. Hopefully, this example will be of some use to you.

What you have seen is that VB 6.0 has two ways to draw shapes: drawing using the native functions or drawing using the GDI API functions.

The native VB 6.0 drawing functions consist of setting various color, line style, and fill parameters for the object you are drawing on. You then call the object's graphics function to draw the shape using the line width, color, and fill color you set up in advance.

The native VB 6.0 drawing functions are constrained in that there is no clipping region available. The clipping region allows you create a shape, such as a rectangle, and only those parts of the rectangle that are inside the clipping region will show up. Without a clipping region, drawing inside a complex shape (such as a circle) is very processor-intensive and slow.

You can use the GDI API functions from within VB 6.0 or C++. These functions contain a clipping region and several more shape functions. Using the GDI API functions to draw the filled fishbowl project in this chapter resulted in a speed over 300 times faster than using native VB 6.0 commands.

The next chapter introduces you to vector graphics using .NET GDI+. I will go into some detail on the features of the System.Drawing namespace. You will see quite an improvement to drawing using GDI+ as opposed to GDI or VB 6.0.

CHAPTER 4

Vector Graphics

Andre, a simple peasant, had only one thing on his mind as he crept along the east wall: "Andre creep . . . Andre creep . . . Andre creep."

—David Allen Janzen, Davis, California

IN CHAPTER 3, you learned how to draw some interesting graphics using VB 6.0 native drawing commands and some GDI graphics commands. I hope I also managed to impress upon you the importance of memory management in GDI. Although you will not use the GDI32 commands or VB 6.0 commands again in this book, I think they provide a nice contrast to how things are done in the GDI+ world.

This chapter introduces you to the most common of the GDI+ graphics capabilities. I provide in-depth coverage of the System.Drawing namespace. I also provide plenty of examples of how to use these new functionalities in both C# and VB .NET.

Coordinate Systems and Transformations

The three types of coordinate spaces in GDI+ are as follows:

- The world coordinate space

- The page coordinate space

- The device coordinate space

These three coordinate spaces and their relationships are key in knowing how .NET will draw in the GDI+ space.

Transforming World Coordinates

World coordinates define how you want your shape to be drawn. These coordinates remain constant irrespective of where the shape is actually drawn and its actual size. What do I mean by this?

Suppose you wanted a line drawn starting at the origin and ending at points 100, 100. Your command would be as follows (assuming that *G* is the Graphics region and the points are in world coordinates):

```
G.DrawLine(Pens.DarkBlue, 0, 0, 100, 100)
```

You would think this would be a diagonal line starting at the top-left corner of the client area and ending 100 pixels down and to the right of the origin. As a default, you would be right. The default page coordinates are the same as the world coordinates, which are the same as the default device coordinates. The default units of measurement are also pixels.

It is possible to apply a transform to the world coordinates so that the line in the previous example would appear in a completely different place. You would do this by using the **TranslateTransform** method.

Apply a transform to the world coordinates to get a different set of page coordinates. Now draw the same line.

```
G.TranslateTransform(20.0F, 20.0F)
G.DrawLine(Pens.DarkBlue, 0, 0, 100, 100)
```

What you get here is a line that actually starts at (20, 20) and ends at (120, 120). The page coordinates are translated 20 pixels in the X direction and 20 pixels in the Y direction. The line is drawn in a completely different area than your line command specified.

You have noticed, I am sure, that the arguments to the **TranslateTransform** method are floats. Why use a float for a transform argument when you are talking pixels? The answer is that it is not necessary to use a float value for pixels. However, the page coordinate system could have units of inches, not pixels. A floating-point argument for a transformation would come in handy for inches or millimeters.

Transforming Device Coordinates

Now you know about world and page coordinates, but what about device coordinates? The smallest unit on a screen is the pixel. The pixel is also the default transformation. This means that unless you change the **PageUnit** property to something other than pixel, your device coordinates will be the same as your page coordinates. What happens if you try the following code?

```
G.PageUnit = GraphicsUnit.Inch
G.TranslateTransform(1.0F, 1.0F)
G.DrawLine(Pens.DarkBlue, 0, 0, 1, 1)
```

You get a line, that's what. Seriously, though, this is how things will shake out:

- World coordinates define the line to start at (0, 0) and end at (1, 1). Units are not defined here.

- Page units have been changed from pixels to inches.

- The page coordinate system has the line starting at (1 inch, 1 inch) and ending at (2 inches, 2 inches).

- The default pen has a width of 1 (1 inch, that is).

- The device coordinates are defined by the vertical and horizontal resolution of your screen. Mine is 96dpi. The device coordinates would be (96, 96) to (192, 192).

This is a pretty fat line. What happens is kind of cool, though. Think of a mapping program. You could draw a map on your screen that's actually drawn to scale.

So, to summarize: If the **PageUnit** property is in pixels, the world, page, and device coordinates are all the same. If the **PageUnit** property is in something other than pixels, a transform is applied to get the actual scaling used. This is enough for now. You will learn about transformations in depth later in this chapter and in subsequent chapters.

Using the System.Drawing Namespace

The GDI+ classes are all encapsulated under the System.Drawing namespace. This is the top-level namespace, and it has several specialized namespaces under it:

- System.Drawing.Drawing2D

- System.Drawing.Imaging

- System.Drawing.Text

- System.Drawing.Printing

- System.Drawing.Design

The 2D namespace is an extension of the capabilities provided by the System.Drawing namespace. Chapter 5 details this namespace.

The System.Drawing.Imaging namespace is all about images such as bitmaps, JPEG files, and so forth. Chapter 6 details this namespace.

The System.Drawing.Text namespace is all about rendering text on the screen. It includes classes to handle existing fonts as well as custom fonts. Chapter 7 details this namespace.

The System.Drawing.Printing namespace is pretty self-explanatory. This namespace provides classes to help in printing. Printing is often the forgotten stepchild of graphics programming. Just press Alt-PrtScn and you are all done, right? Not quite. Chapter 8 details printing.

The last namespace in the System.Drawing namespace list is System.Drawing.Design. This namespace has classes that are helpful in extending the capabilities of the IDE. You can create custom toolbox items and type-specific editors for graphical objects. This namespace is really not necessary for everyday programming of graphics, and I will not discuss it further in this book. Extending the IDE is a subject for another book altogether.

The System.Drawing Classes

The System.Drawing namespace contains 28 classes, 8 structures, 4 delegates, and 10 enumerations. As you can probably guess, each of these classes contains quite a few methods and properties.

Because the structures are designed to hold information necessary for some of the methods in the classes, I do not deal with them separately. Rather, I explain a particular structure if and when it shows up.

Using the Pen Class

You have seen a pen used before in this book. Chapters 1 and 3 contain small drawing examples that use a pen.

A pen is used to draw a line that has a particular width and style. The line need not be straight—it could take on any shape. Drawing a curve, ellipse, or circle requires a Pen object, just as drawing a rectangle or a line does.

Most of the shapes you draw will consist of solid lines. It is possible, however, to draw lines that consist of dashes or dots. The DashStyle enumeration has the following members:

- Custom

- Dash

- DashDot

- DashDotDot

- Dot

- Solid

You can choose one of the standard styles or make up your own using the **Custom** property. You will make a custom line in Chapter 5.

The Pen Constructor

There are four overloaded versions of the Pen constructor:

- Pen (Brush)

- Pen (Brush, width)

- Pen (Color)

- Pen (Color, width)

The standard width for a pen is 1 pixel. If you want a pen with a thicker line, you need to use one of the constructors with a value for the width argument.

The Pen constructor also takes as an argument either a brush or a color. An argument of a simple color gives you a line of a particular width and a solid color.

A pen that has a brush argument basically draws a rectangular line that is filled in according to the Brush object passed to it. If you use the constructor without the width property, you may not be able to see the characteristics of the brush, though. If you were to create a pen based upon a brush and a width of several pixels, you would see a line that looked as though you painted it with a real brush. You would see the texture and richness of the brush stroke in the line instead of just a thick, solid line. The following simple example draws several types of lines on the screen.

First, create a Windows Forms project in either C# or VB. Your project should have a single form, and you will draw directly on that form. You can make the form as large as you want. Figure 4-1 shows my VB Solution Explorer after I created the project.

Figure 4-1. Simple VB project for the pen demonstration

Once you have this project ready, go into the code pane and make sure that your project includes a reference to the System.Drawing namespace. You do this by adding the following code to the top of the code pane:

VB

```
Imports System.Drawing
```

C#

```
Using System.Drawing
```

In order to make the lines you draw have a little more contrast, add the following piece of code to the forms constructor just below the InitializeComponent call:

VB

```
Me.BackColor = Color.Black
```

C#

```
this.BackColor=Color.Black;
```

That's it for modifying the existing code. Now add the **OnPaint** method below the Form_Load event, as shown in Listing 4-1. I found the colorbars.jpg file on my machine and put it in the root directory of my D: drive. You may have to search for yours.

Listing 4-1a. VB Code to Draw a Line on the Form

```
Protected Overrides Sub OnPaint(ByVal e As PaintEventArgs)
  Dim G As Graphics = e.Graphics
  Dim Stripe As Image = New Bitmap("d:\colorbars.jpg")
  Dim B1 As TextureBrush = New TextureBrush(Stripe)
  Dim B2 As SolidBrush = New SolidBrush(Color.Aquamarine)
  Dim P1 As Pen


  P1 = New Pen(B1, 10)
  G.DrawLine(P1, 20, 20, Me.Width - 40, Me.Height - 40)
  System.Threading.Thread.CurrentThread.Sleep(1000)

  P1 = New Pen(B2, 10)
  G.DrawLine(P1, 20, 20, Me.Width - 40, Me.Height - 40)
  System.Threading.Thread.CurrentThread.Sleep(1000)

  P1 = New Pen(Color.BlanchedAlmond, 10)
  G.DrawLine(P1, 20, 20, Me.Width - 40, Me.Height - 40)
  B1.Dispose()
  B2.Dispose()
  P1.Dispose()
End Sub
```

Listing 4-1b. C# Code to Draw a Line on the Form

```
protected override void OnPaint(PaintEventArgs e)
{
  Graphics G  = e.Graphics;
  Image Stripe  = new Bitmap("d:\\colorbars.jpg");
  TextureBrush B1  = new TextureBrush(Stripe);
  SolidBrush B2 =new SolidBrush(Color.Aquamarine);
  Pen P1;

  P1 =new Pen(B1, 10);
  G.DrawLine(P1, 20, 20, this.Width - 40, this.Height - 40);
  System.Threading.Thread.Sleep(1000);

  P1 =new Pen(B2, 10);
  G.DrawLine(P1, 20, 20, this.Width - 40, this.Height - 40);
  System.Threading.Thread.Sleep(1000);
```

```
        P1 = new Pen(Color.BlanchedAlmond, 10);
        G.DrawLine(P1, 20, 20, this.Width - 40, this.Height - 40);
         B1.Dispose();
         B21.Dispose();
         P1.Dispose();
     }
```

I use the OnPaint event because it is automatically called every time the form detects that it needs refreshing. This includes when the form is drawn at start-up. I also use the OnPaint event because the Graphics object is conveniently accessible via the OnPaint argument.

The first thing I do here is create and instantiate a Graphics object. The Graphics object is your canvas, and it consists of the form as a whole. I then create two brushes. One is a texture brush that contains a bitmap as its fill color. The other is a solid brush that just has a single color for its fill color.

Once I've created the pen and brushes, I draw a diagonal line from the top left of the form to the bottom right, pause, and draw the same line again.

This shows you two of the four constructors for the Pen object. You can tell from this example that if you created a solid brush and used it as an argument for the pen, you could get the same result as if you created a pen with a color directly. Try it if you want to see for yourself.

Pen Properties and Methods

You have used the constructor for the pen and were able to draw immediately with it. Like most of the other drawing tools in the GDI+, this is usually enough. However, it is possible to create a pen and change its attributes without having to destroy it and create a new one.

Color

Once you have instantiated the Pen object, you can change the color anytime you like with this method:

VB

```
    Dim P1 As Pen = New Pen(Color.Blue, 10)
    P1.Color = Color.DarkOrange
```

C#

```
Pen P1=new Pen(Color.Blue, 10);
P1.Color=Color.DarkOrange;
```

Width

Changing the width of the pen you draw with is just as easy as changing the color:

VB

```
Dim P1 As Pen = New Pen(Color.Blue, 10)
P1.Width = 5
```

C#

```
Pen P1=new Pen(Color.Blue, 10);
P1.Width=5;
```

Try this: Draw a line using a pen of a particular color and width. Change the color to something different and change the width to something smaller. Redraw the exact same line and you should get a line that looks like it has been drawn with three colors.

Brush

You have already seen the brush used in one way as a color for a Pen object. It is possible to change the brush parameters so that when you draw another line with the same pen, you get a different texture to the line. I want you to consider the next small piece of code carefully, because although it is simple, it is also interesting.

VB

```
Dim P2 As Pen = New Pen(Color.Blue, 10)
G.DrawLine(P2, 20, CInt(Me.Height / 3), Me.Width - 20, CInt(Me.Height / 3))

P2.Brush = New TextureBrush(New Bitmap("d:\colorbars.jpg"))
G.DrawLine(P2, 20, CInt(Me.Height / 2), Me.Width - 20, CInt(Me.Height / 2))
```

C#

```
Pen P2=new Pen(Color.Blue, 10);
G.DrawLine(P2, 20, this.Height/3, this.Width - 20, this.Height/3);
P2.Brush=new TextureBrush(new Bitmap("d:\\colorbars.jpg"));
G.DrawLine(P2, 20, this.Height/2, this.Width - 20, this.Height/2);
```

What happens is that a horizontal blue line is drawn one-third of the way down the form. Another horizontal line is drawn one-half of the way down the form, according to the attributes of the brush. You get two lines. So what is so interesting here? The pen was constructed using a color as an argument, not a brush. Changing the brush from what is essentially null to an actual object overrides the constructor for the pen.

What is also interesting is that the reverse is true as well. If you instantiated a pen with a Brush object and then changed the color of the pen, the next line is drawn according to the color you just chose—not the brush.

Alignment

Alignment is an interesting property. It has to do with whether or not the line you draw for a shape is centered on the shape or is just inside the shape. The two enumerated values for this property are **Center** and **Inset**. If you set the **Alignment** property to **Center** and you draw a circle, the outline of the circle will be in the center of the line. If you set the alignment to **Inset**, the outline of the circle will be the same as the outer edge of the line.

DashStyle

The **DashStyle** property gets or sets the continuity of a line. Normally, a line is solid. Using the **DashStyle** property, you can change the line to consist of dots, dashes, and so on.

VB

```
Dim P2 As Pen = New Pen(Color.Blue, 10)
P2.DashStyle = Drawing.Drawing2D.DashStyle.Dash
G.DrawLine(P2, 20, CInt(Me.Height / 2), Me.Width - 20, CInt(Me.Height / 2))
```

C#

```
Pen P2=new Pen(Color.Blue, 10);
P2.DashStyle=System.Drawing.Drawing2D.DashStyle.Dash;
G.DrawLine(P2, 20, this.Height/2, this.Width - 20, this.Height/2);
```

DashPattern

If you set a pen's **DashPattern** to anything other than null (nothing in VB), then the **DashStyle** property automatically gets set to Custom. If you enter the following code, you will see that setting the **DashStyle** property is not needed.

The **DashPattern** property defines the length of a dash and a space based on sets of floating-point numbers. These numbers should come in pairs. The first of the pair is the line dash length and the second of the pair is the space length. These numbers get multiplied by the width of the line to give an actual length.

For the following sample code, the points (3, 1, 2, 5) get multiplied by the line width of 10 to become (30, 10, 20, 50). This sequence is repeated for the whole line. The number of point pairs you can use is unlimited.

VB

```
Dim P2 As Pen = New Pen(Color.Blue, 10)
Dim pts() As Single = {3, 1, 2, 5}
'If you comment out the line below there Is no difference In the output
P2.DashStyle = Drawing.Drawing2D.DashStyle.Dash
P2.DashPattern = pts
G.DrawLine(P2, 20, CInt(Me.Height / 2), Me.Width - 20, CInt(Me.Height / 2))
```

C#

```
Pen P2=new Pen(Color.Blue, 10);
float[] Pts = {3, 1, 2, 5};
//If you comment out the line below there Is no difference In the output
P2.DashStyle=System.Drawing.Drawing2D.DashStyle.Dash;
P2.DashPattern=Pts;
G.DrawLine(P2, 20, this.Height/2, this.Width - 20, this.Height/2);
```

DashOffset

The **DashOffset** property gets or sets the number of pixels to wait before starting the dash. This means if you start a line at (20, 20) and have a **DashOffset** of 20, your line would not appear to start until (40, 20).

VB

```
Dim P2 As Pen = New Pen(Color.Blue, 6)
Dim pts() As Single = {3, 1, 2, 5}
P2.DashPattern = pts
P2.DashOffset = 40
G.DrawLine(P2, 20, CInt(Me.Height / 2), Me.Width - 20, CInt(Me.Height / 2))
```

C#

```
Pen P2=new Pen(Color.Blue, 6);
float[] Pts = {3, 1, 2, 5};
P2.DashPattern=Pts;
P2.DashOffset=40;
G.DrawLine(P2, 20, this.Height/2, this.Width - 20, this.Height/2);
```

DashCap

Each dash in a dashed line can have one of three styles for the beginning and end of each dash: Flat, Round, or Triangle. So far, you have only seen the default flat-ended dash. These different end caps can add a little more flair to your dashed lines.

VB

```
Dim P2 As Pen = New Pen(Color.Blue, 10)
Dim pts() As Single = {3, 1, 2, 5}
P2.DashStyle = Drawing.Drawing2D.DashStyle.Dash
P2.DashPattern = pts
P2.DashCap = Drawing.Drawing2D.DashCap.Triangle
G.DrawLine(P2, 20, CInt(Me.Height / 2), Me.Width - 20, CInt(Me.Height / 2))
```

C#

```
 Pen P2=new Pen(Color.Blue, 10);
 float[] Pts = {3, 1, 2, 5};
P2.DashStyle=System.Drawing.Drawing2D.DashStyle.Dash;
P2.DashPattern=Pts;
P2.DashCap=System.Drawing.Drawing2D.DashCap.Triangle;
 G.DrawLine(P2, 20, this.Height/2, this.Width - 20, this.Height/2);
```

If you type in this code, you will see a line that has a flat start, triangle dashes, and a flat end. The flat start and end of the line can be adjusted by the **StartCap** and **EndCap** properties. I ought to note here that if the line does not end with a dash, you will not get the flat end. That last part of the line you see is the last dash itself, which will have a triangle end. If this happens, adjust the size of your form so you see the end of the line.

Do not set the **DashCap** property to Triangle if the Pen **Alignment** property is set to **Inset**.

StartCap and EndCap

These properties get and set the style of the two ends of the line drawn by the pen. If the **DashStyle** property was set to something other than solid, the **DashCap** property would define the start and end styles of each dash within that line.

The **StartCap** and **EndCap** properties are defined by the **LineCap** enumeration. You can set the following cap styles:

- AnchorMask

- ArrowAnchor

- Custom

- DiamondAnchor

- Flat

- NoAnchor

- Round

- RoundAnchor

- Square

- SquareAnchor

- Triangle

Try the following code:

VB

```
Dim P2 As Pen = New Pen(Color.Blue, 10)
Dim pts() As Single = {3, 1, 2, 5}
P2.DashStyle = Drawing.Drawing2D.DashStyle.Dash
P2.DashPattern = pts
P2.DashCap = Drawing.Drawing2D.DashCap.Triangle
P2.StartCap = Drawing.Drawing2D.LineCap.Round
P2.EndCap = Drawing.Drawing2D.LineCap.ArrowAnchor
G.DrawLine(P2, 20, CInt(Me.Height / 2), Me.Width - 20, CInt(Me.Height / 2))
```

C#

```
Pen P2=new Pen(Color.Blue, 10);
float[] Pts = {3, 1, 2, 5};
P2.DashStyle=System.Drawing.Drawing2D.DashStyle.Dash;
P2.DashPattern=Pts;
P2.DashCap=System.Drawing.Drawing2D.DashCap.Triangle;
P2.StartCap = System.Drawing.Drawing2D.LineCap.Round;
P2.EndCap = System.Drawing.Drawing2D.LineCap.ArrowAnchor;

G.DrawLine(P2, 20, this.Height/2, this.Width - 20, this.Height/2);
```

Figure 4-2 shows the line drawn by the preceding code.

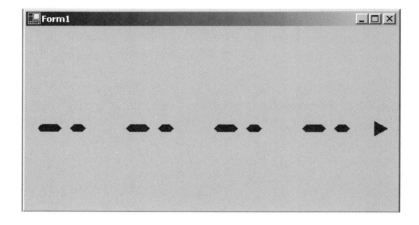

Figure 4-2. Line drawn with different start, dash, and end caps

As you can see from Figure 4-2, the formation of the dash is independent of the ends of the line.

PenType

PenType is a read-only property that determines what style the line was drawn in. If you used a brush for an argument for the pen, this property basically tells you the style of the brush you used. The return value is an enumerated value belonging to the **PenType** enumeration. The values are as follows:

- HatchFill

- LinearGradient

- PathGradient

- SolidColor

- TextureFill

One way to view the **PenType** property is to display the string value of the enumerated value. You can do this by using the **ToString** method that comes with every object. But, but, but . . . this is an integer, is it not? In C, C++, and VB 6.0 this is true. In .NET everything derives from the base object. The object has a few methods, one of which is the **ToString** method. Try the following code:

VB

```
G.Clear(Color.Khaki)
Dim P3 As Pen = New Pen(Color.Blue, 10)
P3.Brush = New TextureBrush(New Bitmap("d:\colorbars.jpg"))
G.DrawLine(P3, 20, CInt(Me.Height / 2), Me.Width - 20, CInt(Me.Height / 2))

lblType.Text = "PenType is " + P3.PenType.ToString
```

C#

```
G.Clear(Color.Khaki);
Pen P3=new Pen(Color.Blue, 10);
P3.Brush=new TextureBrush(new Bitmap("d:\\colorbars.jpg"));
G.DrawLine(P3, 20, this.Height/2, this.Width - 20, this.Height/2);
lblType.Text = "PenType is " + P3.PenType.ToString();
```

I made a form with a single label on it and called the label "lblType". Once I made the pen and changed its **Brush** property, I drew the line on the form. The last line gets the pen type and displays the string value in the label. Figure 4-3 shows my screen after I ran this code.

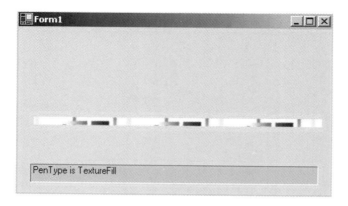

Figure 4-3. Screen showing the pen type after drawing a line

If I had left out the brush definition, the line would have been solid blue and the label would have read "PenType is SolidFill."

CompoundArray

CompoundArray is an interesting property that lets you get or set the values necessary to create multiple parallel lines with one pen.

Recall that I said the width property could simulate drawing three lines by drawing one thin line of color A on top of a thick line of color B. The **CompoundArray** property is a set of floating-point numbers that tells the pen how to draw alternating parallel lines and spaces. These floating-point numbers are percentages of the total width of the pen. Therefore, their values must be between 0 and 1.

In order to draw two lines with one space in between, you would need the following set of numbers:

- *n1:* This number determines the starting point of a line relative to the width of the pen.

- *n2:* This number determines the starting point of a space relative to the width of the pen.

- *n3:* This number determines the starting point of the second line relative to the width of the pen.

- *n4:* This number determines the ending point of the second line relative to the width of the pen.

Make a wide pen and a compound array, and then draw a line with it. Here is the code necessary to draw two parallel lines:

VB

```
G.Clear(Color.Khaki)
P3 = New Pen(Color.Blue, 20)
Dim lines() As Single = {0.0, 0.1, 0.9, 1.0}
P3.CompoundArray = lines
G.DrawLine(P3, 20, CInt(Me.Height / 2), Me.Width - 20, CInt(Me.Height / 2))
```

C#

```
G.Clear(Color.Khaki);
Single[] lines = {0.0f, 0.1f, 0.9f, 1.0f};
P3=new Pen(Color.Blue, 20);
P3.CompoundArray=lines;
G.DrawLine(P3, 20, this.Height/2, this.Width - 20, this.Height/2);
```

The lines' array numbers translate to the following:

- 0.0 is the start of the first line.

- 0.1 is the end of the first line. This translates to a line that is 10 percent of the width of the pen.

- 0.9 is the end of the space between the two lines. This translates to a space that is 80 percent of the width of the pen.

- 1.0 is the end of the last line. This translates to a line that is 10 percent of the width of the pen.

What you get is a line pen that draws two parallel lines, each 10 percent of the width of the pen, separated by a space that is 80 percent of the width of the pen.

So, you may ask, can I draw many more lines like this? The answer is yes. Try this array: (0.0, 0.2, 0.4, 0.6, 0.8, 1.0). What you get is three lines and two spaces. Each of the lines and spaces is 20 percent of the width of the pen.

The Pens Class

This class provides an easy way to get a pen of a particular color. It is probably one of the simplest classes you will come across in .NET.

There are two things you can do with the Pens class. One thing you can do is assign an existing pen to be equal to one of the Pens members. This is a convenient way to change a pen from something complicated to a simple pen of a particular color and width. The following piece of code demonstrates this:

VB

```
P3 = Pens.LightSlateGray
G.DrawLine(P3, 20, CInt(Me.Height / 2), Me.Width - 20, CInt(Me.Height / 2))
```

C#

```
P3 = Pens.LightSlateGray;
G.DrawLine(P3, 20, this.Height/2, this.Width - 20, this.Height/2);
```

This code assumes that you have a pen called P3 already instantiated.

The second thing you can do with a member of the Pens class is use it directly as an argument to a drawing function. This obviates the need to declare a pen, instantiate it, and destroy it. This could save you three lines of code. Big deal, you say? It could be if you forget to destroy your pen and the GC does not clean up after your mess fast enough. Also, as a programmer who started out in the firmware world, economy of code is still a point of pride for me.

The following piece of code shows how to use a Pens member as an argument:

VB

```
G.DrawLine(Pens.Violet, 20, CInt(Me.Height / 2), _
           Me.Width - 20, CInt(Me.Height / 2))
```

C#

```
G.DrawLine(Pens.Violet, 20, this.Height/2,
           this.Width - 20, this.Height/2);
```

Nice, huh? You are probably thinking by now that except for the semicolon in C# code, there is really no difference between VB and C#. Let me assure you that this is not true.

> **NOTE**   *All .NET languages use the common language runtime (CLR). As a result, the languages all use the same set of classes, which makes some of the code from C# and VB identical except for the ending semicolon in C#. When I get to some of the more extensive examples, you will see that there are vast differences between the two languages.*

The SolidBrush Class and the TextureBrush Class

These two classes are derived from the Brush class. The Brush class is an abstract base class. You can derive your own brushes if you want. This is rather advanced, so you will do it in a later chapter.

In describing the Pen object, I also took you through making a SolidBrush and a TextureBrush. While in general a brush is used to fill in a shape, the Pen object used it to draw with. If you think about it, though, the fat pen in the examples was really a filled rectangle in disguise. Remember the VB 6.0 **LineTo** command? If you wanted a rectangle, you just made a fat line.

A solid brush is one that has a solid color. It's simple and not very exciting. It has a single constructor that takes a color. That's it. It also has a member called Color that lets you get or set the color of an existing brush.

A TextureBrush is one that uses a bitmap as its color. It has eight overloaded constructors. It also has three properties you can use:

- Image

- Transform

- WrapMode

The Brushes Class

The Brushes class is much like the Pens class. It provides brushes for all the standard brushes. You can either assign an existing brush to a brush from this class or you can use a brush from this class without instantiating a brush first. The following is some code that assigns a Brushes class to an existing brush and also uses a brush from the Brushes class directly.

VB

```
Protected Overrides Sub OnPaint(ByVal e As PaintEventArgs)
  Dim G As Graphics = e.Graphics

  'Brushes class
  G.Clear(Color.BurlyWood)
  Dim r As Rectangle = New Rectangle(New Point(50, 50), _
                   New Size(CInt(Me.Width - 100), CInt(Me.Height - 100)))
  Dim b As Brush = Brushes.Crimson
  G.FillRectangle(b, r)
  G.FillRectangle(Brushes.Crimson, r)
```

```
        b.Dispose()
    End Sub
```

C#

```csharp
protected override void OnPaint(PaintEventArgs e)
{
  Graphics G  = e.Graphics;

  //Brushes class
  G.Clear(Color.BurlyWood);
  Rectangle r  = new Rectangle(new Point(50, 50),
                    new Size((int)(this.Width - 100),
                    (int)(this.Height - 100)));
  Brush b  = Brushes.Crimson;
  G.FillRectangle(b, r);
  G.FillRectangle(Brushes.Crimson, r);

  b.Dispose();
}
```

Why bother making a solid color brush to fill a shape when you can just use one that comes with .NET to begin with? This is very convenient.

Using the Graphics Class

The Graphics class is arguably the most important class in GDI+. This class encapsulates your canvas and all of the drawing methods necessary to create your work of art.

The object that gets created from the Graphics class is similar to the device context in regular GDI. You can also think of it as one of the many objects you draw on in VB 6.0. As you will see, this is about as far as the similarity goes, though.

Getting the Graphics Object

So, there are all these neat things you can do with a Graphics object, but before you can do anything, you need to get the Graphics object. How do you get it? Not only that, but how do you get it for a particular device? The easiest place is from the **OnPaint** event.

This event-based method of getting the Graphics object is used as the basis for all methods of obtaining the Graphics object. This is because an object's paint event includes the PaintEvent argument each time it is called. The PaintEvent argument has, as one of its members, a reference to the object's Graphics object.

This class has basically two members: a read-only copy of the Graphics class and a read-only clipping rectangle.

Using the OnPaint Method

So far, I have given you one straightforward way to get a Graphics object: through the OnPaint event of the form. The form you are drawing on is the class you are working with in the code pane. Because the .NET wizard gives you the code for this class, it is a simple thing to get the OnPaint event for it. What happens, though, when you have several controls on the form that you want to draw on? You have no way of getting into the class code of those objects, so how would you override an OnPaint event for any control?

Do you recall the discussion on delegates back in Chapter 1? Well, the way to get at the OnPaint event for any control on a form is to create your own delegate for it. The best way to explain this is with a small example.

Start up .NET and create a Windows program in either C# or VB. I provide code for both. Call the project GraphicsObject. Add the following components to your form:

- *Panel:* Call it Panel1.

- *PictureBox:* Call it P1.

- *Button:* Call it B1.

Make these controls fairly large, as you will be drawing a line on each one. Your form should look similar to the one shown in Figure 4-4.

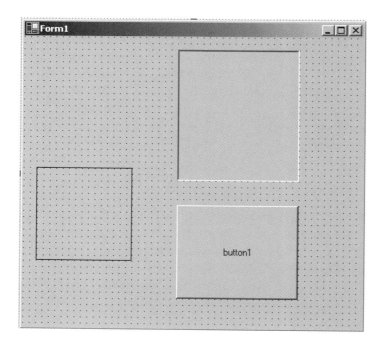

Figure 4-4. Simple form with three controls to draw on

Now go into your code and add the following delegate. It is the same one you have been using for forms throughout this chapter. Add the following code below the Form_Load event:

VB

```vb
Protected Overrides Sub OnPaint(ByVal e As PaintEventArgs)
  Dim G As Graphics = e.Graphics

  G.DrawLine(Pens.Black, 20, 20, 100, 100)
  MyBase.OnPaint(e)
End Sub
```

C#

```csharp
protected override void OnPaint( PaintEventArgs e )
{
  Graphics G = e.Graphics;

  G.DrawLine(Pens.Black,20,20,100,100);
  base.OnPaint(e);
}
```

Compile and run your program. You should get a single diagonal line on your form. Been there, done that. Now for the controls.

For the C# code, add the following methods below the form's **OnPaint** method:

```csharp
void P1Paint( object sender,PaintEventArgs e )
   {
    Graphics G = e.Graphics;

    G.DrawLine(Pens.Black,20,20,100,100);
    base.OnPaint(e);
 }

   void Panel1Paint( object sender,PaintEventArgs e )
   {
     Graphics G = e.Graphics;

     G.DrawLine(Pens.Black,20,20,100,100);
     base.OnPaint(e);
   }

   void ButtonPaint( object sender,PaintEventArgs e )
   {
     Graphics G = e.Graphics;

     G.DrawLine(Pens.Black,20,20,100,100);
     base.OnPaint(e);
   }
```

Now go into the "Windows Form Designer generated code" section and add the following delegate definitions:

For P1

```csharp
       this.P1.Paint += new System.Windows.Forms.PaintEventHandler
                                          (this.P1Paint);
```

For Panel1

```csharp
       this.Panel1.Paint += new System.Windows.Forms.PaintEventHandler
                                          (this.Panel1Paint);
```

For B1

```csharp
       this.B1.Paint += new System.Windows.Forms.PaintEventHandler
                                       (this.ButtonPaint);
```

Notice that the delegate does not use the normal System.EventHandler delegate, but instead uses the System.Windows.Forms.PaintEventHandler. This one is specific to painting.

Now compile and run your program. You should see a diagonal line on the form and in every control on the form. Pretty cool, huh? Getting the Graphics object is half the battle.

For the VB code, add the following methods below the form's **OnPaint** method:

```
Private Sub P1Paint(ByVal sender As System.Object, _
                     ByVal e As PaintEventArgs) Handles P1.Paint
  Dim G As Graphics = e.Graphics

  G.DrawLine(Pens.Black, 20, 20, 100, 100)
  MyBase.OnPaint(e)
End Sub

Private Sub Panel1Paint(ByVal sender As System.Object, _
                     ByVal e As PaintEventArgs) Handles Panel1.Paint
  Dim G As Graphics = e.Graphics

  G.DrawLine(Pens.Black, 20, 20, 100, 100)
  MyBase.OnPaint(e)
End Sub

Private Sub ButtonPaint(ByVal sender As System.Object, _
                     ByVal e As PaintEventArgs) Handles B1.Paint
  Dim G As Graphics = e.Graphics

  G.DrawLine(Pens.Black, 20, 20, 100, 100)
  MyBase.OnPaint(e)
End Sub
```

Now compile and run your VB program. You should get a line on the form and on each of the form's controls.

NOTE *I must say that in comparing delegate handling between C# and VB, I like VB better. It is more compact and it is all done on one line. However, the C# way will appeal to you C++ programmers because it is slightly more obfuscated and looks harder to the person standing over your shoulder. This means you can get paid more.*

This is a lot of code to handle a paint event for all these controls. Suppose you had dozens of them on your form? How would you collapse the code here and accomplish the same thing? Make just one delegate that handles all the controls' paint events. Add the following code at the end of your form:

C#

```
void AllPaint( object sender,PaintEventArgs e )
{
  Graphics G = e.Graphics;

  G.DrawLine(Pens.Black,20,20,100,100);
  base.OnPaint(e);
}
```

VB

```
Private Sub AllPaint(ByVal sender As System.Object, _
                     ByVal e As PaintEventArgs) _
                     Handles B1.Paint, P1.Paint, Panel1.Paint

  Dim G As Graphics = e.Graphics

  G.DrawLine(Pens.Black, 20, 20, 100, 100)
  MyBase.OnPaint(e)
End Sub
```

Okay, you VB folks are done. Just make sure you have commented out the previous delegates. You C# programmers need to change the delegate definitions to the following code:

For P1

```
    this.P1.Paint += new System.Windows.Forms.PaintEventHandler
                                            (this. AllPaint);
```

For Panel1

```
    this.Panel1.Paint += new System.Windows.Forms.PaintEventHandler
                                            (this. AllPaint);
```

For B1

```
this.B1.Paint += new System.Windows.Forms.PaintEventHandler
                                        (this. AllPaint);
```

Now compile and run the code. You should see the same line on each control. You got rid of two of the delegates and made just one handler for all three controls' OnPaint events.

Your next question should be, "How do I use a single delegate to draw something different on each control?" The answer is the Sender object.

Each of these delegates includes as an argument a Sender object. The Sender object identifies who fired the event. Change your **AllPaint** method to paint a different colored line on each object. Listing 4-2 contains the code for the new **AllPaint** method. Note that there is a big difference between the VB code and the C# code here. It is not all just a matter of a semicolon.

Listing 4-2a. Delegate to Handle the Paint Event from Multiple Sources in VB

```
Private Sub AllPaint(ByVal sender As System.Object, _
                    ByVal e As PaintEventArgs) _
                    Handles B1.Paint, P1.Paint, Panel1.Paint

  Dim G As Graphics = e.Graphics

  If sender.GetType Is GetType(Panel) Then
    If CType(sender, Panel).Name = "Panel1" Then
      G.DrawLine(Pens.Red, 20, 20, 100, 100)
    End If
  End If

  If sender.GetType Is GetType(Button) Then
    If CType(sender, Button).Name = "B1" Then
      G.DrawLine(Pens.Green, 20, 20, 100, 100)
    End If
  End If

  If sender.GetType Is GetType(PictureBox) Then
    If CType(sender, PictureBox).Name = "P1" Then
      G.DrawLine(Pens.Blue, 20, 20, 100, 100)
    End If
  End If

  MyBase.OnPaint(e)
End Sub
```

Listing 4-2b. Delegate to Handle the Paint Event from Multiple Sources in C#

```csharp
void AllPaint( object sender, PaintEventArgs e )
{
  Graphics G = e.Graphics;

  if ( sender.GetType() == Panel1.GetType() )
    if ( ((Panel)sender).Name == "Panel1" )
      G.DrawLine(Pens.Red,20,20,100,100);

  if ( sender.GetType() == B1.GetType() )
    if ( ((Button)sender).Name == "B1" )
      G.DrawLine(Pens.Green,20,20,100,100);

  if ( sender.GetType() == P1.GetType() )
    if ( ((PictureBox)sender).Name == "P1" )
      G.DrawLine(Pens.Blue,20,20,100,100);

  base.OnPaint(e);
}
```

This is a case where I think that C# beats VB in code compactness. What happens here is that I first check to see what type of object the sender is. Once I am sure of the object type, I know that type of object has a property called Name. I check the name and draw a line that is unique to that object.

If I never check the object type, I may come across an object that does not have a property called Name and my program will crash.

I want to point out one other thing here about when to draw. VB 6.0 had drawing methods within objects. These drawing methods allowed you to draw at any time you wanted. The object would sense an invalid region and automatically redraw itself with your shape on it.

.NET does not work this way. For that matter, C++ also does not work this way. If .NET senses that there is an invalid region in the Graphics object, it will fire the OnPaint event. I used the OnPaint event in these examples because I know for a fact that it is fired when the program starts. After all, a new object needs something on it. The OnPaint event is also convenient to use because the object firing the event will send along a copy to its Graphics object. This is necessary for you to have something to draw on.

If your desktop has a lot going on, the OnPaint event can get fired quite often. For instance, if you have your example running and drag another window across it, you are invalidating the Graphics region that you are covering. When your project appears from under the window, the OnPaint event gets fired and you see your example in all its glory.

There is also a way to invalidate your object's Graphics region yourself. You do not need to wait around for something to happen in order for you to draw. I discuss this method later in this chapter.

NOTE *At the end of each OnPaint event, I am calling the OnPaint event for the base class. This is necessary to make sure that the base class handles any graphical rendering that I did not.*

While this is the most common method of getting a Graphics object, it is not the only way.

Using the CreateGraphics Method

The **CreateGraphics** method allows you to create a new Graphics object from a form and draw directly on it. As a matter of fact, you can create a Graphics region on any object that can be drawn on. In addition to the **OnPaint** method, the **CreateGraphics** method is very convenient to use.

Go to your project and double-click the big button. VB and C# will make a delegate for you that handles the click event. Enter the following code in your click event:

VB

```
Private Sub B1_Click(ByVal sender As System.Object, _
                    ByVal e As System.EventArgs) Handles B1.Click
   Dim G As Graphics

   G = Me.CreateGraphics
   G.DrawLine(New Pen(Color.DarkMagenta, 10), 50, 10, 50, 100)

   G.Dispose()
End Sub
```

C#

```
private void B1_Click(object sender, System.EventArgs e)
{
  Graphics G;
  G = this.CreateGraphics();
  G.DrawLine ( new Pen(Color.DarkMagenta,10),50,10,50,100 );
  G.Dispose();
}
```

Run the program and click the button. You will see a vertical stripe appear on the screen. Try adding code to create the same slash on each of the objects when the button is clicked. If you get stuck, look at the code I generated myself.

Don't forget to get rid of the objects you created. Calling the **Dispose** method on the pens and brushes you make will obviate the need for the GC to call the **Finalize** method whenever it gets around to it.

Using the Window Handle Method

As all you C++ programmers know, every window has a handle. Most advanced VB programmers also know this. There is a method in the Graphics class that allows you to create a new Graphics object out of the specified handle to the window.

In general, I do not see much use to this method. Perhaps you could use it if a routine passed you a handle to a window and that is all you got. You could then use that handle to draw on the window.

Expand on your click event for the button. Add the following code to create a second Graphics object in addition to the first one you made using the **CreateGraphics** method:

VB

```
Private Sub B1_Click(ByVal sender As System.Object, _
                    ByVal e As System.EventArgs) Handles B1.Click
  Dim G As Graphics
  Dim G2 As Graphics

  G = Me.CreateGraphics
  G.DrawLine(New Pen(Color.DarkMagenta, 10), 50, 10, 50, 100)

  G2 = Graphics.FromHwnd(Me.Handle)
  G2.DrawLine(New Pen(Color.DarkCyan, 10), 70, 10, 70, 100)

  G.Dispose()
  G2.Dispose()
End Sub
```

C#

```
private void B1_Click(object sender, System.EventArgs e)
{
  Graphics G;
  Graphics G2;
```

```
    G = this.CreateGraphics();
    G.DrawLine ( new Pen(Color.DarkMagenta,10),50,10,50,100 );

    G2 = Graphics.FromHwnd(this.Handle);
    G2.DrawLine(new Pen(Color.DarkCyan, 10), 70, 10, 70, 100);

    G.Dispose();
    G2.Dispose();
}
```

This is not too difficult. This method lets you create a Graphics object from one of the basic properties of a window, the handle. If you have nothing else to go on, you will always be able to get a handle to a window.

Using the HDC Method

This method of obtaining a Graphics object is almost as basic as the Window Handle method. It uses the HDC, which is the handle to the device context. Does this sound vaguely familiar? It should, since the HDC is what the regular GDI draws on. It is the GDI equivalent to the Graphics object. This method gets the HDC and turns it into a Graphics object that you can use in GDI+. One thing to note here is that the HDC you get from the Graphics object *is* the Graphics object. If you dispose of it twice you will get an error. You can see this in the code that follows.

Change the button's click event to draw another line on the screen using the HDC as follows:

VB

```
Private Sub B1_Click(ByVal sender As System.Object, _
                     ByVal e As System.EventArgs) Handles B1.Click
    Dim G As Graphics
    Dim G2 As Graphics

    G = Me.CreateGraphics
    G.DrawLine(New Pen(Color.DarkMagenta, 10), 50, 10, 50, 100)

    G2 = Graphics.FromHwnd(Me.Handle)
    G2.DrawLine(New Pen(Color.DarkCyan, 10), 70, 10, 70, 100)

    ' Create new graphics object using handle to device context.
    Dim G3 As Graphics = Graphics.FromHdc(G2.GetHdc())
    G3.DrawLine(New Pen(Color.Black, 10), 85, 10, 85, 100)
    G3.Dispose()

    G.Dispose()
```

```
'    G2.Dispose()
  End Sub
```

C#

```
private void B1_Click(object sender, System.EventArgs e)
{
  Graphics G;
  Graphics G2;

  G = this.CreateGraphics();
  G.DrawLine ( new Pen(Color.DarkMagenta,10),50,10,50,100 );

  G2 = Graphics.FromHwnd(this.Handle);
  G2.DrawLine(new Pen(Color.DarkCyan, 10), 70, 10, 70, 100);

  // Create new graphics object using handle to device context.
  Graphics G3  = Graphics.FromHdc(G2.GetHdc());
  G3.DrawLine(new Pen(Color.Black, 10), 85, 10, 85, 100);
  G3.Dispose();

  G.Dispose();
  // G2.Dispose();
}
```

Compile and run your program. You should now see a third (black) stripe on the form when you click the big button.

Disposing of G2 will cause a runtime error. G2 is the GDI+ reference to the form's Graphics object. It belongs to the system and cannot be disposed of until the form itself is disposed of.

Using the Image Method

This is kind of a cool way to get a Graphics object. You first create an image from a JPEG or other type of image file. You then get a Graphics object for that image. Now you can scribble all over that image if you want. If you are artistic, you can draw a moustache on a picture of someone before you show it on the screen.

Double-click the PictureBox. .NET provides a skeleton click event delegate for you. Add code to this delegate to get an image, draw a strip on it, and load the resulting image into the PictureBox. Your code should look like the code that follows. The crane.jpg file is included with the code for this book in the Downloads section of the Apress Web site (http://www.apress.com).

VB

```
Private Sub P1_Click(ByVal sender As System.Object, _
                        ByVal e As System.EventArgs) Handles P1.Click

    Dim img As Image = Image.FromFile("D:\CRANE.JPG")
    Dim G As Graphics = Graphics.FromImage(img)

    G.DrawLine(New Pen(Color.Aquamarine, 10), 0, CInt(img.Height / 2), _
                                        CInt(img.Width), _
                                        CInt(img.Height / 2))

    P1.Image = img
    G.Dispose()
End Sub
```

C#

```
private void P1_Click(object sender, System.EventArgs e)
{
  Image img = Image.FromFile("d:\\crane.jpg");
  Graphics G = Graphics.FromImage(img);

  G.DrawLine(new Pen(Color.Aquamarine, 10), 0,(int)(img.Height / 2),
                                    (int)(img.Width),
                                    (int)(img.Height / 2));
  P1.Image=img;
  G.Dispose();
}
```

The image I use is one I have in the root of my D: drive. You can use whatever image you want.

Working with the Graphics Region

The Graphics class has many properties and methods available. This section deals with the properties of the client drawing area that is the Graphics object. Some of these properties and methods will seem a bit more obvious than others, but once you see some examples, you will find out just how useful they are.

Starting Fresh

Several properties and methods allow you to start your drawing from a known state:

- Clear

- Dispose

- Save

- Restore

You have already used the **Clear** and **Dispose** methods in previous examples. Here they are again:

VB

```
Protected Overrides Sub OnPaint(ByVal e As PaintEventArgs)
  Dim G As Graphics = e.Graphics

  G.Clear(Color.Bisque)
  G.Dispose()
End Sub
```

C#

```
protected override void OnPaint ( PaintEventArgs e )
{
  Graphics G = e.Graphics;

  G.Clear(Color.Bisque);
  G.Dispose();
}
```

The **Clear** method takes a color as an argument.[1] The **Dispose** method releases not only memory associated with the Graphics object itself, but also memory for any tool such as a pen, brush, and so forth. It is a very convenient way to call a global **Dispose** on all objects having to do with the Graphics object.

The next four methods are used for saving and restoring the state of the Graphics object. Why would you want to do this? Suppose you are drawing a complicated set of shapes that include transforming coordinates and altering the smoothing mode. It could take you quite a while to set your Graphics object up. Now during the middle of all this drawing, you need to put a simple rectangle on the screen. Without undoing all the transforms, you would get a rectangle drawn as defined by all your complicated attributes. If you reset the Graphics object to

---

1. I chose Bisque hoping for lobster . . . It looks like I got tomato.

draw the rectangle, you would need to set it all back up again before continuing on with your complicated drawing.

There is a second reason to save and restore the graphics state. It is not inconceivable to make a routine that takes a reference to a Graphics object as an argument. The first thing you would do in this routine is save the graphics state by storing it. The last thing you would do before leaving is restore the graphics state. This allows you to draw any shape with any attribute on any Graphics object without messing up the routine that called you. By the way, you really, really need to restore the graphics state before you leave. .NET stores and restores graphics states in a last-in last-out method. Not restoring the graphics state could lead to strange bugs. If you encapsulated this store-restore behavior in a class, you could make sure that the graphics state is restored whenever your class leaves the scope of the code you are using it in.

Many of you might be thinking, "Hey, this sounds like the assembler interrupt routines I wrote in elementary school." Well, you would not be far off. Just like saving registers on the stack and restoring them afterward, the graphics state is also stored on the stack.

One other thing about storing and restoring graphics states: The process can be nested. You can save several graphics states and then restore them one by one as you undo the nesting.

Time for a demo. In this example, you will use a single, simple state of the Graphics object. That state is the smoothing mode. You will also use the now-familiar OnPaint event for the form to do all the work. Start out with a new Windows Forms project. With the exception of one other line, the **OnPaint** method is the only code you will add.

Listing 4-3 shows the OnPaint event for both VB and C#. Before you do this, though, go to the top of the code pane for this form and make sure you include a reference to System.Drawing.Drawing2D.

VB

```
Imports System.Drawing.Drawing2D
```

C#

```
using System.Drawing.Drawing2D;
```

I sometimes find the difference in syntax between C# and VB .NET rather strange. They are both essentially new languages that were designed for the .NET CLR. You would think that Microsoft would have come up with some common terms. But I digress. . . .

Listing 4-3a. The OnPaint Event for the Saving State Example in VB

```
Protected Overrides Sub OnPaint(ByVal e As PaintEventArgs)
  Dim G As Graphics = e.Graphics

  'Get a base color for the Graphics region
  G.Clear(Color.Bisque)

  'Change one of the attributes of the Graphics object
  'then save the state.
  G.SmoothingMode = SmoothingMode.AntiAlias
  Dim OldG As GraphicsState = G.Save()

  'Restore the Smoothing mode state and draw a line
  G.SmoothingMode = SmoothingMode.Default
  G.DrawLine(New Pen(Color.DarkMagenta, 20), 10, 50, _
                        CInt(Me.Width - 10), 140)

  'Restore the old Graphics state and draw another line
  G.Restore(OldG)
  G.DrawLine(New Pen(Color.DarkMagenta, 20), 10, 100, _
                        CInt(Me.Width - 10), 190)

  G.Dispose()
End Sub
```

Listing 4-3b. The OnPaint Event for the Saving State Example in C#

```
protected override void OnPaint ( PaintEventArgs e )
{
  Graphics G = e.Graphics;

  G.Clear(Color.Bisque);
  //Change one of the Graphics attributes and save state
  G.SmoothingMode=SmoothingMode.AntiAlias;
  GraphicsState OldG = G.Save();

  //Restore the attribute and draw a line
  G.SmoothingMode=SmoothingMode.Default;
  G.DrawLine(new Pen(Color.DarkMagenta, 20), 10, 50,
                        (int)(this.Width - 10), 140);
```

```
                //Restore the old Graphics state and draw another line
                G.Restore(OldG);
                G.DrawLine(new Pen(Color.DarkMagenta, 20), 10, 100,
                                        (int)(this.Width - 10), 190);

                G.Dispose();
        }
```

Here is what you are doing:

- Changing the smoothing mode of any shape that gets drawn

- Saving the graphics state

- Restoring the smoothing mode to the default

- Drawing a line

- Restoring the graphics state

- Drawing another line

Restoring the graphics state before drawing the last line changed the smoothing mode to antialias. The lines were drawn diagonally so you can see the aliasing effect. Compile and run the program and you should see a screen similar to the one shown in Figure 4-5.

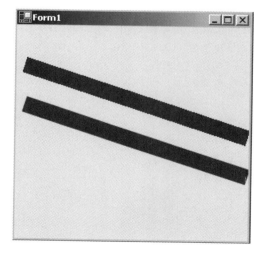

Figure 4-5. Effect of smoothing on diagonal lines

This example actually shows you two things: the saving and restoring of the graphics state, and the benefit of using an antialiasing effect. So, you may ask, why is there even an attribute for this? Antialiasing is far superior—why not use it all the time? The answer is speed. It takes a great deal more time to draw the line with antialiasing than without. A static rectangle would not benefit from antialiasing.

The next two methods are very similar to saving and restoring the Graphics object:

- BeginContainer

- EndContainer

The difference between **BeginContainer** and **Save** is that **BeginContainer** has several overloaded constructors.

The first **BeginContainer** constructor contains no arguments. This is identical to the **Graphics.Save** method. The state for the whole graphics container is saved and the graphics container you work in is identical to the saved one.

The second and third **BeginContainer** constructors contain arguments to set up a scale transform in the units of your choice. One uses integer arguments, and the other uses floating-point arguments for the scale transform.

I bet you are wondering what a scale transformation is. A default graphics container has a scale transformation of 1 in the X direction and 1 in the Y direction. Suppose you drew a rectangle that was 100 pixels wide by 100 pixels tall in the default container. It would be square. Then you applied a scale transform of 1.3 in the X direction and 1.8 in the Y direction and redrew the same rectangle. You would end up with a rectangle that was stretched in both directions. The size in the X direction would be 100?1.3, or 130 pixels. The size in the Y direction would be 100?1.8, or 180 pixels. You would have a rectangle that is taller than it is wide.

There are a few other kinds of transformations, but I cover them later. What I will do now is give you two examples of the **BeginContainer** and **EndContainer** methods. Hopefully, you will see how to use them.

The first thing to do is add two buttons to the bottom of your form. Call them B0 and B1. Also, change the text attributes to B0 and B1, respectively. Now double-click each button to get a click event generated in the code.

Listing 4-4 shows the new click events and two new methods that write to the screen. The original **OnPaint** method for this project stays as is.

Listing 4-4a. BeginContainer VB Code

```
Private Sub B0_Click(ByVal sender As System.Object, _
                     ByVal e As System.EventArgs) Handles B0.Click
    BeginContainerNoArg(Me.CreateGraphics())
End Sub
```

```vb
Private Sub B1_Click(ByVal sender As System.Object, _
                     ByVal e As System.EventArgs) Handles B1.Click
    BeginContainerIntRectArg(Me.CreateGraphics())
End Sub

Public Sub BeginContainerNoArg(ByVal G As Graphics)

    G.Clear(Color.Bisque)

    'Change one of the attributes of the Graphics object
    'then save the state.
    G.SmoothingMode = SmoothingMode.AntiAlias
    Dim OldG As GraphicsContainer = G.BeginContainer()

    'Restore the Smoothing mode state and draw a line
    G.SmoothingMode = SmoothingMode.Default
    G.DrawLine(New Pen(Color.Chocolate, 20), 10, 50, _
                               CInt(Me.Width - 10), 150)

    'Restore the old Graphics state and draw another line
    G.EndContainer(OldG)
    G.DrawLine(New Pen(Color.Chocolate, 20), 10, 100, _
                               CInt(Me.Width - 10), 200)

    G.Dispose()
End Sub

Public Sub BeginContainerIntRectArg(ByVal G As Graphics)

    G.Clear(Color.Bisque)

    ' Define transformation for container.
    Dim srcRect As New Rectangle(0, 0, 200, 200)
    Dim destRect As New Rectangle(0, 0, 100, 100)
    ' Begin graphics container.
    Dim containerState As GraphicsContainer = G.BeginContainer(destRect, _
                                       srcRect, GraphicsUnit.Pixel)

    G.DrawLine(New Pen(Color.DarkOrchid, 20), 10, 100, 200, 100)
    G.EndContainer(containerState)

    G.DrawLine(New Pen(Color.DarkOrchid, 20), 10, 100, 200, 100)

    G.Dispose()
End Sub
```

Listing 4-4b. BeginContainer C# Code

```csharp
private void B0_Click(object sender, System.EventArgs e)
{
  BeginContainerNoArg(this.CreateGraphics());
}

private void B1_Click(object sender, System.EventArgs e)
{
  BeginContainerIntRectArg(this.CreateGraphics());
}

public void BeginContainerNoArg(Graphics G)
{
  G.Clear(Color.Bisque);

  //Change one of the attributes of the Graphics object
  //then save the state.
  G.SmoothingMode = SmoothingMode.AntiAlias;
  GraphicsContainer OldG  = G.BeginContainer();

  //Restore the Smoothing mode state and draw a line
  G.SmoothingMode = SmoothingMode.Default;
  G.DrawLine(new Pen(Color.Chocolate, 20), 10, 50,
                          (int)(this.Width - 10), 150);

  //Restore the old Graphics state and draw another line
  G.EndContainer(OldG);
  G.DrawLine(new Pen(Color.Chocolate, 20), 10, 100,
                          (int)(this.Width - 10), 200);

  G.Dispose();
}

public void BeginContainerIntRectArg(Graphics G)
{
  G.Clear(Color.Bisque);

  // Define transformation for container.
  Rectangle srcRect = new Rectangle(0, 0, 200, 200);
  Rectangle destRect = new Rectangle(0, 0, 100, 100);
  // Begin graphics container.
  GraphicsContainer containerState  = G.BeginContainer(destRect,
                              srcRect, GraphicsUnit.Pixel);
```

```
        G.DrawLine(new Pen(Color.DarkOrchid, 20), 10, 100, 200, 100);
        G.EndContainer(containerState);

        G.DrawLine(new Pen(Color.DarkOrchid, 20), 10, 100, 200, 100);

        G.Dispose();
    }
```

Compile and run your program. You should see the two diagonal lines from the original OnPaint event. Click B0 and you will see the same two diagonal lines, but they are skewed a little and in a different color. Click B1 and you will see two horizontal lines with different origins, widths, and endpoints.

The **ContainerNoArg** method is virtually identical to the OnPaint delegate. This shows you that using the **BeginContainer** method with no arguments is virtually the same as using the **Save** method.

The **ContainerIntRecArg** method is a little different. First off, look at Figure 4-6. It shows the result of clicking the B1 button.

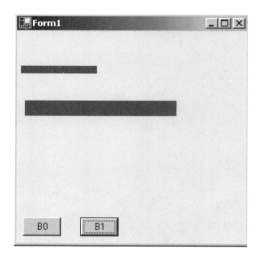

Figure 4-6. Scale transformation of a graphics container

```
public void BeginContainerIntRectArg(Graphics G)
{
  G.Clear(Color.Bisque);

  // Define transformation for container.
  Rectangle srcRect = new Rectangle(0, 0, 200, 200);
  Rectangle destRect = new Rectangle(0, 0, 100, 100);
  // Begin graphics container.
  GraphicsContainer containerState  = G.BeginContainer(destRect,
                                      srcRect, GraphicsUnit.Pixel);

  G.DrawLine(new Pen(Color.DarkOrchid, 20), 10, 100, 200, 100);
  G.EndContainer(containerState);

  G.DrawLine(new Pen(Color.DarkOrchid, 20), 10, 100, 200, 100);

  G.Dispose();
}
```

I create two rectangles. One is considered the source rectangle and one is the destination rectangle. Next, I save the container state. I use the two rectangles to obtain a scale transformation in pixels. There are several other units I could have used as well:

- Display (equates to 1/75 of an inch)

- Document (equates to 1/300 of an inch)

- Inch

- Millimeter

- Pixel

- Point (equates to 1/72 of an inch)

- World

If I had used inches, you would not have seen the second line at all! Okay, now what is the transformation here? The origin of each rectangle is 0. No transformation here. The ends of the first rectangle are 200 for X and 200 for Y. The ends of the second rectangle are 100 for X and 100 for Y. Take the second rectangle's end points and divide them by the first rectangle's end points. You will get a scale transformation of 0.5 in the X direction and 0.5 in the Y direction.

After saving the container, I draw a line, restore the container, and draw the same line again.

Using the **BeginContainer** method saves the old container and gives me a new container to work in with the scale transform dictated by the two rectangles. The first line drawn has the following attributes:

- Its width is 1/2 the defined width of the pen.

- Its starting point is 1/2 the defined starting point of the line.

- Its length is 1/2 the length as defined by the line draw command.

In effect, all calculations in the X direction are 1/2 what they should be and all calculations in the Y direction are 1/2 what they should be.

The second line is drawn after restoring the original graphics container. This line has all the attributes you would expect.

The **BeginContainer/EndContainer** and **Save/Restore** methods can be very powerful indeed. You can use them to provide dramatic perspective changes in a screen drawing. It is a simple matter to nest graphics containers with different perspectives. You could then draw your simple shapes on each container. The drawing as a whole would then be correct for any viewpoint you choose.

> **NOTE** *You have probably noticed that your project returns to the screen defined by the forms **OnPaint** method whenever you place another window in front of it. This is not a bug, it is a feature! Whenever your client area is covered, .NET invalidates that portion of your window. When your client area is shown again, .NET calls the **OnPaint** method for that graphics container—in this case, the whole form. It is automatic.*

Changing the Graphics Container's Qualities

You can greatly affect the speed of rendering in your Graphics object. You do this, however, at the expense of quality. The PixelOffsetMode allows you to get or set the rendering mode according the PixelOffsetMode enumeration. The members of the enumeration are as follows:

- Default

- Half

- HighQuality

- HighSpeed

- Invalid

- None

Setting a graphics container's PixelOffsetMode for HighQuality improves viewing while sacrificing rendering speed.

Know Your Coordinates

At the beginning of this chapter I went over the different coordinate systems: world, page, and device. The next four properties I cover affect the coordinate systems relating to scale.

The first two properties are the read-only vertical and horizontal resolutions:

- Graphics.DpiX

- Graphics.DpiY

Both of these measurements are in dots per inch.

VB

```
Dim x as Single = G.DpiX
```

C#

```
Single x = G.DpiY
```

The next two properties are

- PageScale

- PageUnit

The **PageUnit** property allows you to get or set the mode of transformation between the world and page coordinate systems. Consider the following code:

VB

```vb
Public Sub World2PageXform(ByVal G As Graphics)
  Dim EndX As Int32 = 1
  Dim EndY As Int32 = 1

  G.Clear(Color.Azure)
  G.PageUnit = GraphicsUnit.Inch
  G.TranslateTransform(1, 1)
  G.DrawLine(Pens.Blue, 0, 0, EndX, EndY)

  Dim Xpix As Int32 = EndX * CInt(G.DpiX)
  Dim Ypix As Int32 = EndX * CInt(G.DpiY)
End Sub
```

C#

```csharp
public void World2PageXform(Graphics G)
{
  int EndX = 1;
  int EndY = 1;
  G.Clear(Color.Azure);
  G.PageUnit=GraphicsUnit.Inch;
  G.TranslateTransform(1, 1);
  G.DrawLine(Pens.Blue, 0, 0, EndX, EndY);

  int Xpix = EndX * (int)G.DpiX;
  int Ypix = EndY * (int)G.DpiY;
}
```

What you end up with here is a fat line that looks like the one shown in Figure 4-7.

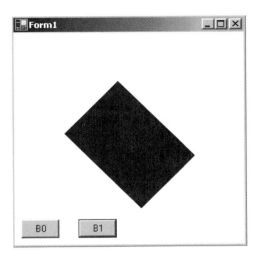

Figure 4-7. Transformed line

The variables Xpix and Ypix contain the actual length of the line in pixels. It ends up being 96 pixels in both the X direction and the Y direction.

Quality Factors

Several quality factors affect how things are drawn. Two of them, **CompostingQuality** and **InterpolationMode**, have to do with the internal calculation necessary to determine which point to render next in a drawing. I do not cover **InterpolationMode** further in this book.

One of the next two properties, **SmoothingMode**, has already been used extensively in this chapter. **SmoothingMode** allows you to set the quality of the shape you draw in your graphics container. A diagonal line as seen on the screen will normally have jagged edges. It will often look like a staircase. You can alleviate this effect by setting the **SmoothingMode** to something other than the default or HighSpeed. Setting the mode to AntiAlias or HighQuality produces a line with no jagged edges or staircase effect.

CompostingMode determines how an image is rendered on the screen. If the **CompostingMode** is set for SourceCopy, it will completely overwrite the affected area of the Graphics container. If the **CompostingMode** is set for SourceOver, the image will be blended with the background color of the graphics container. If you placed a yellow sun on a blue sky with SourceOver, you would end up with a green sun instead.[2]

---

2. Remember this problem from when you colored as a child?

So far everything has been lines, lines, and more lines. What about text? The next two properties of the graphics container have to do with how text is rendered:

- TextContrast

- TextRenderingHint

You will explore text in much more detail in a later chapter, but I will provide a simple example here. Consider the following code:

VB

```vb
Public Sub RenderText(ByVal G As Graphics)
  Dim F As New Font("Arial", 16)
  Dim B As New SolidBrush(Color.Black)

  G.Clear(Color.Azure)
  G.TextRenderingHint = TextRenderingHint.SingleBitPerPixel
  G.DrawString("SingleBitPerPixel", F, B, New PointF(10, 10))

  G.TextRenderingHint = TextRenderingHint.AntiAlias
  G.DrawString("AntiAlias default Contrast", F, B, New PointF(10, 60))

  G.TextContrast = 12 'max value
  G.DrawString("AntiAlias Low Contrast", F, B, New PointF(10, 90))

  G.TextContrast = 1
  G.DrawString("AntiAlias High Contrast", F, B, New PointF(10, 120))
  F.Dispose()
  B.Dispose()
End Sub
```

C#

```csharp
public void RenderText(Graphics G)
{
  Font F = new Font("Arial", 16);
  SolidBrush B = new SolidBrush(Color.Black);

  G.Clear(Color.Azure);
  G.TextRenderingHint = TextRenderingHint.SingleBitPerPixel;
  G.DrawString("SingleBitPerPixel", F, B, new PointF(10, 10));
```

```
G.TextRenderingHint = TextRenderingHint.AntiAlias;
G.DrawString("AntiAlias default Contrast", F, B, new PointF(10, 60));

G.TextContrast = 12; //max value
G.DrawString("AntiAlias Low Contrast", F, B, new PointF(10, 90));

G.TextContrast = 1;
G.DrawString("AntiAlias High Contrast", F, B, new PointF(10, 120));
F.Dispose();
B.Dispose();
}
```

This routine produces the output in Figure 4-8.

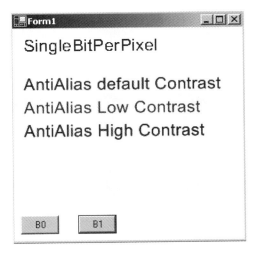

Figure 4-8. Text rendering on a graphics container

What you see here is that using SingleBitPerPixel results in fast and readable text, but nothing you would use for a resume. AntiAlias using a high contrast seems to be best here. However, it is much slower to render.

Shaping the Graphics Region

So far, everything you have drawn has been in the complete client area of the object drawn in. In other words, for a form, the whole form has been available to you to draw in. You could limit your drawing to the area in question by carefully limiting how your shapes are rendered, but that is very time consuming and takes a lot of code.

In Chapter 3 you constructed a fishbowl using regular GDI calls from within VB 6.0. These GDI API calls used the clipping region to turn a rectangle into a circle. Well, GDI+ has clipping regions as well. You might think of them as clipping regions on steroids.

Setting the Clipping Region

There are several ways to set or get a clipping region:

- Clip

- SetClip

- ExcludeClip

- ResetClip

- ClipBounds

- VisibleClipBounds

A *clipping region* is usually an area where you can see the effects of your drawing commands. All areas outside of this zone do not show what you have drawn. There is also, however, an exclusionary clipping zone. This is one where everything outside the clipping region is visible and any drawing inside the clipping region is not visible.

The following example contains three buttons. Each button invokes a form of clipping region. The steps for the example are as follows:

1. Create a new project called ClipDraw. Use VB or C# (or both!).

2. Add a button. Call it B1 with the text "Clip".

3. Add a button. Call it B2 with the text "SetClip".

4. Add a button. Call it B3 with the text "ExcludeClip".

5. Make your form look something like the one in Figure 4-9.

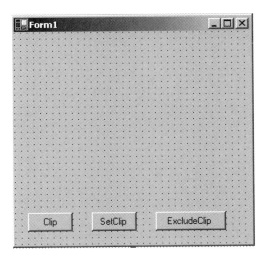

Figure 4-9. Form setup for clipping

Double-click each of the buttons to create event handlers for it. Next, go into the code and add a namespace reference to System.Drawing.Drawing2D. Listing 4-5 shows the code necessary for each event handler.

Listing 4-5a. Event Handlers That Create Clipping Regions in VB

```
Private Sub B1_Click(ByVal sender As System.Object, _
                     ByVal e As System.EventArgs) Handles B1.Click
  Dim G As Graphics = Me.CreateGraphics
  Dim R As New Rectangle(50.0F, 50.0F, 100.0F, 100.0F)

  G.Clear(Color.Gainsboro)
  'Outline the rectangle and create the clipping region
  G.DrawRectangle(Pens.Black, R)
  G.Clip = New Region(R)

  'Draw line the width of the form
  G.DrawLine(Pens.Blue, 0, 75, Me.Width, 75)
  'Draw a circle 1/4 inside clipping region
  G.FillEllipse(Brushes.LawnGreen, New Rectangle(75, 75, 150, 150))

  G.Dispose()
End Sub
```

```
    Private Sub B2_Click(ByVal sender As System.Object, _
                    ByVal e As System.EventArgs) Handles B2.Click
    Dim G As Graphics = Me.CreateGraphics
    Dim R As New Rectangle(20.0F, 20.0F, 100.0F, 100.0F)
    Dim path As New GraphicsPath()

    G.Clear(Color.Gainsboro)
    path.AddEllipse(R)
    G.DrawPath(Pens.Black, path)
    G.SetClip(path)

    ' Draw some clipped strings.
    Dim F As New Font("Arial", 16)
    G.DrawString("ABCDEFGHIJKLM", F, Brushes.DeepPink, 15, 25)
    G.DrawString("NOPQRSTUVWXYZ", F, Brushes.DeepPink, 15, 68)

    path.Dispose()
    F.Dispose()
  End Sub

  Private Sub B3_Click(ByVal sender As System.Object, _
                    ByVal e As System.EventArgs) Handles B3.Click
    Dim G As Graphics = Me.CreateGraphics
    Dim R As New Rectangle(40.0F, 20.0F, 100.0F, 100.0F)
    Dim path As New GraphicsPath()

    G.Clear(Color.Gainsboro)
    path.AddEllipse(R)
    G.DrawPath(Pens.Black, path)

    G.ExcludeClip(New Region(path))

    ' Draw some clipped strings.
    Dim F As New Font("Arial", 16)
    G.DrawString("ABCDEFGHIJKLM", F, Brushes.DeepPink, 15, 25)
    G.DrawString("NOPQRSTUVWXYZ", F, Brushes.DeepPink, 15, 68)

    path.Dispose()
    F.Dispose()
  End Sub
End Class
```

Listing 4-5b. Event Handlers That Create Clipping Regions in C#

```csharp
private void B1_Click(object sender, System.EventArgs e)
{
  Graphics G  = this.CreateGraphics();
  Rectangle R = new Rectangle(50, 50, 100, 100);

  G.Clear(Color.Gainsboro);

  //Outline the rectangle and create the clipping region
  G.DrawRectangle(Pens.Black, R);
  G.Clip = new Region(R);

  //Draw line the width of the form
  G.DrawLine(Pens.Blue, 0, 75, this.Width, 75);
  //Draw a circle 1/4 inside clipping region
  G.FillEllipse(Brushes.LawnGreen, new Rectangle(75, 75, 150, 150));

  G.Dispose();
}

private void B2_Click(object sender, System.EventArgs e)
{
  Graphics G = this.CreateGraphics();
  Rectangle R = new Rectangle(20, 20, 100, 100);
  GraphicsPath path = new GraphicsPath();

  G.Clear(Color.Gainsboro);
  path.AddEllipse(R);
  G.DrawPath(Pens.Black, path);
  G.SetClip(path);

  // Draw some clipped strings.
  Font F = new Font("Arial", 16);
  G.DrawString("ABCDEFGHIJKLM", F, Brushes.DeepPink, 15, 25);
  G.DrawString("NOPQRSTUVWXYZ", F, Brushes.DeepPink, 15, 68);

  path.Dispose();
  F.Dispose();
}
```

```
private void B3_Click(object sender, System.EventArgs e)
{
  Graphics G = this.CreateGraphics();
  Rectangle R = new Rectangle(40, 20, 100, 100);
  GraphicsPath path = new GraphicsPath();

  G.Clear(Color.Gainsboro);
  path.AddEllipse(R);
  G.DrawPath(Pens.Black, path);
  G.ExcludeClip(new Region(path));

  // Draw some clipped strings.
  Font F = new Font("Arial", 16);
  G.DrawString("ABCDEFGHIJKLM", F, Brushes.DeepPink, 15, 25);
  G.DrawString("NOPQRSTUVWXYZ", F, Brushes.DeepPink, 15, 68);

  path.Dispose();
  F.Dispose();
}
```

The delegate for button B1 creates a small rectangle, which is used as the clipping region. To see the outline of the clipping region, I drew the rectangle on the screen. I then created a new region based on the rectangle and at the same time assigned this region as the clip area using the **Graphics.Clip** command. Next, I drew a line from one side of the form to the other. Because drawing a line in a clipping region is not very exciting, I also drew a circle that was bounded by a rectangle that intersected the clipping region. Figure 4-10 shows the result of this method.

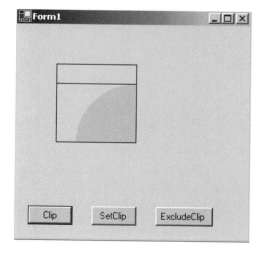

Figure 4-10. Clipping using Graphics.Clip

The delegate for button B2 is a little more involved. Here is what happens:

1. I create a small rectangle to act as the bounds of an ellipse.

2. I create a graphics path and, using the ellipse function, add a circle to that path based on the rectangle I created earlier.

3. I draw the path to make it easy to see the clipping region.

4. I use the **Graphics.SetClip** method to create a clipping region based on the path.

5. I render some text on the screen.

6. I dispose of the graphics container.

Figure 4-11 shows the result of this method.

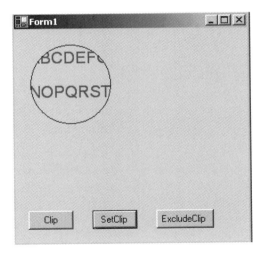

Figure 4-11. Result of using Graphics.SetClip with a path

The third button creates an inverse clipping region where shapes are drawn on the outside and the inside is off limits. The code is almost identical to the code for button B2. Figure 4-12 shows the result of the exclusion clipping region.

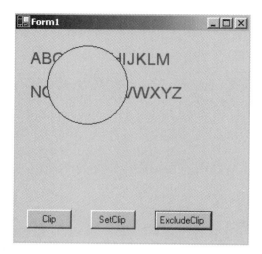

Figure 4-12. Exclusion clipping region

You are probably wondering about now what the difference is between **Graphics.Clip** and **Graphics.SetClip**. **Graphics.Clip** is a property that can be set only to a region. A region can be simple, such as the rectangle I used, or it can be as complicated as you want, such as a region created out of a graphics path. **Graphics.SetClip** is a method. This method has several overloaded variations whose arguments are as follows:

- *Graphics:* Sets the new clipping region to the **Clip** property of the Graphics object.

- *Graphics, CombineMode:* Sets the new clipping region to the **Clip** property of the Graphics object. Renders output according to the combining operation specified by CombineMode.

- *GraphicsPath:* Sets the new clipping region to the specified path.

- *GraphicsPath, CombineMode:* Sets the new clipping region to the specified path. Renders output according to the combining operation specified by **CombineMode**.

- *Rectangle:* Sets the new clipping region to the specified rectangle.

- *Rectangle, CombineMode:* Sets the new clipping region to the specified rectangle. Renders output according to the combining operation specified by **CombineMode**.

- *Region, CombineMode:* Sets the new clipping region to the specified region. Renders output according to the combining operation specified by **CombineMode**.

There is another method that uses RectangleF, but it is identical to Rectangle. The CombineMode argument specifies how a clipping region is to be combined with other clipping regions on the graphics container. The CombineMode enum is defined as follows:

- *Complement:* The existing region is excluded from the new region.

- *Exclude:* The new region is excluded from the existing region. This is the opposite of Complement.

- *Intersect:* The result is the intersection of the two regions.

- *Replace:* The new region replaces the existing region.

- *Union:* The two regions are combined, resulting in their union.

- *Xor:* The region created is outside of the intersection of both regions.

Now, I provide one more SetClip example. This example brings together some of the Graphics methods you've used previously as well:

1. Add another button to the form and call it B4. Set the text to "Intersect".

2. Place the button just above the SetClip button on the form.

3. Double-click the new button to get a new delegate generated for you in your code.

4. Enter the following code in your new B4 click event:

VB

```
Private Sub B4_Click(ByVal sender As System.Object, _
                     ByVal e As System.EventArgs) Handles B4.Click
   Dim G As Graphics = Me.CreateGraphics
   Dim R As New Rectangle(40.0F, 20.0F, 100.0F, 100.0F)
   Dim R2 As New Rectangle(60.0F, 20.0F, 120.0F, 120.0F)
   Dim P1 As New GraphicsPath()
   Dim P2 As New GraphicsPath()
```

```
        G.Clear(Color.Gainsboro)
        P1.AddEllipse(R)
        G.DrawPath(Pens.Black, P1)

        P2.AddEllipse(R2)
        G.DrawPath(Pens.Black, P2)

        G.SetClip(P1)
        G.SetClip(P2, CombineMode.Intersect)

        ' Draw some clipped strings.
        Dim F As New Font("Arial", 16)
        G.DrawString("ABCDEFGHIJKLM", F, Brushes.DeepPink, 15, 25)
        G.DrawString("NOPQRSTUVWXYZ", F, Brushes.DeepPink, 15, 68)

        P1.Dispose()
        P2.Dispose()
        F.Dispose()
    End Sub
```

C#

```
    private void B4_Click(object sender, System.EventArgs e)
    {
      Graphics G = this.CreateGraphics();
      Rectangle R = new Rectangle(40, 20, 100, 100);
      Rectangle R2 = new Rectangle(60, 20, 120, 120);
      GraphicsPath P1 = new GraphicsPath();
      GraphicsPath P2 = new GraphicsPath();

      G.Clear(Color.Gainsboro);
      P1.AddEllipse(R);
      G.DrawPath(Pens.Black, P1);

      P2.AddEllipse(R2);
      G.DrawPath(Pens.Black, P2);

      G.SetClip(P1);
      G.SetClip(P2, CombineMode.Intersect);
```

```
  // Draw some clipped strings.
  Font F = new Font("Arial", 16);
  G.DrawString("ABCDEFGHIJKLM", F, Brushes.DeepPink, 15, 25);
  G.DrawString("NOPQRSTUVWXYZ", F, Brushes.DeepPink, 15, 68);

  P1.Dispose();
  P2.Dispose();
  F.Dispose();
}
```

Okay, who can tell me what's going on here? If you don't know, here it is:

- I cloned the B3 code. I also added some extra lines.

- I created a new rectangle (R2), which acts as the bounds for an ellipse. Because the rectangle is square, the ellipse will be a circle.

- I created a new path (P2), which consists of the circle bounded by R2.

- I set the new clipping region to be an intersecting region with the original one.

Figure 4-13 shows the result of this method.

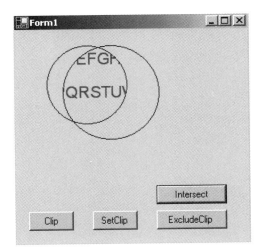

Figure 4-13. Intersected clipping regions

I leave it to you to try out the other combinations. Xor is kind of cool.

The next three properties are pretty self-explanatory:

- IsVisible

- IsClipEmpty

- IsVisibleClipEmpty

The **IsVisible** property determines if a point is inside the visible clip region of a particular graphics container.

The **IsClipEmpty** property determines if the clipping region for the current Graphics object is empty.

The **IsVisibleClipEmpty** property determines if the visible portion of the clipping region is empty. Well, what does the "visible portion" mean? It is possible to have a clipping region for a window and a separate clipping region for a graphics container. The intersection of these two clipping regions is called the *visible clipping region*. This property will tell you if this intersection can have any drawing in it.

Amend your current project and include the following line, which defines a Graphics object that is local to the class:

VB

```
 Private G_obj As Graphics
```

C#

```
  private Graphics G_obj;
```

Now add the event handler that draws inside a Graphics region using the **IsVisible** method:

VB

```
 Private Sub Form1Mouse(ByVal sender As System.Object, _
                        ByVal e As MouseEventArgs) Handles MyBase.MouseMove
   If G_obj Is Nothing Then Exit Sub
   If G_obj.IsVisible(e.X, e.Y) Then
     G_obj.FillRectangle(Brushes.BlueViolet, e.X, e.Y, 1, 1)
   End If
 End Sub
```

C#

```
private void Form1Mouse(System.Object sender , MouseEventArgs e)
{
  if (G_obj == null)
    return;
  if (G_obj.IsVisible(e.X, e.Y))
    G_obj.FillRectangle(Brushes.BlueViolet, e.X, e.Y, 1, 1);
}
```

You will need to instantiate this global Graphics object. Do it inside the B4 delegate. Doing it here will make the Graphics object the intersection of the two graphics paths you created. Add the following line just before the path dispose code in the B4 delegate:

C#

```
G_obj = G;
```

VB

```
G_obj = G
```

There is one more thing to do for the C# project: Add the mouse move delegate definition to the forms constructor. Add the following code in the TODO section of the constructor:

C#

```
this.MouseMove += new MouseEventHandler(this.Form1Mouse);
```

Now compile and run the program. When you click the Intersect button, move the mouse over the graphics container. You will see a line being drawn inside the intersection but not outside of it. This is because I use the **Graphics.IsVisible** method to determine when to draw.

So, are you paying attention? So far in this chapter, I have shown you three types of events—the normal system events, the paint events, and the mouse events—and how to generate delegates for them.

Now add one more button to your current project. Set its text to "IntersectClip" and name it B5. Double-click the button and add the following code to the B5.Click delegate that was made for you:

VB

```vb
Private Sub B5_Click(ByVal sender As System.Object, _
                     ByVal e As System.EventArgs) Handles B5.Click

  'Bail out if not set
  If G_obj Is Nothing Then Exit Sub
  Dim R2 As New Rectangle(75, 75, 150, 150)

  G_obj.IntersectClip(R2)
  G_obj.FillRectangle(New SolidBrush(Color.Blue), 0, 0, 500, 500)

End Sub
```

C#

```csharp
private void B5_Click(object sender, System.EventArgs e)
{
  //Bail out if not set
  if (G_obj == null )
    return;
  Rectangle R2 = new Rectangle(75, 75, 150, 150);

  G_obj.IntersectClip(R2);
  G_obj.FillRectangle(new SolidBrush(Color.Blue), 0, 0, 500, 500);
}
```

The first thing that happens here is that the routine detects if the global Graphics region was already set. If not, you bail out. This means that you must click the Intersect button before you can click the IntersectClip button. The rest of the code just generates a rectangle and sets the Graphics region to be the intersection of the old Graphics region and the new rectangle. You end up with a rather complex Graphics region. Just to prove the point, you fill a large rectangle that would normally cover most of the form. Instead, only the intersected region gets filled in. You end up with a quarter pie for a Graphics region, as shown in Figure 4-14.

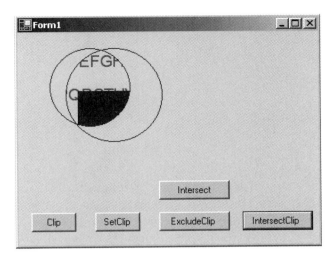

Figure 4-14. Result of the IntersectClip method

That's pretty much it for the simple uses of clipping regions. As you can see, they can be very powerful indeed. You can create a clipping region from any graphics path you can imagine, or you can combine shapes in a Boolean manner to make a new kind of clipping region.

Now onto the real drawing part.

Drawing in the Graphics Region

You can draw quite a few base objects in a Graphics region. I describe each object in this section.

Shapes Defined by Rectangles

Several drawing functions are constrained by the bounds of a rectangle. The rectangle can be defined before the shape is drawn, or the rectangle can be defined as four points that define the corners of the rectangle. The methods are as follows:

- DrawArc

- DrawEllipse

- FillEllipse

- DrawPie

- FillPie

- DrawRectangle

- FillRectangle

- DrawRectangles

- FillRectangles

Each of the preceding methods also takes a Pen object to draw with.

First, let's make a rectangle. A rectangle is a structure that consists of either four integers, which define the top-left corner of the rectangle and the width and height, or by a location point and a size structure. There are also quite a few members of a rectangle:

- Bottom

- Height

- Left

- Top

- Width

- X

- Y

- Location

- Size

- IsEmpty

Here are some examples of rectangle structures you can make using the various rectangle constructors:

VB

```
Dim R1 As New Rectangle(10, 10, 30, 30)
Dim R2 As New Rectangle(New Point(10, 10), New Size(20, 20))
```

C#

```
Rectangle R1 = new Rectangle(10, 10, 30, 30);
Rectangle R2 = new Rectangle(new Point(10, 10), new Size(20, 20));
```

Both of these constructors create the same rectangle.

Drawing Shapes Based on Rectangles

Open a new C# or VB Windows project. Mine is called GraphicsDraw. Make the default form size 450, 350. Enter the code for the standard **OnPaint** method. You have probably done this enough times by now to write it by heart. What you will do is define a single rectangle as the container for all basic shapes that you will draw on the screen. So, you ask, because the rectangle definition contains a starting point, won't all the shapes be drawn on top of each other? The answer is, not if you translate the shapes. Listing 4-6 shows the **OnPaint** method that draws all the shapes based upon a rectangle.

Listing 4-6a. Basic Shapes Based upon a Rectangle in VB

```
Protected Overrides Sub OnPaint(ByVal e As PaintEventArgs)
  Dim R1 As New Rectangle(10, 10, 40, 40)

  e.Graphics.SmoothingMode = SmoothingMode.HighQuality

  e.Graphics.DrawRectangle(Pens.Black, R1)
  e.Graphics.TranslateTransform(50.0F, 0.0F)
  e.Graphics.FillRectangle(Brushes.Black, R1)

  'Draw three rectangles
  Dim ThreeRects() As Rectangle = {New Rectangle(110, 10, 40, 40), _
                    New Rectangle(160, 10, 40, 40), _
                    New Rectangle(210, 10, 40, 40)}
  e.Graphics.ResetTransform()
  e.Graphics.DrawRectangles(Pens.Red, ThreeRects)

  'Draw three filled rectangles
  e.Graphics.ResetTransform()
  e.Graphics.TranslateTransform(100.0F, 0.0F)
  e.Graphics.FillRectangles(Brushes.Red, ThreeRects)
```

```
'Use first rect to bound ellipse as circle
e.Graphics.ResetTransform()
e.Graphics.TranslateTransform(0.0F, 50.0F)
e.Graphics.DrawEllipse(Pens.Green, R1)

'Draw a filled ellipse
e.Graphics.TranslateTransform(50.0F, 0.0F)
e.Graphics.FillEllipse(Brushes.Green, R1)

'Use first rect to bound pie
e.Graphics.ResetTransform()
e.Graphics.TranslateTransform(100.0F, 50.0F)
e.Graphics.DrawPie(Pens.DarkViolet, R1, 0, 60)

'Use first rect to fill pie
e.Graphics.ResetTransform()
e.Graphics.TranslateTransform(150.0F, 50.0F)
e.Graphics.FillPie(Brushes.DarkViolet, R1, 0, 60)

'Use first rect to bound arc
e.Graphics.ResetTransform()
e.Graphics.TranslateTransform(200.0F, 50.0F)
e.Graphics.DrawArc(Pens.DarkBlue, R1, 40, 160)

End Sub
```

Listing 4-6b. Basic Shapes Based upon a Rectangle in C#

```
protected override void OnPaint(PaintEventArgs e)
{
  Rectangle R1 = new Rectangle(10, 10, 40, 40);

  e.Graphics.SmoothingMode=SmoothingMode.HighQuality;

  e.Graphics.DrawRectangle(Pens.Black,R1);
  e.Graphics.TranslateTransform(50.0F, 0.0F);
  e.Graphics.FillRectangle(Brushes.Black,R1);
```

```
        //Draw three rectangles
        Rectangle[] ThreeRects = {new Rectangle(110, 10, 40, 40),
                                  new Rectangle(160, 10, 40, 40),
                                  new Rectangle(210, 10, 40, 40)};
        e.Graphics.ResetTransform();
        e.Graphics.DrawRectangles(Pens.Red, ThreeRects);

        //Draw three filled rectangles
        e.Graphics.ResetTransform();
        e.Graphics.TranslateTransform(100.0F, 0.0F);
        e.Graphics.FillRectangles(Brushes.Red, ThreeRects);


        //Use first rect to bound ellipse as circle
        e.Graphics.ResetTransform();
        e.Graphics.TranslateTransform(0.0F, 50.0F);
        e.Graphics.DrawEllipse(Pens.Green,R1);

        //Draw a filled ellipse
        e.Graphics.TranslateTransform(50.0F, 0.0F);
        e.Graphics.FillEllipse(Brushes.Green,R1);

        //Use first rect to bound pie
        e.Graphics.ResetTransform();
        e.Graphics.TranslateTransform(100.0F, 50.0F);
        e.Graphics.DrawPie(Pens.DarkViolet, R1, 0, 60);

        //Use first rect to fill pie
        e.Graphics.ResetTransform();
        e.Graphics.TranslateTransform(150.0F, 50.0F);
        e.Graphics.FillPie(Brushes.DarkViolet, R1, 0, 60);

        //Use first rect to bound arc
        e.Graphics.ResetTransform();
        e.Graphics.TranslateTransform(200.0F, 50.0F);
        e.Graphics.DrawArc(Pens.DarkBlue, R1, 40, 160);

    }
```

Compile and run the program. If you get a syntax error during compile, it is most likely because you need to include the System.Drawing.Drawing2D namespace at the top of your program. Figure 4-15 shows what you should see.

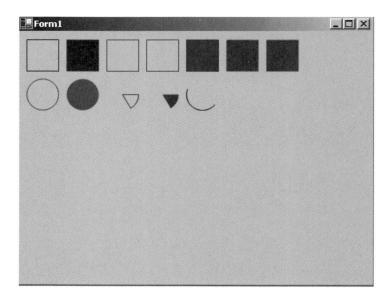

Figure 4-15. Drawing all the basic shapes based upon a rectangle

Take a good look at the code. Except for drawing the three rectangles (used in the call to DrawRectanges), all the shapes are based upon the same rectangle defined at the beginning of the routine. In order to place the shapes at different locations, I use the Graphics.TranslateTransform to move the starting point of the shape.

Shapes Defined by Sets of Points

You can define the nonregular shapes (as well as regular ones) by a set of points along the shape. Often this set of points is an array that can contain as many X, Y pairs as you like. As the shape is being drawn, .NET "connects the dots" and makes a straight line between each pair of points. The endpoint is often connected to the beginning point to make a closed shape. The methods that draw in this manner are as follows:

- DrawBezier

- DrawBeziers

- DrawClosedCurve

- FillClosedCurve

- DrawCurve

- DrawLine

- DrawLines

- DrawPolygon

- FillPolygon

First of all, let's define a set of points. Points are actually .NET structures complete with methods:

- *X:* The X value of the point.

- *Y:* The Y value of the point.

- *Ceiling:* Rounds each value of PointF to the next highest integer.

- *Round:* Rounds each value of PointF to integer.

- *Truncate:* Converts each value of PointF to point structure by truncating floats.

- *Empty:* Generates an empty Point object.

- *Equals:* Determines if two Point objects are equal.

- *Add operator:* Adds two Point objects.

- *Subtract operator:* Subtracts two Point objects.

- *Equal operator:* Boolean comparison. True if equal.

- *Inequality operator:* Boolean comparison. True if not equal.

- Point to Size conversion

- Point to PointF conversion

This seems like quite a few members for what amounts to a pair of values. You will find these members very important, though. The next example will not only draw some different shapes, but it will also use many of these Point members.

Drawing Shapes Based on Points

Add a new method to your new project. This method will be called from the **OnPaint** method and will draw the next few shapes. The new method will be called DrawPoints and take a Graphics object as an argument. This method will be the last line of the OnPaint method. Listing 4-7 makes use of sets of points for all the drawing functions. Note also that some of the Point functions translate the origins of the shapes.

Listing 4-7a. Drawing Shapes Based on Points in C#

```csharp
private void PointDraw( Graphics G )
{
  //Start with clean slate
  G.ResetClip();
  G.ResetTransform();

  //Separate sections
  G.DrawLine(Pens.Black,10,110,this.Width-10,110);

  //------------ Draw Line -----------------------
  //Generate start and end points
  Point StartPt = new Point(10,130);
  Point EndPt = new Point(200,130);
  Pen P = new Pen(Brushes.CadetBlue, 5);
  G.DrawLine(P, StartPt, EndPt);

  //------------- Draw lines ----------------------
  //Translate in the Y Direction
  Size Xlate_Y = new Size(0,40);
  //Translate in the X Direction
  Size Xlate_X = new Size(200,0);
  Point Pt = StartPt;
  //Generate set of points based on offsets of original point
  Point[] ManyPoints = { (Pt + Xlate_X),
                         (Pt = Pt + Xlate_X + Xlate_Y),
                         (Pt = Pt + Xlate_X) };
  P.Color=Color.Firebrick;
  G.DrawLines(P, ManyPoints);
```

```
//------------ DrawBezier and Polygon -------------------
StartPt.X=10;
StartPt.Y=250;
Point CtlPtA = new Point(50,150);
Point CtlPtB = new Point(350,300);
EndPt.X=400;
EndPt.Y=250;
Point[] PolyPoints = { StartPt, CtlPtA, EndPt, CtlPtB };
//Draw the controlling shape of the Bezier spline
G.DrawPolygon ( Pens.DarkSeaGreen, PolyPoints );

//Draw the actual Spline
P.Color=Color.DarkSeaGreen;
P.Width=3;
G.DrawBezier( P, StartPt, CtlPtA, CtlPtB, EndPt );

//---------- Draw two Bezier splines --------------------
Size Y = new Size(0,40);
Size X = new Size(20,0);
//Y Translated start of first spline
//Same control points for first spline,
//X,Y Translated end of first spline,
//X Translate control points for second spline,
//X,Y New end point for second spline
Point[] TwoSplines = { StartPt+Y,
                       CtlPtA,
                       CtlPtB,
                       EndPt+Y-new Size(200,0),
                       CtlPtA+X,
                       CtlPtB+X,
                       EndPt+Y+X };
P.Color=Color.Gold;
G.DrawBeziers (P, TwoSplines);

//---------- Draw a closed curve -----------
PolyPoints[0] = new Point(100, 350);
PolyPoints[1] = new Point(250, 300);
PolyPoints[2] = new Point(250, 400);
PolyPoints[3] = new Point(150, 400);
P.Color=Color.Olive;
//Curve traces outside of polygon
//Curve is closed cardinal spline & hits all points
G.DrawPolygon (P, PolyPoints);
G.DrawClosedCurve(P,PolyPoints);
```

```csharp
        //Uncomment next line to fill the egg shape
        // G.FillClosedCurve(Brushes.AliceBlue,PolyPoints);

        //---------- Draw an open cardinal curve -----------
        Point[] CardPoints = { new Point( 310, 350 ),
                               new Point( 330, 360 ),
                               new Point( 360, 320 ),
                               new Point( 390, 370 ),
                               new Point( 400, 350 ),
                               new Point( 480, 340 )};
        P.Color=Color.DarkOrange;
        G.DrawCurve(P, CardPoints);

        P.Dispose();
    }
```

Listing 4-7b. Drawing Shapes Based on Points in VB.NET

```vbnet
    Private Sub PointDraw(ByVal G As Graphics)
        'Start with clean slate
        G.ResetClip()
        G.ResetTransform()

        'Separate sections
        G.DrawLine(Pens.Black, 10, 110, Me.Width - 10, 110)

        '------------ Draw Line -----------------------
        'Generate start and end points
        Dim StartPt As Point = New Point(10, 130)
        Dim EndPt As Point = New Point(200, 130)
        Dim P As Pen = New Pen(Brushes.CadetBlue, 5)
        G.DrawLine(P, StartPt, EndPt)

        '------------- Draw lines ----------------------
        'Translate in the Y Direction
        Dim Xlate_Y As Size = New Size(0, 40)
        'Translate in the X Direction
        Dim Xlate_X As Size = New Size(200, 0)
        Dim Pt As Point = StartPt
        'Generate set of points based on offsets of original point
        Dim ManyPoints As Point() = {Point.op_Addition(Pt, Xlate_X), _
                                Point.op_Addition(Pt, _
                                Size.op_Addition(Xlate_X, Xlate_Y)), _
                                Point.op_Addition(Pt, Xlate_X)}
```

```
P.Color = Color.Firebrick
G.DrawLines(P, ManyPoints)


'------------ DrawBezier and Polygon ------------------
StartPt.X = 10
StartPt.Y = 250
Dim CtlPtA As Point = New Point(50, 150)
Dim CtlPtB As Point = New Point(350, 300)
EndPt.X = 400
EndPt.Y = 250
Dim PolyPoints As Point() = {StartPt, CtlPtA, EndPt, CtlPtB}
'Draw the controlling shape of the Bezier spline
G.DrawPolygon(Pens.DarkSeaGreen, PolyPoints)


'Draw the actual Spline
P.Color = Color.DarkSeaGreen
P.Width = 3
G.DrawBezier(P, StartPt, CtlPtA, CtlPtB, EndPt)


'---------- Draw two Bezier splines --------------------
Dim Y As Size = New Size(0, 40)
Dim X As Size = New Size(20, 0)
'Y Translated start of first spline
'Same control points for first spline,
'X,Y Translated end of first spline,
'X Translate control points for second spline,
'X,Y New end point for second spline
Dim TwoSplines As Point() = {Point.op_Addition(StartPt, Y), _
                    CtlPtA, _
                    CtlPtB, _
                    Point.op_Addition(EndPt, _
                    Size.op_Subtraction(Y, New Size(200, 0))), _
                    Point.op_Addition(CtlPtA, X), _
                    Point.op_Addition(CtlPtB, X), _
                    Point.op_Addition(EndPt, Size.op_Addition(Y, X))}


P.Color = Color.Gold
G.DrawBeziers(P, TwoSplines)


'---------- Draw a closed curve -----------
PolyPoints(0) = New Point(100, 350)
PolyPoints(1) = New Point(250, 300)
PolyPoints(2) = New Point(250, 400)
PolyPoints(3) = New Point(150, 400)
P.Color = Color.Olive
```

```
'Curve traces outside of polygon
'Curve is closed cardinal spline & hits all points
G.DrawPolygon(P, PolyPoints)
G.DrawClosedCurve(P, PolyPoints)
'Uncomment next line to fill the egg shape
'G.FillClosedCurve(Brushes.AliceBlue, PolyPoints)

'---------- Draw an open cardinal curve -----------
Dim CardPoints As Point() = {New Point(310, 350), _
                    New Point(330, 360), _
                    New Point(360, 320), _
                    New Point(390, 370), _
                    New Point(400, 350), _
                    New Point(480, 340)}
P.Color = Color.DarkOrange
G.DrawCurve(P, CardPoints)

P.Dispose()
End Sub
```

Before you compile and run the code, make sure that your form is sized to fit all the shapes that will be drawn on it. Make your form's size equal 512 wide by 650 high. If you have entered everything correctly, you should be able to see quite a few shapes on the screen in addition to those shown in Figure 4-15. Figure 4-16 shows the new shapes.

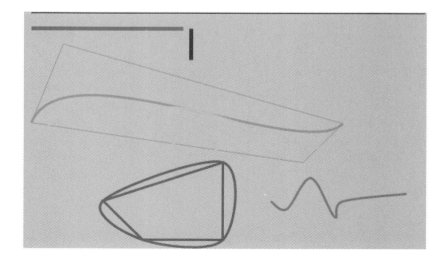

Figure 4-16. Shapes based on sets of points

So, what do you think so far? Except for the lines, these shapes are a bit more complicated and interesting. The Bezier spline is interesting in that the curve is controlled by two sets of points that are not part of the curve. These points are shown as the outline of the rectangle that borders the spline. You can see how the curve of the line heads toward the control points.

The ClosedCurve is similar to the Bezier spline. The difference is that the curve runs through each defined point and there is no start or end.

The plural shapes DrawBeziers and DrawLines draw subsequent shapes where the start of the next shape is the end of the previous shape.

Let's look at the code in a little detail. You will note that I started out with a set of points and with subsequent shapes I translated the start and end points using two size objects. One for X and one for Y. This was not necessary for this procedure but it is instructive in that it shows how to use the methods provided by the Point and Size structures to modify the position of the shapes.

Note the difference between the C# code and the VB code. In this case, I find the C# code to be easier to both write and understand. Consider the case of translating a Point structure by a Size structure. The objective is to add or subtract the X and Y values of the Size structure to or from the X and Y values of the Point structure. The C# language overloads the + operator for this operation. VB .NET has no overloaded + or – operator for adding Size structures to Point structures. Compare the following code to the preceding code and see which one you prefer.

VB

```
Dim TwoSplines As Point() = {Point.op_Addition(StartPt, Y), _
                      CtlPtA, _
                      CtlPtB, _
                      Point.op_Addition(EndPt, _
                      Size.op_Subtraction(Y, New Size(200, 0))), _
                      Point.op_Addition(CtlPtA, X), _
                      Point.op_Addition(CtlPtB, X), _
                      Point.op_Addition(EndPt, Size.op_Addition(Y, X))}
```

C#

```
Point[] TwoSplines = { StartPt+Y,
                      CtlPtA,
                      CtlPtB,
                      EndPt+Y-new Size(200,0),
                      CtlPtA+X,
                      CtlPtB+X,
                      EndPt+Y+X };
```

As you can see, using the + and – operators makes for less cumbersome code. Of course in real life I would not have done it this way—I would have defined a new set of points. But then I would not have been able to show you this code.[3]

> **NOTE** *I used Option Strict in my VB code. This is why the DIM xxx definitions contain the "As <something>" clause. It is best to let the compiler know exactly what you mean.*

Shapes Defined by a Path

Instead of using a point array, you can often create a shape by giving it a graphics path to trace. A graphics path can be one of the basic shapes or it can be a shape made up from a set of points. What makes this method different than the previous methods is that a path can also be additive. What do I mean by that? You can make a path out of a rectangle and then add another shape, such as a circle, to get a new path. You can keep adding shapes as long as you like and the path will get more and more complex. This is a very powerful method of drawing indeed. The path drawing methods are as follows:

- DrawPath

- FillPath

Each of these drawing methods needs a GraphicsPath object to provide the points necessary to draw the final shape. The graphics path in this example will be fairly simple. I go into more detail with the graphics path in Chapter 5. The following code demonstrates adding shapes to a GraphicsPath and then drawing and filling in the GraphicsPath.

VB

```vb
Private Sub PathDraw(ByVal G As Graphics)
  'Start with clean slate
  G.ResetClip()
  G.ResetTransform()

  'Separate sections
  G.DrawLine(Pens.Black, 10, 420, Me.Width - 10, 420)
```

---

3. You will find that VB does some things better and C# wins on other points.

```
    'Make a blank path and add shapes to it
    Dim gp As GraphicsPath = New GraphicsPath()
    Dim P As Pen = New Pen(Brushes.ForestGreen, 3)
    gp.AddRectangle(New Rectangle(10, 450, 100, 100))
    gp.AddEllipse(120, 450, 100, 100)
    gp.AddPie(70, 500, 100, 100, 25, 120)
    'Draw the outline of the path and fill it in
    G.DrawPath(P, gp)
    G.FillPath(Brushes.Bisque, gp)

    P.Dispose()
  End Sub
```

C#

```
    private void PathDraw( Graphics G )
    {
      //Start with clean slate
      G.ResetClip();
      G.ResetTransform();

      //Separate sections
      G.DrawLine(Pens.Black, 10, 420, this.Width-10, 420);

      //Make a blank path and add shapes to it
      GraphicsPath gp = new GraphicsPath();
      Pen P = new Pen(Brushes.ForestGreen,3);
      gp.AddRectangle(new Rectangle(10, 450, 100, 100));
      gp.AddEllipse(120, 450, 100, 100);
      gp.AddPie ( 70, 500, 100, 100, 25, 120 );
      //Draw the outline of the path and fill it in
      G.DrawPath (P, gp );
      G.FillPath(Brushes.Bisque,gp);

      P.Dispose();
    }
```

As with the last example, you need to add a call to this procedure as the last line of the **OnPaint** method.

When you run this code, you will see that three shapes are drawn and they are all filled in at the same time with the same color. While these shapes may look separate, they are all actually part of the same path.

Rendering Images and Text

Along with drawing shapes of varying complexity, you can draw images or text within a Graphics region. The methods for doing this are as follows:

- DrawIcon

- DrawIconUnstretched

- DrawText

- DrawImage

- DrawImageUnscaled

The **DrawImage** method has 27 overloaded versions. The **DrawImageUnscaled** method has 4 overloaded versions. These methods are interesting indeed. Basically, they allow you to create a rectangle anywhere on the form and drop an image in that rectangle. There is no need to use a container such as the PictureBox control. The image can be drawn either with the original size or as a scaled image.

There are two versions of the **DrawIcon** method. The first one draws the icon within the bounds of a supplied rectangle. This method sizes the icon accordingly. The other draws the icon with its normal size at a supplied point.

The method **DrawIconUnstretched** simply draws the icon within the boundary of a supplied rectangle but in the original size. If the rectangle is smaller than the icon, the icon will be clipped.

 NOTE *I have found that the **DrawIconUnstretched** method does not clip the icon. If the rectangle is smaller than the icon, the icon is still drawn normal size.*

The next example originally used the **DrawImage** and **DrawIcon** methods. However, as I started to write the code, I got rather involved and came up with an example that was a little more complex than I planned for.[4] All you developers can identify with that, can't you? But anyway, this example allows you to use the mouse to draw a rectangle on the screen and put an image in that rectangle.

First, create a new Windows Forms project. Mine is called IconImageDraw. Size the form large enough for you to play with. Mine is 500×400. There are no extraneous controls added to this project.

---

4. The best laid plans of mice and men. . . .

The code in Listing 4-8 shows the use of three mouse events: MouseDown, MouseUp, and MouseMove. It also shows how to invalidate a graphics container and force the OnPaint method. This listing does not show the Windows Form Designer generated code. This code is produced by the wizard when making the project and is unchanged for this example.

Listing 4-8a. VB Code to Draw an Image Inside a Supplied Rectangle

```
Imports System.Drawing
Imports System.Drawing.Imaging
Imports System.Drawing.Drawing2D

Public Class Form1
  Inherits System.Windows.Forms.Form

#Region " Windows Form Designer generated code "

  '"R" holds the image, "Box" is the new image home currently being drawn by
  'holding the mouse down and dragging
  Private R As Rectangle = Rectangle.Empty
  Private Box As Rectangle = Rectangle.Empty
  Private I As Image = Image.FromFile("D:\\sample.jpg")
  Private ThisIcon As Icon = New Icon("d:\\usa.ico")
  Private OK2Paint As Boolean = False

  Private Sub Form1_Load(ByVal sender As System.Object, _
                    ByVal e As System.EventArgs) _
                    Handles MyBase.Load

  End Sub

  Protected Overrides Sub OnPaint(ByVal e As PaintEventArgs)

    'Always draw the icon
    e.Graphics.DrawIcon(ThisIcon, 1, 1)

    'Bail if rectangle is empty
    If R.IsEmpty Then
      Return
    End If
```

```
      If Not OK2Paint Then
        Return
      End If


      Dim P As Pen = New Pen(Brushes.Black, 3)
      e.Graphics.DrawRectangle(P, R)
      ' Draw image based on rectangle.
      e.Graphics.DrawImage(I, R)


      P.Dispose()

  End Sub


  Private Sub DrawBox(ByVal sender As System.Object, _
                      ByVal m As MouseEventArgs) Handles MyBase.MouseMove
     'Prints the x,y coordinates directly on the screen
     Dim G As Graphics = Me.CreateGraphics()
     Dim TextR As RectangleF = New RectangleF(10, Me.Height - 50, 100, 20)
     Dim B As SolidBrush = New SolidBrush(Me.BackColor)

     G.FillRectangle(B, TextR)
     G.DrawString(m.X.ToString() + ", " + m.Y.ToString(), _
                  New Font("Arial", 10), _
                  Brushes.Black, TextR, _
                  StringFormat.GenericDefault)

     B.Dispose()

     'Draw the box as the mouse drags
     If m.Button = MouseButtons.Left Then
       If Not Box.IsEmpty Then
         Dim P As Pen = New Pen(New SolidBrush(Me.BackColor), 1)
         G.DrawRectangle(P, Box)
         P.Dispose()
       End If
       Box = New Rectangle(R.X, R.Y, m.X - R.X, m.Y - R.Y)
       G.DrawRectangle(Pens.Black, Box)
     End If

  End Sub
```

```vb
  Private Sub StartBox(ByVal sender As System.Object, _
                       ByVal m As MouseEventArgs) Handles MyBase.MouseDown
    If m.Button = MouseButtons.Left Then
      R.X = m.X
      R.Y = m.Y
      OK2Paint = False
    End If
  End Sub

  Private Sub EndBox(ByVal sender As System.Object, _
                     ByVal m As MouseEventArgs) Handles MyBase.MouseUp
    R.Width = m.X - R.X
    R.Height = m.Y - R.Y
    OK2Paint = True
    Me.Refresh()
  End Sub
End Class
```

Listing 4-8b. C# Code to Draw an Image Inside a Supplied Rectangle

```csharp
using System;
using System.Drawing;
using System.Drawing.Imaging;
using System.Drawing.Drawing2D;
using System.Collections;
using System.ComponentModel;
using System.Windows.Forms;
using System.Data;

namespace IconImageDraw_c
{
  public class Form1 : System.Windows.Forms.Form
  {
    /// <summary>
    /// Required designer variable.
    /// </summary>
    private System.ComponentModel.Container components = null;
```

```csharp
public Form1()
{
  //
  // Required for Windows Form Designer support
  //
  InitializeComponent();

  this.MouseMove += new MouseEventHandler(this.DrawBox);
  this.MouseDown += new MouseEventHandler(this.StartBox);
  this.MouseUp += new MouseEventHandler(this.EndBox);
}

/// <summary>
/// Clean up any resources being used.
/// </summary>
protected override void Dispose( bool disposing )
{
  if( disposing )
  {
    if (components != null)
    {
      components.Dispose();
    }
  }
  base.Dispose( disposing );
}

#region Windows Form Designer generated code

/// <summary>
/// The main entry point for the application.
/// </summary>
///

//"R" holds the image, "Box" is the new image home currently being
//drawn by holding the mouse down and dragging
private Rectangle R = Rectangle.Empty;
private Rectangle Box = Rectangle.Empty;
private Image I = Image.FromFile("D:\\sample.jpg");
private Icon ThisIcon = new Icon("d:\\usa.ico");
private bool OK2Paint = false;
```

```
[STATh)read]
static void Main()
{
  Application.Run(new Form1());
}

private void Form1_Load(object sender, System.EventArgs e)
{
}

protected override void OnPaint ( PaintEventArgs e )
{
  //Always draw the icon
  e.Graphics.DrawIcon(ThisIcon, 1, 1);

  //Bail if rectangle is empty
  if ( R == Rectangle.Empty )
    return;

  if ( !OK2Paint )
    return;

  Pen P = new Pen(Brushes.Black, 3);
  e.Graphics.DrawRectangle(P, R);
  // Draw image based on rectangle.
  e.Graphics.DrawImage(I, R);

  P.Dispose();
}

private void DrawBox ( System.Object sender , MouseEventArgs m )
{
  //Prints the x,y coordinates directly on the screen
  Graphics G = this.CreateGraphics();
  Rectangle TextR = new Rectangle(10, this.Height-50, 100, 20 );
  SolidBrush B = new SolidBrush(this.BackColor);

  G.FillRectangle(B, TextR);
  G.DrawString ( m.X.ToString() + ", " + m.Y.ToString(),
                 new Font("Arial", 10),
                 Brushes.Black, TextR, StringFormat.GenericDefault );

  B.Dispose();
```

```
    //Draw the box as the mouse drags
    if ( m.Button == MouseButtons.Left )
    {
      if ( Box != Rectangle.Empty )
      {
        Pen P = new Pen(new SolidBrush(this.BackColor),1);
        G.DrawRectangle ( P, Box );
        P.Dispose();
      }
      Box = new Rectangle ( R.X, R.Y, m.X - R.X, m.Y - R.Y );
      G.DrawRectangle( Pens.Black, Box );
    }
}

private void StartBox( System.Object sender , MouseEventArgs m )
{
  if ( m.Button == MouseButtons.Left )
  {
    R.X=m.X;
    R.Y=m.Y;
    OK2Paint = false;
  }
}
private void EndBox( System.Object sender , MouseEventArgs m )
{
  R.Width = m.X - R.X;
  R.Height = m.Y - R.Y;
  OK2Paint = true;
  this.Refresh();
}
    }
}
```

The C# code is a little harder to understand than the VB code, mainly because of having to declare the delegate in the forms constructor.

Compile and run the code. You will see several things:

- The form comes up and an icon is placed at position 1, 1.

- Run the mouse over the form and the mouse position is drawn using the DrawText function, directly on the screen.

- Hold the left button of the mouse down on the form and drag it diagonally across the form. You will see a rectangle being generated.

- Lift up the mouse button and the rectangle will be replaced by an image.

NOTE *I used two images that are part of the .NET samples. I put them on my D: drive for my own convenience. You can use any images you like.*

The code you wrote in this example is indicative of things you will need to do in the world of graphics programming. Drawing rectangles with the mouse is common. Moving images around the screen is also common. Enabling or disabling the OnPaint delegate is necessary to both force a repaint and prevent scribbling on the screen. Also, being able to handle mouse events is key to just about any graphics program you can think of.

One final note about this example. Examine how I draw the position of the mouse to the screen. If I do not blank out the rectangle that contains the text, I will soon have an unintelligible scribble of text on the form. Because I use the existing background color of the form for the **FillRectangle** method, the user can change form colors and will never know that the text is being erased and redrawn.

For those not faint of heart, try drawing a rectangle on the form from the bottom right to the top left. You will see an inverted image. The image is always rendered from the origin of the rectangle to the end of the rectangle. You can do some cool things with this. Chapter 7 has an example on rubber banding a rectangle. By the way, the **DrawRectangle** method does not take a rectangle that has been defined with a negative width or height.

Objects Belonging to the System

There are a set of system parameters that describe various colors and icons. When you set up your desktop colors, you are assigning a color to a particular attribute of the desktop. Some of these color attributes are as follows:

- ActiveBorder

- DeskTop

- HighLightText

- Control

There are quite a few more system colors you can use. I suggest looking in the system help to see what else is available.

Instead of trying to guess what the system color you need is, you can actually get the color of the attribute you want. Suppose that the computer user changes the color of a particular attribute such as the ActiveBorder. If you have code that paints some text the ActiveBorder color, your text color will change to match.

There are four classes in the System.Drawing namespace you can use to get system colors for common operations:

- SystemBrushes

- SystemColors

- SystemIcons

- SystemPens

Any objects you instantiated from these classes would be used the same way you have been using them in this chapter. Consider the following code snippet:

C#

```
Brush B = SystemBrushes.HighlightText;
Color C = SystemColors.Desktop;
Pen   P = SystemPens.ControlDarkDark;
Icon  I = SystemIcons.Hand;
```

VB

```
Dim B As Brush = SystemBrushes.HighlightText
Dim C As Color = SystemColors.Desktop
Dim P As Pen = SystemPens.ControlDarkDark
Dim I As Icon = SystemIcons.Hand
```

Summary

This chapter introduced you to the System.Drawing namespace. Coverage of the Graphics class and its members took up most of this chapter. The Graphics class is probably the most important class in the GDI+ realm.

Numerous examples in this chapter took you from drawing simple lines all the way to managing complex images and where they are rendered on the screen. Now that you have finished this chapter, here is what you should know how to do (and it is quite a bit):

- Convert back and forth between coordinate systems

- Use pens

- Use brushes, including solid and texture brushes

- Draw various kinds of lines

- Change the end shape of lines

- Understand the importance of the Graphics class

- Get a reference to an object's Graphics region

- Adjust the quality of drawing in the Graphics region

- Handle the **OnPaint** method

- Generate and manipulate clipping regions

- Draw within clipping regions

- Transform clipping regions

- Draw all the stock shapes

- Draw shapes using graphics paths

- Use the Point structure

- Render images on a Graphics region

- Draw text on a Graphics region

- Handle and respond to mouse events

- Use the system-supplied drawing tools

While this chapter may seem fairly inclusive, you have only just learned the basics of GDI+ and how to use it. The next chapter focuses on the more advanced aspects of GDI+ drawing. There are some pretty cool ideas in the next chapter.

CHAPTER 5
Advanced Graphics

Dolores breezed along the surface of her life like a flat stone forever skipping across smooth water, rippling reality sporadically but oblivious to it consistently, until she finally lost momentum, sank, and due to an overdose of fluoride as a child which caused her to lie forever on the floor of her life as useless as an appendix and as lonely as a five-hundred-pound barbell in a steroid-free fitness center.

—Linda Vernon, Newark, California (1990 Winner)

HELLO, AND WELCOME to Chapter 5.

In Chapter 4 I took you through most of the System.Drawing namespace. The majority of this namespace is devoted to the Graphics class and its members. This chapter delves a little deeper into some of the more esoteric aspects of pens and brushes. It also goes much deeper into drawing itself.

In this chapter, you will be introduced to some of the more complicated vector graphics drawing concepts, such as

- Matrix transforms

- Color blending

- Gradients

- Drawing and filling in shapes made from Graphics paths

While some of the classes in this chapter are from the System.Drawing namespace, most of the chapter is devoted to the System.Drawing.Drawing2D namespace.

More About Pens, Lines, and Brushes

Chapter 4 had quite a bit of information on pens and brushes. However, some of the Pen members are more than a little basic, so I decided to leave them to this chapter. The Pen members I'm referring to are as follows:

- Pen.LineJoin

- Pen.CustomEndCap

- Pen.CustomStartCap

Along with these Pen members, there are also a couple of other related classes:

- CustomLineCap

- AdjustableArrowCap

As you can probably guess, these methods, properties, and classes have to do with how the pen looks as it is drawing lines or other shapes. Let's start with the **LineJoin** method.

Start a new project in either C# or VB. Size the form to be 400×400. Go into the code and type in the skeleton for the **OnPaint** method. The **OnPaint** method should be ingrained in your brain by now. It is without a doubt the most important method in any graphics program. Enter the code shown in Listing 5-1.

 NOTE *Be sure to include the following namespaces in all your code for this chapter: System.Drawing and System.Drawing.Drawing2D.*

Listing 5-1a. Different LineJoin Methods in VB

```
Protected Overrides Sub OnPaint(ByVal e As PaintEventArgs)
   Dim G As Graphics = e.Graphics
   Dim PtsA As Point() = {New Point(10, 10), _
                         New Point(150, 150), _
                         New Point(400, 10)}
   Dim PtsB As Point() = {New Point(10, 40), _
                         New Point(150, 180), _
                         New Point(400, 40)}
   Dim PtsC As Point() = {New Point(10, 70), _
                         New Point(150, 210), _
                         New Point(400, 70)}
   Dim PtsD As Point() = {New Point(10, 100), _
                         New Point(150, 240), _
                         New Point(400, 100)}
   Dim P As Pen = New Pen(Color.Blue, 10)
```

```
    G.SmoothingMode = SmoothingMode.AntiAlias
    P.LineJoin = LineJoin.Bevel
    G.DrawLines(P, PtsA)

    P.LineJoin = LineJoin.Miter
    G.DrawLines(P, PtsB)

    P.LineJoin = LineJoin.MiterClipped
    G.DrawLines(P, PtsC)

    P.LineJoin = LineJoin.Round
    G.DrawLines(P, PtsD)
  End Sub
```

Listing 5-1b. Different LineJoin Methods in C#

```csharp
    protected override void OnPaint ( PaintEventArgs e )
    {
      Graphics G = e.Graphics;
      Point[] PtsA = { new Point(10, 10),
                       new Point(150, 150),
                       new Point(400, 10) };
      Point[] PtsB = { new Point(10, 40),
                       new Point(150, 180),
                       new Point(400, 40) };
      Point[] PtsC = { new Point(10, 70),
                       new Point(150, 210),
                       new Point(400, 70) };
      Point[] PtsD = { new Point(10, 100),
                       new Point(150, 240),
                       new Point(400, 100) };
      Pen P = new Pen(Color.Blue, 10);

      G.SmoothingMode=SmoothingMode.AntiAlias;
      P.LineJoin=LineJoin.Bevel;
      G.DrawLines(P, PtsA);

      P.LineJoin=LineJoin.Miter;
      G.DrawLines(P, PtsB);

      P.LineJoin=LineJoin.MiterClipped;
      G.DrawLines(P, PtsC);

      P.LineJoin=LineJoin.Round;
      G.DrawLines(P, PtsD);
    }
```

Here you're making a set of points that describe line segments. You then set the smoothing mode to AntiAlias so you can see a straight line. Next, you draw lines that are connected according to the LineJoin enumeration.

There are four LineJoin enumerations:

- *Bevel:* Joins two lines with a bevel on the outside of the joint.

- *Miter:* Joins two lines with a miter joint. This bisects the angle of the two lines.

- *MiterClipped:* Joins two lines with a miter joint if the length of the miter exceeds the MiterLimit. Joins two lines with a bevel if the length of the miter is within the MiterLimit.

- *Round:* Joins two lines with a smooth, round corner.

The result of running the code in Listing 5-1 is shown in Figure 5-1.

Figure 5-1. Result of different corners joining two lines

Back in Chapter 4 I discussed several kinds of start and end caps that you can put on a line. These caps are far more interesting than the normal straight, boxed ends. Next, you will define your own start and end caps.

You define a custom cap using the CustomLineCap class. This class has four overloaded constructors as well as five properties. The constructors' arguments are as follows:

- GraphicsPath defines the fill. GraphicsPath defines the outline.

- GraphicsPath defines the fill. GraphicsPath defines the outline. LineCap defines the base of the custom cap.

- GraphicsPath defines the fill. GraphicsPath defines the outline. LineCap defines the base of the custom cap. Inset defines the distance between the line and the cap.

The properties of the CustomLineCap class basically make up the individual arguments of the constructors. They are as follows:

- *BaseCap:* The LineCap enumeration on which this cap is based.

- *BaseInset:* The distance between the end of the line and the cap.

- *StrokeJoin:* The LineJoin enumeration that determines how lines in the cap are joined.

- *WidthScale:* The scaling factor of the cap to the pen width.

Listing 5-2 shows an example of how to create a custom line caps. Start with a new project and do all the work in the **OnPaint** method.

Listing 5-2a. CustomLineCap Example in C#

```csharp
protected override void OnPaint ( PaintEventArgs e )
{
  Graphics G = e.Graphics;
  Pen P = new Pen(Color.Blue, 1 );
  Point[] Pts = { new Point( 10, 10 ),
                  new Point( 15, 10 ),
                  new Point( 20, 15 ),
                  new Point( 20, 20 ),
                  new Point( 15, 25 ),
                  new Point( 10, 25 ),
                  new Point( 5, 20 ),
                  new Point( 5, 15 ),
                  new Point( 10, 10 )};
  GraphicsPath Path = new GraphicsPath();

  Path.AddLines (Pts);
```

```
    G.SmoothingMode=SmoothingMode.AntiAlias;
    CustomLineCap Lc = new CustomLineCap( null, Path );
    Lc.BaseInset=0;
    Lc.WidthScale=1;
    Lc.StrokeJoin=LineJoin.Miter;
    P.CustomEndCap = Lc;
    P.CustomStartCap=Lc;

    G.DrawLine ( P, 50, 150, 200, 150 );
    G.DrawLine ( P, 150, 50, 150, 200 );

    Lc.Dispose();
    Path.Dispose();
    P.Dispose();
}
```

Listing 5-2b. CustomLineCap Example in VB

```
Protected Overrides Sub OnPaint(ByVal e As PaintEventArgs)
  Dim G As Graphics = e.Graphics
  Dim P As Pen = New Pen(Color.Blue, 1)
  Dim Pts() As Point = {New Point(10, 10), _
                  New Point(15, 10), _
                  New Point(20, 15), _
                  New Point(20, 20), _
                  New Point(15, 25), _
                  New Point(10, 25), _
                  New Point(5, 20), _
                  New Point(5, 15), _
                  New Point(10, 10)}
  Dim Path As GraphicsPath = New GraphicsPath()

  Path.AddLines(Pts)

  G.SmoothingMode = SmoothingMode.AntiAlias
  Dim Lc As CustomLineCap = New CustomLineCap(Nothing, Path)
  Lc.BaseInset = 0
  Lc.WidthScale = 1
  Lc.StrokeJoin = LineJoin.Miter
  P.CustomEndCap = Lc
  P.CustomStartCap = Lc
```

```
G.DrawLine(P, 50, 150, 200, 150)
G.DrawLine(P, 150, 50, 150, 200)

Lc.Dispose()
Path.Dispose()
P.Dispose()

End Sub
```

Using the Hatch Brush

So far, you have used a SolidBrush and a TextureBrush. The SolidBrush is one where the whole width of the brush stroke is a single, solid color. The TextureBrush is one where the fill of the brush consists of a supplied bitmap. The HatchBrush is one that is made up of repeating patterns. Table 5-1 shows the HatchBrush's available patterns. This table contains the members of the HatchStyle enumeration.

Table 5-1. HatchBrush Patterns

Style	Description
BackwardDiagonal	A pattern of lines on a diagonal from the upper right to the lower left.
Cross	Specifies horizontal and vertical lines that cross.
DarkDownwardDiagonal	Specifies diagonal lines that slant to the right from top points to bottom points, and are spaced 50 percent closer together than and are twice the width of ForwardDiagonal. This hatch pattern is not antialiased.
DarkHorizontal	Specifies horizontal lines that are spaced 50 percent closer together than Horizontal and are twice the width of HatchStyleHorizontal.
DarkUpwardDiagonal	Specifies diagonal lines that slant to the left from top points to bottom points, are spaced 50 percent closer together than BackwardDiagonal, and are twice its width, but the lines are not antialiased.
DarkVertical	Specifies vertical lines that are spaced 50 percent closer together than Vertical and are twice its width.
DashedDownwardDiagonal	Specifies dashed diagonal lines that slant to the right from top points to bottom points.

Table 5-1. HatchBrush Patterns (Continued)

Style	Description
DashedHorizontal	Specifies dashed horizontal lines.
DashedUpwardDiagonal	Specifies dashed diagonal lines that slant to the left from top points to bottom points.
DashedVertical	Specifies dashed vertical lines.
DiagonalBrick	Specifies a hatch that has the appearance of layered bricks that slant to the left from top points to bottom points.
DiagonalCross	Specifies forward diagonal and backward diagonal lines that cross. The lines are antialiased.
Divot	Specifies a hatch that has the appearance of divots.
DottedDiamond	Specifies forward diagonal and backward diagonal lines, each of which is composed of dots that cross.
DottedGrid	Specifies horizontal and vertical lines, each of which is composed of dots that cross.
ForwardDiagonal	A pattern of lines on a diagonal from upper left to lower right.
Horizontal	A pattern of horizontal lines.
HorizontalBrick	Specifies a hatch that has the appearance of horizontally layered bricks.
LargeCheckerBoard	Specifies a hatch that has the appearance of a checkerboard with squares that are twice the size of SmallCheckerBoard.
LargeConfetti	Specifies a hatch that has the appearance of confetti and is composed of larger pieces than SmallConfetti.
LargeGrid	Specifies the hatch style Cross.
LightDownwardDiagonal	
LightHorizontal	Specifies horizontal lines that are spaced 50 percent closer together than Horizontal.
LightUpwardDiagonal	Specifies diagonal lines that slant to the left from top points to bottom points and are spaced 50 percent closer together than BackwardDiagonal, but they are not antialiased.

Table 5-1. HatchBrush Patterns (Continued)

Style	Description
LightVertical	Specifies vertical lines that are spaced 50 percent closer together than Vertical.
Max	Specifies the hatch style SolidDiamond.
Min	Specifies the hatch style.
NarrowHorizontal	Specifies horizontal lines that are spaced 75 percent closer together than the hatch style Horizontal (or 25 percent closer together than LightHorizontal).
NarrowVertical	Specifies vertical lines that are spaced 75 percent closer together than the hatch style Vertical (or 25 percent closer together than LightVertical).
OutlinedDiamond	Specifies forward diagonal and backward diagonal lines that cross but are not antialiased.
Percent05	Specifies a 5 percent hatch. The ratio of foreground color to background color is 5:100.
Percent10	Specifies a 10 percent hatch. The ratio of foreground color to background color is 10:100.
Percent20	Specifies a 20 percent hatch. The ratio of foreground color to background color is 20:100.
Percent25	Specifies a 25 percent hatch. The ratio of foreground color to background color is 25:100.
Percent30	Specifies a 30 percent hatch. The ratio of foreground color to background color is 30:100.
Percent40	Specifies a 40 percent hatch. The ratio of foreground color to background color is 40:100.
Percent50	Specifies a 50 percent hatch. The ratio of foreground color to background color is 50:100.
Percent60	Specifies a 60 percent hatch. The ratio of foreground color to background color is 60:100.
Percent70	Specifies a 70 percent hatch. The ratio of foreground color to background color is 70:100.
Percent75	Specifies a 75 percent hatch. The ratio of foreground color to background color is 75:100.

Table 5-1. HatchBrush Patterns (Continued)

Style	Description
Percent80	Specifies an 80 percent hatch. The ratio of foreground color to background color is 80:100.
Percent90	Specifies a 90 percent hatch. The ratio of foreground color to background color is 90:100.
Plaid	Specifies a hatch that has the appearance of a plaid material.
Shingle	Specifies a hatch that has the appearance of diagonally layered shingles that slant to the right from top points to bottom points.
SmallCheckerBoard	Specifies a hatch that has the appearance of a checkerboard.
SmallConfetti	Specifies a hatch that has the appearance of confetti.
SmallGrid	Specifies horizontal and vertical lines that cross and are spaced 50 percent closer together than the hatch style Cross.
SolidDiamond	Specifies a hatch that has the appearance of a checkerboard placed diagonally.
Sphere	Specifies a hatch that has the appearance of spheres laid adjacent to one another.
Trellis	Specifies a hatch that has the appearance of a trellis.
Vertical	A pattern of vertical lines.
Wave	Specifies horizontal lines that are composed of tildes.
Weave	Specifies a hatch that has the appearance of a woven material.
WideDownwardDiagonal	Specifies diagonal lines that slant to the right from top points to bottom points, have the same spacing as the hatch style ForwardDiagonal, and are triple its width, but are not antialiased.
WideUpwardDiagonal	Specifies diagonal lines that slant to the left from top points to bottom points, have the same spacing as the hatch style BackwardDiagonal, and are triple its width, but are not antialiased.
ZigZag	Specifies horizontal lines that are composed of zigzags.

Listing 5-3 shows an **OnPaint** method that draws on the screen using a HatchBrush.

Listing 5-3a. HatchBrush in C#

```csharp
protected override void OnPaint ( PaintEventArgs e )
{
  HatchBrush h = new HatchBrush(HatchStyle.BackwardDiagonal,
                                Color.Black,
                                Color.Cyan);
  Pen P = new Pen(h, 20);

  e.Graphics.Clear(Color.AliceBlue);
  e.Graphics.SmoothingMode = SmoothingMode.AntiAlias;

  e.Graphics.DrawLine(P, 80, 90, 80, 200 );
  e.Graphics.FillEllipse(h, 50, 50, 50, 30 );
  P.Dispose();
  h.Dispose();
}
```

Listing 5-3b. HatchBrush in VB

```vb
Protected Overrides Sub OnPaint(ByVal e As PaintEventArgs)
  Dim h As HatchBrush = New HatchBrush(HatchStyle.BackwardDiagonal, _
                                Color.Black, _
                                Color.Cyan)
  Dim P As Pen = New Pen(h, 20)

  e.Graphics.Clear(Color.AliceBlue)
  e.Graphics.SmoothingMode = SmoothingMode.AntiAlias

  e.Graphics.DrawLine(P, 80, 90, 80, 200)
  e.Graphics.FillEllipse(h, 50, 50, 50, 30)

  P.Dispose()
  h.Dispose()
End Sub
```

The result of this program is shown in Figure 5-2.

Figure 5-2. HatchBrush example

It is easy to see a wide range of possibilities for this brush. There are two other brushes that have to do with color blending. I consider these to be the coolest of the brushes. I explain them in detail in the next section.

Blending Colors

There are basically two types of blending in GDI+: blending and alpha blending. *Alpha blending* is the process of creating a Pen, Brush, or Image that has attributes that determine its transparency. *Blending* is the process of drawing a line or filling a shape with a color that starts out at one end of the spectrum and ends at the other.

An example of alpha blending would be creating an image on the screen and then drawing a shape on top of the image that still allows the image to show through. You would perhaps do this in an architecture program that layers successive detail on a base drawing.

An example of blending would be drawing an ellipse that is filled starting with blue and ending with red. Where would you use this? Well, you could use it in a thermal imaging program that shows the temperature of an object as red in the center and fades to blue at the edges.

Alpha Blending

It is possible to create a brush that blends its color with that of the background. The same goes for a Pen or an Image. You will need to become familiar with the following terms and ideas before you can start using this feature effectively:

- Alpha factor

- Compositing mode

- Gamma correction

The *alpha factor* determines the transparency of the color. This is an 8-bit value that ranges from 0 to 255. Zero represents a fully transparent color and 255 represents a completely opaque color. So far in this book, all the colors you have used have had an alpha factor of 255; they have all been solid colors.

The *compositing mode* is slightly different from the alpha factor. It has to do with how images are blended in a transparent manner rather than single colors. The Graphics class has an enumeration called Graphics.CompositingMode. This enumeration has two values:

- CompositingMode.SourceCopy defines that the source image completely overwrites the background colors.

- CompositingMode.SourceOver defines that the source image is blended with the background image, depending on the alpha blending factor.

Often the compositing mode is used in conjunction with the alpha factor. The compositing mode is used as a switch to turn on or off the transparency of the source image.

The MSDN help for .NET defines *gamma correction* as describing the shape of the brightness transfer function for one or more stages in an imaging pipeline. *What?!* In English, gamma correction refers to the brightness of the image. Useful values can range from 0.1 to about 5.0, but normal values are between 1.0 and 2.2. A value of 1.0 is "standard." The lower the gamma value, the brighter the image.

So now that you know some terms, how about an example? This example will not be as simple as previous ones. It includes the following aspects of a .NET program:

- A couple of controls with delegates assigned to the events

- Variables that are local to the class itself

- Initialization code for constituent controls

- Disposal of class-local objects

- Try-Finally block for handling disposal of local objects

Open a new Windows Forms project in either C# or VB. I called mine Blend. Place two horizontal scroll bars on the form. Call one AlphaScroll and call the other one GammaScroll. Do not worry about placement right now, as you will write code to place these scroll bars correctly.

Once you have placed the scroll bars on the screen, double-click each one to force the code wizard to generate the scroll delegate for you. You could change the name of the delegate, or even combine both into one, but for now just accept what the wizard made for you.

This example contains code that reads an image from the disk. I chose the color bars hatch image because it shows a multitude of distinct colors without being fuzzy when expanded. I put this image in the root of my D: drive to make it easy to get to. You can find this image in the samples that come with .NET.

Listing 5-4 shows the code necessary for this example. I do not include the "Windows Form Designer generated code" section. Be sure to include the System.Drawing, System.Drawing.Drawing2D, and System.Drawing.Imaging namespaces.

NOTE *It is, of course, entirely possible to write the code for all the examples in this book without adding references to namespaces. However, you would need to fully qualify every method and class, which can lead to overly verbose code and confusion.*

Listing 5-4a. Alpha Blend, Compositing, and Gamma Correction Example in C#

```
using System;
using System.Drawing;
using System.Drawing.Imaging;
using System.Drawing.Drawing2D;
using System.Collections;
using System.ComponentModel;
using System.Windows.Forms;
using System.Data;

namespace Blend_c
{
```

```csharp
public class Form1 : System.Windows.Forms.Form
{
  private System.Windows.Forms.HScrollBar AlphaScroll;
 /// <summary>
 /// Required designer variable.
 /// </summary>
 private System.ComponentModel.Container components = null;

  private int AlphaFactor = 255;
  private float GammaFactor = 1.0f;
  private Rectangle R = new Rectangle(40, 20, 100, 100 );
  private Image I = Image.FromFile("d:\\Colorbars.jpg");
  private int ImWidth;
  private int ImHeight;
  private System.Windows.Forms.HScrollBar GammaScroll;
  private ImageAttributes Ia = new ImageAttributes();

  public Form1()
  {
    //
    // Required for Windows Form Designer support
    //
    InitializeComponent();

      AlphaScroll.Minimum = 20;
      AlphaScroll.Maximum = 245;
      AlphaScroll.SmallChange = 5;
      AlphaScroll.LargeChange = 5;
      AlphaScroll.Left = R.Left;
      AlphaScroll.Width = R.Width;
      AlphaScroll.Top = R.Bottom;

      GammaScroll.Minimum=1;
      GammaScroll.Maximum = 50;
      GammaScroll.SmallChange=1;
      GammaScroll.LargeChange=5;
      GammaScroll.Left = R.Left;
      GammaScroll.Top = R.Top - GammaScroll.Height;
      GammaScroll.Width = R.Width;

      ImWidth = I.Width;
      ImHeight = I.Height;
```

```
        AlphaScroll.Value = (AlphaScroll.Maximum-AlphaScroll.Minimum )/2;
        GammaScroll.Value = (GammaScroll.Maximum-GammaScroll.Minimum )/2;
        AlphaFactor = AlphaScroll.Value;
        GammaFactor = (float)GammaScroll.Value / 10;


    }

  protected override void Dispose( bool disposing )
  {
   if( disposing )
   {
    if (components != null)
    {
     components.Dispose();
    }
        if ( I != null )
          I.Dispose();
        if ( Ia != null )
          Ia.Dispose();
   }

   base.Dispose( disposing );
  }

  /// <summary>
  /// The main entry point for the application.
  /// </summary>
  [STAThread]
  static void Main()
  {
   Application.Run(new Form1());
  }

    private void Form1_Load(object sender, System.EventArgs e)
    {
    }
    protected override void OnPaint(PaintEventArgs e)
    {
      AlphaBlend(e.Graphics);
      base.OnPaint(e);
    }
```

```csharp
private void AlphaBlend( Graphics G )
{
  //AlphaFactor is depeneding upon scroll bars
  Pen P = new Pen( Color.FromArgb (AlphaFactor, 200, 0, 100 ), 20);
  Bitmap bmp = new Bitmap( 120, 120 );
  Graphics G2 = Graphics.FromImage(bmp);
  Brush B = new SolidBrush(Color.FromArgb( AlphaFactor, 50, 200, 50 ));

  try
  {
    // Set the brightness while rendering image
    Ia.SetGamma( GammaFactor );
    G.DrawImage(I, R, 0, 0, ImWidth, ImHeight, GraphicsUnit.Pixel, Ia);
    //Draw transparent line on top of image
    G.DrawLine(P, 10, 100, 200, 100 );

    // Draw inside the image contained in memory
    G2.FillEllipse( B, 0, 0, 75, 75 );
    G.DrawImage( I, new Rectangle(140, 140, 120, 120 ) );
    G.CompositingQuality = CompositingQuality.GammaCorrected;
    G.CompositingMode = CompositingMode.SourceOver;
    G.DrawImage( bmp, new Rectangle( 150, 150, 150, 150 ) );
  }
  finally
  {
    if (bmp != null )
      bmp.Dispose();
    if ( G2 != null )
      G2.Dispose();
    if ( B != null )
      B.Dispose();
    if ( P != null )
      P.Dispose();
  }
}

private void AlphaScroll_Scroll(object sender,
                        System.Windows.Forms.ScrollEventArgs e)
{
  AlphaFactor = AlphaScroll.Value;
  this.Refresh();
}
```

```
      private void GammaScroll_Scroll(object sender,
                                   System.Windows.Forms.ScrollEventArgs e)
   {
     GammaFactor = (float)GammaScroll.Value / 10;
     this.Refresh();
   }


 }
}
```

Listing 5-4b. Alpha Blend, Compositing, and Gamma Correction Example in VB

```
Option Strict On

Imports System.Drawing
Imports System.Drawing.Drawing2D
Imports System.Drawing.Imaging

Public Class Form1
  Inherits System.Windows.Forms.Form

  Private AlphaFactor As Int32 = 255
  Private GammaFactor As Single = 1.0F
  Private R As Rectangle = New Rectangle(40, 20, 100, 100)
  Private I As Image = Image.FromFile("d:\\Colorbars.jpg")
  Private ImWidth As Int32
  Private ImHeight As Int32
  Private Ia As ImageAttributes = New ImageAttributes()

#Region " Windows Form Designer generated code "

  Public Sub New()
    MyBase.New()

    'This call is required by the Windows Form Designer.
    InitializeComponent()

    AlphaScroll.Minimum = 20
    AlphaScroll.Maximum = 245
    AlphaScroll.SmallChange = 5
    AlphaScroll.LargeChange = 5
    AlphaScroll.Left = R.Left
    AlphaScroll.Width = R.Width
    AlphaScroll.Top = R.Bottom
```

```
   GammaScroll.Minimum = 1
   GammaScroll.Maximum = 50
   GammaScroll.SmallChange = 1
   GammaScroll.LargeChange = 5
   GammaScroll.Left = R.Left
   GammaScroll.Top = R.Top - GammaScroll.Height
   GammaScroll.Width = R.Width


   ImWidth = I.Width
   ImHeight = I.Height


   AlphaScroll.Value = CType((AlphaScroll.Maximum - AlphaScroll.Minimum) / 2, _
                       Int32)
   GammaScroll.Value = CType((GammaScroll.Maximum - GammaScroll.Minimum) / 2, _
                       Int32)
   AlphaFactor = AlphaScroll.Value
   GammaFactor = CType(GammaScroll.Value, Single) / 10

End Sub


'Form overrides dispose to clean up the component list.
Protected Overloads Overrides Sub Dispose(ByVal disposing As Boolean)
   If disposing Then
     If Not (components Is Nothing) Then
       components.Dispose()
     End If
     If Not I Is Nothing Then I.Dispose()
     If Not Ia Is Nothing Then Ia.Dispose()
   End If
   MyBase.Dispose(disposing)
End Sub
Friend WithEvents GammaScroll As System.Windows.Forms.HScrollBar
Friend WithEvents AlphaScroll As System.Windows.Forms.HScrollBar


'Required by the Windows Form Designer
Private components As System.ComponentModel.IContainer

'NOTE: The following procedure is required by the Windows Form Designer
'It can be modified using the Windows Form Designer.
'Do not modify it using the code editor.
<System.Diagnostics.DebuggerStepThrough()> Private Sub InitializeComponent()
…
#End Region
```

```vb
          Private Sub Form1_Load(ByVal sender As System.Object, _
                                 ByVal e As System.EventArgs) _
                                 Handles MyBase.Load

          End Sub

          Protected Overrides Sub OnPaint(ByVal e As PaintEventArgs)

            AlphaBlend(e.Graphics)

          End Sub

          Private Sub AlphaBlend(ByVal G As Graphics)
            'AlphaFactor is variable depeneding upon scroll bars
            Dim P As Pen = New Pen(Color.FromArgb(AlphaFactor, 200, 0, 100), 20)
            Dim bmp As Bitmap = New Bitmap(120, 120)
            Dim G2 As Graphics = Graphics.FromImage(bmp)
            Dim B As Brush = New SolidBrush(Color.FromArgb(AlphaFactor, 50, 200, 50))

            Try
              ' Set the brightness while rendering image
              Ia.SetGamma(GammaFactor)
              G.DrawImage(I, R, 0, 0, ImWidth, ImHeight, GraphicsUnit.Pixel, Ia)
              'Draw transparent line on top of image
              G.DrawLine(P, 10, 100, 200, 100)

              ' Draw inside the image contained in memory
              G2.FillEllipse(B, 0, 0, 75, 75)
              G.DrawImage(I, New Rectangle(140, 140, 120, 120))
              G.CompositingQuality = CompositingQuality.GammaCorrected
              G.CompositingMode = CompositingMode.SourceOver
              G.DrawImage(bmp, New Rectangle(150, 150, 150, 150))

            Finally
              If Not bmp Is Nothing Then bmp.Dispose()
              If Not G2 Is Nothing Then G2.Dispose()
              If Not B Is Nothing Then B.Dispose()
              If Not P Is Nothing Then P.Dispose()
            End Try

          End Sub
```

```
Private Sub GammaScroll_Scroll(ByVal sender As System.Object, _
                    ByVal e As System.Windows.Forms.ScrollEventArgs) _
                    Handles GammaScroll.Scroll
    GammaFactor = CType(GammaScroll.Value / 10, Single)
    Me.Refresh()

End Sub

Private Sub AlphaScroll_Scroll(ByVal sender As System.Object, _
                    ByVal e As System.Windows.Forms.ScrollEventArgs) _
                    Handles AlphaScroll.Scroll
    AlphaFactor = AlphaScroll.Value
    Me.Refresh()

End Sub
End Class
```

Compile and run the program. You should start out with a screen that looks like the one shown in Figure 5-3. Once you see this, start scrolling the scroll bars. The top one is the gamma correction for the top image and the bottom one is the alpha blend for the line.

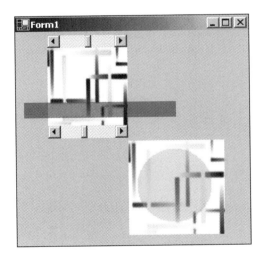

Figure 5-3. Alpha and gamma images

If you scroll the top bar all the way to the left, the top image will be almost invisible, as the brightness will be very high. Scrolling it all the way to the right makes the image darker.

If you scroll the bottom bar all the way to the left, the line will be almost invisible, as will the circle in the lower image. This is because the opacity of both will be almost zero. If you scroll the bottom bar all the way to the right you will see the line get more opaque in the top image and the circle get more opaque in the lower image. Figure 5-4 shows the form with both scroll bars all the way to the right.

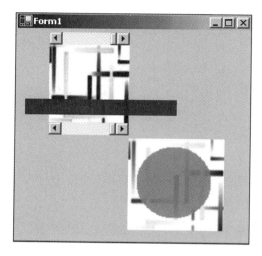

Figure 5-4. Form showing maximum opacity and brightness

Now it is time to dissect the code a little.

The form's constructor contains code that sets up the scroll bars and positions them on the screen at the top and bottom of the top image. Once this is done, I set both scroll bars' positions to the middle. I also set the gamma and alpha values to the mid ranges. What this does is make the bar half opaque and the top image normal brightness.

The **OnPaint** method for the form calls the **AlphaBlend()** method for the example. After this, it calls the base class' **OnPaint** method. You will need to call the base **OnPaint** method because you have overridden it here. There may be some extra painting or housecleaning that goes on in the base method that you are not aware of.

Every time the upper scroll bar is moved, its delegate **GammaScroll_Scroll** gets called. Inside this method I make the GammaFactor variable equal to potion of the scroll bar divided by ten. This gives me a fine-grained change of the gamma factor. Once this is done, I call the form's **OnPaint** method. Doing this, of course, calls the overridden **OnPaint** method, at which point I repaint the screen with objects based on the new values.

The lower scroll bar is essentially the same as the upper one except that it changes the alpha blend factor for both the line and the circle. When the **OnPaint** method is called, the CompositingMode is set to SourceOver, which blends the image being drawn with the background of the space it is drawn on. If I had set the CompositingMode to SorceCopy, the image of the circle would have completely overlaid the background image of the color bars. Try it if you don't believe me!

The last thing I do in this example is run code in the form's **Dispose** method that calls the **Dispose** methods of the class-local Image and ImageAttributes objects. I suppose it is not strictly necessary in this example, as the memory will get reclaimed as soon as the program ends, but I feel it is always wise to clean up after yourself.[1]

You will notice that in both the C# and VB code examples I used a Try-Finally block to contain the drawing code. The Finally block has code that tests the objects to see if they are real, and then calls the **Dispose** method on each. This is the way your code should look at all times. As I mentioned in a previous chapter, C# has a **Using** statement that can take the place of the Finally block of code. I chose not to do this here so you could compare the C# code to the VB code.

My Friend Flicker

I think it is a good time to go over another aspect of painting shapes on forms. I am talking about speed. As you no doubt noticed, there was a problem in viewing the last example. As you moved the pointer on the scroll bar, you saw a lot of flicker on the screen. This is not pretty.

Up to this point you have seen only the simplest way to force the form to repaint. This is accomplished calling the **Refresh** method of the form. Most other controls also have a **Refresh** method. All you VB programmers know that this method very well. It is a part of most of the constituent VB 6.0 controls.

It is not uncommon in VB 6.0 to call a control's **Refresh** method to force something to appear on the screen. As you have seen, I have also been calling the **Refresh** method for the form every time I need to show something on the screen. There is a problem, however, with calling the form's **Refresh** method.

Calling a form's **Refresh** method forces a repaint of everything on that form. If you have a complex form with quite a few painted shapes, calling the **Refresh** method on the whole form when only one area needs repainting is a waste of time

---

1. I keep hearing my mother say this: "Clean up after yourself!"

and quite often results in flicker. So the question is, how do you repaint only the area of the form that needs it? What you do is invalidate a certain area of the form.

Invalidating Regions

There is an **Invalidate** method for every control, including the form. This **Invalidate** method has six overloaded forms:

- *Invalidate():* Causes the whole control to be repainted

- *Invalidate(boolean):* Causes the whole control to be repainted and optionally any child controls

- *Invalidate(Rectangle):* Causes the area of the control contained within the rectangle to be repainted

- *Invalidate(Rectangle, boolean):* Causes the area of the control contained within the rectangle to be repainted and optionally any child controls

- *Invalidate(Region):* Causes the area of the control contained within the region to be repainted

- *Invalidate(Region, boolean):* Causes the area of the control contained within the region, and optionally any child controls, to be repainted

You can see that there are three basic ways to invalidate a form. Using a rectangle or a region allows you to be very specific about the area you invalidate. Calling **Invalidate** with no arguments is essentially the same as calling **Refresh**. Invalidating a region is the finest control you have in deciding which part of a form to repaint. As you discovered in Chapter 4, a region can consist of a graphics path, which can itself be any shape you can think of. If you like, you can invalidate a portion of the screen shaped like a heart.

Suppose you had a form with all kinds of shapes on it and you changed the fill color of just one of those shapes. Here are the steps to repaint just that shape on the form. This is just one way to accomplish this goal.

1. Create the shapes and note the coordinates and size of each shape on the form.

2. Make a change to the fill color of one of the shapes.

3. Make a rectangle with the noted coordinates and size.

4. Call the form's **Invalidate** method and pass in the rectangle.

These steps will result in the single shape (and anything else inside the bounding rectangle) being redrawn while the rest of the form is left alone. Consider the following snippet of code:

VB

```
Me.Invalidate(New Rectangle(New Point(10, 10), _
                            New Size(50, 50)))
Invalidate(New Rectangle(10, 10, 50, 50))
Me.Invalidate(New Region(New Rectangle(10, 10, 50, 50)))
```

C#

```
this.Invalidate( new Rectangle( new Point(10, 10),
                                new Size(50, 50)));
Invalidate( new Rectangle( 10, 10, 50, 50 ));
this.Invalidate( new Region( new Rectangle(10, 10, 50, 50)));
```

Each of these calls to the Invalidate event does the same thing: It invalidates a rectangle that starts at 10, 10 and whose width and height are 50 pixels. You can also see from this code that you do not need to qualify the Invalidate event with the form's identity. Calling **Invalidate** is the same as calling **Me.Invalidate** for VB or **this.Invalidate** for C#.

So is this it? Will this eliminate flicker? Like most things, the answer is maybe. If you have a small enough invalid region and what you are doing is not complex, then this may eliminate flicker. However, while this method goes a long way to solving the problem, there is more that you can do to smooth out the drawing process.

Using Control Styles to Reduce Flicker

The ControlStyles enumeration is a set of bit fields whose bitwise combination defines how the screen is painted. Table 5-2 shows the bit fields and their meanings. There are quite a few members of this enumeration, and only those that have to do with painting are shown in Table 5-2.

Table 5-2. ControlStyles Enumeration Members

Name	Description
AllPaintingInWmPaint	WM_ERASEBKGND message is ignored to reduce flicker.
CacheText	Control keeps a copy of text instead of getting it from the text handle.
DoubleBuffer	Drawing is done in the background buffer and then sent to the screen.
Opaque	Control is drawn opaque. Background is not redrawn.
ResizeRedraw	Control is redrawn when it is resized.
SupportsTransparentBackColor	Control accepts a BackColor whose alpha is less than 255.
UserPaint	Control paints itself rather than the operating system.

If the AllPaintingInWmPaint bit is set, the control's **OnPaint** and **OnPaintBackground** methods are called directly from the WM_PAINT message. This can greatly reduce flicker.

Double buffering is probably the best way to reduce flicker. All painting is done in a background buffer that mimics the screen's buffer. After the painting is done in the background, the information is blasted to the foreground.[2] To fully enable double buffering, you must set the AllPaintingInWmPaint, DoubleBuffer, and UserPaint control bits.

The method for setting these bits is through the **SetStyle** and **GetStyle** members of a control class. The following piece of code shows how this is done:

VB

```
Dim a As Boolean = Me.GetStyle(ControlStyles.AllPaintingInWmPaint)
Dim b As Boolean = Me.GetStyle(ControlStyles.DoubleBuffer)
Me.SetStyle(ControlStyles.AllPaintingInWmPaint, True)
Me.SetStyle(ControlStyles.DoubleBuffer, True)
```

---

2. Usually during the vertical blanking interrupt.

C#

```
bool a = this.GetStyle(ControlStyles.AllPaintingInWmPaint);
bool b = this.GetStyle(ControlStyles.DoubleBuffer);
this.SetStyle ( ControlStyles.AllPaintingInWmPaint, true);
this.SetStyle ( ControlStyles.DoubleBuffer, true);
```

 NOTE   *This ControlStyles enumeration is valid only for those objects that derive from the System.Windows.Forms.Control class. Yes, Windows Forms do derive from this class and therefore have the **SetStyle** and **GetStyle** members available.*

The next example shows control styles in action.

Painting the Background

There is one last thing you can do to help eliminate flicker. It is possible to paint just the background of a form without touching the foreground images. Why do this? Suppose you needed to change the color of the background based on a user preference. You can do this using the **OnPaintBackground** method.

This method can be overridden like the OnPaint delegate, and it also takes the same PaintEventArgs argument. This method is not, however, a real event. There is no PaintBackgound event, and a derived class is not required to call the base class' **OnPaintBackground** method.

So how do you invoke this method? You need to call the control's **InvokePaintBackgound** method:

```
this.InvokePaintBackground(this, e );
```

So this is it for speeding up your painting process. In Chapter 6 I show another process for speeding up drawing: bit block transfer.

Blending

You probably think of color blending as adding blue to yellow and coming up with green. While you can do that in .NET (as you shall soon see), the true power of blending is where you start out filling a shape with a particular color and ending the fill with another color. The entire fill in between the start and end colors are even steps of color. For instance, a light blue to red fill would go through all the shades of blue, through purple, and all the way to red.

The two classes that deal with setting up color blends are as follows:

- Blend

- ColorBlend

The two classes that use the blend objects are as follows:

- LinearGradientBrush

- PathGradientBrush

Using these four classes, you can create some truly impressive drawings.

New Blends

The LinearGradientBrush is a brush that has a start color and an end color. It also has a repeat pattern defined by a start point and an end point on the screen. The LinearGradientBrush has eight overloaded constructors that allow you to specify the start and end points as either a rectangle or Point structures. Each of these constructors also allows you to specify the start and end colors.

The linear gradient part of the brush means that the color is interpolated linearly between the start color and the end color along the length of the repeat pattern. The repeat pattern is defined for the whole graphics container. What this means is that a shape drawn with a LinearGradientBrush will have its start color be the same as the color of the brush's color at that point in the repeat pattern. Are you confused yet?

In other words, suppose you made a brush that started out blue at point 0, 0 and ended up red at point 100, 100. Now say you drew a rectangle using that brush that started at 50, 50. The first color of your rectangle would be some shade of purple. This is because you started the rectangle at the point where the brush was changing from blue to red.

Well, this is kind of neat, but suppose you wanted to use three or more colors before the pattern repeated? Suppose you wanted to determine where along the pattern the brushes changed colors? A couple of methods in the LinearGradientBrush class allow you to do just that:

- Blend

- InterpolationColors

The **Blend** method takes as an argument a Blend object. This object is made up of a set of blending factors and blending positions.

A *blending factor* is the percentage of the starting and ending colors that are used at the corresponding blending positions.

Blending positions are floating-point values that relate to a percentage of distance along the gradient line. The combination of blending factors and blending positions allows you to create a staircase gradient that goes from a start color to an end color in discrete steps.

InterpolationColors is a method that gets or sets a ColorBlend object that defines how the gradient is formed. The ColorBlend object includes a set of colors and positions. The ColorBlend object is similar to the Blend object, except that instead of defining color factors it defines actual colors to be used at the positions provided. Using **InterpolationColors** nullifies any colors and positions previously defined for the brush.

The following example is fairly complicated and demonstrates how do to several things, such as

- Use a LinearGradientBrush with default values

- Skew a linear gradient brush

- Draw several shapes along the gradient path

- Shows the complete gradient path

- Change a two-color gradient path

- Change alpha values for a LinearGradientBrush

- Use the **Invalidate** method to speed up redraw

- Use ControlStyles to speed up redraw

- Use a ColorBlend object to define a set of gradient colors and positions

- Change the gradient using the **InterpolationColors** method

- Use event handling for scroll bars

Okay, now start a new VB or C# Windows project. Mine is called GradientBlend. Perform the following steps:

1. Size the form to be 400×400.

2. Set the form's start-up position to be center screen.

3. Add a horizontal scroll bar. Name it BlendWidth. Placement is not critical.

4. Add a horizontal scroll bar. Name it Skew. Placement is not critical.

5. Add a button. Name it cmdDoubleBuffer. Placement is not critical.

The controls will be moved via code, so it does not matter where you put them on the form.

Next, double-click the controls to get the wizard-generated scroll and button click event handlers. For my C# code, I changed the handler for the Skew control to SkewColor. The handler for the BlendWidth control is called BlendChange. I accepted the default handlers for the VB code. Now go into the code pane and enter the code shown in Listing 5-5. The code shown here is for the whole program except for the form's **InitializeComponent** method. This is generated by the wizard and was not touched.

Listing 5-5a. LinearGradientBrush Example in VB

```
Option Strict On

Imports System
Imports System.Drawing
Imports System.Drawing.Imaging
Imports System.Drawing.Drawing2D

Public Class Form1
  Inherits System.Windows.Forms.Form

  Private BlWidth As Int32
  Private SkewVal As Int32
  Private EL1Rect As Rectangle
  Private EL2Rect As Rectangle
  Private EL1Region As Region
  Private EL2Region As Region
  Private EL3Region As Region
```

```vbnet
#Region " Windows Form Designer generated code "

  Public Sub New()
    MyBase.New()

    'This call is required by the Windows Form Designer.
    InitializeComponent()

    'Set up rectangles to draw ellipses in
    EL1Rect = New Rectangle(10, 10, 150, 50)
    EL2Rect = EL1Rect
    'I could make a new rectangle but I can offset without knowing
    'anything about the previous rectangle.
    EL2Rect.Offset(200, 0)

    'Set up Regions for invalidation
    EL1Region = New Region(EL1Rect)
    EL2Region = New Region(EL2Rect)
    EL3Region = New Region(New Rectangle(New Point(0, 65), _
                                         New Size(Me.Width, 50)))

    'Set up the blend scroll bar
    BlendWidth.Top = 120
    BlendWidth.Left = CType(Me.Width / 3, Int32)
    BlendWidth.Width = CType(Me.Width / 3, Int32)
    BlendWidth.Minimum = 10
    BlendWidth.Maximum = 200
    BlendWidth.SmallChange = 1
    BlendWidth.LargeChange = 10
    BlendWidth.Value = BlendWidth.Minimum

    'Set up the Skew Scroll Bar
    Skew.Top = 145
    Skew.Left = CType(Me.Width / 3, Int32)
    Skew.Width = CType(Me.Width / 3, Int32)
    Skew.Minimum = 10
    Skew.Maximum = 40
    Skew.SmallChange = 1
    Skew.LargeChange = 10
    Skew.Value = Skew.Minimum
```

```
'Set up the double buffer button
cmdDoubleBuffer.Top = Skew.Top + Skew.Height + 5
cmdDoubleBuffer.Width = Skew.Width
cmdDoubleBuffer.Left = Skew.Left
cmdDoubleBuffer.Text = "Allow Flicker"

BlWidth = BlendWidth.Value
SkewVal = Skew.Value

' Set up for double buffering.
'This, along with invalidating only those areas that need it, TOTALLY
'eliminates flicker in this program
Me.SetStyle(ControlStyles.AllPaintingInWmPaint, True)
Me.SetStyle(ControlStyles.DoubleBuffer, True)
Me.SetStyle(ControlStyles.UserPaint, True)

End Sub

'Form overrides dispose to clean up the component list.
Protected Overloads Overrides Sub Dispose(ByVal disposing As Boolean)
  If disposing Then
    If Not (components Is Nothing) Then
      components.Dispose()
    End If
    'Dispose of our own objects
    EL1Region.Dispose()
    EL2Region.Dispose()
    EL3Region.Dispose()
  End If
  MyBase.Dispose(disposing)
End Sub

'Required by the Windows Form Designer
Private components As System.ComponentModel.IContainer

'NOTE: The following procedure is required by the Windows Form Designer
'It can be modified using the Windows Form Designer.
'Do not modify it using the code editor.
Friend WithEvents cmdDoubleBuffer As System.Windows.Forms.Button
Friend WithEvents Skew As System.Windows.Forms.HScrollBar
Friend WithEvents BlendWidth As System.Windows.Forms.HScrollBar
<System.Diagnostics.DebuggerStepThrough()> Private Sub InitializeComponent()
 …
 …
End Sub
```

```
#End Region

    Private Sub Form1_Load(ByVal sender As System.Object, _
                           ByVal e As System.EventArgs) _
                           Handles MyBase.Load
    End Sub

    Protected Overrides Sub OnPaint(ByVal e As PaintEventArgs)

        e.Graphics.SmoothingMode = SmoothingMode.AntiAlias

        StandardGradient(e.Graphics)
        e.Graphics.DrawLine(Pens.Black, 0, cmdDoubleBuffer.Bottom + 10, Me.Width, _
                           cmdDoubleBuffer.Bottom + 10)
        InterpolateGradient(e.Graphics)

        MyBase.OnPaint(e)

    End Sub

    Private Sub StandardGradient(ByVal G As Graphics)
        'This brush defines how the color is distributed across the whole
        'graphics container. Any filled object that gets drawn in the container
        'will pick up the color starting with the color gradient at that
        'particular point on the screen.
        Dim B As LinearGradientBrush = New LinearGradientBrush(New PointF(0, 20), _
                                       New PointF(BlWidth, SkewVal), _
                                       Color.Blue, _
                                       Color.Red)

        'Draw an image inside the second rectangle
        G.DrawImage(Image.FromFile("D:\\Colorbars.jpg"), EL2Rect)

        'Draw a line across the screen with the brush
        'to show the repeating pattern
        Dim P As Pen = New Pen(B, 15)
        G.DrawLine(P, 0, 75, Me.Width, 75)
        'Draw a filled ellipse to show how the colors are used
        G.FillEllipse(B, EL1Rect)
```

```
'Change the starting and ending colors
'Set the alpha so the image below shows through
Dim c() As Color = {Color.FromArgb(100, Color.LightBlue), _
               Color.FromArgb(100, Color.DarkBlue)}
B.LinearColors = c
P.Brush = B
G.DrawLine(P, 0, 100, Me.Width, 100)
G.FillEllipse(B, EL2Rect)

'Reclaim some memory
c = Nothing
If Not P Is Nothing Then
  P.Dispose()
End If
If Not B Is Nothing Then
  B.Dispose()
End If
End Sub

Private Sub InterpolateGradient(ByVal G As Graphics)
'Make a set of colors to use in the blend
Dim EndColors() As Color = {Color.Green, _
                  Color.Yellow, _
                  Color.Yellow, _
                  Color.Blue, _
                  Color.Red, _
                  Color.Red}

'These are the positions of the colors along the Gradient line
Dim ColorPositions() As Single = {0.0F, 0.2F, 0.4F, 0.6F, 0.8F, 1.0F}

'Fill the blend object with the colors and their positions
Dim C_Blend As ColorBlend = New ColorBlend()
C_Blend.Colors = EndColors
C_Blend.Positions = ColorPositions

'Make the linear brush and assign the custom blend to it
Dim B As LinearGradientBrush = New LinearGradientBrush(New Point(10, 110), _
                                      New Point(140, 110), _
                                      Color.White, _
                                      Color.Black)
B.InterpolationColors = C_Blend
```

```
  'Make a graphics path that we can fill and show custom blended fill
  Dim Pth As GraphicsPath = New GraphicsPath()
  Pth.AddEllipse(20, 210, 120, 50)
  Pth.AddString("Filled String", New FontFamily("Impact"), _
                CType(FontStyle.Italic, Int32), 30, New Point(200, 220), _
                StringFormat.GenericDefault)
  G.FillPath(B, Pth)

  Dim P As Pen = New Pen(B, 20)
  G.DrawLine(P, 0, 300, Me.Width, 300)

  If Not P Is Nothing Then
    P.Dispose()
  End If
  If Not B Is Nothing Then
    B.Dispose()
  End If
  If Not Pth Is Nothing Then
    Pth.Dispose()
  End If
End Sub

Private Sub BlendWidth_Scroll(ByVal sender As System.Object, ByVal e As
System.Windows.Forms.ScrollEventArgs) Handles BlendWidth.Scroll

  BlWidth = BlendWidth.Value
  'Redraw the first ellipse
  Me.Invalidate(EL1Region)
  'Redraw the second ellipse
  Me.Invalidate(EL2Region)
  'Redraw the lines
  Me.Invalidate(EL3Region)
End Sub

Private Sub Skew_Scroll(ByVal sender As System.Object, _
                   ByVal e As _
       System.Windows.Forms.ScrollEventArgs) _
                   Handles Skew.Scroll
```

```
            SkewVal = Skew.Value
            'Redraw the first ellipse
            Me.Invalidate(EL1Region)
            'Redraw the second ellipse
            Me.Invalidate(EL2Region)
            'Redraw the lines
            Invalidate(EL3Region)
        End Sub


        Private Sub cmdDoubleBuffer_Click(ByVal sender As System.Object, _
                        ByVal e As System.EventArgs) Handles cmdDoubleBuffer.Click

          If Me.GetStyle(ControlStyles.AllPaintingInWmPaint) And _
             Me.GetStyle(ControlStyles.DoubleBuffer) And _
             Me.GetStyle(ControlStyles.UserPaint) Then
            cmdDoubleBuffer.Text = "Eliminate Flicker"
            Me.SetStyle(ControlStyles.AllPaintingInWmPaint, False)
            Me.SetStyle(ControlStyles.DoubleBuffer, False)
          Else
            cmdDoubleBuffer.Text = "Allow Flicker"
            Me.SetStyle(ControlStyles.AllPaintingInWmPaint, True)
            Me.SetStyle(ControlStyles.DoubleBuffer, True)
          End If

      End Sub
  End Class
```

Listing 5-5b. LinearGradientBrush Example in C#

```
using System;
using System.Drawing;
using System.Drawing.Imaging;
using System.Drawing.Drawing2D;
using System.Collections;
using System.ComponentModel;
using System.Windows.Forms;
using System.Data;
```

```csharp
namespace GradientBlend_c
{
  /// <summary>
  /// Summary description for Form1.
  /// </summary>
  public class Form1 : System.Windows.Forms.Form
  {
    private System.Windows.Forms.HScrollBar BlendWidth;
    private System.ComponentModel.Container components = null;
    private System.Windows.Forms.HScrollBar Skew;
    private System.Windows.Forms.Button cmdDoubleBuffer;

    private int BlWidth;
    private int SkewVal;
    private Rectangle EL1Rect;
    private Rectangle EL2Rect;
    private Region EL1Region;
    private Region EL2Region;
    private Region EL3Region;

    public Form1()
    {
      //
      // Required for Windows Form Designer support
      //
      InitializeComponent();

      //Set up rectangles to draw ellipses in
      EL1Rect = new Rectangle(10, 10, 150, 50);
      EL2Rect = EL1Rect;
      //I could make a new rectangle but I can offset without knowing
      //anything about the previous rectangle.
      EL2Rect.Offset(200, 0);

      //Set up Regions for invalidation
      EL1Region = new Region(EL1Rect);
      EL2Region = new Region(EL2Rect);
      EL3Region = new Region( new Rectangle(new Point(0, 65),
                                      new Size(this.Width, 50)));
```

```
      //Set up the blend scroll bar
      BlendWidth.Top = 120;
      BlendWidth.Left = this.Width/3;
      BlendWidth.Width = this.Width/3;
      BlendWidth.Minimum = 10;
      BlendWidth.Maximum = 200;
      BlendWidth.SmallChange = 1;
      BlendWidth.LargeChange = 10;
      BlendWidth.Value = BlendWidth.Minimum;

      //Set up the Skew Scroll Bar
      Skew.Top = 145;
      Skew.Left = this.Width/3;
      Skew.Width = this.Width/3;
      Skew.Minimum = 10;
      Skew.Maximum = 40;
      Skew.SmallChange = 1;
      Skew.LargeChange = 10;
      Skew.Value = Skew.Minimum;

      //Set up the double buffer button
      cmdDoubleBuffer.Top = Skew.Top + Skew.Height + 5;
      cmdDoubleBuffer.Width = Skew.Width;
      cmdDoubleBuffer.Left = Skew.Left;
      cmdDoubleBuffer.Text = "Allow Flicker";

      BlWidth = BlendWidth.Value;
      SkewVal = Skew.Value;

      // Set up for double buffering.
      //This, along with invalidating only those areas that need it, TOTALLY
      //eliminates flicker in this program
      this.SetStyle ( ControlStyles.AllPaintingInWmPaint, true);
      this.SetStyle ( ControlStyles.DoubleBuffer, true);
      this.SetStyle ( ControlStyles.UserPaint, true);

   }
```

```csharp
/// <summary>
/// Clean up any resources being used.
/// </summary>
protected override void Dispose( bool disposing )
{
  if( disposing )
  {
    if (components != null)
    {
      components.Dispose();
    }
    //Dispose of our own objects
    EL1Region.Dispose();
    EL2Region.Dispose();
    EL3Region.Dispose();
  }
  base.Dispose( disposing );
}

#region Windows Form Designer generated code
/// <summary>
/// Required method for Designer support - do not modify
/// the contents of this method with the code editor.
/// </summary>
private void InitializeComponent()
{
  this.BlendWidth = new System.Windows.Forms.HScrollBar();
  this.Skew = new System.Windows.Forms.HScrollBar();
  this.cmdDoubleBuffer = new System.Windows.Forms.Button();
  this.SuspendLayout();
  //
  // BlendWidth
  //
  this.BlendWidth.Location = new System.Drawing.Point(32, 224);
  this.BlendWidth.Name = "BlendWidth";
  this.BlendWidth.Size = new System.Drawing.Size(192, 16);
  this.BlendWidth.TabIndex = 0;
  this.BlendWidth.Scroll += new
            System.Windows.Forms.ScrollEventHandler
            (this.BlendChange);
```

```
            //
            // Skew
            //
            this.Skew.Location = new System.Drawing.Point(192, 272);
            this.Skew.Name = "Skew";
            this.Skew.Size = new System.Drawing.Size(104, 16);
            this.Skew.TabIndex = 1;
            this.Skew.Scroll += new
                    System.Windows.Forms.ScrollEventHandler
                    (this.SkewColor);
            //
            // cmdDoubleBuffer
            //
            this.cmdDoubleBuffer.Location = new System.Drawing.Point(40, 304);
            this.cmdDoubleBuffer.Name = "cmdDoubleBuffer";
            this.cmdDoubleBuffer.Size = new System.Drawing.Size(248, 24);
            this.cmdDoubleBuffer.TabIndex = 2;
            this.cmdDoubleBuffer.Text = "button1";
            this.cmdDoubleBuffer.Click += new
                                System.EventHandler
                                (this.cmdDoubleBuffer_Click);
            //
            // Form1
            //
            this.AutoScaleBaseSize = new System.Drawing.Size(5, 13);
            this.ClientSize = new System.Drawing.Size(392, 373);
            this.Controls.AddRange(new System.Windows.Forms.Control[]
                    {this.cmdDoubleBuffer, this.Skew,
                     this.BlendWidth});
            this.Name = "Form1";
            this.StartPosition = System.Windows.Forms.FormStartPosition.CenterScreen;
            this.Text = "Form1";
            this.Load += new System.EventHandler(this.Form1_Load);
            this.ResumeLayout(false);

        }
        #endregion
```

```
/// <summary>
/// The main entry point for the application.
/// </summary>
[STAThread]
static void Main()
{
  Application.Run(new Form1());
}

private void Form1_Load(object sender, System.EventArgs e)
{
}

protected override void OnPaint ( PaintEventArgs e )
{
  e.Graphics.SmoothingMode=SmoothingMode.AntiAlias;

  StandardGradient( e.Graphics );
  e.Graphics.DrawLine(Pens.Black, 0, cmdDoubleBuffer.Bottom+10, this.Width,
                      cmdDoubleBuffer.Bottom+10);
  InterpolateGradient( e.Graphics );

  base.OnPaint(e);
}

private void StandardGradient( Graphics G )
{
  //This brush defines how the color is distributed across the whole
  //graphics container. Any filled object that gets drawn in the container
  //will pick up the color starting with the color gradient at that
  //particular point on the screen.
  LinearGradientBrush B = new LinearGradientBrush(new PointF(0, 20),
                                    new PointF(BlWidth, SkewVal),
                                    Color.Blue,
                                    Color.Red);

  //Draw an image inside the second rectangle
  G.DrawImage(Image.FromFile("D:\\Colorbars.jpg"), EL2Rect);

  //Draw a line across the screen with the brush
  //to show the repeating pattern
  Pen P = new Pen(B, 15);
  G.DrawLine ( P, 0, 75, this.Width, 75 );
  //Draw a filled ellipse to show how the colors are used
  G.FillEllipse(B, EL1Rect);
```

```
    //Change the starting and ending colors
    //Set the alpha so the image below shows through
    Color[] c = {Color.FromArgb(100, Color.LightBlue),
               Color.FromArgb(100, Color.DarkBlue)};
    B.LinearColors = c;
    P.Brush = B;
    G.DrawLine ( P, 0, 100, this.Width, 100 );
    G.FillEllipse(B, EL2Rect );

    //Reclaim some memory
    c = null;
    P.Dispose();
    B.Dispose();
}

private void InterpolateGradient ( Graphics G )
{
    //Make a set of colors to use in the blend
    Color[] EndColors = {Color.Green,
                        Color.Yellow,
                        Color.Yellow,
                        Color.Blue,
                        Color.Red,
                        Color.Red};

    //These are the positions of the colors along the Gradient line
    float[] ColorPositions = {0.0f, .20f, .40f, .60f, .80f, 1.0f};

    //Fill the blend object with the colors and their positions
    ColorBlend C_Blend = new ColorBlend();
    C_Blend.Colors = EndColors;
    C_Blend.Positions = ColorPositions;

    //Make the linear brush and assign the custom blend to it
    LinearGradientBrush B = new LinearGradientBrush ( new Point(10, 110),
                                                      new Point(140, 110),
                                                      Color.White,
                                                      Color.Black );
    B.InterpolationColors = C_Blend;
```

```
    //Make a graphics path that we can fill and show custom blended fill
    GraphicsPath Pth = new GraphicsPath();
    Pth.AddEllipse(20, 210, 120, 50);
    Pth.AddString("Filled String", new FontFamily("Impact"),
                (int)FontStyle.Italic, 30, new Point(200, 220),
                StringFormat.GenericDefault );
    G.FillPath(B, Pth);

    Pen P = new Pen(B, 20);
    G.DrawLine ( P, 0, 300, this.Width, 300 );

    if (P != null)
      P.Dispose();
    if (B != null)
      B.Dispose();
    if (Pth != null)
      Pth.Dispose();
}
private void BlendChange(object sender,
                        System.Windows.Forms.ScrollEventArgs e)
{
  BlWidth = BlendWidth.Value;
  //Redraw the first ellipse
  this.Invalidate(EL1Region);
  //Redraw the second ellipse
  this.Invalidate(EL2Region);
  //Redraw the lines
  this.Invalidate(EL3Region);
}

private void SkewColor(object sender,
                        System.Windows.Forms.ScrollEventArgs e)
{
  SkewVal = Skew.Value;
  //Redraw the first ellipse
  this.Invalidate(EL1Region);
  //Redraw the second ellipse
  this.Invalidate(EL2Region);
  //Redraw the lines
  Invalidate(EL3Region);
}
```

```
private void cmdDoubleBuffer_Click(object sender, System.EventArgs e)
{
  if (  this.GetStyle( ControlStyles.AllPaintingInWmPaint ) &&
    this.GetStyle( ControlStyles.DoubleBuffer ) &&
    this.GetStyle( ControlStyles.UserPaint ) )
  {
    cmdDoubleBuffer.Text = "Eliminate Flicker";
    this.SetStyle ( ControlStyles.AllPaintingInWmPaint, false);
    this.SetStyle ( ControlStyles.DoubleBuffer, false);
  }
  else
  {
    cmdDoubleBuffer.Text = "Allow Flicker";
    this.SetStyle ( ControlStyles.AllPaintingInWmPaint, true);
    this.SetStyle ( ControlStyles.DoubleBuffer, true);
  }
  }
 }
}
```

This seems like a big program for such a limited example. Or is it? I could have written the standard "draw a simple static shape using defaults" example. I believe, however, you will learn a lot more than just some GDI programming from this example. It also teaches you how to weave quite a few concepts together. This is just as important, I think, as the concepts themselves.

By the way, if you want, you can download the code from Downloads section of the Apress Web site (http://www.apress.com) if you do not want to enter it manually.[3]

So what does this example look like when it runs? Figure 5-5 shows the screen as it starts up.

As you can see, there are quite a few things on the screen. The screen is also divided into two sections. First of all, look at the top part of the screen. The upper scroll bar changes the repeat distance of the color pattern. The lower scroll bar changes the skew of the pattern. The pattern is skewed to the left. The button below the scroll bars changes some of the painting parameters to prevent flicker.

Try running the program and playing with the scroll bars and antiflicker button. Pretty cool stuff. You will see that the top right-hand ellipse has an alpha component to it and is drawn as a transparent image on top of the color bars' picture. Figure 5-6 shows this screen with the blend scroll bar to the right and the skew as vertical. The blend repeat pattern is much longer.

---

3. I encourage you to enter as much as you can. You will learn so much more from making mistakes than not trying.

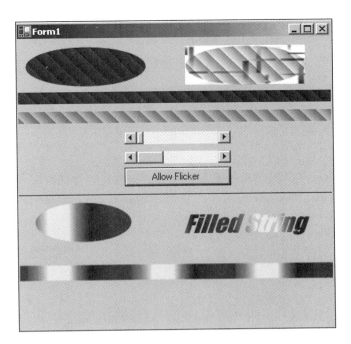

Figure 5-5. Starting screen of the LinearGradientBrush example

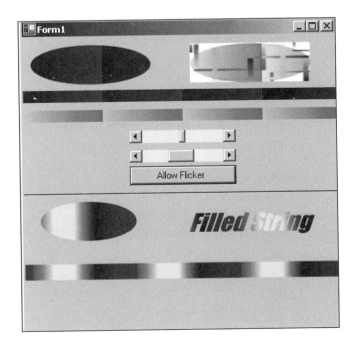

Figure 5-6. Longer blend repeat pattern and no skew

Turn off the antiflicker and you will see the top half of the screen flicker as you move the scroll bars. You will also notice that the bottom images do not flicker. This is because you are invalidating only those portions of the screen that are affected by the scroll bars. Turn on the antiflicker and the painting will be very smooth. No tearing or flicker.

The bottom half of the screen is painted only once. It is a LinearGradientBrush that has four colors for its pattern. Also, the pattern repeats at odd intervals to create an interesting gradient. The string and ellipse are part of the same path. When this path is filled, both the ellipse and the string get filled at the same time using just one call.

The antiflicker is accomplished by setting the **ControlStyles** properties to enable double buffering. As you can see, this is very effective.

Creating a PathGradientBrush

I said I would talk about the last two brushes, and so far I have only mentioned one of them: the LinearGradientBrush. The last one is called the PathGradientBrush.

Where a LinearGradientBrush started out with one color at the start point and ended with another color at the end point, the PathGradientBrush starts with a color at the center of a path and ends with another color at the outer edge of the path.

The classic example is comparing a line that starts out as blue and ends with red to a circle whose center is blue and whose outer edges end with red. Both kinds of brushes can have an unlimited number of colors between the start and end colors and they can place those colors anywhere along the gradient path.

My personal opinion is that the PathGradientBrush is the cooler of the two brushes, and the next two examples will show you just one application of this brush. For now, though, I think it is best to explain the behavior of this brush in detail.

The PathGradientBrush has five overloaded constructors. All the constructors take either a path or an array of points. Since a path can be made up of an array of points, in this case, they are the same. Two of the constructors take an extra argument called a WrapMode.

What is a WrapMode? Basically, it is a way of telling the drawing method how a gradient is to be tiled when the object lies outside the gradient area. As you will see, the gradient path has a size that can be different from the size of the shape you are filling.

Table 5-3 shows the WrapMode enumeration and describes what each member means.

Table 5-3. WrapMode Enumeration

Name	Description
Clamp	Clamps the gradient to the edges of the filled shape
Tile	Tiles the gradient
TileFlipX	Reverses the gradient in the X axis, and then tiles the gradient
TileFlipY	Reverses the gradient in the Y axis, and then tiles the gradient
TileFlipXY	Reverses the gradient in both axes, and then tiles the gradient

The default value for WrapMode is Clamp. This means that if the gradient fill area is less than the shape you are drawing, any part of the shape that is outside of the gradient area will not be shown. This is very much like a clipping region.

Perhaps a small example is in order. Figure 5-7 shows a rectangle that defines the size of the PathGradientBrush. Inside this rectangle is a small circle whose color gradient starts in the middle and flows out evenly to the edges of the circle. Outside of the rectangle is a large circle. The fill of the large circle shows the path gradient in a tiled fashion.

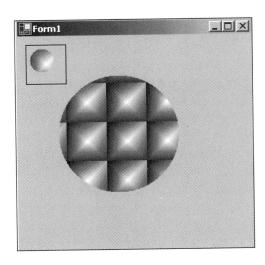

Figure 5-7. Tiled WrapMode for a PathGradientBrush

The constructor I am using for this brush has a WrapMode set to WrapMode.Tile. The C# code for this small example is shown in Listing 5-6. This is all done in the **OnPaint** method of a blank form.

Listing 5-6. C# Code for Demonstrating a Tiled WrapMode

```
protected override void OnPaint( PaintEventArgs e )
{
  GraphicsPath Path = new GraphicsPath();
  Rectangle R = new Rectangle(10, 10, 50, 50);
  e.Graphics.DrawRectangle(Pens.Black,R);
  Path.AddRectangle(R);

//    PathGradientBrush B = new PathGradientBrush(Path.PathPoints);
  PathGradientBrush B = new PathGradientBrush(Path.PathPoints,
                                        WrapMode.Tile);
  Color[] c = { Color.Blue, Color.Aqua, Color.Red };

  B.CenterColor = Color.White;
  B.SurroundColors = c;

  //Small circle inside gradient path
  e.Graphics.FillEllipse(B, 15, 15, 30, 30);
  //Large circle outside gradient path
  e.Graphics.FillEllipse(B, 50, 50, 150, 150);
}
```

Comment out the constructor for the PathGradientBrush and uncomment the one in Listing 5-6. Now run the program again and you should see just the small circle. The WrapMode is defaulted to WrapMode.Clamp and anything outside the gradient area is not shown.

As you have no doubt surmised, the PathGradientBrush is used to fill objects from the center on out. The PathGradientBrush has enough intelligence to figure out the centroid of a path. After all, not everything is a rectangle or an ellipse. Some paths can be quite complex indeed. Think of the computation needed to figure the center of a path made up of a line of text![4]

Let's look at some more detail regarding the PathGradientBrush. For one thing, it needs more setup than can be provided by constructor arguments. This is very different from all the pens and brushes you have dealt with so far. They can all be constructed using just one line of code. The PathGradientBrush needs at least

---

4. Well, I could, but why bother?

two more pieces of information: the center color and the color array that leads to the outer color.

Several properties to this brush can greatly change the way it behaves:

- Blend

- CenterColor

- CenterPoint

- FocusScales

- InterpolationColors

- Rectangle

- SurroundColors

- Transform

- WrapMode

You have already seen WrapMode. You also know about **CenterColor** from the example in Listing 5-6. Transform is a subject you will deal with a little later in this chapter.

The Blend object and **InterpolationColors** were explained in the previous section about the LinearGradientBrush.

The Rectangle object defines the rectangle that surrounds the gradient path. Even though the path may be complex and convoluted, this method returns the rectangle structure that surrounds that path. Often this rectangle is called the *bounding rectangle.*

SurroundColors is an array of colors that corresponds with the array of points that make up the path.

The **CenterPoint** is calculated by the object itself from the path given at construction. This property can be written to as well. You can change the center point to be anywhere in world coordinate space. Yes, this means that the center of the gradient path can be outside of the path itself. You will take advantage of this fact in the next example.

The **FocusScales** property is interesting indeed. It acts as a lens on the center of the gradient. It creates a scaled path inside the original gradient path whose color is the center color. The **FocusScales** property is a PointF structure whose first value is the scaling factor in the X direction. The second value is the scaling factor in the Y direction. Both values are normalized and range from 0 to 1.

Using the **FocusScales** property, you can create a cat's eye by defining a horizontal ellipse whose **FocusScales** property is larger in the Y direction than in the X direction. The MSDN help on PathGradients has a good example of using this property.

Now you know all the theory behind a PathGradientBrush. I have given you a small, static example of drawing a shape outside the gradient to see what happens. As you have probably guessed, though, I am not a big fan of static examples. You are not about to go drawing simple pictures your whole career. You also need to know how to use some of what I am talking about in an interactive program. The LinearGradientBrush example was interactive and showed you how you could use **OnPaint** method effectively in a real situation.

The next example is also interactive. It will, however, be somewhat more difficult. Because of this, it will also be very cool. This example contains two shape objects. One of those objects will be contained in its own class. This is what the C++ guys call a "wrapper."

Why wrap a shape in a class? One of the points to object-oriented programming is information hiding. This class will accomplish some complicated things and it will also know how to draw itself on the screen. All this functionality is hidden behind a very simple interface. This shape object will move around the screen and respond to mouse events. The shape that is not wrapped in a class is static. I draw it on the screen in the same place all the time. Only some of the properties change. No need for a class here.

So, let's begin. Here are some features you will see in this program:

- Your own class

- Overloaded constructors

- Read/Write properties

- ReadOnly properties

- Class methods

- Mouse events

- Mouse tracking

- PathGradientBrush

- AntiFlicker redraw

- Changes in the centroid of a shape object

Start a new VB or C# project. My examples are called PathBlend-c and PathBlend-vb. There are no controls for this form, so accept the defaults and go straight into the code pane.

The next step is to add a new class. There are several ways to do this—here is one way:

1. Right-click the project name in the Solution Explorer.

2. Choose Add and then choose Add Class.

3. Name the class Centroid.

This procedure is the same for VB and for C#.

 NOTE *I encourage you to enter the code for both language versions of this example. This example brings out some of the disparate syntax between both languages. It is interesting to see how C# and VB accomplish the same thing.*

Your Solution Explorer should have one form and one class. It should look like Figure 5-8.

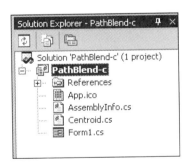

Figure 5-8. Solution Explorer for Listing 5-7

The VB classes will have an extension of .vb.

Bring up the Centroid class and enter the code shown in Listing 5-7a. This class is a wrapper for a circle that will act as the centroid for a much larger circle.

Listing 5-7a. Code for the Centroid Wrapper Class

C#

```csharp
using System;
using System.Drawing;
using System.Drawing.Drawing2D;

namespace PathBlend_c
{
    /// <summary>
    /// This class acts a centroid for another shape
    /// There is no Dispose() method for this class
    /// because it consumes
    /// no resources
    /// </summary>
    public class Centroid
    {
     const int w = 20;
     const int h = 20;

     private int m_StartX;   // Top left X
     private int m_StartY;   // Top left Y
     private Rectangle r;    // Rectangle that holds the circle

     #region Constructors / Destructors
     public Centroid()
     {
       m_StartX = 10;
       m_StartY = 10;
       r.X = 10;
       r.Y = 10;
       r.Width = w;
       r.Height = h;
     }

     public Centroid( int X, int Y )
     {
       m_StartX = X;
       m_StartY = Y;
       r.X = X;
       r.Y = Y;
       r.Width = w;
       r.Height = h;
     }
```

```csharp
#endregion

#region Properties

public int X
{
  get { return m_StartX; }
  set
  {
    m_StartX = value;
    r.X = value;
  }
}

public int Y
{
  get { return m_StartY; }
  set
  {
    m_StartY = value;
    r.Y = value;
  }
}

public Rectangle Rect
{
  get { return r; }
}
public Point Center
{
  get { return (new Point((r.Left+r.Width/2), r.Top+r.Height/2)); }
}

#endregion

#region Methods

public void Draw( Graphics G )
{
  G.FillEllipse(Brushes.Aqua, r);
}
```

```csharp
      public bool Relocate( System.Windows.Forms.MouseEventArgs e )
      {
        if ( e.Button == System.Windows.Forms.MouseButtons.Left )
        {
          if ( (e.X > r.Left) && (e.X < r.Right) &&
               (e.Y > r.Top) &&  (e.Y < r.Bottom) )
          {
            //Must make the center of the rectangle = x,y
            //If you don't you will lose track of the ball
            r.X = e.X - r.Width/2;
            m_StartX = r.X;
            r.Y = e.Y - r.Height/2;
            m_StartY = r.Y;
            return(true);
          }
        }
        return(false);
      }

    #endregion

  }
}
```

VB

```vb
Option Strict On

Imports System
Imports System.Drawing
Imports System.Drawing.Drawing2D

Public Class Centroid

  Const w As Int32 = 20
  Const h As Int32 = 20

  Private m_StartX As Int32        ' Top left X
  Private m_StartY As Int32        ' Top left Y
  Private r As Rectangle           ' Rectangle that holds the circle
```

```vb
#Region "Constructor/Destructor"
  Public Sub New()
    m_StartX = 10
    m_StartY = 10
    r.X = 10
    r.Y = 10
    r.Width = w
    r.Height = h
  End Sub

  Public Sub New(ByVal X As Int32, ByVal Y As Int32)
    m_StartX = X
    m_StartY = Y
    r.X = X
    r.Y = Y
    r.Width = w
    r.Height = h
  End Sub
#End Region

#Region "Properties"
  Public Property X() As Int32
    Get
      Return m_StartX
    End Get
    Set(ByVal Value As Int32)
      m_StartX = Value
    End Set
  End Property

  Public Property Y() As Int32
    Get
      Return m_StartY
    End Get
    Set(ByVal Value As Int32)
      m_StartY = Value
    End Set
  End Property

  Public ReadOnly Property Center() As PointF
    Get
      Return (New PointF((r.Left + CInt(r.Width / 2)), _
                         r.Top + CInt(r.Height / 2)))
    End Get
  End Property
```

```
    Public ReadOnly Property Rect() As Rectangle
      Get
        Return r
      End Get
    End Property
  #End Region


  #Region "Methods"
    Public Sub Draw(ByVal G As Graphics)
      G.FillEllipse(Brushes.Aqua, r)
    End Sub


    Public Function Relocate(ByVal e As System.Windows.Forms.MouseEventArgs) _
                        As Boolean
      If e.Button = System.Windows.Forms.MouseButtons.Left Then
        If ((e.X > r.Left) And (e.X < r.Right) And _
           (e.Y > r.Top) And (e.Y < r.Bottom)) Then
          'Must make the center of the rectangle = x,y
          'If you don't you will lose track of the ball
          r.X = e.X - CInt(r.Width / 2)
          m_StartX = r.X
          r.Y = e.Y - CInt(r.Height / 2)
          m_StartY = r.Y
          Return (True)
        End If
      End If
      Return (False)
    End Function
  #End Region
End Class
```

This class has two overloaded constructors. The default one makes the centroid at a fixed place on the screen. The second one takes *x* and *y* coordinates to make the centroid anywhere on the screen you want.

This class also has several accessor properties and two methods. One of the methods tells the object to relocate itself on the screen according to mouse coordinates and the other method tells the object to draw itself.

Once you are able to compile this code, switch back to the form's code pane. This is where all the action happens. Listing 5-7b shows the code for this form. All the code, including the wizard code, is shown here.

Listing 5-7b. Code for the Main Form

C#

```csharp
using System;
using System.Drawing;
using System.Drawing.Drawing2D;
using System.Collections;
using System.ComponentModel;
using System.Windows.Forms;
using System.Data;

namespace PathBlend_c
{
 public class Form1 : System.Windows.Forms.Form
 {
  /// <summary>
  /// Required designer variable.
  /// </summary>
  private System.ComponentModel.Container components = null;

    private Point CenterPoint;
    private Rectangle R;
    private Centroid Moon = new Centroid(50, 50);

  public Form1()
  {
   InitializeComponent();

      Graphics G = Graphics.FromHwnd(this.Handle);
      G.SmoothingMode=SmoothingMode.AntiAlias;

      this.SetStyle(ControlStyles.AllPaintingInWmPaint, true);
      this.SetStyle(ControlStyles.DoubleBuffer, true);
      this.SetStyle(ControlStyles.UserPaint, true);

      //Rectangle R holds the ellipse
      R = new Rectangle( this.Width/6, this.Height/6,
                         this.Width/3*2, this.Height/3*2 );
      CenterPoint.X = Moon.X;
      CenterPoint.Y = Moon.Y;
  }
```

```csharp
/// <summary>
/// Clean up any resources being used.
/// </summary>
protected override void Dispose( bool disposing )
{
 if( disposing )
 {
  if (components != null)
  {
   components.Dispose();
  }
 }
 base.Dispose( disposing );
}

#region Windows Form Designer generated code
/// <summary>
/// Required method for Designer support - do not modify
/// the contents of this method with the code editor.
/// </summary>
private void InitializeComponent()
{
    //
    // Form1
    //
    this.AutoScaleBaseSize = new System.Drawing.Size(5, 13);
    this.ClientSize = new System.Drawing.Size(292, 273);
    this.MinimizeBox = false;
    this.Name = "Form1";
    this.SizeGripStyle = System.Windows.Forms.SizeGripStyle.Hide;
    this.StartPosition = System.Windows.Forms.FormStartPosition.CenterScreen;
    this.Text = "Moon Over Mars";
    this.Load += new System.EventHandler(this.Form1_Load);
    this.MouseMove += new
                      System.Windows.Forms.MouseEventHandler(this.GetCoord);

}
#endregion

/// <summary>
/// The main entry point for the application.
/// </summary>
[STAThread]
static void Main()
```

```
{
 Application.Run(new Form1());
}

  private void Form1_Load(object sender, System.EventArgs e)
  {
  }

  protected override void OnPaint( PaintEventArgs e)
  {
    GraphicsPath path = new GraphicsPath();
    path.AddEllipse( R );

    // Use the path to construct a path gradient brush.
    PathGradientBrush B = new PathGradientBrush(path);
    B.CenterColor = Color.Aqua;
    B.CenterPoint = CenterPoint;
    Color[] c = {Color.Red};

    B.SurroundColors = c;

    // Fill the path with the path gradient brush.
    e.Graphics.FillPath(B, path);

    Moon.Draw( e.Graphics );
  }

  private void GetCoord(object sender, System.Windows.Forms.MouseEventArgs e)
  {
    this.Invalidate(Moon.Rect);
    if ( Moon.Relocate(e) )
    {
      CenterPoint = Moon.Center;
      //Redraw the centroid
      this.Invalidate(Moon.Rect);
      //Redraw the main ellipse
      this.Invalidate( R );
    }
  }
}
}
```

VB

```
Option Strict On

Imports System
Imports System.Drawing
Imports System.Drawing.Drawing2D

Public Class Form1
  Inherits System.Windows.Forms.Form

  Private CenterPoint As PointF
  Private R As Rectangle
  Private Moon As Centroid = New Centroid(50, 50)

#Region " Windows Form Designer generated code "

  Public Sub New()
    MyBase.New()

    'This call is required by the Windows Form Designer.
    InitializeComponent()

    Dim G As Graphics = Graphics.FromHwnd(Me.Handle)
    G.SmoothingMode = SmoothingMode.AntiAlias

    Me.SetStyle(ControlStyles.AllPaintingInWmPaint, True)
    Me.SetStyle(ControlStyles.DoubleBuffer, True)
    Me.SetStyle(ControlStyles.UserPaint, True)

    'Rectangle R holds the ellipse
    R = New Rectangle(CInt(Me.Width / 6), CInt(Me.Height / 6), _
                    CInt(Me.Width / 3 * 2), CInt(Me.Height / 3 * 2))
    CenterPoint.X = Moon.X
    CenterPoint.Y = Moon.Y
  End Sub


  'Form overrides dispose to clean up the component list.
  Protected Overloads Overrides Sub Dispose(ByVal disposing As Boolean)
    If disposing Then
      If Not (components Is Nothing) Then
        components.Dispose()
      End If
    End If
```

```
    MyBase.Dispose(disposing)
  End Sub


  'Required by the Windows Form Designer
  Private components As System.ComponentModel.IContainer

  'NOTE: The following procedure is required by the Windows Form Designer
  'It can be modified using the Windows Form Designer.
  'Do not modify it using the code editor.
  <System.Diagnostics.DebuggerStepThrough()> Private Sub InitializeComponent()
    '
    'Form1
    '
    Me.AutoScaleBaseSize = New System.Drawing.Size(5, 13)
    Me.ClientSize = New System.Drawing.Size(292, 273)
    Me.Name = "Form1"
    Me.StartPosition = System.Windows.Forms.FormStartPosition.CenterScreen
    Me.Text = "Moon Over Mars"
  End Sub

#End Region

  Private Sub Form1_Load(ByVal sender As System.Object, _
                       ByVal e As System.EventArgs) Handles MyBase.Load
  End Sub

  Protected Overrides Sub OnPaint(ByVal e As PaintEventArgs)
    Dim path As GraphicsPath = New GraphicsPath()

    path.AddEllipse(R)

    ' Use the path to construct a path gradient brush.
    Dim B As PathGradientBrush = New PathGradientBrush(path)
    B.CenterColor = Color.Aqua
    B.CenterPoint = CenterPoint
    Dim c() As Color = {Color.Red}
    B.SurroundColors = c

    ' Fill the path with the path gradient brush.
    e.Graphics.FillPath(B, path)

    Moon.Draw(e.Graphics)

  End Sub
```

```
Public Sub GetCoord(ByVal sender As Object, _
                    ByVal e As System.Windows.Forms.MouseEventArgs) _
                    Handles MyBase.MouseMove

  Me.Invalidate(Moon.Rect)
  If Moon.Relocate(e) Then
    CenterPoint = Moon.Center
    'Redraw the centroid
    Me.Invalidate(Moon.Rect)
    'Redraw the main ellipse
    Me.Invalidate(R)
  End If
End Sub
End Class
```

This form's code sets up the painting parameters so redrawing the form will be very fast. It also draws a large red circle on the form that is filled with a PathGradientBrush. This brush has its center defined by the center of the moon. The moon is, of course, the object constructed by the new class you made.

You can move the moon by pressing the left mouse key while inside the moon boundary and dragging the moon to another position. While you are dragging the moon, the centroid of the PathGradientBrush is changed and the large circle is repainted to reflect this. The effect you get is a reflection of the satellite object on the stationary object.

Compile and run the program. Figure 5-9 shows the form as it first comes up.

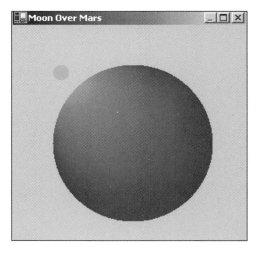

Figure 5-9. Starting position of the centroid example

Try grabbing the moon and moving it slowly around and through the large circle. You will see the color gradient change according to the center point of the path. Figure 5-10 shows the form after moving the satellite just to the outside of the circle.

Figure 5-10. Gradient after the satellite is moved

Isn't this example better than just a plain old static one? While it's kind of neat in itself, you may not see right away some of the applications. Eventually, when you start programming for real, you'll need to do things on a common basis such as

- Find the center of an object

- Respond to mouse events based on several parameters

- Move an object around the screen[5]

- Draw smoothly on the screen

---

5. This is probably one of the most common things you will do in graphics programming.

More Transforms

Remember the cool movie called *The Matrix*? This section covers the mathematical matrix as it relates to transforms in graphics space. It has nothing to do with the movie.[6]

A *matrix* is a set of numbers arranged in *m* rows and *n* columns. GDI+ uses a 3×3 matrix to store values that correspond to a rotation of a shape and a translation of that shape.

How about a little matrix math? A linear transformation is known as *rotation*. This is defined by multiplying a point structure by a 2×2 matrix. A translation is defined by adding a point structure to a 1×2 matrix. Suppose you had a point at (20, 45) and you wanted to rotate it by 90 degrees. The math would look like Figure 5-11.

$$\begin{bmatrix} 20 & 45 \end{bmatrix} \times \begin{bmatrix} 0 & 1 \\ -1 & 0 \end{bmatrix} = \begin{bmatrix} -45 & 20 \end{bmatrix}$$

Figure 5-11. Matrix equation for multiplying a 1×2 matrix by a 2×2 matrix

The single point (20, 45) can be thought of as a 1×2 matrix. The transformation is a 2×2 matrix. Multiplying the two gives you a transformed point. So, how do you do this multiplication? Use a calculator . . . just kidding.

You take the dot product which is taking the Ith row of the A matrix and multiplying it by the jth column of the B matrix. The number of columns in the A matrix must equal the number of rows in the B matrix. I learned this in school. Here is what it means in plain English:

- First of all, if you are multiplying a matrix *m* by another matrix *p*, the number of columns in *m* must equal the number of rows in *p*. For the previous example, *m* has two columns and *p* has two rows.

- Multiply each of the numbers in the *m* column by its corresponding row in the *p* row.

- Add the resulting row × column entries to get the resulting matrix.

---

6. *The Matrix* was one of my favorite movies. I await the sequels with great anticipation.

So the dot product of the previous example is $(20×0)+(45×∠1)$, $(20×1)+(45×0)$ = $(-45, 20)$.

Okay. Now you know how to transform a point. How about translating a point? What is translation anyway? *Translation* is moving a point in the X and/or Y direction. You have done translation already in a few examples in Chapter 4. A matrix translation is not done by multiplication, but by addition of the individual element of a matrix.

A point is a 1×2 matrix. Translating that point to another point consists of adding another point to it. Suppose you had a point of (4, 5). If you added another point to it of (3, 0) you would end up with a point of (7, 5). You have translated the original point by 3 in the X direction.

Linear transformation (multiplication) and translation (addition) are the two things you can do to a point in the GDI+ space. The combination of a transform and a translation is called an *affine transformation.*

It would be nice to be able to represent an affine transformation by one matrix. GDI+ has the Matrix object, which is a 3×3 matrix representing an affine transformation.

So, you ask, how can a 3×3 matrix represent a 1×2 matrix multiplied by a 2×2 matrix and added to another 1×2 matrix? Well, a point in the plane needs to be stored in a 1×3 matrix with a dummy third coordinate. Making the third coordinate of the original point and the third coordinate of the translation point equal to 1 does this.

Take the point of (20, 45). This is represented by a matrix of [20 45 1], with 1 being the dummy third coordinate. Now suppose you wanted to transform it by 90 degrees and translate it by 7 in the X direction and by 12 in the Y direction. The affine transformation would look like Figure 5-12.

$$\begin{bmatrix} 20 & 45 & 1 \end{bmatrix} \times \begin{bmatrix} 0 & 1 & 0 \\ -1 & 0 & 0 \\ 7 & 12 & 1 \end{bmatrix} = \begin{bmatrix} -38 & 32 \end{bmatrix}$$

Figure 5-12. Affine transformation of point (20, 45)

Adding the third dummy coordinate ensures that the number of columns in the first matrix equals the number of rows in the second matrix. The third column of an affine matrix will always contain the numbers (0, 0, 1).

It stands to reason that you would want to make several transformations in series. For instance, you could transform a point by 60 degrees, scale it by a factor of 3 in the Y direction, and then translate it by 32 in the X direction. This sequence of transformation can all be multiplied together to make a singe 3×3 matrix. What this means is that a sequence of transformations can also be stored in the Matrix object.

The Matrix class has several methods that allow you to do certain things to a point structure. Some of these methods are as follows:

- Multiply

- Rotate

- RotateAt

- Scale

- Shear

- TransformVectors

- TranslatePoints

I bet you thought you would have to do this matrix math yourself. The matrix math I have shown you only touches on the subject of linear algebra. I feel that it is good, however, to know something about what is going on behind the scenes.

The **TransformVectors** method applies the 3×3 matrix multiply to affect only the transform. Remember, a transform consists of rotation and scaling, not translation. It does this by ignoring the third coordinate. The **TransformPoints** method applies the 3×3 matrix multiply to affect both a transform and translation of a point. Consider the following example, which applies an affine transform to simulate the formula shown in Figure 5-12. This example transforms the point (20, 45) by 90 degrees and translates it by 7 in the X direction and 12 in the Y direction.

Create a new console application, either in VB or C#. Mine is called Matrix. Once you have created this application, set a reference in the Solution Explorer to System.Drawing. You will need this so you can import the System.Drawing and System.Drawing.Drawing2d namespaces. Listing 5-8 shows the code for this example.

Listing 5-8a. C# Code Showing an Affine Transform

```
using System;
using System.Drawing;
using System.Drawing.Drawing2D;

namespace Matrix_c
{
```

```
class Class1
{
 [STAThread]
 static void Main(string[] args)
 {
     Matrix m = new Matrix();
     m.Rotate(90, MatrixOrder.Append);
     m.Translate(7, 12, MatrixOrder.Append);
     Point[] p = {new Point(20, 45)};
     Console.WriteLine(p.GetValue(0).ToString());
     m.TransformPoints(p);
     Console.WriteLine(p.GetValue(0).ToString());

     Console.ReadLine();
   }
 }
}
```

Listing 5-8b. VB Code Showing an Affine Transformation

```
Option Strict On

Imports System.Drawing
Imports System.Drawing.Drawing2D

Module Module1
  Sub Main()
    Dim m As Matrix = New Matrix()
    m.Rotate(90, MatrixOrder.Append)
    m.Translate(7, 12, MatrixOrder.Append)
    Dim p() As Point = {New Point(20, 45)}
    Console.WriteLine(p.GetValue(0).ToString())
    m.TransformPoints(p)
    Console.WriteLine(p.GetValue(0).ToString())

    Console.ReadLine()
  End Sub
End Module
```

The first thing you do is make a matrix whose elements are set to rotate a point by 90 degrees and translate it by (7, 12). Once this is done, you write out the original points to the screen, tell the Matrix object to transform the points, and write out the results of the transformation. The results of running this example are as follows:

```
{X=20,Y=45}
{X=-38,Y=32}
```

No need for any math on your part. So now you know about matrix math and the Matrix class. What can you do with it? The following list details some of the classes that use the Matrix object:

- Pen.Transform

- Pen.MultiplyTransform

- Graphics.MultiplyTransform

- Graphics.Transform

- GraphicsPath.Flatten

- GraphicsPath.GetBounds

- GraphicsPath.Warp

- GraphicsPath.Widen

- LinearGradientBrush.Transform

- LinearGradientBrush.MultiplyTransform

- PathGradientBrush.Transform

- PathGradientBrush.MultiplyTransform

- TextureBrush.Transform

- TextureBrush.MultiplyTransform

- Region.Transform

How about another example showing how to use a Matrix object in a drawing situation? Open up a new project in either VB or C#. Mine is called MatrixDraw.

Place a vertical scroll bar on the right side of the form and call it "xlate". Place a horizontal scroll bar at the bottom of the form and call it "rotate". Your screen should look like the one shown in Figure 5-13.

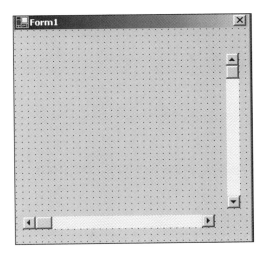

Figure 5-13. MatrixDraw form setup

Next, double-click each of the scroll bars to get the event handler generated for you. The default handler is okay here.

Go into the code pane and enter the code from Listing 5-9. The VB code includes only the constructor code from the wizard-generated code. The rest of the wizard code is not changed, so I did not include it here. The C# code does not include any of the wizard-generated code.

Listing 5-9a. C# Code for the MatrixDraw Example

```csharp
using System;
using System.Drawing;
using System.Drawing.Drawing2D;
using System.Collections;
using System.ComponentModel;
using System.Windows.Forms;
using System.Data;

namespace MatrixDraw_c
{
  public class Form1 : System.Windows.Forms.Form
  {
    internal System.Windows.Forms.HScrollBar rotate;
    internal System.Windows.Forms.VScrollBar xlate;
  /// <summary>
  /// Required designer variable.
  /// </summary>
```

```csharp
    private System.ComponentModel.Container components = null;

      int XlateY;
      float Angle;
      Rectangle DrawingRect = new Rectangle(25, 25, 225, 225);

    public Form1()
    {
     //
     // Required for Windows Form Designer support
     //
     InitializeComponent();

        Angle = 0;
        XlateY = 0;
        xlate.Minimum = -50;
        xlate.Maximum = 50;
        xlate.SmallChange = 1;
        xlate.LargeChange = 5;
        xlate.Value = 0;

        rotate.Minimum = -180;
        rotate.Maximum = 180;
        rotate.SmallChange = 1;
        rotate.LargeChange = 10;
        rotate.Value = 0;

        this.SetStyle(ControlStyles.AllPaintingInWmPaint, true);
        this.SetStyle(ControlStyles.DoubleBuffer, true);
        this.SetStyle(ControlStyles.UserPaint, true);
      }
    /// <summary>
    /// Clean up any resources being used.
    /// </summary>
    protected override void Dispose( bool disposing )
    {
     if( disposing )
     {
      if (components != null)
      {
       components.Dispose();
      }
     }
     base.Dispose( disposing );
    }
```

```
   #region Windows Form Designer generated code
…

…

#end region

   /// <summary>
   /// The main entry point for the application.
   /// </summary>
   [STAThread]
   static void Main()
   {
    Application.Run(new Form1());
   }

     private void Form1_Load(object sender, System.EventArgs e)
     {
     }

     protected override void OnPaint(PaintEventArgs e)
     {
       Graphics G  = e.Graphics;
       G.SmoothingMode = SmoothingMode.AntiAlias;

       // Create a graphics path, add a rectangle, set colors
       GraphicsPath Path = new GraphicsPath();
       Path.AddRectangle(new Rectangle(75, 100, 100, 75));
       PointF[] Pts  = Path.PathPoints;
       PathGradientBrush B = new PathGradientBrush(Pts);
       B.CenterColor = Color.Aqua;
       Color[] SColor = {Color.Blue};
       B.SurroundColors = SColor;

       //We will translate the brush!  NOT the rectangle!
       Matrix m = new Matrix();
       m.Translate(0, XlateY, MatrixOrder.Append);
       m.RotateAt(Angle, B.CenterPoint, MatrixOrder.Append);
       B.MultiplyTransform(m, MatrixOrder.Append);
       G.FillRectangle(B, DrawingRect);

       m.Dispose();
       B.Dispose();
       Path.Dispose();
     }
```

```
        private void xlate_Scroll(object sender,
                            System.Windows.Forms.ScrollEventArgs e)
        {
          XlateY = xlate.Value;
          this.Invalidate(DrawingRect);
        }

        private void rotate_Scroll(object sender,
                            System.Windows.Forms.ScrollEventArgs e)
        {
          Angle = rotate.Value;
          this.Invalidate(DrawingRect);
        }
    }
}
```

Listing 5-9b. VB Code for the MatrixDraw Example

```
Option Strict On

Imports System.Drawing
Imports System.Drawing.Drawing2D

Public Class Form1
  Inherits System.Windows.Forms.Form

  Dim XlateY As Int32
  Dim Angle As Single
  Dim DrawingRect As Rectangle = New Rectangle(25, 25, 225, 225)

#Region " Windows Form Designer generated code "

  Public Sub New()
    MyBase.New()

    'This call is required by the Windows Form Designer.
    InitializeComponent()

    Angle = 0
    Xlatey = 0
    xlate.Minimum = -50
    xlate.Maximum = 50
    xlate.SmallChange = 1
    xlate.LargeChange = 5
    xlate.Value = 0
```

```vb
        rotate.Minimum = -180
        rotate.Maximum = 180
        rotate.SmallChange = 1
        rotate.LargeChange = 10
        rotate.Value = 0

        Me.SetStyle(ControlStyles.AllPaintingInWmPaint, True)
        Me.SetStyle(ControlStyles.DoubleBuffer, True)
        Me.SetStyle(ControlStyles.UserPaint, True)

    End Sub
…
…


#End Region

    Private Sub Form1_Load(ByVal sender As System.Object, _
                           ByVal e As System.EventArgs) _
                           Handles MyBase.Load

    End Sub

    Protected Overrides Sub OnPaint(ByVal e As PaintEventArgs)
        Dim G As Graphics = e.Graphics

        G.SmoothingMode = SmoothingMode.AntiAlias

        ' Create a graphics path, add a rectangle, set colors
        Dim Path As New GraphicsPath()
        Path.AddRectangle(New Rectangle(75, 100, 100, 75))
        Dim Pts As PointF() = Path.PathPoints
        Dim B As New PathGradientBrush(Pts)
        B.CenterColor = Color.Aqua
        Dim SColor As Color() = {Color.Blue}
        B.SurroundColors = SColor

        'We will translate the brush!  NOT the rectangle!
        Dim m As New Matrix()
        m.Translate(0, Xlatey, MatrixOrder.Append)
        m.RotateAt(Angle, B.CenterPoint, MatrixOrder.Append)
        B.MultiplyTransform(m, MatrixOrder.Append)
        G.FillRectangle(B, DrawingRect)
```

```
        m.Dispose()
        B.Dispose()
        Path.Dispose()

    End Sub

    Private Sub xlate_Scroll(ByVal sender As System.Object, _
                            ByVal e As System.Windows.Forms.ScrollEventArgs) _
                            Handles xlate.Scroll

        Xlatey = xlate.Value
        Me.Invalidate(DrawingRect)

    End Sub

    Private Sub rotate_Scroll(ByVal sender As System.Object, _
                            ByVal e As System.Windows.Forms.ScrollEventArgs) _
                            Handles rotate.Scroll

        Angle = rotate.Value
        Me.Invalidate(DrawingRect)

    End Sub
End Class
```

Compile and run the program. You should get a screen like the one shown in Figure 5-14.

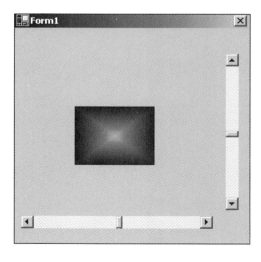

Figure 5-14. MatrixDraw start-up screen

The vertical scroll bar translates the image in the Y direction; the horizontal scroll bar transforms the image by rotating it between –180 and +180 degrees. The center point for the rotation is the center of the PathGradientBrush.

Try moving the scroll bars. If at first you move the vertical one you will see the image go up and down. Rotate the image using the horizontal bar and then move it using the vertical bar. You will see the image move in the rotated Y direction. Figure 5-15 shows this effect after rotating the image 45 degrees and moving it up.

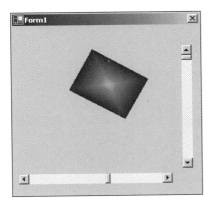

Figure 5-15. Rotated and translated MatrixDraw image

Why am I making a big deal about this? Because I am not moving the image at all! Take a close look at the code and you will see that the matrix is applied to the PathGradientBrush, *not* the shapes' rectangle. It is the brush's rectangle that I am changing. The rectangle that I am filling never has its coordinates changed. Wrap your brain around that!

Miscellaneous Extras

I have taken you through most of the complicated drawing that you will need to know. What follows in this section are some of the miscellaneous methods and classes that round out this chapter. There are not too many of them, but they do come in handy:

- GetNearestColor method

- ColorTranslator class

- GraphicsPathIterator

- RegionData

The **GetNearestColor** method returns a Color structure that is the nearest system color to the color that you have specified. For instance, you might specify a color like this:

```
Color MyColor = Color.FromArgb( 255, 100, 100 , 100);
```

Now suppose you want to get the next color up that was a known system color. You would do this:

```
Color ActualColor = e.Graphics.GetNearestColor(MyColor);
```

Translating Colors

The ColorTranslator class has the following public methods:

- FromHtml

- FromOle

- FromWin32

- ToHtml

- ToOle

- ToWin32

As you can probably guess, this class allows you to go from one type of color definition to another. When would you use this? How about when you are accessing a COM object using the COM Interop with a .NET class? This COM object hands you a color that it wants your .NET client to use in rendering a form. The **ColorTranslator.FromOle** method would be used here. This is because colors in the COM world are defined as OLECOLOR.

Tracing a Path

Okay, you have generated this complicated path made up of all kinds of shapes. Now you want to traverse that path. To do this, you use the GraphicsPathIterator class. The next example generates a path and uses the GraphicsPathIterator class to display some information about that path. This is only one use of the GraphicsPathIterator class.

Make a new VB or C# program. Mine is called Misc2D. Make the form 300?400 and then drop a list box and three labels on the form. Accept the default names. All the code for this project is done inside the **OnPaint** method. Listing 5-10 shows the **OnPaint** method for both VB and C#. Don't forget to add the namespaces System.Drawing and System.Drawing2D.

Listing 5-10a. VB Code for the Misc2D Example

```vb
Protected Overrides Sub OnPaint(ByVal e As PaintEventArgs)
  Dim G As Graphics = e.Graphics

  Dim p As GraphicsPath = New GraphicsPath()
  Dim pts() As PointF = {New PointF(50.0F, 50.0F), _
                   New PointF(150.0F, 25.0F), _
                   New PointF(200.0F, 50.0F)}
  p.AddCurve(pts)
  p.AddRectangle(New Rectangle(60, 60, 50, 50))
  p.AddPie(100, 100, 80, 80, 0, 35)
  G.DrawPath(Pens.Black, p)

  Dim iter As GraphicsPathIterator = New GraphicsPathIterator(p)
  label1.Text = "Num pts in path = " + iter.Count.ToString()
  label2.Text = "Num subpaths in path = " + iter.SubpathCount.ToString()
  label3.Text = "Path has curve = " + iter.HasCurve().ToString()

  Dim StartIndex As Int32
  Dim EndIndex As Int32
  Dim i As Int32
  Dim IsClosed As Boolean
  ' Rewind the Iterator.
  iter.Rewind()
  ' List the Subpaths.
  For i = 0 To iter.SubpathCount - 1
    iter.NextSubpath(StartIndex, EndIndex, IsClosed)
    listBox1.Items.Add("Start: " + StartIndex.ToString() + _
                  " End: " + EndIndex.ToString() + _
                  " IsClosed: " + IsClosed.ToString())
  Next
End Sub
```

Listing 5-10b. C# Code for the Misc2D Example

```csharp
protected override void OnPaint(PaintEventArgs e)
{
  Graphics G = e.Graphics;

  GraphicsPath p = new  GraphicsPath();
  PointF[] pts = { new PointF(50,  50),
                   new PointF(150, 25),
                   new PointF(200, 50)};
  p.AddCurve(pts);
  p.AddRectangle(new Rectangle(60, 60, 50, 50));
  p.AddPie(100, 100, 80, 80, 0, 35);
  G.DrawPath(Pens.Black,p);

  GraphicsPathIterator iter = new GraphicsPathIterator(p);
  label1.Text = "Num pts in path = " + iter.Count.ToString();
  label2.Text = "Num subpaths in path = " + iter.SubpathCount.ToString();
  label3.Text = "Path has curve = " + iter.HasCurve().ToString();

  int StartIndex;
  int EndIndex;
  int i;
  bool IsClosed;
  // Rewind the Iterator.
  iter.Rewind();
  // List the Subpaths.
  for(i=0;i<iter.SubpathCount;i++)
  {
    iter.NextSubpath(out StartIndex, out EndIndex, out IsClosed);
    listBox1.Items.Add("Start: " + StartIndex.ToString() +
                       " End: " + EndIndex.ToString() +
                       " IsClosed: " + IsClosed.ToString());
  }
}
```

Compile and run the program. Your output should match that shown in Figure 5-16.

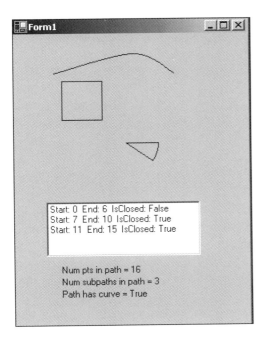

Figure 5-16. Result of the Misc2D example

As you can see from this example, you generate a GraphicsPath that is made up of three shapes. Each of these shapes is referred to as a subpath. You will also see that the iterator tells you if the shape is closed and what the start and end indexes are.

There is quite a bit more you can do with the GraphicsPathIterator class. I have shown you just a little here. Walking a path is something you will probably need to do at some time. I suggest you familiarize yourself more with this class via the MSDN documents.

Looking at Your Region's Data

Remember the clipping regions from Chapter 4? You used them to encapsulate drawing to a particular area of the screen. You have also used regions in this chapter to speed up the drawing process by invalidating regions of the screen.

You can get information about any region that you have created by using the RegionData class. This class has one member: Data. This member returns an array of bytes that describe the region. The following snippet of code demonstrates how to use it:

```
Rectangle regionRect = new Rectangle(20, 20, 100, 100);
Region myRegion = new Region(regionRect);
RegionData Rd = myRegion.GetRegionData();
int RdLength = Rd.Data.Length;
```

You can keep the RegionData object in memory, fiddle with the data itself, and create a new region from this data.

Summary

Well, you have learned quite a bit in this chapter. In Chapter 4, I showed you some of the basic drawing functionality. This chapter extended that by demonstrating more of the depth of GDI+. Here is a summary of what you learned:

- *Pen and brush end caps:* These end caps represent a new way to change the shape of a line.

- *HatchBrush:* This brush is made up of repeating hatch patterns.

- *Alpha blend:* This is about transparency in shapes, colors, and images.

- *Gamma correction:* This refers to the brightness and contrast of images and how to change them.

- *Flicker:* I spent quite a bit of time on how to paint with no flicker, including using the ControlStyles enumeration and invalidating regions.

- *LinearGradientBrush:* This brush is made up of colors that change gradually from a start color to an end color in a linear fashion.

- *PathGradientBrush:* This brush is made up of colors that change from a center point out to another color at the edges of a shape. I supplied examples on wrapping and changing the centroid of a gradient.

- *Transforms:* I covered the 3×3 matrix called an affine transformation. This allows you to rotate, scale, and translate an image or a brush.

- *GraphicsPathIterator:* This class allows you to walk a graphics path and find information about that path.

This chapter contained a lot of information to digest. Hopefully, I have provided you with enough examples to make it clear not only how *to* use some of this functionality, but also how you *could* use it.

The next chapter is about imaging. This is where you will learn about bitmaps, JPEG files, and so forth, and how to manipulate them. Remember the satellite over the planet example? The next chapter will show you how to speed up this program even more.

CHAPTER 6

Working with Images

Although Sarah had an abnormal fear of mice, it did not keep
her from eeking out a living at a local pet store.

—Richard W. O'Bryan, Perrysburg, Ohio

ANYONE WHO HAS DONE any graphics programming using GDI has the same growing fear in mind when looking through the GDI+ documentation for the first time:

Q: Oh my God, they took away the BitBlt!

A: No, they didn't. It just morphed.

Now you can rest easy and go through this chapter knowing that you can still transfer images to the screen at high speed.

The rest of you are wondering, "What's BitBlt?" Don't worry, by the end of this chapter you'll be blitting your way across the screen with the best of them. I explain the bit block transfer soon enough.

In this chapter I cover some of the leftover classes from the System.Drawing and System.Drawing2D namespaces. There are only a few of these, though. Most of this chapter deals with the classes contained in the System.Drawing.Imaging namespace.

 TIP *I present many examples in this chapter that load pictures from disk. You are more than welcome to substitute any picture you want. However, the icons and bitmaps I use are included either with the operating system or with .NET itself.*

Images Files Explained

Remember that in Chapter 1 I said everything is an object? Here I will say something equally wide-ranging: All images are bitmaps. That is a pretty sweeping statement considering that you can get pictures in quite a few formats. Perhaps I should clarify that statement a little: All images held in memory are bitmaps.

247

The dots on your screen are called *pixels*. A *bitmap* consists of a rectangular array of pixel data. This data contains the color attributes of the pixel in question. The number of colors for a pixel corresponds to the number of bits per pixel available. Table 6-1 shows a common range of bitmap color resolutions and the number of bits needed to represent them.

Table 6-1. Bitmap Color Resolution

Bits per Pixel	Colors Available per Pixel
1	2^1 = 2 colors
2	2^2 = 4 colors
4	2^4 = 16 colors
8	2^8 = 256 colors
16	2^16 = 65,536 colors
24	2^24 = 16,777,216 colors
32	2^32 = 4,294,967,296 colors

Twenty-four-bit color and 32-bit color are often referred to as *true color*. 16-bit color is often called *high color*. Does this sound familiar? It should. If you right-click your desktop and choose Settings, a drop-down box appears in which you can choose the number of colors your screen will display.

The number of screen colors is inversely proportional to the resolution setting of your screen. This is because your graphics card has a limited amount of memory to parse out screen size and colors. Table 6-2 shows a comparison of memory size to colors and resolution.

Table 6-2. Memory Size According to Resolution and Number of Colors

Screen Resolution	Colors	Memory Needed
800×600	256	480K
800×600	64K	960K
800×600	16 million	1.44MB
1024×768	256	787K
1024×768	64K	1.57MB

Table 6-2. Memory Size According to Resolution and Number of Colors (Continued)

Screen Resolution	Colors	Memory Needed
1024×768	16 million	2.3MB
1280×1024	256	1.3MB
1280×1024	64K	2.5MB
1280×1024	16 million	3.9MB

As you can see, the more memory your video card has, the more colors you are able to display and the higher the resolution you can display them at.

When a bitmap is saved as a BMP file, it is saved with no compression. This takes up the most space on disk but also ensures an absolutely accurate (and fast recalling) image. If you were to save a picture that was 400×400 pixels using a 24-bit bitmap, you would need almost 470K of space. This may not seem like much in these days of multigigabyte storage, but these images add up. Also, with the Internet as the transfer medium, you need to very conscious of speed. Speed equals size. If you have a Web page that is trying to render three or four 24-bit BMP files, your customers could soon lose interest while waiting for the page to render.

Storing Bitmaps As BMP Files

You can store a bitmap on disk in a few ways. One way is to store bitmaps with 24 bits per pixel. This gives you the largest storage space for an image and requires no color table lookup.

Another way to store bitmap images is to store the pixel information along with a block of information that represents a color table. If you used a 16-color table, you would need only 4 bits per pixel to store an image. Each color in the table, however, would need 24 bits. Add the pixel information to the color table itself and you would have a very small disk file. This type of bitmap is called a *palette-indexed* bitmap.

While most bitmaps are stored in a top-down manner, it is not uncommon to see some bitmaps stored in a bottom-up arrangement. In this case, the first row of pixels in the file corresponds to the bottom row of pixels in the image.

Storing Bitmaps As Other File Types

So now you know a little about bitmaps and how BMP files are stored. You know that they are large, but they also have fast access because there is no manipulation involved. What about other file types? Here are the other types supported directly by GDI+:

- GIF

- JPEG

- EXIF

- PNG

- TIFF

GIF File Storage

GIF stands for *Graphics Interchange Format.* This is a common format for displaying images on Web pages. GIF files use a lossless compression technique that stores at most 8 bits per pixel. According to Table 6-1, this means that GIF files can store at most 256 colors.

A lossless compression algorithm ensures that no information is lost during compression and that the reconstructed image is exactly the same as the original.

A GIF file can have an image with one color designated as transparent. Usually, this color is the background color of the image, so it will appear normal on any Web page. The background of the Web page becomes the background of the GIF image.

GIF files are good for storing images with very few colors and sharp delineations between colors. You can also store multiple GIF files in a single file. This means that you can have an animated GIF.

JPEG File Storage

JPEG stands for *Joint Photographic Experts Group.* JPEG files are commonly stored with the extension .jpg. JPEG is a lossy compression technique that can greatly reduce the size of an image. By "lossy," I mean that some of the original information is discarded during compression. If an image such as a nature scene is compressed using JPEG compression, you will probably not even see the loss of information.

JPEG compression is usually configurable, and a 20:1 compression ratio is not uncommon. JPEG files use 24 bits per pixel, which means that they can store more than 16 million colors. However, JPEG files do not support transparency or animation. JPEG files are used quite often in Web pages.

Because JPEG is a lossy compression scheme, it does not do well with pictures that have sharp boundaries between colors. An artist's drawing of a red and blue checkerboard, for example, is better suited to a GIF file than a JPEG file.[1]

EXIF File Storage

EXIF, which stands for *Exchangeable Image File,* is an interesting format that is not well known. It is a bitmap file that has been compressed using JPEG compression but also includes some extra information. EXIF files are used often for digital camera photos. Some of the extra information EXIF files carry is as follows:

- Shutter speed

- F-stop

- Date taken

- Camera manufacturer

- Camera model

The list goes on.

PNG File Storage

PNG stands for *Portable Network Graphics.* PNG files are pretty much the same as GIF files, but without some of the drawbacks. For instance, PNG files can store colors with 8, 24, or 48 bits per pixel and grayscales with 1, 2, 4, 8, or 16 bits per pixel. PNG files can also store an alpha component for each pixel.[2] GIF files can only store one completely transparent color.

PNG files can also store gamma correction and color correction information. This allows the file to be displayed correctly on any kind of display.

---

1. By the way, JPEG is a compression scheme, not a file format.
2. If you do not know what an alpha value is, read Chapter 5.

TIFF File Storage

TIFF stands for *Tagged Image File Format.* This format is commonly used in the publishing industry. In fact, all the images contained in this book started out life as TIFF images.

The tags refer to how extra information about the image is stored in the file. Some of the information that can be stored in the file is as follows:

- Computer type

- Samples per pixel

- Compression type

TIFF files can store images with a wide variety of compression algorithms and any number of bits per pixel. TIFF files can also store several images in one multipage TIFF file.

Working with Image Classes

Now you have a working knowledge of how images are stored on disk. The rest of this chapter shows you how to manipulate those images.

First, though, you need to know something about how .NET has set up the image classes. Three classes you will work with in .NET have to do with images:

- Bitmap

- Icon

- Metafile

All three of these classes derive from the same abstract base class, Image. The Image base class provides the interface that the Bitmap, Icon, and Metafile classes must implement.

Now, most of you C++ programmers know what abstract base classes are. You VBers have never had this programming construct to work with before.[3] I think it is worth taking a little time to go over a simple explanation of abstract base classes.

Base classes are designed to provide a common set of functionality. Customization of this functionality is done through extending the base class via inheritance. Base classes often contain methods and properties that have implementation

---

3. No, implementation inheritance in VB 6.0 is not the same thing.

code. It is possible for derived classes to inherit this code or ignore it by overriding the base class' method or property. You have seen this already in just about every example in this book.

Remember the **OnPaint** method? There is basic functionality in the base class, but in each example I have overridden the base class and created my own **OnPaint** method. This is why I call the base class' **OnPaint** method before I leave my own **OnPaint** method. If I did not do this, the base class code would never run.

Well, that is the very short definition of a base class. However, I started out talking about the Image class and it is an *abstract* base class. The abstract part is interesting.

"Abstract" refers to a class that is somewhat or totally incomplete. An abstract class generally has some methods or properties that have no implementation. The members are marked as needing to be overridden. Any class that inherits from the abstract base class must override any abstract members and thereby provide the implementation for those members. Abstract classes are not allowed to be marked as Sealed (C#) or NotInheritable (VB). Interestingly enough, abstract classes are not required to have abstract members.

Abstract base classes cannot be instantiated directly. You cannot use the keyword new to make an Image object. You can only use the keyword new with descendent classes of the Image class. You can create an Image object using some static methods in the Image class.

Okay, so what you have here is the Image class with a whole bunch of properties and methods. Some members are abstract and others are not. It just so happens that those members that are not abstract are static members. These static members are members that are implemented in the base class and can be called directly by referencing them through the base class. Again, you have seen this numerous times in previous examples in this book. Remember this C# construct:

```
Image I = Image.FromFile("D:\\colorbars.jpg");
```

This construct creates an Image object in memory by using the static method **FromFile**.

The Bitmap Class

This class derives from the Image class. It provides functionality for every abstract Image method and adds a few of its own. Let's start out with something you'll undoubtedly need to do: constructing a bitmap. The Bitmap class has 12 overloaded constructors that allow you to make a bitmap in any number of ways. Here are a few of the more common ways:

- Create a bitmap from an image.

- Create a bitmap from a file.

- Create a bitmap with the same resolution as a Graphics object.

- Create a bitmap from a set of pixel data.

Most of the constructors also allow you to set the size of the resulting bitmap. The following code shows you three different ways to create a bitmap:

VB

```vb
Dim I As Image = Image.FromFile("D:\\colorbars.jpg")
Dim bt1 As Bitmap = New Bitmap(I)
Dim bt2 As Bitmap = New Bitmap("D:\\colorbars.jpg")

Dim g As Graphics = Me.CreateGraphics()
Dim bt3 As Bitmap = New Bitmap(100, 100, g)
```

C#

```csharp
Image I = Image.FromFile("D:\\colorbars.jpg");
Bitmap bt1 = new Bitmap(I);
Bitmap bt2 = new Bitmap("D:\\colorbars.jpg");

Graphics g  = this.CreateGraphics();
Bitmap bt3 = new Bitmap(100, 100, g);
```

As you can see, just one line of code can convert a JPEG file into a bitmap. Not bad. In Chapters 4 and 5 I showed you examples that included drawing bitmaps and images to the screen. While I extend upon that in this chapter, I want to first show you what information you could get from bitmaps as well as how to manipulate bitmaps.

Bitmap Properties

Getting a bitmap in memory and onto the screen is relatively easy. What if you wanted to change some aspects of the bitmap before you put it on the screen? Quite a few properties and methods in the Bitmap class allow you to view all kinds of information about that bitmap:

- Size

- Width

- Height

- HorizontalResolution

- VerticalResolution

- PhysicalDimension

- GetBounds

- PixelFormat

- SetResolution

Width and **Height** are integers indicating the width and height of the bitmap in pixels. **Size** returns a Size structure whose integer elements are the width and height of the bitmap in pixels. **PhysicalDimension** returns a SizeF structure. This holds the floating-point values of the width and height of the bitmap.

HorizontalResolution and **VerticalResolution** return the dots per inch (dpi) as a floating-point number. **SetResolution** allows you to change the dpi of the bitmap.

GetBounds returns a Rectangle structure that bounds the bitmap. This is commonly referred to as the *bounding box*.

PixelFormat returns an enum value. This value is part of the PixelFormat enumeration that contains in-depth color information about the bitmap.

You can use just these properties and methods to show a user all kinds of information about a particular picture.

Start a new VB or C# Windows Forms project. Mine is called ImageClass. Perform the following steps before you enter in any code:

1. Size the form to 400×400. This should be big enough to show small graphics.

2. Add a button to the bottom of the form. Call it cmdOpen. Set the text to "Open".

3. Add a button to the bottom of the form. Call it cmdSetRes. Set the text to "Reset Resolution".

4. Add a GroupBox to the form. It should be about 225×225. Set the text to "Attributes".

5. Add an OpenFile dialog box to the form. Call it odfBitmap.

 NOTE   *Adding invisible controls such as the OpenFile dialog box does not put them on the form as in VB 6.0. You will find them on the panel just below the Forms Designer panel.*

Your form should look somewhat like the one shown in Figure 6-1.

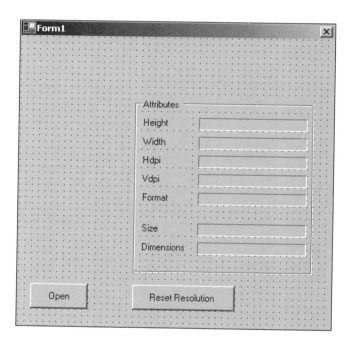

Figure 6-1. Layout of the ImageClass form

Double-click the Open button to get the wizard-generated event handler for the click event. Change the name of the handler to "OpenFile". Remember to change the C# delegate definition in the wizard-generated code. You have done this many times before in this book.

Next, double-click the Reset Resolution button to the event handler for the click event for this button. Change the name of this handler to "SetRes". While this changes the actual resolution, you may not see any change on the screen.

Now you are ready to enter code. Listing 6-1 shows the code necessary for this program. The "Windows Form Designer generated code" region for this example is rather long, and besides changing the C# delegate definition, you will not even need to see it. This code block is not shown here. You are, of course, welcome to download this example, along with all the examples in this book, from the Downloads section of the Apress Web site (http://www.apress.com).

Listing 6-1a. C# Code for a Bitmap Information Program

```
using System;
using System.Drawing;
using System.Drawing.Drawing2D;
using System.Drawing.Imaging;
using System.Collections;
using System.ComponentModel;
using System.Windows.Forms;
using System.Data;

namespace ImageClass
{
  /// <summary>
  /// Summary description for Form1.
  /// </summary>
  public class Form1 : System.Windows.Forms.Form
  {
    private System.Windows.Forms.OpenFileDialog ofdBitmap;
    private System.Windows.Forms.Button cmdOpen;
    /// <summary>
    /// Required designer variable.
    /// </summary>
    private System.ComponentModel.Container components = null;
    private System.Windows.Forms.GroupBox groupBox1;
    private System.Windows.Forms.Label label1;
    private System.Windows.Forms.Label label2;
    private System.Windows.Forms.Label label3;
    private System.Windows.Forms.Label label4;
    private System.Windows.Forms.Label label5;
    private System.Windows.Forms.Label lblHT;
    private System.Windows.Forms.Label lblWidth;
    private System.Windows.Forms.Label lblHdpi;
    private System.Windows.Forms.Label lblVdpi;
```

```csharp
        private System.Windows.Forms.Label lblFormat;
        private System.Windows.Forms.Label label6;
        private System.Windows.Forms.Label lblSize;
        private System.Windows.Forms.Label lblDIM;
        private System.Windows.Forms.Label label8;
        private System.Windows.Forms.Button cmdSetRes;

        #region Class local variables
        Bitmap Bmp;
        RectangleF BMPContainer;
        #endregion

        public Form1()
        {
          //
          // Required for Windows Form Designer support
          //
          InitializeComponent();

          ofdBitmap.Filter= "Image Files(*.BMP;*.JPG;*.GIF)|*.BMP;*.JPG;*.GIF";
          ofdBitmap.InitialDirectory = "D:";
        }

        /// <summary>
        /// Clean up any resources being used.
        /// </summary>
        protected override void Dispose( bool disposing )
        {
          If( disposing )
          {
            if (components != null)
            {
              components.Dispose();
            }

          Bmp.Dispose();
          base.Dispose( disposing );
        }

        #region Windows Form Designer generated code
        …
        …
        …
        #endregion
```

```csharp
/// <summary>
/// The main entry point for the application.
/// </summary>
[STAThread]
static void Main()
{
  Application.Run(new Form1());
}

private void Form1_Load(object sender, System.EventArgs e)
{
}

protected override void OnPaint( PaintEventArgs e)
{
  Graphics G = e.Graphics;
  if ( Bmp != null )
  {
    //OK Folks. This is a BitBlt!
    G.DrawImage(Bmp, BMPContainer);
  }

  base.OnPaint(e);
}

private void cmdOpen_Click(object sender, System.EventArgs e)
{
  ofdBitmap.ShowDialog();
}

private void OpenFile(object sender,
                     System.ComponentModel.CancelEventArgs e)
{
  //Wondering what sender is?  Use reflection!
  if ( !( sender is System.Windows.Forms.OpenFileDialog ) )
    return;

  Bmp = new Bitmap( ofdBitmap.FileName );
  if ( Bmp != null )
  {
    ShowStats();
    DrawBMP();
  }
}
```

```csharp
        private void SetRes(object sender, System.EventArgs e)
        {
          if ( Bmp != null )
          {
            Bmp.SetResolution(150, 150);
            DrawBMP();
          }
        }

        private void DrawBMP()
        {
          if ( Bmp != null )
          {
            //Invalidate only the area where the image will be drawn
            Graphics G = this.CreateGraphics();
            GraphicsUnit GU = G.PageUnit;
            BMPContainer = Bmp.GetBounds( ref GU ); //X,Y = 0
            ShowStats();
            this.Invalidate( Rectangle.Round( BMPContainer ) );
            G.Dispose();
          }
        }
        private void ShowStats()
        {
          if ( Bmp != null )
          {
            //Show some properties here
            lblHT.Text = Bmp.Height.ToString();
            lblWidth.Text = Bmp.Width.ToString();
            lblVdpi.Text = Bmp.VerticalResolution.ToString();
            lblHdpi.Text = Bmp.HorizontalResolution.ToString();
            lblFormat.Text = Bmp.PixelFormat.ToString();
            lblSize.Text = Bmp.Size.ToString();
            lblDIM.Text = Bmp.PhysicalDimension.ToString();
          }
        }
      }
    }
```

Listing 6-1b. VB Code for a Bitmap Information Program

```vb
Option Strict On

Imports System.Drawing
Imports System.Drawing.Drawing2D
Imports System.Drawing.Imaging

Public Class Form1
  Inherits System.Windows.Forms.Form

#Region "Class local variables"
  Dim Bmp As Bitmap
  Dim BMPContainer As RectangleF
#End Region

#Region " Windows Form Designer generated code "

  Public Sub New()
    MyBase.New()

    'This call is required by the Windows Form Designer.
    InitializeComponent()

    ofdBitmap.Filter = "Image Files(*.BMP;*.JPG;*.GIF)|*.BMP;*.JPG;*.GIF"
    ofdBitmap.InitialDirectory = "D:"

  End Sub

  'Form overrides dispose to clean up the component list.
  Protected Overloads Overrides Sub Dispose(ByVal disposing As Boolean)
    If disposing Then
      If Not (components Is Nothing) Then
        components.Dispose()
      End If
    End If
    Bmp.Dispose()
    MyBase.Dispose(disposing)
  End Sub

  …
  …   'Designer code here
  …
```

```
#End Region

  Private Sub Form1_Load(ByVal sender As System.Object, _
                        ByVal e As System.EventArgs) Handles MyBase.Load

  End Sub

  Protected Overrides Sub OnPaint(ByVal e As PaintEventArgs)
    Dim G As Graphics = e.Graphics

    If Not Bmp Is Nothing Then
      'OK Folks. This is a BitBlt!
      G.DrawImage(Bmp, BMPContainer)
    End If

    MyBase.OnPaint(e)
  End Sub

  Private Sub Open(ByVal sender As System.Object, _
                   ByVal e As System.EventArgs) Handles cmdOpen.Click
    ofdBitmap.ShowDialog()
  End Sub

  Private Sub OpenFile(ByVal sender As System.Object, _
                   ByVal e As System.ComponentModel.CancelEventArgs) _
                                         Handles ofdBitmap.FileOk
    'Wondering what sender is?  Use reflection!
    If Not sender.GetType() Is GetType(System.Windows.Forms.OpenFileDialog) Then
      Return
    End If

    Bmp = New Bitmap(ofdBitmap.FileName)
    If Not Bmp Is Nothing Then
      ShowStats()
      DrawBMP()
    End If
  End Sub
```

```
Private Sub SetRes(ByVal sender As System.Object, _
                   ByVal e As System.EventArgs) Handles cmdSetRes.Click
   If Not Bmp Is Nothing Then
     Bmp.SetResolution(150, 150)
     DrawBMP()
   End If

End Sub


Private Sub DrawBMP()
   If Not Bmp Is Nothing Then
     'Invalidate only the area where the image will be drawn
     Dim G As Graphics = Me.CreateGraphics()
     Dim GU As GraphicsUnit = G.PageUnit
     BMPContainer = Bmp.GetBounds(GU) 'x,y=0
     ShowStats()
     Me.Invalidate(Rectangle.Round(BMPContainer))
     G.Dispose()
   End If
End Sub


Private Sub ShowStats()
   If Not Bmp Is Nothing Then
     'Show some properties here
     lblHT.Text = Bmp.Height.ToString()
     lblWidth.Text = Bmp.Width.ToString()
     lblVdpi.Text = Bmp.VerticalResolution.ToString()
     lblHdpi.Text = Bmp.HorizontalResolution.ToString()
     lblFormat.Text = Bmp.PixelFormat.ToString()
     lblSize.Text = Bmp.Size.ToString()
     lblDIM.Text = Bmp.PhysicalDimension.ToString()
   End If
 End Sub
End Class
```

Compile and run the code. After you click the Open button and select a picture, your screen should look similar to the one shown in Figure 6-2. (Of course, you may have chosen another graphic.)

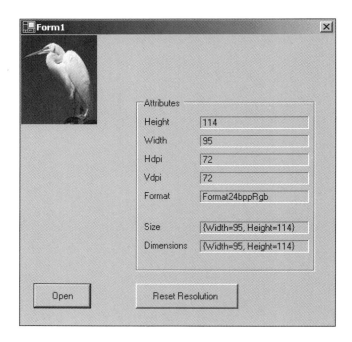

Figure 6-2. ImageClass form showing bitmap properties

First off, no, this program is not perfect. For starters, I draw the image according to its native size in pixels. If you choose a large image, it may overflow into the frame's region or even be bigger than the form itself. This program is only a demo.

As you can see from the attribute's frame, I am displaying the image's size several times. Each time I display the size of the image, I am using a different method to get the size.

Let's take a closer look at the code. I will point out some interesting things that you should know.

First of all, notice that I am using my own region to block out class local variables. Regions are simple to define. They can greatly increase the readability of your code by allowing you to collapse or expand the region in the editor as needed.

I am using a Common dialog box provided by .NET to access the pictures I want to see. This dialog box works pretty much the same as what you would find in VB 6.0 with one very important exception. The .NET version has events. The Common dialog box in VB 6.0 is modal. Once you called the dialog box up, all processing in your program would halt until the dialog box was exited. Any results from the dialog box would need to be obtained by code that runs immediately after the dialog box was released.

The .NET Common dialog box is modal as well. However, the necessary code to determine what happened in the dialog box (OK or Cancel, for instance) disappears.

Instead, you get an event based upon the action taken in the dialog box. You can see this by looking at the code for the cmdOpen click event. All I do in there is call up the File Open dialog box. There is no code in this method that processes the results of the dialog box. Instead, there is a delegate that handles the FileOK event. If I were interested in the user clicking Cancel, I would have a delegate for that as well.

I think this makes for much neater and more readable code, don't you? In fact, I would go further than this. If I had a program that included a few different Common dialog boxes, I would create just one delegate to handle all the dialog boxes' FileOK events. You can do this by chaining the Handles keyword in VB and by referring to the same function using the "+=" operator in C#. Central processing can be a wonderful thing.

One more thing about the Common dialog box's FileOK delegate. I said you could use one delegate to have the events from multiple dialog boxes. To do this, the first thing you need to know is who sent the event. Well, there is a really neat thing in .NET called *reflection*. Basically, reflection allows you to interrogate an object to find out basic properties about it.

NOTE *Reflection is not within the scope of this book, but it is vital to a good understanding of how .NET works and how you can use it effectively. My book* Internationalization and Localization Using Microsoft .NET *(Apress, 2002) has a neat program that gets information about all the methods in a .NET DLL using reflection. I suggest you learn about reflection. You will find many uses for it.*

Here is the code again for the FileOK event in both VB and C#:

VB

```
Private Sub OpenFile(ByVal sender As System.Object, _
                ByVal e As System.ComponentModel.CancelEventArgs) _
                                        Handles ofdBitmap.FileOk
    'Wondering what sender is?  Use reflection!
    If Not sender.GetType() Is GetType(System.Windows.Forms.OpenFileDialog) Then
        Return
    End If

    Bmp = New Bitmap(ofdBitmap.FileName)
    If Not Bmp Is Nothing Then
        ShowStats()
        DrawBMP()
    End If
End Sub
```

C#

```
private void OpenFile(object sender,
                    System.ComponentModel.CancelEventArgs e)
{
  //Wondering what sender is?  Use reflection!
  if ( !( sender is System.Windows.Forms.OpenFileDialog ) )
    return;

  Bmp = new Bitmap( ofdBitmap.FileName );
  if ( Bmp != null )
  {
    ShowStats();
    DrawBMP();
  }
}
```

The first thing I do in this method is find out who fired the event. More to the point, I find out *what* fired the event. I use the "is" operator in C# to see if the sender is a Common dialog box. VB is a little more convoluted in that I need to explicitly get the type of each object before using the "is" operator.[4]

What I did not do here is find out which dialog box fired the event. I leave that up to you. By the way, I need to know what fired the event because several controls have the same event signature as the Common dialog box control. I could have used this delegate to handle events from a number of different controls, some of which could have the same name.

The next thing I want to draw your attention to is the **DrawBMP** method. It is in here that I find out the size of the picture and invalidate the rectangle that holds that picture. Remember, always try to paint only the region you need to paint. Painting takes time, and the faster you can make it, the sooner you can get back to your program.

Let's look at the **DrawBMP** method again. There is some interesting code in here. Here is the C# code again (the VB code is virtually the same):

```
private void DrawBMP()
{
  if ( Bmp != null )
  {
    //Invalidate only the area where the image will be drawn
    Graphics G = this.CreateGraphics();
    GraphicsUnit GU = G.PageUnit;
```

---

4. Here C# is the winner in clarity. Usually it is VB.

```
    BMPContainer = Bmp.GetBounds( ref GU ); //X,Y = 0
    ShowStats();
    this.Invalidate( Rectangle.Round( BMPContainer ) );
    G.Dispose();
  }
}
```

The first thing I do, of course, is make sure that I am working with a valid bitmap. I could have caught any error with a Try-Catch block, but it is always better to test for validity, if you can, rather than just catching the problem.

In order to invalidate a section of the screen for repainting purposes, I first need to find that area. The best method in the case of this bitmap is using a rectangle. I could have generated a new rectangle using any of the size methods of the bitmap, but I chose the **GetBounds** method instead.[5] This method returns a RectangleF structure sized to hold the bitmap in question. However, this method requires a reference to a **GraphicsUnit** used by the Graphics object. It needs this information to determine if you are working in inches, millimeters, pixels, or whatever. The **GraphicsUnit** currently used by the Graphics object is exposed through the object's **PageUnit** property.

Okay, the key word in the last paragraph is *reference*. If you worked with the VB code, you would have no idea that you passed a reference or the actual value to this method. VB takes care of that behind the scenes for you.[6] C# needs you to make sure you know what you are doing here. You can see that I use the keyword ref. This indicates that you are sending a reference to the argument. (You certainly should know the difference between sending a reference as opposed to sending a value.)

I could have forced the argument to the **GetBounds** method to be any kind of **GraphicsUnit** I wanted. However, because I am working with the form's Graphics container, it is best to use the same one the form is using.

Once I have the RectangleF structure, I change it to a rectangle by using the static method **Rectangle.Round** and pass it to the **Invalidate** method. I do this because there is no overloaded version of **Invalidate** that takes a floating-point rectangle.

This **DrawBMP** method invalidates the area of the screen defined by the size of the bitmap. It is dynamic and I could use this method in any number of programs that need to display bitmaps.

---

5. This is, after all, an instructional book.
6. Personally, I think you ought to know this is going on.

Bitmap Methods

The previous example showed you how to get information about a bitmap. It also showed you how to change the resolution of the bitmap. There was nothing really hard about any of this, and it was also mostly a passive program. This section delves into some of the methods you can use to manipulate bitmaps.

First of all, I want to talk about alternate ways to create a bitmap. So far, the only creation method I discussed was via the constructor. However, once you get into animation, thumbnails, icons, and the need for speed, you will need other ways to create bitmaps. The following list is what the Bitmap class provides to address these needs:

- FromIcon

- FromResource

- Clone

- GetThumbnailImage

- RotateFlip

The **FromResource** method is interesting. This method looks inside an executable file and extracts the named bitmap. What is the purpose of this? Globalization. When a program is localized to a particular country, you normally create a resource file for it in the form of a DLL. You could go as far as having a single resource DLL contain all the graphics for a particular program. The strings could be held in a separate DLL altogether. This is not how I would do it, but I have seen it done this way.

 NOTE *My book* Internationalization and Localization Using Microsoft .NET *(Apress, 2002) deals with resource files and localization techniques. Among other things, it includes in-depth examples on using bitmaps and icons in resource files.*

Anyway, this **FromResource** method could be used to get a bitmap from a resource DLL without using any of the classes in the System.Resources namespace. By the way, this method is static. What are static methods again . . . anyone? They are methods that are invoked from the class itself, not the object created from the class. Static methods do not operate on a specific instance of the class.

The **FromIcon** static method translates an icon to a bitmap and returns the bitmap to you. This method requires the windows handle to the icon as an argument.

You can get this handle in a number of ways. One way is to use the PInvoke capability of .NET and call the API command LoadImage. This method returns a handle to the icon you load. I suppose this is okay, but an easier method is to load the icon using a .NET method and get the handle that way. No need to resort to the API. Consider the following code snippet that uses this method:

VB

```
Dim ico As Icon = New Icon("d:\\usa.ico")
Dim b As Bitmap = Bitmap.FromHicon(ico.Handle)
```

C#

```
Icon ico = new Icon("d:\\usa.ico");
Bitmap b = Bitmap.FromHicon(ico.Handle);
```

Okay, I got those two out of the way—now on to the more exciting methods. Let's start with the thumbnail. You have all seen thumbnail images before in photo programs. In fact, Windows can display thumbnail images in Windows Explorer if you so choose.

A *thumbnail* image is just a smaller version of a full-size bitmap. That's it. Try creating a small program with an overridden **OnPaint** method:

VB

```
Protected Overrides Sub OnPaint(ByVal e As PaintEventArgs)
  Dim B As Image = Bitmap.FromFile("d:\\sample.jpg")
  Dim Tom As Image = B.GetThumbnailImage(100, 100, Nothing, New IntPtr())

  e.Graphics.DrawImage(Tom, New Point(10, 10))
End Sub
```

C#

```
protected override void OnPaint(PaintEventArgs e)
{
  Image B = Bitmap.FromFile("d:\\sample.jpg");
  Image Tom  = B.GetThumbnailImage(100, 100, null, new IntPtr());

  e.Graphics.DrawImage(Tom, new Point(10, 10));
}
```

Run the program and you will see a thumbnail image on the screen. The **GetThumbnailImage** method requires that you provide it with the name of a delegate. The documentation mentions that version 1 of GDI+ does not actually call this delegate. You can make a dummy one if you like, or you can do what I did and send it a null pointer.

The **RotateFlip** method is pretty self-explanatory. It takes an image and rotates it, flips it, or both. This method takes an enumerated value from the RotateFlipType enumeration. Table 6-3 shows this enumeration and the manipulations you can perform.

Table 6-3. RotateFlipType Enumeration

Enumerator	Description
RotateNoneFlipNone	No rotation, no flip
RotateNoneFlipX	No rotation with X-axis flip
RotateNoneFlipY	No rotation with Y-axis flip
RotateNoneFlipXY	No rotation with X-axis and Y-axis flip
Rotate90FlipNone	Rotate 90 degrees with no flip
Rotate90FlipX	Rotate 90 degrees with X-axis flip
Rotate90FlipY	Rotate 90 degrees with Y-axis flip
Rotate90FlipXY	Rotate 90 degrees with X-axis and Y-axis flip
Rotate180FlipNone	Rotate 180 degrees with no flip
Rotate180FlipX	Rotate 180 degrees with X-axis flip
Rotate180FlipY	Rotate 180 degrees with Y-axis flip
Rotate180FlipXY	Rotate 180 degrees with X-axis and Y-axis flip
Rotate270FlipNone	Rotate 270 degrees with no flip
Rotate270FlipX	Rotate 270 degrees with X-axis flip
Rotate270FlipY	Rotate 270 degrees with Y-axis flip
Rotate270FlipXY	Rotate 270 degrees with X-axis and Y-axis flip

The first enumerator (no rotation, no flip) seems kind of useless to me. The first program I thought of that uses the flip and rotate feature was Visio.[7] Visio is basically a flowcharting tool. It allows you to flip and rotate images on its screen.

---

7. The .NET architect version comes with Visio as its UML designer.

The next example builds upon all you know about bitmaps, events, and fast drawing. I add one extra twist, though: the ImageAttributes class.

The **ImageAttributes** class contains information about how an image is to be rendered. This class is instantiated completely separately from any individual drawing element. When that drawing element is rendered, you can use this class to define how the colors of that element are manipulated. I talk about drawing elements. This is because **ImageAttributes** can apply to any of the following objects:

- Bitmap

- Brush

- Pen

- Text

The **ImageAttributes** class has many methods, all of which pertain to how colors are rendered during drawing. The method I use in the next example is one that sets the ColorMatrix for the image.

The **ColorMatrix** is a 5×5 matrix of values that represent red, green, blue, alpha, and w. The value for w is always 1. The properties for the **ColorMatrix** object let you get or set values for any point in the matrix. For instance, one of the properties is **ColorMatrix.Matrix23**. This represents the element of the second row of the third column of the matrix.

Because an **ImageAttributes** object can apply to a whole bitmap I can set the transparency for the whole bitmap. You will see from the next example that I use the **ImageAttributes** class for a pretty cool effect.

Time for the example. Open a new VB or C# Windows project. Mine is called BitmapExt. Before you add any code, perform the following steps:

1. Resize the form to 400×400.

2. Remove the MinimizeBox and MaximizeBox.

3. Set the start-up position to CenterScreen.

4. Add a button to the bottom right-hand corner of the form. Call it cmdGo and set the text property to "GO".

5. Add a timer to the form and call it T1.

6. Double-click the timer and accept the default event handler.

7. Double-click the button and change the name of the event handler to "Explode".

271

Now it is time to add code. First of all, what this example does is create a bitmap from a picture on disk. (I used one from my D: drive. You should use one of similar size.) When you click the GO button, the picture explodes into four pieces that spin off while fading into oblivion. I think this is a pretty cool example, and if you think about it, the techniques I use here can apply to any number of situations.

Listing 6-2 shows the code for this example in both VB and C#. Again, I limit the amount of wizard-generated code shown here because you will never touch most of it. The class constructor and class **Dispose** methods for any VB project are within the "Windows Form Designer generated code" region. I will show these two methods here.

Listing 6-2a. C# Code for the Bitmap Explode Example

```
using System;
using System.Drawing;
using System.Drawing.Drawing2D;
using System.Drawing.Imaging;
using System.Collections;
using System.ComponentModel;
using System.Windows.Forms;
using System.Data;

namespace BitMapExt_c
{
  public class Form1 : System.Windows.Forms.Form
  {

    #region Class Local Variables

    private Bitmap WholeBMP;
    private Bitmap SaveBMP;
    private Bitmap TLBMP;
    private Bitmap TRBMP;
    private Bitmap BLBMP;
    private Bitmap BRBMP;

    private Rectangle DrawRect;
    private Point TLpt;
    private Point TRpt;
    private Point BLpt;
    private Point BRpt;
    private int Counter = 0;
```

```
private ImageAttributes Ia;


#endregion
private System.ComponentModel.IContainer components;
private System.Windows.Forms.Timer T1;


private System.Windows.Forms.Button cmdGo;


public Form1()
{
  InitializeComponent();

  this.SetStyle(ControlStyles.DoubleBuffer, true);
  this.SetStyle(ControlStyles.AllPaintingInWmPaint, true);

  WholeBMP = new Bitmap("D:\\crane.jpg");
  DrawRect = new Rectangle(0, 0, WholeBMP.Width, WholeBMP.Height);
  DrawRect.X = this.Width/2 - WholeBMP.Width/2;
  DrawRect.Y = this.Height/2 - WholeBMP.Height/2;
  T1.Interval = 75;
  T1.Enabled = false;
}


protected override void Dispose( bool disposing )
{
  if( disposing )
  {
    if (components != null)
    {
      components.Dispose();
    }
  }
  If (WholeBMP != null)
    WholeBMP.Dispose();
  If (SaveBMP != null)
    SaveBMP.Dispose();
  If (TLBMP != null)
    TLBMP.Dispose();
  If (TRBMP != null)
    TRBMP.Dispose();
  If (BLBMP != null)
    BLBMP.Dispose();
  If (BRBMP != null)
    BRBMP.Dispose();
```

```
      If (Ia != null)
        Ia.Dispose();
      base.Dispose( disposing );
    }

    #region Windows Form Designer generated code
...
...
...
    #endregion

    [STAThread]
    static void Main()
    {
      Application.Run(new Form1());
    }

    private void Form1_Load(object sender, System.EventArgs e)
    {
    }

    protected override void OnPaint(PaintEventArgs e)
    {
      Graphics G = e.Graphics;

      if ( WholeBMP != null )
      {
        G.DrawImage(WholeBMP, DrawRect);
        return;
      }

      if ( TLBMP != null )
        G.DrawImage( TLBMP, new Rectangle(TLpt, TLBMP.Size),
          0, 0,
          TLBMP.Width, TLBMP.Height,
          GraphicsUnit.Pixel,
          Ia );

      if ( TRBMP != null )
        G.DrawImage( TRBMP, new Rectangle(TRpt, TRBMP.Size),
          0, 0,
          TRBMP.Width, TRBMP.Height,
          GraphicsUnit.Pixel,
          Ia );
```

```
  if ( BLBMP != null )
    G.DrawImage( BLBMP, new Rectangle(BLpt, BLBMP.Size),
      0, 0,
      BLBMP.Width, BLBMP.Height,
      GraphicsUnit.Pixel,
      Ia );

  if ( BRBMP != null )
    G.DrawImage( BRBMP, new Rectangle(BRpt, BRBMP.Size),
      0, 0,
      BRBMP.Width, BRBMP.Height,
      GraphicsUnit.Pixel,
      Ia );
  }

private void Explode(object sender, System.EventArgs e)
{
  if ( WholeBMP != null )
  {
    cmdGo.Enabled = false;
    int L = 0;
    int T = 0;
    int Cx = (int)(WholeBMP.Width/2);
    int Cy = (int)(WholeBMP.Height/2);

    SaveBMP = WholeBMP;
    TLBMP = WholeBMP.Clone(new Rectangle( L, T, Cx, Cy ),
                           WholeBMP.PixelFormat);
    TRBMP = WholeBMP.Clone(new Rectangle( Cx, T, Cx, Cy ),
                           WholeBMP.PixelFormat);
    BLBMP = WholeBMP.Clone(new Rectangle( L, Cy, Cx, Cy ),
                           WholeBMP.PixelFormat);
    BRBMP = WholeBMP.Clone(new Rectangle( Cx, Cy, Cx, Cy ),
                           WholeBMP.PixelFormat);

    WholeBMP = null;

    int Gap = 10;
    TLpt = new Point( DrawRect.Left-Gap, DrawRect.Top-Gap );
    TRpt = new Point( DrawRect.Left+Cx+Gap, DrawRect.Top-Gap );
    BLpt = new Point( DrawRect.Left-Gap, DrawRect.Top+Cy+Gap );
    BRpt = new Point( DrawRect.Left+Cx+Gap, DrawRect.Top+Cy+Gap );
```

```
      T1.Enabled = true;
      Invalidate();
   }
}

private void T1_Tick(object sender, System.EventArgs e)
{
  Counter += 1;
  if ( Counter == 62 )
  {
    Counter = 0;
    cmdGo.Enabled = true;
    T1.Enabled = false;
    WholeBMP = SaveBMP;
  }

  TLpt.X-=1;
  TLpt.Y-=1;

  TRpt.X+=1;
  TRpt.Y-=1;

  BLpt.X-=1;
  BLpt.Y+=1;

  BRpt.X+=1;
  BRpt.Y+=1;

  // Initialize a color matrix.
  //Set the alpha for the whole image
  float[][] m ={new float[] {1, 0, 0, 0, 0},
                new float[] {0, 1, 0, 0, 0},
                new float[] {0, 0, 1, 0, 0},
                new float[] {0, 0, 0, (1-(float)Counter/62), 0},
                new float[] {0, 0, 0, 0, 1}};
  ColorMatrix cm = new ColorMatrix(m);

  // Create an ImageAttributes object and set its color matrix.
  Ia = new ImageAttributes();
  Ia.SetColorMatrix( cm, ColorMatrixFlag.Default,
                          ColorAdjustType.Bitmap);
```

```
      TLBMP.RotateFlip(RotateFlipType.Rotate90FlipNone);
      TRBMP.RotateFlip(RotateFlipType.Rotate90FlipNone);
      BLBMP.RotateFlip(RotateFlipType.Rotate90FlipNone);
      BRBMP.RotateFlip(RotateFlipType.Rotate90FlipNone);

      Invalidate();
    }
  }
}
```

Listing 6-2b. VB Code for the Exploding Bitmap Example

```
Option Strict On

Imports System.Drawing
Imports System.Drawing.Drawing2D
Imports System.Drawing.Imaging

Public Class Form1
  Inherits System.Windows.Forms.Form

#Region "Class Local Variables"

  Private WholeBMP As Bitmap
  Private SaveBMP As Bitmap
  Private TLBMP As Bitmap
  Private TRBMP As Bitmap
  Private BLBMP As Bitmap
  Private BRBMP As Bitmap

  Private DrawRect As Rectangle
  Private TLpt As Point
  Private TRpt As Point
  Private BLpt As Point
  Private BRpt As Point
  Private Counter As Int32 = 0

  Private Ia As ImageAttributes

 #End Region

 #Region " Windows Form Designer generated code "
```

```vb
Public Sub New()
  MyBase.New()

  'This call is required by the Windows Form Designer.
  InitializeComponent()

  Me.SetStyle(ControlStyles.DoubleBuffer, True)
  Me.SetStyle(ControlStyles.AllPaintingInWmPaint, True)

  T1.Interval = 75
  T1.Enabled = False

  WholeBMP = New Bitmap("D:\\crane.jpg")
  DrawRect = New Rectangle(0, 0, WholeBMP.Width, WholeBMP.Height)
  DrawRect.X = CInt(Me.Width / 2 - WholeBMP.Width / 2)
  DrawRect.Y = CInt(Me.Height / 2 - WholeBMP.Height / 2)

End Sub

'Form overrides dispose to clean up the component list.
Protected Overloads Overrides Sub Dispose(ByVal disposing As Boolean)
  If disposing Then
    If Not (components Is Nothing) Then
      components.Dispose()
    End If
  End If
  If not WholeBMP Is Nothing then
    WholeBMP.Dispose()
  EndIf
  If not SaveBMP Is Nothing then
    SaveBMP.Dispose()
  EndIf
  If not TLBMP Is Nothing then
    TLBMP.Dispose()
  EndIf
  If not TRBMP Is Nothing then
    TRBMP.Dispose()
  EndIf
  If not BLBMP Is Nothing then
    BLBMP.Dispose()
  EndIf
  If not BRBMP Is Nothing then
    BRBMP.Dispose()
  EndIf
```

```
    If not Ia Is Nothing then
      Ia.Dispose()
    EndIf
    MyBase.Dispose(disposing)
  End Sub


  'Required by the Windows Form Designer
  Private components As System.ComponentModel.IContainer

...

...

...

#End Region

  Private Sub Form1_Load(ByVal sender As System.Object, _
                       ByVal e As System.EventArgs) Handles MyBase.Load
  End Sub

  Protected Overrides Sub OnPaint(ByVal e As PaintEventArgs)
    Dim G As Graphics = e.Graphics

    If Not WholeBMP Is Nothing Then
      G.DrawImage(WholeBMP, DrawRect)
      Return
    End If

    If Not TLBMP Is Nothing Then
      G.DrawImage(TLBMP, New Rectangle(TLpt, TLBMP.Size), _
        0, 0, _
        TLBMP.Width, TLBMP.Height, _
        GraphicsUnit.Pixel, _
        Ia)
    End If


    If Not TRBMP Is Nothing Then
      G.DrawImage(TRBMP, New Rectangle(TRpt, TRBMP.Size), _
        0, 0, _
        TRBMP.Width, TRBMP.Height, _
        GraphicsUnit.Pixel, _
        Ia)
    End If
```

```
      If Not BLBMP Is Nothing Then
        G.DrawImage(BLBMP, New Rectangle(BLpt, BLBMP.Size), _
            0, 0, _
            BLBMP.Width, BLBMP.Height, _
            GraphicsUnit.Pixel, _
            Ia)
      End If


      If Not BRBMP Is Nothing Then
        G.DrawImage(BRBMP, New Rectangle(BRpt, BRBMP.Size), _
            0, 0, _
            BRBMP.Width, BRBMP.Height, _
            GraphicsUnit.Pixel, _
            Ia)
      End If


  End Sub


  Private Sub Explode(ByVal sender As System.Object, _
                      ByVal e As System.EventArgs) Handles cmdGo.Click

    If Not WholeBMP Is Nothing Then
      cmdGo.Enabled = False
      Dim L As Int32 = 0
      Dim T As Int32 = 0
      'Round down is safer
      Dim Cx As Int32 = CInt(Math.Floor(WholeBMP.Width / 2))
      Dim Cy As Int32 = CInt(Math.Floor(WholeBMP.Height / 2))

      SaveBMP = WholeBMP
      TLBMP = WholeBMP.Clone(New Rectangle(L, T, Cx, Cy), WholeBMP.PixelFormat)
      TRBMP = WholeBMP.Clone(New Rectangle(Cx, T, Cx, Cy), WholeBMP.PixelFormat)
      BLBMP = WholeBMP.Clone(New Rectangle(L, Cy, Cx, Cy), WholeBMP.PixelFormat)
      BRBMP = WholeBMP.Clone(New Rectangle(Cx, Cy, Cx, Cy), WholeBMP.PixelFormat)
      WholeBMP = Nothing

      Dim Gap As Int32 = 10
      TLpt = New Point(DrawRect.Left - Gap, DrawRect.Top - Gap)
      TRpt = New Point(DrawRect.Left + Cx + Gap, DrawRect.Top - Gap)
      BLpt = New Point(DrawRect.Left - Gap, DrawRect.Top + Cy + Gap)
      BRpt = New Point(DrawRect.Left + Cx + Gap, DrawRect.Top + Cy + Gap)
```

```
      T1.Enabled = True
      Invalidate()
    End If

End Sub

Private Sub T1_Tick(ByVal sender As System.Object, _
                    ByVal e As System.EventArgs) Handles T1.Tick

    Counter += 1
    If Counter = 62 Then
      Counter = 0
      cmdGo.Enabled = True
      T1.Enabled = False
      WholeBMP = SaveBMP
    End If

    TLpt.X -= 1
    TLpt.Y -= 1

    TRpt.X += 1
    TRpt.Y -= 1

    BLpt.X -= 1
    BLpt.Y += 1

    BRpt.X += 1
    BRpt.Y += 1

    ' Initialize a color matrix.
    'Set the alpha for the whole image
    Dim m()() As Single = {New Single() {1, 0, 0, 0, 0}, _
                New Single() {0, 1, 0, 0, 0}, _
                New Single() {0, 0, 1, 0, 0}, _
                New Single() {0, 0, 0, (1 - CType(Counter, Single) / 62), 0}, _
                New Single() {0, 0, 0, 0, 1}}
    Dim cm As ColorMatrix = New ColorMatrix(m)

    ' Create an ImageAttributes object and set its color matrix.
    Ia = New ImageAttributes()
    Ia.SetColorMatrix(cm, ColorMatrixFlag.Default, _
                      ColorAdjustType.Bitmap)
```

```
      TLBMP.RotateFlip(RotateFlipType.Rotate90FlipNone)
      TRBMP.RotateFlip(RotateFlipType.Rotate90FlipNone)
      BLBMP.RotateFlip(RotateFlipType.Rotate90FlipNone)
      BRBMP.RotateFlip(RotateFlipType.Rotate90FlipNone)

      Invalidate()

   End Sub
End Class
```

Compile and run the program. If you used the same picture as I did (Crane.jpg is on your system somewhere), then you will see a picture of a bird centered on the form. Click the GO button and you will see the picture fracture into quarters and each piece fly off diagonally while spinning and fading out. When the pieces disappear, the form returns to its starting state. Figure 6-3 shows the form about one-third of the way though its cycle.

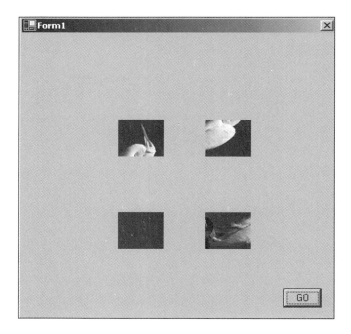

Figure 6-3. Exploding bitmap

Pretty cool, huh? Now it is time to dissect the code. I start with the form's constructor. Notice that I set the form up for high-speed painting using double buffering. You have seen this in previous examples. I also use the properties of the bitmap to create a rectangle within which I draw the picture. This rectangle is centered on the form.

Let's look at the **OnPaint** method. The VB version is repeated here:

```
Protected Overrides Sub OnPaint(ByVal e As PaintEventArgs)
  Dim G As Graphics = e.Graphics

  If Not WholeBMP Is Nothing Then
    G.DrawImage(WholeBMP, DrawRect)
    Return
  End If

  If Not TLBMP Is Nothing Then
    G.DrawImage(TLBMP, New Rectangle(TLpt, TLBMP.Size), _
      0, 0, _
      TLBMP.Width, TLBMP.Height, _
      GraphicsUnit.Pixel, _
      Ia)
  End If


  If Not TRBMP Is Nothing Then
    G.DrawImage(TRBMP, New Rectangle(TRpt, TRBMP.Size), _
      0, 0, _
      TRBMP.Width, TRBMP.Height, _
      GraphicsUnit.Pixel, _
      Ia)
  End If

  If Not BLBMP Is Nothing Then
    G.DrawImage(BLBMP, New Rectangle(BLpt, BLBMP.Size), _
      0, 0, _
      BLBMP.Width, BLBMP.Height, _
      GraphicsUnit.Pixel, _
      Ia)
  End If

  If Not BRBMP Is Nothing Then
    G.DrawImage(BRBMP, New Rectangle(BRpt, BRBMP.Size), _
      0, 0, _
      BRBMP.Width, BRBMP.Height, _
      GraphicsUnit.Pixel, _
      Ia)
  End If
End Sub
```

I use the **DrawImage** method to get each of the four bitmaps on the screen. The main bitmap is called WholeBMP and is drawn using a version of the **DrawImage** method that doesn't use an ImageAttributes object. This is because I want to draw it completely opaque.

The other images are drawn using a version of the **DrawImage** method that accepts an ImageAttributes object. This is how I make the four quadrants fade out.

Notice that I test for a current instance of each object before I draw it. This is because I set the individual bitmaps to null at certain times in the code. Why draw what I do not need to draw?

Okay, I mentioned the four quadrant images. These are created in the **Explode** method. This method is the click event handler for the button. The VB version is repeated here:

```
Private Sub Explode(ByVal sender As System.Object, _
                    ByVal e As System.EventArgs) Handles cmdGo.Click

    If Not WholeBMP Is Nothing Then
      cmdGo.Enabled = False
      Dim L As Int32 = 0
      Dim T As Int32 = 0
      'Round down is safer
      Dim Cx As Int32 = CInt(Math.Floor(WholeBMP.Width / 2))
      Dim Cy As Int32 = CInt(Math.Floor(WholeBMP.Height / 2))

      SaveBMP = WholeBMP
      TLBMP = WholeBMP.Clone(New Rectangle(L, T, Cx, Cy), WholeBMP.PixelFormat)
      TRBMP = WholeBMP.Clone(New Rectangle(Cx, T, Cx, Cy), WholeBMP.PixelFormat)
      BLBMP = WholeBMP.Clone(New Rectangle(L, Cy, Cx, Cy), WholeBMP.PixelFormat)
      BRBMP = WholeBMP.Clone(New Rectangle(Cx, Cy, Cx, Cy), WholeBMP.PixelFormat)
      WholeBMP = Nothing

      Dim Gap As Int32 = 10
      TLpt = New Point(DrawRect.Left - Gap, DrawRect.Top - Gap)
      TRpt = New Point(DrawRect.Left + Cx + Gap, DrawRect.Top - Gap)
      BLpt = New Point(DrawRect.Left - Gap, DrawRect.Top + Cy + Gap)
      BRpt = New Point(DrawRect.Left + Cx + Gap, DrawRect.Top + Cy + Gap)

      T1.Enabled = True
      Invalidate()
    End If
End Sub
```

In this method I find out the necessary sizes of the rectangle needed to hold one-fourth of the picture. I then use the **Bitmap.Clone** method to create those four quadrant bitmaps. I save the original bitmap and then set it to nothing. The **OnPaint** method detects this and does not try to draw the original bitmap.

The Point structures are where I hold the locations of where each of the four bitmaps is to be drawn. The gap variable represents the starting fracture space between each bitmap. Once I have filled in the Point structures, I enable the timer and invalidate the form so these images will be painted.

The last function in this example is the timer tick event handler. I set the timer to go off every 75 milliseconds. Each time this happens, I change the location of each bitmap, rotate each bitmap by 90 degrees, and increase the fading of each bitmap. I then invalidate the form and wait for the next timer tick. The VB code showing the timer tick event handler is as follows:

```
Private Sub T1_Tick(ByVal sender As System.Object, _
                    ByVal e As System.EventArgs) Handles T1.Tick

    Counter += 1
    If Counter = 62 Then
      Counter = 0
      cmdGo.Enabled = True
      T1.Enabled = False
      WholeBMP = SaveBMP
    End If

    TLpt.X -= 1
    TLpt.Y -= 1

    TRpt.X += 1
    TRpt.Y -= 1

    BLpt.X -= 1
    BLpt.Y += 1

    BRpt.X += 1
    BRpt.Y += 1
```

```
' Initialize a color matrix.
'Set the alpha for the whole image
Dim m()() As Single = {New Single() {1, 0, 0, 0, 0}, _
            New Single() {0, 1, 0, 0, 0}, _
            New Single() {0, 0, 1, 0, 0}, _
            New Single() {0, 0, 0, (1 - CType(Counter, Single) / 62), 0}, _
            New Single() {0, 0, 0, 0, 1}}
Dim cm As ColorMatrix = New ColorMatrix(m)

' Create an ImageAttributes object and set its color matrix.
Ia = New ImageAttributes()
Ia.SetColorMatrix(cm, ColorMatrixFlag.Default, _
                    ColorAdjustType.Bitmap)

TLBMP.RotateFlip(RotateFlipType.Rotate90FlipNone)
TRBMP.RotateFlip(RotateFlipType.Rotate90FlipNone)
BLBMP.RotateFlip(RotateFlipType.Rotate90FlipNone)
BRBMP.RotateFlip(RotateFlipType.Rotate90FlipNone)

Invalidate()
End Sub
```

Let's go a little deeper into this method. The first thing I do is increment the counter to a certain point. When I am finished with the timer, I turn off the timer, re-enable the button, and restore the original bitmap.

You can see that I am spreading the starting locations of the four bitmaps farther out each time I enter this function. This is what gives the appearance of an explosion.

The next thing I do after spreading out the bitmaps some more is change the alpha value of each bitmap through the ColorMatrix object. One thing to notice here is that I use the following equation to determine the alpha value of the bitmap:

```
(1 - CType(Counter, Single) / 62)
```

Why do I subtract the value from 1? I leave that to you to experiment with.[8]

The last thing I do before I invalidate the form is rotate each image by 90 degrees. All of this makes it look like the image is spinning off while fading away. Any clues as to how you would make the images look like they are spinning off into the distance? You know enough about GDI+ by now to figure this one out.

---

8. If I did not subtract from 1, the images would start out invisible and end up visible.

Bitmap Speed

Drawing bitmaps to the screen is probably the most common and yet time-consuming task in graphics programming. It would be, anyhow, without the BitBlt function.

Anyone who has done graphics programming has eventually needed to dip down into the Win32 API and use the **BitBlt** method to draw a bitmap to the screen. This is probably one of the most used API commands for VB 6.0 programmers. **BitBlt** stands for *bit block transfer*.

All bitmaps consist of a rectangular block of pixels. Windows has a function to take that rectangular block and copy it directly from one part of memory to another part. This is the transfer. The **BitBlt** method of drawing bitmaps is so ubiquitous that most graphics cards are tuned to handle this type of transfer. In fact, it can often be done in one cycle.

I said at the beginning of this chapter that the **BitBlt** was not gone in GDI+, it had just morphed. The **DrawImage** and **DrawImageUnscaled** methods use the **BitBlt** API command internally.

.NET was designed to be as complete as possible so programmers would not need to resort to API calls. Encapsulating the **BitBlt** is just further proof of that.

Working with Bitmap Colors

Four methods allow you to directly manipulate the colors of individual pixels:

- Bitmap.Palette

- Bitmap.GetPixel

- Bitmap.SetPixel

- Bitmap.MakeTransparent

Each of these methods either takes or returns a Color object. In the case of **Palette**, what you get in return is an array of Color objects in the form of a ColorPalette object.

Here is how you would use the **Bitmap.Palette** method:

VB

```
Dim cp As ColorPalette
Dim s As String
Dim bmp As Bitmap = New Bitmap("D:\\lock.bmp")
```

```
cp = bmp.Palette
Dim c As Color
For Each c In cp.Entries
  s = c.ToString()
Next
```

C#

```
ColorPalette cp;
String s;
Bitmap bmp = new Bitmap("D:\\lock.bmp");

cp = bmp.Palette;
foreach (Color c in cp.Entries)
{
  s = c.ToString();
}
```

I said that the ColorPalette object contains an array of colors. This array can be iterated as shown in the previous code snippet. Look closely and you will see that I used a For Each construct. Fans of VB 6.0 collections will be familiar with this code. However, in VB 6.0 you could only iterate natively over collections. .NET allows you to iterate using the For Each construct over collections *or* arrays. This is most welcome for someone like me who is one of the world's biggest fans of collections.

For those of you unfamiliar with the For Each construct, notice that nowhere do I try to discover the bounds of the array. If there is nothing in the array, this loop will fall through; otherwise, the loop will be entered for each member of the array.

 NOTE *I urge you to discover collections, arrays, and iterators in .NET. They will make your programming life simpler and your code easier to read.*

Let's try setting the colors of some individual pixels. The **GetPixel** method returns a Color structure and the **SetPixel** method takes a Color structure as an argument. You can do some interesting things with these two methods. The next small example changes the color of every pixel on the screen by adding a fixed amount to the blue component. Start a new project in either VB or C#. This project will be very small, so I will only show the **OnPaint** method in Listing 6-3.

Listing 6-3a. VB Code for the OnPaint Method for the BitmapColor Example

```vb
Protected Overrides Sub OnPaint(ByVal e As PaintEventArgs)
  Dim bmp As Bitmap = New Bitmap("D:\\crane.jpg")
  Dim c As Color
  Dim x, y As Int32

  e.Graphics.DrawImage(bmp, 10, 30)

  For x = 0 To bmp.Width - 1
    For y = 0 To bmp.Height - 1
      c = bmp.GetPixel(x, y)
      c = Color.FromArgb(c.ToArgb() + 100)
      bmp.SetPixel(x, y, c)
    Next
  Next

  e.Graphics.DrawImage(bmp, 150, 30)
End Sub
```

Listing 6-3b. C# Code for the OnPaint Method for the BitmapColor Example

```csharp
protected override void OnPaint(PaintEventArgs e)
{
  Bitmap bmp = new Bitmap("D:\\crane.jpg");
  Color c;

  e.Graphics.DrawImage( bmp, 10, 30 );

  for ( int x=0; x<bmp.Width-1; x++ )
  {
    for ( int y=0; y<bmp.Height-1; y++ )
    {
      c = bmp.GetPixel( x, y );
      c = Color.FromArgb( c.ToArgb() + 100 );
      bmp.SetPixel( x, y, c );
    }
  }
  e.Graphics.DrawImage( bmp, 150, 30 );
}
```

The ARGB 32-bit sequence is AARRGGBB, where AA are the alpha bits, RR are the red bytes, GG are the green bits, and BB are the blue bits. As you can see from the code, I am increasing the blue component of each pixel by 100. This gives a neat reverse color effect. Try running it and fooling around with the color component. Try altering every third byte.

I will say this about the previous example: If you change the least significant bit of the ARGB 32-bit value in each pixel, the human eye will not notice any difference in the picture. This applies mostly to complicated pictures, such as nature scenes. So what, you say? Think about this: What could you do by stealing a single bit in each pixel of a picture? Perhaps hide some information? Hiding information inside a picture comes under the topic of Steganography.

Saving Bitmaps

Want to see how easy it is to save a bitmap in another format? All along I have been creating a bitmap with a constructor that takes a JPEG file (or any other supported file type) as an argument. Now I will show you how to convert a JPEG file to a BMP file:

VB

```
Dim bmp As Bitmap = New Bitmap("D:\\Crane.jpg")
bmp.Save("d:\crane.bmp", ImageFormat.Bmp)
```

C#

```
Bitmap bmp = new Bitmap("d:\\crane.jpg");
bmp.Save("d:\\crane.bmp", ImageFormat.Bmp);
```

Voila! You have converted the JPEG file to a BMP file. The file formats you can save images in are as follows:

- ImageFormat.Bmp

- ImageFormat.Emf

- ImageFormat.Exif

- ImageFormat.Gif

- ImageFormat.Icon

- ImageFormat.Jpeg

- ImageFormat.MemoryBmp

- ImageFormat.Png

- ImageFormat.Tiff

- ImageFormat.Wmf

- ImageFormat.Guid

This last one is interesting. This GUID refers to a 128-bit unique number that represents an ImageFormat object. It is possible to encode your own format (and many companies do), and then save your bitmap to a file using this format.[9]

The Icon Class

So what is an icon, anyway? Well, an *icon* is a small bitmap. In fact, it is a transparent bitmap whose size is set by the system. Often you will find icons that are 16×16 or 32×32 pixels. These are often considered small and large icons, respectively.

The Icon class has four properties:

- Height

- Width

- Size

- Handle

Besides being able to save and create icons, you are able to convert an icon into a bitmap with the **ToBitmap** method. Why convert an icon? Suppose you did not like the colors in your icon. You could convert the icon to a bitmap, change the colors, and then save it as an icon again. Easy.

.NET allows you to create a special icon: NotifyIcon. This class is actually in the System.Windows.Forms namespace, which should give you some clue as to its purpose.

A NotifyIcon icon sits in the system tray at the bottom right of your task bar. It is normally used when there is no constant user interface to a program. An antivirus program is one such example.

---

9. COM programmers know all about GUIDs. .NET uses them extensively for other things.

These icons have their own events and methods that allow you to create tool tip text and pop-up menus. They also have a **Visible** property that allows the user to see the icon or not. Here is a C# sample of how to use it:

```
NotifyIcon i = new NotifyIcon();
i.Icon = new Icon("d:\\usa.ico");
i.Visible=true;
i.Text="Hello, status bar";
```

Make a program with these four lines of code and you will see your icon in the status bar. Move your mouse over it and you will see the tool tip text pop-up with the words "Hello, status bar".

Vector-Based Images

The last type of image I cover in this chapter is a *metafile.* A metafile does not really contain an image per se; rather, it contains a set of instructions on how to create an image. Mostly, the types of images I am referring to are line drawings.

Let me provide a little background here. A normal image, such as a bitmap, JPEG, TIFF, or GIF, is called a *raster image.* Raster images contain information about each individual pixel that must be rendered on the screen. For the most part, an image such as a metafile is called a *vector image.* A vector image is one that contains the drawing instructions itself.

Creating Metafiles

Because metafiles are vector-based files, they can contain as many drawing instructions as you like. It is possible using .NET to enumerate through each instruction one at a time and to carry out that drawing instruction or not. Because a metafile is derived from an image, it can also be displayed using the **DrawImage** method. Metafiles come in the following formats:

- Windows metafile (.wmf)

- Enhanced metafile (.emf)

- EMF+

Version 1 of GDI+ is unable to record metafiles in the .wmf format. There are two versions of the EMF+ format: the EMF+-only version and the EMF+ dual version. The "only" version can only be displayed by GDI+ (and not GDI). The "dual" version can be displayed by both GDI+ and GDI.

You can create a metafile any number of ways. In fact, there are 39 overloaded constructors for creating metafiles.

You can, of course, instantiate a metafile from a disk file and draw it using the **DrawImage** method. This is no different from loading and displaying a bitmap or GIF file. Been there, done that.

What is not so easy or intuitive is how to create a metafile and record drawing instructions. The next example shows you how to do this. Basically, this example follows these steps:

1. Create a Graphics object from the current form.

2. Create a handle to the Graphics object.

3. Create a new metafile with a file name. Use the handle created in step 2.

4. Create a new Graphics object based on the metafile.

5. Draw stuff on the new Graphics object.

That's it. As you draw on the new metafile Graphics object, your drawing instructions will get recorded in the metafile. Listing 6-4 shows the code for an example that creates and displays a metafile.

Start a new Windows Forms project in either VB or C#. Mine is called Metafile. This example is very simple, so I will show the Form_Load event and the OnPaint event only.

Listing 6-4a. VB Code Showing How to Create a Metafile

```
Private Sub Form1_Load(ByVal sender As System.Object, _
                       ByVal e As System.EventArgs) Handles MyBase.Load

    ' Create a graphics object from the form's graphics object
    ' and get the handle to it.
    Dim FormGraphics As Graphics = Me.CreateGraphics()
    Dim hdc As IntPtr = FormGraphics.GetHdc()

    ' Now create a blank metafile using the graphics handle
    ' This is the metafile where all drawing instructions will
    ' be recorded.
    Dim mf As Metafile = New Metafile("d:\\mymeta.emf", hdc)
```

```
    ' In order to record drawing commands we need to draw on something
    ' That something is a new graphics object
    Dim MetaGraphics As Graphics = Graphics.FromImage(mf)

    MetaGraphics.SmoothingMode = SmoothingMode.AntiAlias

    'Now we are ready to draw on the metagraphics object
    MetaGraphics.DrawRectangle(Pens.Black, 10, 10, 100, 50)
    MetaGraphics.DrawLine(Pens.Orange, 10, 70, 150, 100)

    'Dispose of temporary stuff
    MetaGraphics.Dispose()
    mf.Dispose()
    FormGraphics.ReleaseHdc(hdc)
    FormGraphics.Dispose()

  End Sub

  Protected Overrides Sub OnPaint(ByVal e As PaintEventArgs)

    Dim mf As Metafile = New Metafile("d:\\mymeta.emf")
    e.Graphics.DrawImage(mf, New Point(10, 10))

  End Sub
```

Listing 6-4b. C# Code Showing How to Create a Metafile

```
    private void Form1_Load(object sender, System.EventArgs e)
    {
      // Create a graphics object from the form's graphics object
      // and get the handle to it.
      using (Graphics FormGraphics = this.CreateGraphics())
      {
        IntPtr hdc = FormGraphics.GetHdc();

        // Now create a blank metafile using the graphics handle
        // This is the metafile where all drawing instructions will
        // be recorded.
        Metafile mf = new Metafile("d:\\mymeta.emf", hdc);
```

```
    // In order to record drawing commands we need to draw on something
    // That something is a new graphics object
    using (Graphics MetaGraphics = Graphics.FromImage(mf))
    {
      using ( mf )
      {
        MetaGraphics.SmoothingMode = SmoothingMode.AntiAlias;

        //Now we are ready to draw on the metagraphics object
        MetaGraphics.DrawRectangle(Pens.Black, 10, 10, 100, 50 );
        MetaGraphics.DrawLine(Pens.Orange, 10, 70, 150, 100 );
      }
    }
    FormGraphics.ReleaseHdc(hdc);
  }
}

protected override void OnPaint( PaintEventArgs e )
{
  Metafile mf = new Metafile("d:\\mymeta.emf");
  e.Graphics.DrawImage(mf, new Point(10,10));
}
```

As you can see, I create a file using the HDC for the current form's Graphics
object. I then create another Graphics object on which to draw. This new Graphics
object is based on the metafile. Once this is done, I can use any of the drawing
functions and release the objects when I am done.

Look closely at the code. You will see that I am changing the smoothing mode
of the MetaGraphics object. This command is also getting saved in the metafile.
When I display the file in the **OnPaint** method, the line is smooth. I think this is
pretty neat.

I would like to draw your attention to the C# code. Notice that I do not explicitly
dispose of any objects. This is because I am using the **Using** statement. Some time
back, I said that you could use this statement to automatically call D**ispose** on an
object when it goes out of scope. It makes for less code and it also means that I
do not have to remember to dispose of my objects. Notice that I use the **Using**
statement both during object instantiation and in the case of the metafile, after it
has been instantiated and used once. This is perfectly valid.

Enumerating Metafiles

So what else can you do with a metafile? How about enumerating it? If a metafile is a set of drawing commands and graphics settings, it stands to reason that you should know what those commands are and display them. In fact, you can do this with a method for the Graphics class called **EnumerateMetafile**. You may think it strange that the metafile class itself does not have this method, but if you think about it, this makes sense. The Graphics object is responsible for drawing everything, and enumerating a metafile is nothing more than drawing the individual records contained in the metafile.

I played around quite a bit with metafiles trying to figure out the best way to draw individual records contained within a metafile. The documentation is rather scant on this subject, and after some experimentation I found that some things do not work. Do not fret, though, as I have discovered a method that does work and I will show it to you shortly.

Basically, what is supposed to happen is this:

1. Create a callback method that does something with each record from a metafile.

2. Pass this callback method as an argument to the **Graphics.Enumerate-Metafile** method.

3. This method sends each individual record to your callback method, which is responsible for doing something with it.

Now, this sounds simple enough until you see what the signature of the callback method is:

```
private bool MetafileCallback( EmfPlusRecordType recordType, int flags,
                               int dataSize, IntPtr data,
                               PlayRecordCallback callbackData);
```

Note that this delegate signature contains as the last argument another delegate. This is very unusual, to say the least. So what is this other delegate? Well, it is one that is supplied by the .NET Framework to play individual records. Fine. Listing 6-5 shows a snippet of a C# program that sets up the callback method necessary for enumerating records in a metafile.

Listing 6-5. Metafile Enumeration Delegate Definition

```
// Define callback method.
private bool MetafileCallback( EmfPlusRecordType recordType, int flags,
                                   int dataSize, IntPtr data,
                                   PlayRecordCallback callbackData)
{
  if ( dataSize > 0 )
  {
    // Play metafile record.
    callbackData(recordType, flags, dataSize, data);
  }
  return true;
}
```

Alas, this does not work. Such promise, too. It seems that the folks at Microsoft left something out here. There is no such internal method that will play the metafile record. Perhaps it will be included in the next version.

What to do? What could you replace the **callbackData** method with? Look in the documentation for the metafile class and you will see a method called **PlayRecord**. This looks promising, except for one thing: It takes an array of data bytes as an argument. The EnumerateMetafileProc needs a delegate with a particular signature. Unfortunately, you only have access to the handle, which only points to the data.

The method I used is rather advanced and not really for the faint of heart. I used the InteropServices Marshal class to copy the data into my own array, and then I passed that array to the **PlayRecord** method. Listing 6-6 shows the same C# callback method that now uses the **PlayRecord** method of displaying records.

NOTE   *The InteropServices are a whole other ball of wax. As you can see, familiarity with this namespace and all its classes comes in handy for things other than making your program work with VB 6.0 legacy apps.*

Listing 6-6. Working Metafile Delegate Definintion

```
// Define callback method.
private bool MetafileCallback( EmfPlusRecordType recordType, int flags,
                                        int dataSize, IntPtr data,
                                        PlayRecordCallback callbackData)
{
  if ( dataSize > 0 )
  {
    byte[] D = new byte[dataSize];
    Marshal.Copy(data, D, 0, dataSize);
    mf.PlayRecord(recordType, flags, dataSize, D);
  }
  return true;
}
```

I have bypassed the nonworking **callbackData** method and replaced it with my own. There is one drawback to this method, though. The **PlayRecord** method is part of an instance of a particular metafile. Because I am prohibited from passing in the metafile, it must be local to the class as a whole. (Sigh.)

So, one of the parameters to this delegate is the **EmfPlusRecordType** member that tells you what the current record is supposed to do. Using this flag, you can selectively play records from a metafile. Suppose you had a metafile with lots of different shapes, including lines, and you wanted to display all the shapes *except* for lines. You would do something like this:

```
if (recordType != EmfPlusRecordType.DrawLines)
{
  byte[] D = new byte[dataSize];
  Marshal.Copy(data, D, 0, dataSize);
  mf.PlayRecord(recordType, flags, dataSize, D);
}
```

In this case, "Just *Don't* Do It."

The next example is a short one, but it shows you some basic concepts having to do with displaying metafiles. This example displays the metafile you made using the example code in Listing 6-4. This metafile is very small in that it only contains two drawing instructions. The first is to draw a rectangle and the next one is to draw a line. It also sets the antialiasing mode of the Graphics object. This example also displays the steps that are taken by the metafile rendering method.

First, make a new C# or VB project. Mine is called MetaEnum. Add a list box and call it LB. Listing 6-7 shows the fairly minimal code for this example.

Listing 6-7a. VB Code to Enumerate a Metafile

```vb
Option Strict On

Imports System.Drawing
Imports System.Drawing.Drawing2D
Imports System.Drawing.Imaging
Imports System.Runtime.InteropServices

Public Class Form1
  Inherits System.Windows.Forms.Form

  Dim mf As Metafile = New Metafile("d:\\mymeta.emf")

#Region " Windows Form Designer generated code "

  Public Sub New()
    MyBase.New()
    InitializeComponent()
  End Sub

  'Form overrides dispose to clean up the component list.
  Protected Overloads Overrides Sub Dispose(ByVal disposing As Boolean)
    If disposing Then
      If Not (components Is Nothing) Then
        components.Dispose()
      End If
    End If
    mf.Dispose()
    MyBase.Dispose(disposing)
  End Sub

  ...
  ...


#End Region

  Private Sub Form1_Load(ByVal sender As System.Object, _
                   ByVal e As System.EventArgs) Handles MyBase.Load

  End Sub
```

```
        Protected Overrides Sub OnPaint(ByVal e As PaintEventArgs)
          Dim G As Graphics = e.Graphics
          G.EnumerateMetafile(mf, New Point(50, 50), _
                     New Graphics.EnumerateMetafileProc _
                     (AddressOf Me.MetafileCallback))
        End Sub

        Private Function MetafileCallback(ByVal recordType As EmfPlusRecordType, _
                                     ByVal flags As Int32, _
                                     ByVal dataSize As Int32, _
                                     ByVal data As IntPtr, _
                                     ByVal callbackData As PlayRecordCallback) _
                                     As Boolean
          LB.Items.Add(recordType)
          If dataSize > 0 Then
            Dim D(dataSize) As Byte
            Marshal.Copy(data, D, 0, dataSize)
            mf.PlayRecord(recordType, flags, dataSize, D)
          End If
          Return True
        End Function
    End Class
```

Listing 6-7b. C# Code to Enumerate a Metafile

```csharp
using System;
using System.Drawing;
using System.Drawing.Drawing2D;
using System.Drawing.Imaging;
using System.Collections;
using System.ComponentModel;
using System.Windows.Forms;
using System.Data;
using System.Runtime.InteropServices;

namespace MetaEnum_c
{
  public class Form1 : System.Windows.Forms.Form
  {
    private System.ComponentModel.Container components = null;
    private System.Windows.Forms.ListBox LB;

    Metafile mf = new  Metafile("d:\\mymeta.emf");
```

```
public Form1()
{
  InitializeComponent();
}

protected override void Dispose( bool disposing )
{
  if( disposing )
  {
    if (components != null)
    {
      components.Dispose();
    }
  }
  mf.Dispose();
  base.Dispose( disposing );
}

#region Windows Form Designer generated code
...
...
#endregion

[STAThread]
static void Main()
{
  Application.Run(new Form1());
}

private void Form1_Load(object sender, System.EventArgs e)
{
}

protected override void OnPaint(PaintEventArgs e)
{
  Graphics G = e.Graphics;
  G.EnumerateMetafile( mf, new Point( 50, 50 ),
              new Graphics.EnumerateMetafileProc(this.MetafileCallback) );

}
```

```
// Define callback method.
private bool MetafileCallback( EmfPlusRecordType recordType, int flags,
                                        int dataSize, IntPtr data,
                                        PlayRecordCallback callbackData)
{
  LB.Items.Add(recordType);
  if ( dataSize > 0 )
  {
    byte[] D = new byte[dataSize];
    Marshal.Copy(data, D, 0, dataSize);
    mf.PlayRecord(recordType, flags, dataSize, D);
  }
  return true;
}
  }
}
```

The output for this program should look like Figure 6-4.

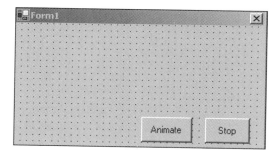

Figure 6-4. Result of metafile enumeration

Remember how to do this. I have not found this method anywhere. Notice that even though each figure in the metafile was generated at certain points on the screen, you are able to change the starting coordinates when you play it back.

So what else could you do with the ability to play back records of a metafile individually rather than just using the **DrawImage** method? How about a form of animation? Try this:

1. Make a structure that holds the four pieces of data needed by the **PlayRecord** method.

2. Instantiate and fill in this structure each time you enter the callback routine.

3. Save these structures in a collection or array.

You now have a set of structures that represent each record of the metafile. You can then use a timer to play back each drawing at a timed interval.

There is a better way to animate, though, using a different type of graphics file.

Simple Animation

Earlier in this chapter I covered the types of images that .NET supports. If you recall, I said that GIF files are able to hold a number of images. The reason for this is animation. Each image can represent a frame in an animation sequence. Each image can also be given a delay time in hundredths of a second. This allows you to create and show time-based animation.

Anyone who connects to the Internet sees animated GIFs. Whether it is some casino slot machine rolling all sevens or a page with a waving flag, you are seeing an animated GIF. Another place you see animation is the Copy dialog box in Windows Explorer. It shows two file cabinets with a piece of paper flying from one to the other.

What simple animation is *not* is a complete cartoon. Seamless animation like this requires a minimum of 15 frames per second. This is way too much bandwidth for a GIF file.

So, how do you animate a GIF file? You do it using a new class called ImageAnimator. This class has four static members:

- CanAnimate

- Animate

- StopAnimate

- UpdateFrames

The **CanAnimate** method returns a Boolean that indicates whether a particular image can be animated.

The **Animate** method takes as arguments the image to be animated and a delegate to another function that gets called when the next image needs to be displayed. This delegate is really a callback function for the animator code.

The **StopAnimate** function terminates the process and disconnects the delegate. It therefore needs the same argument list as the **Animate** function.

The **UpdateFrames** method tells the animator to index the next frame in the animation sequence. If there is no argument to this method, all the currently animated images will be bumped up to the next frame. If you like, you can supply the image name as an argument, which forces only that image to be bumped up to the next frame.

It is possible to have quite a few images animated at the same time. The **UpdateFrames** method allows you to update all of them at once with a single call.

I know the next question you have: "How do I create an animated GIF?" A number of programs are available on the Internet to help you do just this. Some are free, but most are inexpensive shareware. I used a simple shareware program to generate the image in the next example. Of course, the next question you might have is "But can I do this in .NET?"

The answer is kind of. The code to generate an animated GIF needs to work with image encoders and the **Image.SaveAdd** method. However, there are built-in image encoders for saving JPEG files and TIFF files as multiframe files only. There is an EncoderValue enumeration in GDI+ that specifies a value for VersionGif87 and VersionGif89. Unfortunately, GDI+ version 1 does not support these two versions natively. Perhaps version 2 will. So all you can do with what GDI+ offers is save multiframe TIFF files. I will say this, though: You can build your own encoder to save time-based, multiframe GIF files as animations. This is beyond the scope of this book, however.[10]

The following example takes an animated GIF and displays it on the screen. The GIF is not one you will readily find anywhere, as I made it specifically for this example. You will find the GIF included with this example when you download the code for this book from the Downloads section of the Apress Web site (http://www.apress.com).

Start a new C# or VB project. Mine is called Animate. Perform the following steps before you enter in any code:

1. Size the form to be 320×184.

2. Make the form's position be CenterScreen.

3. Remove the form's Maximize and Minimize buttons. They are not needed.

4. Add a button to the bottom right of the screen called cmdStop. Change the text to "Stop".

---

10. UniSys owns the patent on LZW compression, which is used to compress GIF files. If you make a GIF animator, be sure you do not violate any patents.

5. Add a button next to the Stop button called cmdGo. Change the text to "Animate".

6. Double-click both buttons to get the event handler code.

I am not sure why Microsoft decided to make the default position for a form random. I find this annoying, so I always make the default position either center screen or center parent. Anyway, you now have a form ready to go. It should look like the one shown in Figure 6-5.

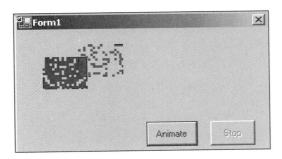

Figure 6-5. Basic form for animation example

The next step in this process is to enter code. Listing 6-8 shows the code for both the VB version and C# version of this example. The C# version will not show any code from the "Windows Form Designer generated code" region. The VB code will show the constructor and **Dispose** methods of the "Windows Form Designer generated code" region only.

Listing 6-8a. C# Code for the Animate Example

```csharp
using System;
using System.Drawing;
using System.Drawing.Drawing2D;
using System.Drawing.Imaging;
using System.Collections;
using System.ComponentModel;
using System.Windows.Forms;
using System.Data;
```

```
namespace Animate_c
{
  public class Form1 : System.Windows.Forms.Form
  {
    private System.Windows.Forms.Button cmdGo;
    /// <summary>
    /// Required designer variable.
    /// </summary>
    ///

    Bitmap RotatingBlocks;
    Point DrawHere;
    Rectangle InvalidRect;
    bool InProcess = false;
    private System.Windows.Forms.Button cmdStop;

    private System.ComponentModel.Container components = null;

    public Form1()
    {
      InitializeComponent();

      RotatingBlocks = new Bitmap("blocks.gif");
      DrawHere = new Point(10, 10);
      InvalidRect = new Rectangle(DrawHere, RotatingBlocks.Size);

      this.SetStyle(ControlStyles.AllPaintingInWmPaint,true);
      this.SetStyle(ControlStyles.DoubleBuffer,true);
      cmdStop.Enabled = false;
    }

    protected override void Dispose( bool disposing )
    {
      if( disposing )
      {
        if (components != null)
        {
          components.Dispose();
        }
      }
      RotatingBlocks.Dispose();
      base.Dispose( disposing );
    }
```

```csharp
    #region Windows Form Designer generated code
.. .auto code here
…

    #endregion

    [STAThread]
    static void Main()
    {
      Application.Run(new Form1());
    }

    private void Form1_Load(object sender, System.EventArgs e)
    {
    }

    private void OnFrameChanged(object o, EventArgs e)
    {
      //Force a call to the Paint event handler.
      this.Invalidate(InvalidRect);
    }

    protected override void OnPaint(PaintEventArgs e)
    {
      if ( !InProcess )
        return;

      //Get the next block ready to display.
      ImageAnimator.UpdateFrames(RotatingBlocks);
      //Draw the next frame in the RotatingBlocks animation.
      e.Graphics.DrawImage(RotatingBlocks, DrawHere);
    }

    private void cmdGo_Click(object sender, System.EventArgs e)
    {
      if (!InProcess)
      {
        if ( ImageAnimator.CanAnimate(RotatingBlocks) )
        {
          //Begin the animation only once.
          ImageAnimator.Animate(RotatingBlocks,
                              new EventHandler(this.OnFrameChanged));
          InProcess = true;
          cmdGo.Enabled = false;
          cmdStop.Enabled = true;
```

```
          }
        }
      }

    private void cmdStop_Click(object sender, System.EventArgs e)
    {
      ImageAnimator.StopAnimate(RotatingBlocks,
                           new EventHandler(this.OnFrameChanged));
      InProcess = false;
      cmdGo.Enabled = true;
      cmdStop.Enabled = false;
    }
  }
}
```

Listing 6-8b. VB Code for the Animate Example

```
Option Strict On

Imports System.Drawing
Imports System.Drawing.Drawing2D
Imports System.Drawing.Imaging

Public Class Form1
  Inherits System.Windows.Forms.Form

  Dim RotatingBlocks As Bitmap
  Dim DrawHere As Point
  Dim InvalidRect As Rectangle
  Dim InProcess As Boolean = False

#Region " Windows Form Designer generated code "

  Public Sub New()
    MyBase.New()

    'This call is required by the Windows Form Designer.
    InitializeComponent()

    RotatingBlocks = New Bitmap("blocks.gif")
    DrawHere = New Point(10, 10)
    InvalidRect = New Rectangle(DrawHere, RotatingBlocks.Size)
```

```
    Me.SetStyle(ControlStyles.AllPaintingInWmPaint, True)
    Me.SetStyle(ControlStyles.DoubleBuffer, True)
    cmdStop.Enabled = False


  End Sub


  'Form overrides dispose to clean up the component list.
  Protected Overloads Overrides Sub Dispose(ByVal disposing As Boolean)
    If disposing Then
      If Not (components Is Nothing) Then
        components.Dispose()
      End If
    End If
    RotatingBlocks.Dispose()
    MyBase.Dispose(disposing)
  End Sub

… more code here
…

…

#End Region

  Private Sub Form1_Load(ByVal sender As System.Object, _
                         ByVal e As System.EventArgs) Handles MyBase.Load
  End Sub

  Protected Overrides Sub OnPaint(ByVal e As PaintEventArgs)

    If Not InProcess Then Return

    'Get the next block ready to display.
    ImageAnimator.UpdateFrames(RotatingBlocks)
    'Draw the next frame in the RotatingBlocks animation.
    e.Graphics.DrawImage(RotatingBlocks, DrawHere)
  End Sub

  Private Sub OnFrameChanged(ByVal o As Object, ByVal e As EventArgs)
    'Force a call to the Paint event handler.
    Me.Invalidate(InvalidRect)
  End Sub
```

```
Private Sub cmdGo_Click(ByVal sender As System.Object, _
                        ByVal e As System.EventArgs) Handles cmdGo.Click
   If Not InProcess Then
     If ImageAnimator.CanAnimate(RotatingBlocks) Then
       'Begin the animation only once.
       ImageAnimator.Animate(RotatingBlocks, AddressOf Me.OnFrameChanged)
       InProcess = True
       cmdGo.Enabled = False
       cmdStop.Enabled = True
     End If
   End If

End Sub

Private Sub cmdStop_Click(ByVal sender As System.Object, _
                          ByVal e As System.EventArgs) Handles cmdStop.Click
   ImageAnimator.StopAnimate(RotatingBlocks, AddressOf Me.OnFrameChanged)
   InProcess = False
   cmdGo.Enabled = True
   cmdStop.Enabled = False
 End Sub
End Class
```

The sequence of events is as follows:

1. The user clicks the Animate button.

2. The code checks if the animation process is already running. If not, it then checks to see if the loaded bitmap can even handle animation.

3. The code tells the Image animator class which image to animate and also gives the name of the callback method.

4. The image animator calls up the next frame in the image and makes a function call to the callback method given.

5. The callback method **OnFrameChanged** invalidates the rectangle that holds the image. This forces a repaint of the form.

6. The Form's Paint method checks to see if the animation process is running. If not, it bails out.

7. The current frame is drawn on the form.

8. Lather, rinse, repeat. Steps 4 through 7 repeat until the user clicks Stop.

What would happen if I did not check the status of the animation process when entering the **OnPaint** method?[11] Try it out then see the footnote.

Notice that in the VB code, a delegate is designated using the AddressOf operator. In VB 6.0 the AddressOf operator was also used as a function pointer with one major drawback: Only processes outside of VB could use this function. The AddressOf operator in VB 6.0 was mainly designed as a way to send a callback function to those Windows API calls that needed it. VB .NET now allows you to use function pointers to call methods from within your VB program itself.

> **NOTE** *Anyone who has done extensive coding in C or C++ has used function pointers to dynamically call methods without actually knowing which method was being called. Tables of function pointers are used heavily in the C and C++ worlds. In fact, a Vtable in COM is a table of function pointers. VB developers are behind the times using this construct. Learn it!*

The image I used for this example is a series of frames depicting a block that moves in a circle and changes colors as it rotates. The last block in the sequence dissolves into the first block in the sequence and the process is repeated. Figure 6-6 shows the form during animation when the last block is changing over to the first block.

The code for this example also tries to be speedy by only invalidating the dirty rectangle and by setting the correct **ControlStyles** property.

---

11. The first frame of the image would be shown at start-up. Always handle initial conditions.

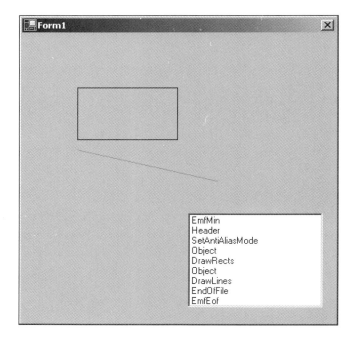

Figure 6-6. The last block dissolves into the first block.

Using Controls to Draw Images

Well, you're coming to the end of this chapter on imaging. Some of the things you've seen so far were fairly simple and straightforward and some were more involved. However, I would be remiss if I didn't point out that there are even easier ways to display images. You could use some of the constituent controls that come with .NET. I'll explain briefly the PictureBox and the Panel controls in this section.

The PictureBox is a simple way to hold a picture and control the picture's properties with the PictureBox properties. The PictureBox will scale, stretch, and clip the picture for you. You can change most of these properties at runtime or at design time. That is about all I am going to say about the PictureBox. It is so easy to use. Here is how you would load a picture in it:

```
Bitmap b = new Bitmap("d:\\crane.jpg");
//PictureBox is "p"
p.Image = (Image)b;
```

The next control is the Panel control. While at first glance this control does not appear to have anything to do with imaging, if you think about it, you could use it to display an unlimited number of thumbnail images. The Panel has an autoscroll capability built in that will let you view all your images. Here is what you could do:

1. Drop a panel on your form.

2. Make a PictureBox for each image you want to display. Do this in code.

3. Add each PictureBox to the Panel's control collection.

4. Arrange the PictureBoxes nicely within the panel for easy viewing.

Now when the user looks at the Panel, he or she sees a scrollable control with all his or her pictures in it in thumbnail size. Listing 6-9 shows three methods from a program I made a while ago that uses the Panel just for this purpose. This code is in C# and will not be repeated in VB. It is easy enough to understand for any programming language.

Listing 6-9. C# Code Showing How to Use a Panel to Display PictureBoxes

```csharp
private void FillPicList()
{
  PicPanel.AutoScroll = true;
  pic.Image = null;
  foreach(ResImage ResImg in m_Pictures)
  {
    //Make a new picture box and add it to the
    //panels control array
    AddPic2Panel(ResImg);
  }
  ArrangePictures();
}

private void AddPic2Panel(ResImage ResImg)
{
  PictureBox Pic;

  Pic = new PictureBox();
  Pic.Size = new Size(PICSIZE, PICSIZE);
  Pic.Location = new Point(10, 10);
  Pic.SizeMode = PictureBoxSizeMode.StretchImage;
  Pic.Image = ResImg.image;
  Pic.Tag = ResImg.Name;
  PicPanel.Controls.Add(Pic);
}
```

```
private void ArrangePictures()
{
  int x;
  int y = 0;

  //Number of pictures in a row.
  //DO not show a picture if it means we get a horizontal
  //scroll bar
  int NumPicsInWidth  = (int)((PicPanel.Size.Width - PICSPACE) /
                              (PICSIZE + PICSPACE)) - 1;
  //Control collections are zero based.
  //VB type collections are 1 based.
  for (int k = 0; k<= PicPanel.Controls.Count - 1; k++)
  {
    //determine if we are in a new row
    if (k % (NumPicsInWidth) == 0 )
        x = PICSPACE;
    else
        x = PicPanel.Controls[k - 1].Location.X + PICSIZE + PICSPACE;

    if (k < NumPicsInWidth )
        y = PICSPACE;
    else if (k % (NumPicsInWidth) == 0 )
        y = PicPanel.Controls[k - 1].Location.Y + PICSIZE + PICSPACE;

    PicPanel.Controls[k].Location = new Point(x, y);
  }
}
```

Let me explain what is going on here. First of all, the images are kept in a collection I named m_Pictures. The **FillPicList** function enumerates the collection and sends each picture to a function called **AddPic2Panel**. This function instantiates a new PictureBox that holds the image sent to it. I position each PictureBox at (10, 10), all on top of each other. Once all the pictures are generated, I then call **ArrangePictures**. This function does a little math to make sure that each picture has a border around it. It also makes sure to place the pictures in such a manner in the panel that only a vertical scroll bar is needed.

Notice that there is nothing in this code that determines how many pictures I have. This is the beauty of collections and the **foreach** method of enumeration. I need to note here that C# has no built-in collection class like VB does. I therefore made my own collection class in C#. The VB version of this code used the built-in VB collection class.

Summary

This was quite a chapter. You learned all about loading and saving different kinds of images. You also learned how to manipulate those images on the screen. Here is a short list of the topics this chapter covered:

- Image types and their attributes

- The Image base class

- The Bitmap class

- Properties of bitmaps

- Bitmap conversion to other image types

- The ColorMatrix and the ImageAttributes class

- Bitmap cloning

- Bitmap speed and **BitBlt** functionality

- Bitmap data and how to work directly with it

- Icons

- Metafile types

- Metafile enumeration

- Metafile creation

- Simple animation with GIF files

- Other drawing controls

The next chapter discusses how to draw text using the System.Drawing.Text namespace.

CHAPTER 7

Drawing Text

Stanley looked quite bored and somewhat detached, but then penguins often do.

—John Witschey, Alexandria, Virginia

THIS CHAPTER IS the last one that deals with putting information on the screen. So far, you have learned about simple drawing, complicated drawing, and working with image files. Along the way I also included a smattering of text.

You may think that this is enough GDI+ stuff. After all, there are a number of controls that handle text input very well. Why draw the text directly on the screen? Perhaps the following reasons will rouse your interest about this chapter:

- Drawing text whose letters are filled in with a gradient brush

- Drawing text directly on a bitmap image for annotation

- Drawing text at an angle

- Drawing text within a shape

- Making a simple (or complex) word processing program

I can think of quite a few other reasons, but by now you should be able to as well. As you head into this chapter, I hope you will find answers to some questions you already have or perhaps you will find some inspiration to add new features to a program you are working on.

As with all the examples in the book, you can download the code for this chapter's examples from the Downloads section of the Apress Web site (http://www.apress.com). I encourage you to try typing in the code, but if that gets too frustrating, by all means load the working copy.

Font Characteristics

When someone asks you what font you are using, you probably answer something along the lines of "Oh, Times Roman." You are only somewhat correct, though. The question you have just answered is, "What font *family* are you using?" There is quite a bit more to a font than just a name.

Using the Correct Vernacular

There are a few terms relating to fonts that you should know. I refer to these terms throughout the rest of this book:

- Font

- Font family

- Font style

- Font size

- Font units

A *font* is an individual member of a font family. For instance, a font would be Times New Roman, 24 pixels, regular style.

The *font family* refers to the name. In the previous case, the font family is Times New Roman.

The *font style* refers to the appearance of the font as it is rendered. Font style is independent of the font you use. GDI has a FontStyle enumeration that contains the following members:

- *Bold:* This produces bold text.

- *Italic:* This produces italic text.

- *Regular:* This produces normal text.

- *Strikeout:* This produces text with a line through it.

- *Underline:* This produces underlined text.

All of these values can be bitwise combined to produce combinations such as bold-italic.

The *font size* refers to the height of the font. However, the height units are not specified in .NET. Size can be in any of the GraphicsUnits available. The GraphicsUnits enumeration contains the following members:

- Display (1/75 of an inch)

- Document (1/300 of an inch)

- Inch

- Millimeter

- Pixel (resolution dependent)

- Point (1/72 of an inch)

- World (uses world units)

More often than not, when you talk about font size you are talking about points. This GraphicsUnit setting is the Font Unit. If a font size is specified as 16 and the units are in inches, you will have some mighty big letters.

Specifying the FontFamily

Now that you know what a font is and how to describe it, you probably would like to know how to specify one. There are two classes you need to instantiate to be able to draw text with a font: the FontFamily class and the Font class. Both of these classes are contained in the System.Drawing namespace. Let's start out with the FontFamily class.

 NOTE *Technically, it is not true that you need to instantiate the FontFamily and Font classes to be able to draw text with a font. There are constructors for the Font class that do not need a FontFamily object. However, without a FontFamily class, you will not be able to obtain any of the font metrics. You really limit yourself by instantiating a Font object without using a FontFamily object.*

A FontFamily is an object that encapsulates some generic information about a certain typeface. All fonts within this font family pretty much have the same design. The three constructors available for this class allow you to

- Create a font family from a user-supplied string.

- Create a font family from a generic font family.

- Create a font family from a font collection.

Now, as you most likely know, not all fonts are available on all machines. However, there are certain kinds of system fonts that come with all flavors of Windows. These are referred to as *generic fonts*. The GenericFontFamilies enumeration has the following members:

- Monospace

- SansSerif

- Serif

These families are totally uninteresting, but you should keep them in mind as a final backup font to use when your program cannot find the font it is looking for. The Monospace fonts are fonts whose characters each take up the same amount of space. Courier is a monospace font. Serif fonts are those that have a little tail (serif) at the end of each mark on a character. SansSerif fonts are those that are without (sans) the serifs.

If you know the name of the font you need, you can supply this name as a string to one of the FontFamily constructors.

Providing a font collection allows you to pick a named font from a certain collection of fonts. Font collections are explained in detail a little later in this chapter.

Okay, suppose you had this piece of code:

```
FontFamily fontFamily = new FontFamily("Arial");
```

You would instantiate a FontFamily class with attributes pertaining to the Arial font. Now suppose you had this piece of code:

```
FontFamily fontFamily = new FontFamily("Nicks Font");
```

Your program would explode. You would, in fact, get a runtime error telling you that this font could not be found on your machine. There are two things you need to do here. The first is to figure out if the font family you want exists, and the next is to provide some sort of fallback in case it does not. I talk about determining the existence of a font on your machine in a little while. First, though, let's handle the error. Listing 7-1 shows the setup of fallback handler for the FontFamily.

Listing 7-1a. Fallback Handler for Instantiating the FontFamily in C#

```csharp
void GetFamily()
{
  FontFamily MyFamily;
  try
  {
    MyFamily = new FontFamily("Nicks Font");
  }
  catch ( System.ArgumentException ex )
  {
    //Catch the more specific exception
    MyFamily = new FontFamily(GenericFontFamilies.Monospace);
  }

  // Do something fun with your family
  MyFamily.Dispose();
}
```

Listing 7-1b. Fallback Handler for Instantiating the FontFamily in VB

```vb
Private Sub Getfamily()
  Dim MyFamily As FontFamily

  Try
    MyFamily = New FontFamily("Nicks Font")
  Catch ex As System.ArgumentException
    'Catch the more specific exception
    MyFamily = New FontFamily(GenericFontFamilies.Monospace)
  End Try

  ' Do something fun with your family
  MyFamily.Dispose()
End Sub
```

I advised you earlier to remember the generic fonts. Here is where they come in handy. If you absolutely must display some text on the screen, then you can try to get the font family you want, but your Try-Catch block will provide a fallback to a guaranteed-to-be-there generic font. Notice that in this piece of code, I catch the most specific exception possible. I could have caught the generic exception, but I would need to do all kinds of testing to determine what caused it. In this case, because it was a bad argument, I can safely assume GDI+ could not find the font . . . for whatever reason.

So, there you go. Two out of the three ways to instantiate a font family. As I mentioned, using a font collection will come later. But what can you do with a font family?

Specifying the Font

Once you have a FontFamily, you can then get one of the fonts that belongs to that family. For instance, in its simplest form, you could get a font like this:

```
FontFamily ff = FontFamily.GenericSansSerif;
Font font = new Font(ff, 12);
```

I used one of the static methods of FontFamily to get a generic SansSerif font family. I then instantiated a font from this family whose size is 12 points. It does not get much simpler than that. It is also pretty much guaranteed to work, as the font family is a system font.

Of course this is not the only way to instantiate a Font object. There are 13 overloaded constructors for the Font class. Some of them do not even require a FontFamily object—just the name of the family. The following simple bit of code allows you to draw text on the current form. It uses the current graphics container to draw in.

```
Dim ff As FontFamily = New FontFamily("Times New Roman")
Dim fnt As Font = New Font(ff, 12, FontStyle.Bold)

e.Graphics.DrawString("Hello Font", Font, Brushes.Black, 10, 10)
```

I suppose that for very simple purposes, this is all you really need to know. However, you won't make much of a living as a top-shelf programmer if you limit yourself to this kind of simple code. There is so much more, as you will soon see.

Using FontFamily Members

Several methods and properties in the FontFamily class allow you to get detailed information about the characteristics of fonts in this family. Some of these characteristics are the font metrics.

What are *font metrics?* They are the key measurements about how a font is constructed. The metric information you can get from a FontFamily is as follows:

- Cell ascent

- Cell descent

- Line spacing

- Em height

Cell ascent refers to how high above the baseline a font reaches. *Cell descent* refers to how low below the baseline a font reaches. The *em height* is the height of the em square. Huh? The em (element) square is the box in which a glyph is placed. The em square is exactly equal to the actual value of the font size. It takes into consideration any rounding or clipping needed to actually display the font image.

These four values are given in design units. Font design units are independent of individual font units or size.

You can probably see the use of the ascent, descent, and line spacing, but what would you use the em height for? Well, it would be nice to perhaps get the line spacing in pixels rather than design units. This way, you can see how many lines fit in a rectangle. The conversion factor is the size of the font divided by the em height of the font family. The code for this equation is as follows:

```
Dim ls As Single = ff.GetLineSpacing(FontStyle.Regular) * _
                fnt.Size / ff.GetEmHeight(FontStyle.Regular)
```

The one thing you will notice abut this line of code is that the answer you get is style dependent. All of these metrics give you slightly different values for different font styles. How about an example to illustrate what these font metrics are?

Showing Font Metrics

There's a nifty graphic in the .NET help that shows a letter annotated with the font metrics. It's pretty good, but there's nothing like figuring this stuff out for yourself. I've constructed an example for you that shows some letters from several different font families and graphically displays the metrics. What's neat about this example is that it's totally independent of the font family or font style you want to show.

This example will pull together several things, such as

- Calculating font metrics in any style

- Translating points (remember Chapter 4?)

- Drawing lines and strings

- Creating a Graphics object

Start a new C# or VB Windows project. Mine is called FontMetrics. Before you add any code, perform the following steps:

1. Size the form to be 500×300.

2. Make the start-up position CenterScreen.

3. Add a button and name it cmdRoman. Set the text to "Times Roman".

4. Add a button and name it cmdArial. Set the text to "Arial Black".

5. Add a button and name it cmdComic. Set the text to "Comic Sans MS".

6. Add a button and name it cmdCourier. Set the text to "Courier New".

Your screen should look like the one shown in Figure 7-1.

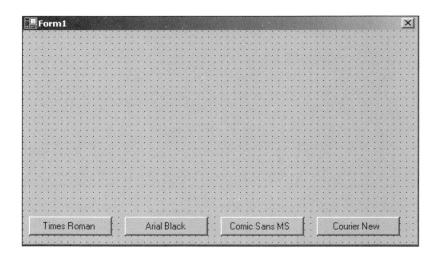

Figure 7-1. Screen setup for the font metrics example

Double-click each of the buttons to get a click event handler generated for each one.

Listing 7-2 shows the code for this example. I am not overriding the **OnPaint** method, nor am I adding any class local variables. The code I show is the event handler code and the **DisplayFontMetrics** method that I create.

Listing 7-2a. C# Code Showing How to Display Font Metrics

```csharp
private void DisplayFontMetrics(FontFamily ff, Font fnt)
{
  //Create graphics object and make it pretty
  Graphics G = this.CreateGraphics();
  G.SmoothingMode=SmoothingMode.AntiAlias;
  G.TextRenderingHint=TextRenderingHint.AntiAlias;

  //Get some metrics
  int LineSpace = (int)(ff.GetLineSpacing(fnt.Style)*
                        fnt.Size/ff.GetEmHeight(fnt.Style));
  int Descent = (int)(ff.GetCellDescent(fnt.Style)*
                        fnt.Size/ff.GetEmHeight(fnt.Style));
  int Ascent = (int)(ff.GetCellAscent(fnt.Style)*
                        fnt.Size/ff.GetEmHeight(fnt.Style));

  //Create the base line to sit the text on
  Point BaseLineStart = new Point ( 15, this.Height*3/5);
  Point BaseLineEnd = new Point ( this.Width-15, this.Height*3/5);
  //Top left corner of text is the ascent
  Point StringPoint = new Point(75, (int)(BaseLineStart.Y-Ascent));

  //Clear the screen and draw the string on a base line
  G.Clear(Color.AliceBlue);
  G.DrawString("A j Q", fnt, Brushes.Blue, StringPoint);
  G.DrawLine(Pens.Black, BaseLineStart, BaseLineEnd);

  //Draw the annotation lines
  Size LineSize = new Size(0, LineSpace);
  Size AscentSize = new Size(0, Ascent);
  Size DescentSize = new Size(0, Descent);
  G.DrawLine(Pens.Black, BaseLineStart-LineSize, BaseLineEnd-LineSize);
  G.DrawLine(Pens.Red, BaseLineStart-AscentSize, BaseLineEnd-AscentSize);
  G.DrawLine(Pens.DarkGreen, BaseLineStart+DescentSize,
                          BaseLineEnd+DescentSize);

  //Annotate
  Font AnnoFont = new Font("Arial", 10);
  G.DrawString("Line Space = " + LineSpace.ToString(), AnnoFont,
    Brushes.Black,
    20,
    (int)(BaseLineStart.Y-LineSpace-12));
```

```
      G.DrawString("Ascent = " + Ascent.ToString(), AnnoFont,
        Brushes.Red,
        250,
        (int)(BaseLineStart.Y-Ascent-12));

      G.DrawString("Descent = " + Descent.ToString(), AnnoFont,
        Brushes.DarkGreen,
        350,
        (int)(BaseLineStart.Y+Descent/8));
    }

    private void cmdRoman_Click(object sender, System.EventArgs e)
    {
      FontFamily ff = new FontFamily("Times New Roman");
      Font f = new Font(ff, 75, FontStyle.Regular, GraphicsUnit.Pixel);

      DisplayFontMetrics(ff, f);
    }

    private void cmdArial_Click(object sender, System.EventArgs e)
    {
      FontFamily ff = new FontFamily("Arial Black");
      Font f = new Font(ff, 75, FontStyle.Regular, GraphicsUnit.Pixel);

      DisplayFontMetrics(ff, f);
    }

    private void cmdComic_Click(object sender, System.EventArgs e)
    {
      FontFamily ff = new FontFamily("Comic Sans MS");
      Font f = new Font(ff, 75, FontStyle.Regular, GraphicsUnit.Pixel);

      DisplayFontMetrics(ff, f);
    }

    private void cmdCourier_Click(object sender, System.EventArgs e)
    {
      FontFamily ff = new FontFamily("Courier New");
      Font f = new Font(ff, 75, FontStyle.Regular, GraphicsUnit.Pixel);

      DisplayFontMetrics(ff, f);
    }
```

Listing 7-2b. VB Code Showing How to Display Font Metrics

```vb
Private Sub DisplayFontMetrics(ByVal ff As FontFamily, ByVal fnt As Font)
  'Create graphics object and make it pretty
  Dim G As Graphics = Me.CreateGraphics()
  G.SmoothingMode = SmoothingMode.AntiAlias
  G.TextRenderingHint = TextRenderingHint.AntiAlias

  'Get some metrics
  Dim LineSpace As Int32 = CInt(ff.GetLineSpacing(fnt.Style) * _
                    fnt.Size / ff.GetEmHeight(fnt.Style))
  Dim Descent As Int32 = CInt(ff.GetCellDescent(fnt.Style) * _
                    fnt.Size / ff.GetEmHeight(fnt.Style))
  Dim Ascent As Int32 = CInt(ff.GetCellAscent(fnt.Style) * _
                    fnt.Size / ff.GetEmHeight(fnt.Style))

  'Create the base line to sit the text on
  Dim BaseLineStart As Point = New Point(15, CInt(Me.Height * 3 / 5))
  Dim BaseLineEnd As Point = New Point(Me.Width - 15, CInt(Me.Height * 3 / 5))
  'Top left corner of text is the ascent
  Dim StringPoint As Point = New Point(75, CInt(BaseLineStart.Y - Ascent))

  'Clear the screen and draw the string on a base line
  G.Clear(Color.AliceBlue)
  G.DrawString("A j Q", fnt, Brushes.Blue, Point.op_Implicit(StringPoint))
  G.DrawLine(Pens.Black, BaseLineStart, BaseLineEnd)

  'Draw the annotation lines
  Dim LineSize As Size = New Size(0, LineSpace)
  Dim AscentSize As Size = New Size(0, Ascent)
  Dim DescentSize As Size = New Size(0, Descent)
  G.DrawLine(Pens.Black, Point.op_Subtraction(BaseLineStart, LineSize), _
                    Point.op_Subtraction(BaseLineEnd, LineSize))
  G.DrawLine(Pens.Red, Point.op_Subtraction(BaseLineStart, AscentSize), _
                    Point.op_Subtraction(BaseLineEnd, AscentSize))
  G.DrawLine(Pens.DarkGreen, Point.op_Addition(BaseLineStart, DescentSize), _
                      Point.op_Addition(BaseLineEnd, DescentSize))

  'Annotate
  Dim AnnoFont As Font = New Font("Arial", 10)
  G.DrawString("Line Space = " + LineSpace.ToString(), AnnoFont, _
    Brushes.Black, _
    20, _
    CInt(BaseLineStart.Y - LineSpace - 12))
```

```
      G.DrawString("Ascent = " + Ascent.ToString(), AnnoFont, _
        Brushes.Red, _
        250, _
        CInt(BaseLineStart.Y - Ascent - 12))

      G.DrawString("Descent = " + Descent.ToString(), AnnoFont, _
        Brushes.DarkGreen, _
        350, _
        CInt(BaseLineStart.Y + Descent / 8))
  End Sub


  Private Sub cmdRoman_Click(ByVal sender As System.Object, _
                            ByVal e As System.EventArgs) Handles cmdRoman.Click
    Dim ff As FontFamily = New FontFamily("Times New Roman")
    Dim f As Font = New Font(ff, 75, FontStyle.Regular, GraphicsUnit.Pixel)

    DisplayFontMetrics(ff, f)

  End Sub

  Private Sub cmdArial_Click(ByVal sender As System.Object, _
                            ByVal e As System.EventArgs) Handles cmdArial.Click
    Dim ff As FontFamily = New FontFamily("Arial Black")
    Dim f As Font = New Font(ff, 75, FontStyle.Regular, GraphicsUnit.Pixel)

    DisplayFontMetrics(ff, f)

  End Sub

  Private Sub cmdComic_Click(ByVal sender As System.Object, _
                            ByVal e As System.EventArgs) Handles cmdComic.Click
    Dim ff As FontFamily = New FontFamily("Comic Sans MS")
    Dim f As Font = New Font(ff, 75, FontStyle.Regular, GraphicsUnit.Pixel)

    DisplayFontMetrics(ff, f)

  End Sub
```

```
Private Sub cmdCourier_Click(ByVal sender As System.Object, _
                            ByVal e As System.EventArgs) _
                            Handles cmdCourier.Click
    Dim ff As FontFamily = New FontFamily("Courier New")
    Dim f As Font = New Font(ff, 75, FontStyle.Regular, GraphicsUnit.Pixel)

    DisplayFontMetrics(ff, f)
End Sub
```

After you enter in all this code or download the code from the Downloads section of the Apress Web site (http://www.apress.com), you should compile and run the program. Click a button and you will see a line of text with its corresponding metrics. Figure 7-2 shows the Comic Sans MS font.

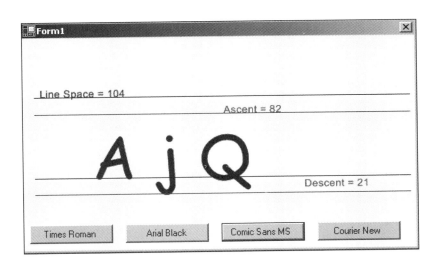

Figure 7-2. Font metrics for the Comic Sans MS font

Personally, I think this is a pretty cool program. There's not much use for it other than as a learning tool, but you get to use the knowledge you gained from previous chapters. By the way, notice that if you cover the form with another window and then uncover it, your form will be blank. Why? You ought to know the answer to that one by now![1]

---

1. Because the **OnPaint** method knows nothing about these graphics.

As far as printing text goes with the **DrawString** function, the line space metric is probably the one you will use most. I put the line space metric to good use in the next example.

Enumerating Fonts

This operation of enumerating fonts installed on your machine is a classic. I have seen it done dozens of times and it always seems to be done the same way. *Boring!* Enumerating fonts and displaying the name in some text box or label is trivial. It also does not make for interesting code.

The next example is one that I came up with to enumerate the installed fonts . . . but with a twist. You will be using the knowledge you gained from Chapters 4 and 6 as well as this chapter. Here is the problem: How would you list all the fonts using the **Graphics.DrawString** method in a scrollable control? Not only that, but it would be nice to draw the name of the font using that font's typeface and style. My solution involves the knowledge of the Graphics object you obtained from Chapter 4 and the knowledge of bitmaps and images you gained from Chapter 6.

While this example is not the only solution, I think that because it builds upon what you have already learned, it is the most instructive. It may also give you some ideas of not-so-obvious ways to use the GDI+ classes.

Start out with a new C# or VB Windows Forms project. Mine is called FontAttr. Before you enter in any code, perform the following steps:

1. Size the default form to be 350×350.

2. Remove the Max and Min buttons from this form.

3. Make the start-up position of the form Center.

4. Add a panel to the form. Name it P1.

5. Make the panel's border style Fixed3D.

6. Add a button to the form. Name it cmdGo and change the text to "GO".

Your form should look like the one shown in Figure 7-3.

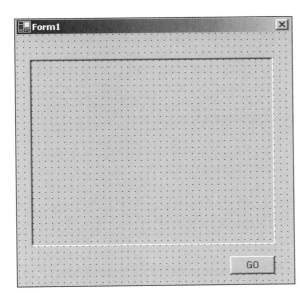

Figure 7-3. Layout of the font enumeration program

Once you have this layout correct, double-click the cmdGO button to get the click event handler generated in code. Now go into the code pane.

First of all, be sure to include the following namespaces:

- System.Drawing

- System.Drawing.Imaging

- System.Drawing.Text

These three namespaces will pretty much be in all the programs for this chapter.

Okay, usually at this point I tell you to override the **OnPaint** method of the form. Not this time, however. You are going to generate your own Graphics object based on a **PictureBox** control that you make via code. Here is what happens:

1. The GO button invokes a method called **EnumInstalledFonts**.

2. The **EnumInstalledFonts** method gets the list of font families and tests each one to see if any of the font styles are available for this font.

3. If a style is available, another procedure called **AddString** is invoked.

4. The AddString procedure generates a font based on the passed-in style and in a fixed size.

5. A PictureBox is generated and sized according to some font metrics.

6. A bitmap is generated and drawn on by obtaining its Graphics object and using the **Graphics.DrawString** procedure.

7. The PictureBox image is set to the bitmap and the PictureBox is then installed as one of the controls in the panel.

These are the basic metasteps—I explain each method fully after you enter the code in Listing 7-3. The only code I show here is for the **cmdGo_Click**, **AddString**, and **EnumInstalledFonts** methods.

Listing 7-3a. C# Code for the Three Main Methods of the FontAttr Example

```
private void EnumInstalledFonts()
{
  FontStyle Style;
  int y = 0;

  foreach (FontFamily ff in FontFamily.Families)
  {
    if ( ff.IsStyleAvailable(Style = FontStyle.Regular) )
      AddString(ff, ref y, Style);
    if ( ff.IsStyleAvailable(Style = FontStyle.Bold) )
      AddString(ff, ref y, Style);
    if ( ff.IsStyleAvailable(Style = FontStyle.Italic) )
      AddString(ff, ref y, Style);
    if ( ff.IsStyleAvailable(Style = FontStyle.Strikeout) )
      AddString(ff, ref y, Style);
    if ( ff.IsStyleAvailable(Style = FontStyle.Underline) )
      AddString(ff, ref y, Style);
  }
}

private void AddString(FontFamily ff, ref int y, FontStyle Style)
{
  using ( Font fnt = new Font(ff, 12, Style, GraphicsUnit.Pixel) )
  {
    int LineSpace = (int)(ff.GetLineSpacing(Style) *
                     fnt.Size / ff.GetEmHeight(Style));
    y += LineSpace + 2;
```

```
        PictureBox P = new PictureBox();
        P.Height = LineSpace;
        P.Width = P1.Width;
        Bitmap B = new Bitmap(P.Width, P.Height);
        using (Graphics G = Graphics.FromImage(B))
        {
          G.DrawString(ff.Name + " : Style = " + Style.ToString(),
                    fnt, Brushes.Black, 0, 0);
        }
        P.Image=B;
        P1.Controls.Add(P);
        P1.Controls[P1.Controls.Count-1].Location = new Point(2, y);
        if ( y < P1.Height )
          P1.Refresh();
    }
  }

  private void cmdGo_Click(object sender, System.EventArgs e)
  {
    P1.Controls.Clear();
    EnumInstalledFonts();
  }
```

Listing 7-3b. VB Code for the Three Main Methods of the FontAttr Example

```
Private Sub EnumInstalledFonts()
  Dim Style As FontStyle
  Dim y As Int32 = 0
  Dim ff As FontFamily

  For Each ff In FontFamily.Families
    Style = FontStyle.Regular
    If ff.IsStyleAvailable(Style) Then
      AddString(ff, y, Style)
    End If
    Style = FontStyle.Bold
    If ff.IsStyleAvailable(Style) Then
      AddString(ff, y, Style)
    End If
    Style = FontStyle.Italic
    If ff.IsStyleAvailable(Style) Then
      AddString(ff, y, Style)
    End If
    Style = FontStyle.Strikeout
```

```
      If ff.IsStyleAvailable(Style) Then
        AddString(ff, y, Style)
      End If
      Style = FontStyle.Underline
      If ff.IsStyleAvailable(Style) Then
        AddString(ff, y, Style)
      End If
    Next
  End Sub

  Private Sub AddString(ByVal ff As FontFamily, ByRef y As Int32, _
                        ByVal Style As FontStyle)
    Dim fnt As Font = New Font(ff, 12, Style, GraphicsUnit.Pixel)
    Dim LineSpace As Int32 = CInt((ff.GetLineSpacing(Style)) * _
                             fnt.Size / ff.GetEmHeight(Style))
    y += LineSpace + 2

    Dim P As PictureBox = New PictureBox()
    P.Height = LineSpace
    P.Width = P1.Width
    Dim B As Bitmap = New Bitmap(P.Width, P.Height)
    Dim G As Graphics = Graphics.FromImage(B)
    G.DrawString(ff.Name + " : Style = " + Style.ToString(), _
                 fnt, Brushes.Black, 0, 0)
    P.Image = B
    P1.Controls.Add(P)
    P1.Controls(P1.Controls.Count - 1).Location = New Point(2, y)
    If y < P1.Height Then
      P1.Refresh()
    End If

    fnt.Dispose()
    G.Dispose()
  End Sub

  Private Sub cmdGo_Click(ByVal sender As System.Object, _
                          ByVal e As System.EventArgs) Handles cmdGo.Click
    P1.Controls.Clear()
    EnumInstalledFonts()
  End Sub
```

After you have either entered the code or downloaded it from the Apress Web site, compile and run it. You should see a screen similar to the one shown in Figure 7-4.

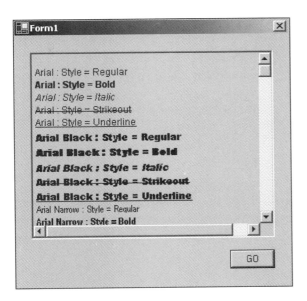

Figure 7-4. Result of running the font enumeration program

You see that the panel now has a scroll bar that enables you to view every font in the system as rendered by that font. I can see using this technique in a small word processing program. Let's look a little more closely at things. I use the C# code for detailed analysis here. The **EnumInstalledFonts** method is as follows:

```
private void EnumInstalledFonts()
{
  FontStyle Style;
  int y = 0;

  foreach (FontFamily ff in FontFamily.Families)
  {
    if ( ff.IsStyleAvailable(Style = FontStyle.Regular) )
      AddString(ff, ref y, Style);
    if ( ff.IsStyleAvailable(Style = FontStyle.Bold) )
      AddString(ff, ref y, Style);
    if ( ff.IsStyleAvailable(Style = FontStyle.Italic) )
      AddString(ff, ref y, Style);
    if ( ff.IsStyleAvailable(Style = FontStyle.Strikeout) )
      AddString(ff, ref y, Style);
    if ( ff.IsStyleAvailable(Style = FontStyle.Underline) )
      AddString(ff, ref y, Style);
  }
}
```

I use the static function **FontFamily.Families** to get an array of font families that .NET knows about for this Graphics object. At the same time, I enumerate though each family using the foreach construct.

> **TIP**   *I have said it before and I will say it again. Enumerating over collections and arrays using the foreach construct will be something you need to do quite often. Learn it.*

Within the iteration code, I test to see if the current font family supports each of the styles. If it does, I call another function called **AddString**. Notice that I pass in a reference to the variable *y*. This variable is the vertical placement of each line of text. It will need to be incremented for each line of text.

The **AddString** method is as follows:

```
private void AddString(FontFamily ff, ref int y, FontStyle Style)
{
  using ( Font fnt = new Font(ff, 12, Style, GraphicsUnit.Pixel) )
  {
    int LineSpace = (int)(ff.GetLineSpacing(Style) *
                          fnt.Size / ff.GetEmHeight(Style));
    y += LineSpace + 2;

    PictureBox P = new PictureBox();
    P.Height = LineSpace;
    P.Width = P1.Width;
    Bitmap B = new Bitmap(P.Width, P.Height);
    using (Graphics G = Graphics.FromImage(B))
    {
      G.DrawString(ff.Name + " : Style = " + Style.ToString(),
                 fnt, Brushes.Black, 0, 0);
    }
    P.Image=B;
    P1.Controls.Add(P);
    P1.Controls[P1.Controls.Count-1].Location = new Point(2, y);
    if ( y < P1.Height )
      P1.Refresh();
  }
}
```

Before I start dissecting this method, notice that I use the "using" keyword with the Graphics object and the Font object. This makes sure that these object are properly disposed of when I am done with them.

After creating a font of size 12 pixels in the style that is passed in, I calculate the line spacing for that font. This allows me to properly size the picture box and to properly place the picture box in the panel. I could have done the easy thing and used something like 20 pixels for the line spacing, but you will need to figure this out if you ever want to properly draw text to the screen.

Once I have the sizing correct, I make a new PictureBox in memory according to the size I just calculated. What I do next is the interesting part.

I make a bitmap in memory of the exact size of the PictureBox. I then obtain a Graphics object from this bitmap (a bitmap is an image, don't forget) and I draw the text I want on this Graphics object. Next, I set the **Image** property of the PictureBox to the bitmap I just made. Presto! Just add water and you have instant text! Really, I just add this PictureBox to the control collection of the panel at the correct position and that is it.

The last thing I do in this method is refresh the screen so the user gets some immediate feedback. Once the list of picture boxes goes out of sight, I speed up the process by *not* refreshing the screen.[2]

Now, if you are astute and you like to play around, you may have the following question: "Why not just write directly on the panel?" Well you can . . . up to a point. The panel only works properly if you add controls to it. Drawing text on the panel means nothing to it. If you keep writing on the panel, it will not know to produce scroll bars and you will only see the text that the panel's native size can hold.

What I have done in this example is make a graphical representation of some text as a bitmap and then use that bitmap as the display medium. All this without the **OnPaint** method!

Other Font Properties

Well, you have put the FontFamily and Font classes to some rudimentary uses. The real power, though, lies in using these classes in something like a small word processing program. Doing something as simple as putting a word in bold font in a sentence can drastically change how the sentence looks. For instance, putting a word in bold font may require you to wrap the sentence at a new point. A bold word generally takes up more space than the same word in a regular style.

---

2. Sometimes it's the little things that count.

Before I take you into measuring and formatting text, you should be familiar with some of the other properties of the Font class listed in Table 7-1.

Table 7-1. Properties of the Font Class That Return Characteristics

Member	Description
Bold	A Boolean that indicates if the current font is bold
FontFamily	Gets the font family object that the current font belongs to
Italic	A Boolean that indicates if the current font is italic
SizeInPoints	Point size of the current font independent of the units
Style	Style of the current font
Underline	A Boolean that indicates if the current font is underlined
Unit	Units of measure for the current font

Using all of these members along with the ones you have seen in the previous examples will tell you everything you need to know about the text you are writing to the screen.

Collections of Fonts

There are three collections of fonts in the System.Drawing.Text namespace:

- InstalledFontCollection

- FontCollection

- PrivateFontCollection

I have already shown you how to enumerate through the InstalledFontCollection. The only thing is I did it a slightly different way than the standard enumerate-the-fonts-in-your-system example. I used the static **FontFamily.Families** method, which gives you the same set of font families as the InstalledFontCollection class does, only with less effort.[3]

---

3. Always find the programmer's easy way out if you can.

The FontCollection is the abstract base class for the InstalledFontFontCollection and the PrivateFontCollection classes. It provides a method for getting the array of FontFamilies.

The InstalledFontCollection class gives you access to all the fonts installed on your computer. As I said, you have already been through this one.

The PrivateFontCollection allows you to include installed fonts as well as fonts that are not installed. You can build up a collection of fonts that are private to this collection.

There is an example in the .NET help that shows you how to use an installed font collection. However, I think this example is much like the installed font enumeration example .NET provides. It is not very exciting and does not really lead you toward any practical use. After all, once you are done with the private font collection example, you may find yourself wondering "Yeah . . . so?" I decided to use the PrivateFontCollection class in a slightly different but very useful way.

Remember the Brushes class and the Pens class? These two classes have properties that provide you with stock brushes or pens. Using a static property of the Pens class bypasses all that code you need to write to get a Pen, such as instantiating a Brush with a certain color and then instantiating a Pen with the Brush you just made and giving it a width of 1 pixel. And, oh, by the way, don't forget to dispose of the Brush and Pen once you've finished with them.

Anyway, when I saw that the mechanics for generating a Font are basically the same as those for generating a Pen, I immediately started looking for a Fonts class. No such thing. This is something that I would find very handy and would use quite a bit. This is what the next example is going to do: make a Fonts class based on the PrivateFontCollection class.

Let's start with a little background on the Pens and Brushes classes. Look in the documentation and you will see that there are three things common to both classes:

- Neither of them can be instantiated as objects.

- Neither of them is inheritable.

- Both of them only contain static properties.

I want my new Fonts class to have these same properties. Here is what I need to do to accomplish this goal:

- Make the new class constructor static.

- Make the new class sealed (not inheritable in VB).

- Make all the properties static.

Once you get though the code, you will see how much easier it is to use this new Fonts class than getting a font the classic way.

The PrivateFontCollection class allows you to load fonts that are included in your system and fonts that are not. I chose to do both because I am a fan of unusual fonts. It did not take me long to search the Internet for a site that provides free TrueType fonts. In fact, I found a font that I thought was pretty unusual, so I picked it to be my nonstandard font for this example. If you downloaded the code for this example, this font is included. It is called ChainLetters. Each letter is made up of links of chain. If you want, you may substitute a font of your own liking.

So now for the example. Start a new Windows Forms project in C# or VB. Mine is called FontClass. There are no controls for this project. Size your form to be about 300×350. Now enter the code pane.

Add a class called Fonts. Include the following namespaces in both the form and in the class:

- System.Drawing

- System.Drawing.Text

Listing 7-4 shows the complete code for the Fonts class. You will notice that I load the system fonts from my C: drive and the nonstandard font from my D:\Temp\Fonts directory. You will need to supply the correct directories for your system.

Listing 7-4a. C# Code for the Fonts Class

```
using System;
using System.Drawing;
using System.Drawing.Text;

namespace FontsClass_c
{

  public sealed class Fonts
  {
    private static PrivateFontCollection PFC;
    private static FontFamily Arial_FF;
    private static FontFamily Comic_FF;
    private static FontFamily Chain_FF;
```

```csharp
static Fonts()
{
  PFC = new PrivateFontCollection();
  PFC.AddFontFile("C:\\WINNT\\Fonts\\Arial.ttf");
  Arial_FF = PFC.Families[0];
  PFC.AddFontFile("d:\\temp\\fonts\\chainletters.ttf");
  Chain_FF = PFC.Families[1];
  PFC.AddFontFile("C:\\WINNT\\Fonts\\comic.ttf");
  Comic_FF = PFC.Families[2];
}

public static FontFamily[] Families
{
  get{ return PFC.Families; }
}

#region Arial Font
public static Font Arial_20
{
  get {return new Font(Arial_FF, 20, FontStyle.Regular, GraphicsUnit.Point);}
}
public static Font ArialItalic_20
{
  get {return new Font(Arial_FF, 20, FontStyle.Italic, GraphicsUnit.Point);}
}
#endregion

#region Chain font
public static Font Chain_20
{
  get {return new Font(Chain_FF, 20, FontStyle.Regular, GraphicsUnit.Point);}
}
public static Font ChainItalic_20
{
  get {return new Font(Chain_FF, 20, FontStyle.Italic, GraphicsUnit.Point);}
}
#endregion
```

```
      #region Comic Font
      public static Font Comic_20
      {
        get {return new Font(Comic_FF, 20, FontStyle.Regular, GraphicsUnit.Point);}
      }
      public static Font ComicItalic_20
      {
        get {return new Font(Comic_FF, 20, FontStyle.Italic, GraphicsUnit.Point);}
      }
      #endregion
  }
}
```

Listing 7-4b. VB Code for the Fonts Class

```
Option Strict On

Imports System
Imports System.Drawing
Imports System.Drawing.Text

Public NotInheritable Class Fonts

  Private Shared PFC As PrivateFontCollection
  Private Shared Arial_FF As FontFamily
  Private Shared Comic_FF As FontFamily
  Private Shared Chain_FF As FontFamily

  Shared Sub New()
    PFC = New PrivateFontCollection()
    PFC.AddFontFile("C:\\WINNT\\Fonts\\Arial.ttf")
    Arial_FF = PFC.Families(0)
    PFC.AddFontFile("d:\\temp\\fonts\\chainletters.ttf")
    Chain_FF = PFC.Families(1)
    PFC.AddFontFile("C:\\WINNT\\Fonts\\comic.ttf")
    Comic_FF = PFC.Families(2)
  End Sub

  Shared ReadOnly Property Families() As FontFamily()
    Get
      Return PFC.Families
    End Get
  End Property
```

```vb
#Region "Arial Font"
  Shared ReadOnly Property Arial_20() As Font
    Get
      Return New Font(Arial_FF, 20, FontStyle.Regular, GraphicsUnit.Point)
    End Get
  End Property

  Shared ReadOnly Property ArialItalic_20() As Font
    Get
      Return New Font(Arial_FF, 20, FontStyle.Italic, GraphicsUnit.Point)
    End Get
  End Property
#End Region

#Region "Chain letter font"
  Shared ReadOnly Property Chain_20() As Font
    Get
      Return New Font(Chain_FF, 20, FontStyle.Regular, GraphicsUnit.Point)
    End Get
  End Property

  Shared ReadOnly Property ChainItalic_20() As Font
    Get
      Return New Font(Chain_FF, 20, FontStyle.Italic, GraphicsUnit.Point)
    End Get
  End Property
#End Region

#Region "Comic Font"
  Shared ReadOnly Property Comic_20() As Font
    Get
      Return New Font(Comic_FF, 20, FontStyle.Regular, GraphicsUnit.Point)
    End Get
  End Property

  Shared ReadOnly Property ComicItalic_20() As Font
    Get
      Return New Font(Comic_FF, 20, FontStyle.Italic, GraphicsUnit.Point)
    End Get
  End Property
#End Region
End Class
```

Of course you need to be able to test this class. Listing 7-5 shows the code for the **OnPaint** method. This is all that you need to add to the form.

Listing 7-5a. C# Code for the OnPaint Method in the Form to Test the Fonts Class

```csharp
protected override void OnPaint(PaintEventArgs e)
{
  Graphics G = e.Graphics;
  G.TextRenderingHint=TextRenderingHint.AntiAlias;
  int y = 0;

  G.DrawString("Regular", Fonts.Arial_20, Brushes.Black, 50, y+=40);
  G.DrawString("Italic", Fonts.ArialItalic_20, Brushes.Black, 50, y+=40);
  G.DrawString("Regular", Fonts.Chain_20, Brushes.Black, 50, y+=40);
  G.DrawString("Italic", Fonts.ChainItalic_20, Brushes.Black, 50, y+=40);
  G.DrawString("Regular", Fonts.Comic_20, Brushes.Black, 50, y+=40);
  G.DrawString("Italic", Fonts.ComicItalic_20, Brushes.Black, 50, y+=40);
}
```

Listing 7-5b. VB Code for the OnPaint Method in the Form to Test the Fonts Class

```vb
Protected Overrides Sub OnPaint(ByVal e As PaintEventArgs)
  Dim G As Graphics = e.Graphics
  G.TextRenderingHint = Drawing.Text.TextRenderingHint.AntiAlias
  Dim y As Int32 = 0

  y += 40
  G.DrawString("Regular", Fonts.Arial_20, Brushes.Black, 50, y)
  y += 40
  G.DrawString("Italic", Fonts.ArialItalic_20, Brushes.Black, 50, y)
  y += 40
  G.DrawString("Regular", Fonts.Chain_20, Brushes.Black, 50, y)
  y += 40
  G.DrawString("Italic", Fonts.ChainItalic_20, Brushes.Black, 50, y)
  y += 40
  G.DrawString("Regular", Fonts.Comic_20, Brushes.Black, 50, y)
  y += 40
  G.DrawString("Italic", Fonts.ComicItalic_20, Brushes.Black, 50, y)
End Sub
```

I find it rather annoying that in VB I have to increment *y* outside of the **DrawString** statement. Anyway, compile and run the program. If you have your fonts set up correctly, you should see a screen like the one shown in Figure 7-5.

Figure 7-5. Result of testing the Fonts class

Let's do a little code dissection. First, the class is marked so it cannot be inherited. It is the only class of its kind allowed.

Second, the constructor is marked as being static (shared in VB). This means that the first time you use any property of this class, the constructor automatically gets called. Also, the constructor only gets called once no matter how many times you access the class.

Third, each property is read-only and is marked as static (shared in VB). This means that each property can be called directly from the class rather than an instance of the class.

Look at the code for the form:

```
G.DrawString("Regular", Fonts.Arial_20, Brushes.Black, 50, y+=40);
G.DrawString("Italic", Fonts.ArialItalic_20, Brushes.Black, 50, y+=40);
G.DrawString("Regular", Fonts.Chain_20, Brushes.Black, 50, y+=40);
G.DrawString("Italic", Fonts.ChainItalic_20, Brushes.Black, 50, y+=40);
G.DrawString("Regular", Fonts.Comic_20, Brushes.Black, 50, y+=40);
G.DrawString("Italic", Fonts.ComicItalic_20, Brushes.Black, 50, y+=40);
```

Each time I use the **DrawString** function, I get an instance of the correct font directly from the class. This is exactly like using the Pens class or the Brushes class.

The Fonts class only returns fonts that are available in the internal PrivateFontCollection class. There is no need for the form to determine what fonts are available or which styles they may be available in. The Fonts class does all this for you.

I think I will keep this one.

Changing Perspective on Text

This section deals with the problem of drawing text at all kinds of different angles. Using the StringFormat class, it is possible to draw text horizontally or vertically directly on the screen. This class is a helper class that encapsulates text layout information. Several of the **Graphics.DrawString** overloaded methods take a StringFormat object as an argument. I'll cover the StringFormat class in detail in a little while.

Anyway, how would you draw text at an angle? How do you draw text so it looks like it is heading away from you into the distance? This kind of drawing is done all the time in professional programs, and you will undoubtedly need to do it too.

You may be thinking that you could use an affine transformation to rotate and skew the text, and you would be on the right track. However, there are no overloaded versions of the **DrawString** function that use any kind of Matrix object. Nor is there any capability in the StringFormat class that takes a Matrix object.

The trick to drawing text at any angle is to draw directly onto a bitmap, and then draw that bitmap on the screen. You have seen this method already in the example that enumerated the installed fonts. In that case, the bitmap was a vehicle used to get an image into a PictureBox control. I use it here to actually draw the text to the screen.

This next example uses quite a few concepts already presented in previous examples, but in a different way. Again, showing you how you could use a method is often more instructive than showing how to just call a method. This is what you will do in the next example:

- Create a Graphics object from an image.

- Create a bitmap in memory and adjust individual pixels.

- Make a single color for the whole bitmap transparent.

- Draw on the Graphics object, effectively drawing on the bitmap.

- Use the TextRenderingHint.

- Set up the form for high-speed drawing.

- Use a parallelogram to skew an image.

You could use an affine transformation to rotate, translate, and skew an image, but that would require some calculation on your part. Also, as you saw from previous examples, it includes quite a few lines of code. There is an alternative method to creating an affine transform (other than using a Matrix): You use a parallelogram.

If you remember your basic math, a parallelogram is a shape that has four sides. The two sets of opposite sides are both parallel and equal in length. The classic parallelogram shape is that of a rectangle leaning over. Figure 7-6 shows several parallelograms.

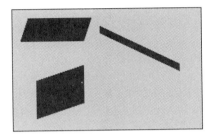

Figure 7-6. Several parallelograms

If you were to fit some text in each of these shapes, it would take on the characteristics of these shapes. You would see skewed text.

For the sake of the **Graphics.DrawImage** method, the parallelogram needs to be defined by an array of three Point structures. The first one must represent the upper left corner of the parallelogram, the second one must represent the upper right corner, and the third one must represent the lower left corner. The lower right corner is extrapolated from the other three points.

If you were to define the parallelogram such that the upper left corner is below the lower left corner, your image would appear to be flipped upside down. If the upper right corner were defined as being to the left of the upper left corner, your image would appear backward—a mirror image.

The next example is rather simple, as it does not really require a lot of code. It is powerful, though, in relation to what it does. It takes a line of text and shows it on the screen rotating around a pole. There is a vertical slider control that is used to skew the text by moving the upper right corner Point up or down.

Start out with a new project in either VB or C#. Mine is called TextRotate. Before you add any code, perform the following steps:

1. Size the form to 400×400.

2. Add a vertical scroll bar to the right of the form. Name it Skew.

3. Add a timer to the form and name it T1.

4. Double-click the slider to get the wizard-generated scroll event handler.

5. Double-click the timer to get the wizard-generated tick event handler.

The code you need to add ranges from class local variables to modifying the **Dispose** method to adding new methods. Listing 7-6 shows the code for the complete form. The C# code does not show the Windows Form Designer generated code, as nothing is added to this section. The VB code shows only the constructor and **Dispose** methods of the Windows Form Designer generated code.

Listing 7-6a. C# Code Showing Rotating Text

```csharp
using System;
using System.Drawing;
using System.Drawing.Drawing2D;
using System.Drawing.Imaging;
using System.Drawing.Text;
using System.Collections;
using System.ComponentModel;
using System.Windows.Forms;
using System.Data;

namespace TextRotate_c
{
  public class Form1 : System.Windows.Forms.Form
  {
    Bitmap bmp;
    Point UL, UR, BL;
    Rectangle InvRect;
    int Direction = -1;
    String s = "ROTATING TEXT";
    Font fnt = new Font("Arial", 12);

    private System.Windows.Forms.VScrollBar Skew;
    private System.Windows.Forms.Timer T1;
    private System.ComponentModel.IContainer components;
```

```csharp
public Form1()
{
  InitializeComponent();

  Skew.Minimum = 50;
  Skew.Maximum = 250;
  Skew.SmallChange = 1;
  Skew.LargeChange = 10;
  Skew.Value = 150;

  using (Graphics G = this.CreateGraphics())
  {
    SizeF sz = G.MeasureString(s, fnt);
    bmp = new  Bitmap((int)sz.Width, (int)sz.Height);
  }

  for ( int k=0; k<bmp.Height; k++ )
  {
    for ( int j=0; j<bmp.Width; j++ )
      bmp.SetPixel(j, k, Color.White);
  }
  bmp.MakeTransparent(Color.White);

  UL = new Point(150, 150);
  UR = new Point(UL.X+bmp.Width, Skew.Value);
  BL = new Point(150, UL.Y+bmp.Height);
  InvRect = new  Rectangle(-UR.X, Skew.Minimum, 2*UR.X, Skew.Maximum);

  using (Graphics G = Graphics.FromImage(bmp))
  {
    G.SmoothingMode = SmoothingMode.AntiAlias;
    G.TextRenderingHint = TextRenderingHint.AntiAlias;
    G.DrawString(s, fnt, Brushes.Black, 0, 0);
  }

  this.SetStyle(ControlStyles.AllPaintingInWmPaint, true);
  this.SetStyle(ControlStyles.DoubleBuffer, true);

  T1.Interval=10; //milliseconds
  T1.Enabled=false;
}
```

```csharp
protected override void Dispose( bool disposing )
{
  if( disposing )
  {
    if (components != null)
    {
      components.Dispose();
    }
  }
  bmp.Dispose();
  fnt.Dispose();
  base.Dispose( disposing );
}

#region Windows Form Designer generated code
#endregion

[STAThread]
static void Main()
{
  Application.Run(new Form1());
}

private void Form1_Load(object sender, System.EventArgs e)
{
}

protected override void OnPaint(PaintEventArgs e)
{
  Point[] dest = {UL, UR, BL};

  // Draw the image mapped to the parallelogram.
  e.Graphics.DrawImage(bmp, dest);
  e.Graphics.DrawLine(Pens.Black, UL, BL+new Size(0, 20));
  if (T1.Enabled==false)
    T1.Enabled=true;
}

private void Skew_Scroll(object sender,
                         System.Windows.Forms.ScrollEventArgs e)
{
  UR.Y = Skew.Value;
}
```

```
    private void T1_Tick(object sender, System.EventArgs e)
    {
      UR.X += Direction;
      if ( UR.X == UL.X + bmp.Width*Direction )
        Direction *=-1;

      Invalidate(InvRect);
    }
  }
}
```

Listing 7-6b. VB Code Showing Rotating Text

```
Option Strict On

Imports System
Imports System.Drawing
Imports System.Drawing.Drawing2D
Imports System.Drawing.Imaging
Imports System.Drawing.Text

Public Class Form1
  Inherits System.Windows.Forms.Form

  Dim bmp As Bitmap
  Dim UL, UR, BL As Point
  Dim InvRect As Rectangle
  Dim Direction As Int32 = -1
  Dim s As String = "ROTATING TEXT"
  Dim fnt As Font = New Font("Arial", 12)

#Region " Windows Form Designer generated code "

  Public Sub New()
    MyBase.New()

    'This call is required by the Windows Form Designer.
    InitializeComponent()

    Skew.Minimum = 50
    Skew.Maximum = 250
    Skew.SmallChange = 1
    Skew.LargeChange = 10
    Skew.Value = 150
```

```
      Dim G As Graphics = Me.CreateGraphics()
      Dim sz As Size = Size.Truncate(G.MeasureString(s, fnt))
      bmp = New Bitmap(CInt(sz.Width), CInt(sz.Height))

      Dim k, j As Int32
      For k = 0 To bmp.Height - 1
        For j = 0 To bmp.Width - 1
          bmp.SetPixel(j, k, Color.White)
        Next
      Next
      bmp.MakeTransparent(Color.White)

      UL = New Point(150, 150)
      UR = New Point(UL.X + bmp.Width, Skew.Value)
      BL = New Point(150, UL.Y + bmp.Height)
      InvRect = New Rectangle(-UR.X, Skew.Minimum, 2 * UR.X, Skew.Maximum)

      G = Graphics.FromImage(bmp)
      G.SmoothingMode = SmoothingMode.AntiAlias
      G.TextRenderingHint = TextRenderingHint.AntiAlias
      G.DrawString(s, fnt, Brushes.Black, 0, 0)
      G.Dispose()

      Me.SetStyle(ControlStyles.AllPaintingInWmPaint, True)
      Me.SetStyle(ControlStyles.DoubleBuffer, True)

      T1.Interval = 10 'milliseconds
      T1.Enabled = False

    End Sub

    'Form overrides dispose to clean up the component list.
    Protected Overloads Overrides Sub Dispose(ByVal disposing As Boolean)
      If disposing Then
        If Not (components Is Nothing) Then
          components.Dispose()
        End If
      End If
      bmp.Dispose()
      fnt.Dispose()
      MyBase.Dispose(disposing)
    End Sub
```

```
...
...
...


#End Region

  Private Sub Form1_Load(ByVal sender As System.Object, _
                         ByVal e As System.EventArgs) Handles MyBase.Load


  End Sub

  Protected Overrides Sub OnPaint(ByVal e As PaintEventArgs)
    Dim dest() As Point = {UL, UR, BL}

    ' Draw the image mapped to the parallelogram.
    e.Graphics.DrawImage(bmp, dest)
    e.Graphics.DrawLine(Pens.Black, UL, Point.op_Addition(BL, New Size(0, 20)))
    If T1.Enabled = False Then
      T1.Enabled = True
    End If

  End Sub

  Private Sub Skew_Scroll(ByVal sender As System.Object, _
                          ByVal e As System.Windows.Forms.ScrollEventArgs) _
                          Handles Skew.Scroll
    UR.Y = Skew.Value
  End Sub

  Private Sub T1_Tick(ByVal sender As System.Object, _
                      ByVal e As System.EventArgs) Handles T1.Tick

    UR.X += Direction
    If UR.X = UL.X + bmp.Width * Direction Then
      Direction *= -1
    End If

    Invalidate(InvRect)
  End Sub
End Class
```

Compile and run the program. You should see a line of text rotating around a pole. Move the scroll bar and the text will skew. Figure 7-7 shows what this should look like.

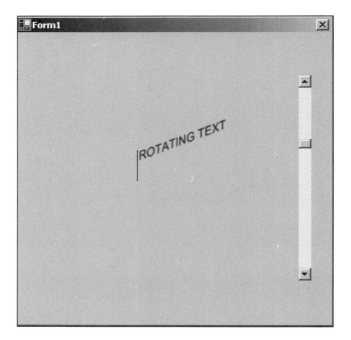

Figure 7-7. Rotating and skewing text

I would like to point out a couple of things about this program. The first is that the bitmap is sized to exactly hold the text. I do this by making a call the **Graphics.MeasureString** method. This method has some powerful calculations going on behind the scenes. It is this method that you would use to figure out line breaks in a text editor program.

I also generate a white bitmap and make the color white transparent. This gives the effect you see of only the text appearing on the screen. I also make sure the invalidation rectangle is only as big as it needs to be. This speeds up repainting, as you already know.

The timer tick event has a small algorithm that notes when the x coordinate of the upper right point is symmetric around the x coordinate of the upper left point. When this happens, I change the direction of the rotation.

Now this is definitely not as far as you could go with a program like this. For instance, the text looks like it is flapping left and right rather than rotating. You could adjust several other parameters as the text is moving to simulate a real rotation. This will be your homework.

Formatting Text

There is a helper class called StringFormat. This class is used in much the same way as the ImageAttributes class is used. That is to say, these classes are used when rendering text and images.

Often the format for a bunch of text strings is the same. In this case, you can set up a StringFormat class and pass it to the **Graphics.DrawString** method every time you draw any string. Table 7-2 details some of the more important members of this class.

Table 7-2. StringFormat Members

Member	Description
Alignment	Uses the StringAlignment enumeration to determine horizontal alignment
LineAlignment	Uses the StringAlignment enumeration to determine vertical alignment
GenericDefault	Static function passes back a generic default StringFormat object
GenericTypographic	Static function passes back a generic Typographics StringFormat object
GetTabStops	Gets an array of floats that define the tab stops for this object
SetTabStops	Uses an array of floats to define the tabs stops for this object
Trimming	Determines how letters are displayed when touching the bounding rectangle
FormatFlags	Gets/sets a number that is the bitwise combination of the StringFormatFlags enumeration

The StringFormatFlags enumeration has several members that determine how a string is rendered inside a bounding rectangle. It allows you far more control than just setting the tabs or the alignment. For instance, it allows you to change the direction of text to right to left. You would use this for different languages that read from right to left.

Measuring the text and fitting it neatly inside a rectangle is quite an undertaking. This class along with the **DrawString** method does it all for you.

The StringAlignment enumeration has the values Near, Far, and Center. Usually, you would think of alignment as left, right, or center. This thinking is definitely Western, though, as it does not take into account that some Eastern languages are written from right to left. What would left-aligned mean in this case? With .NET you can say it is Near-aligned, which is conceptually the same thing in any language.

The next example is an interesting one in that it lays one of the building blocks for the project in Chapter 10. The example has the user draw a rectangle on the screen and then type some text into the rectangle. You actually do this all the time in programs such as Visio.

The example demonstrates something I have not dealt with yet in this book: handling keyboard events. For the most part, they are handled the same as other events, such as the mouse events or even the OnPaint event. There is a major gotcha, though, when trying to handle keyboard input directly on a form. I illustrate this with a small C# program. (The concept is the same for VB.)

Open a new program and go straight into the form's code pane. Override the OnKeyPress event using the following code:

```
protected override void OnKeyPress(KeyPressEventArgs e)
{
  MessageBox.Show("Key Pressed = " + e.KeyChar.ToString());
}
```

This is all you need to add. Now compile and run the program. Press a key and you should see a message box display that indicates which key you pressed. Very simple, huh? Now add a button to the form. Without changing a thing, run the program again.

Press some keys and you get nothing. Put a breakpoint in the code on the message box line and the program never breaks here. What is going on?

What is happening is that the button is getting the focus, not the form. Anytime you put any control on a form, the form can no longer get keypresses directly. This is mainly because you cannot set the focus back to the form once there is a control on it. So how do you get around this problem? Well, you could subclass the form's controls and steal the events, but this would be quite a bit of work, and as it turns out it is quite unnecessary.

Add the following line of code to the form's load event handler:

```
this.KeyPreview=true;
```

Now run the program, press a key, and the message box appears again. You have just told the program that you want to see all keypresses before the controls get them.

This is an exceedingly simple solution, but if you are not aware of it, you could spend quite a bit of time trying to figure out why your program compiles just fine but the code never runs. I learned this the hard way when I first started playing with .NET.

Typing Text in a Rectangle

Time for an example that shows how to draw a rectangle on the form using the mouse, how to change the cursor to an IBeam, and how to type text directly in the rectangle.

Start a new Windows project in either C# or VB. Mine is called TextFormat. You will need to add some controls before adding any code. Perform the following steps to get the form ready for programming:

1. Size the form to 400×400.

2. Center the form upon start-up.

3. Delete the Max and Min buttons.

4. Add a button called cmdNew to the bottom of the screen. Change the text to "New".

5. Add a button called cmdLeft to the bottom of the screen. Change the text to "Center Left Align".

6. Add a button called cmdTop to the bottom of the screen. Change the text to "Top Left Align".

Your form should look like the one shown in Figure 7-8.

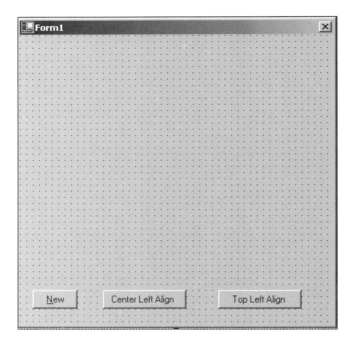

Figure 7-8. Form layout for the string format example

Go into the code pane and add the code in Listing 7-7. The C# code will not include any Windows Form Designer generated code. The VB code will only include the constructor and **Dispose** methods from the Windows Form Designer generated code.

This listing is fairly involved and I encourage you to download the program form the Downloads section of the Apress Web site (http://www.apress.com). I'll also say that the code in Listing 7-7 is not complete and bug-free. It isn't meant to be a program so much as an illustrative example. It applies quite a few of the concepts you've learned over the past few chapters.

Listing 7-7a. C# Code for the String Format Example

```
using System;
using System.Drawing;
using System.Drawing.Drawing2D;
using System.Drawing.Text;
using System.Collections;
using System.ComponentModel;
using System.Windows.Forms;
using System.Data;
```

```csharp
namespace TextFormat_c
{
  public class Form1 : System.Windows.Forms.Form
  {

    #region Class Local Variables
    Rectangle UserRect      = Rectangle.Empty;
    bool RectStarted        = false;
    bool RectFinished       = false;
    bool Typing             = false;
    bool InsideRect         = false;
    Cursor ClientCursor     = Cursors.Default;
    string RectText         = string.Empty;
    StringFormat BoxFormat  = StringFormat.GenericDefault;
    #endregion

    private System.Windows.Forms.Button cmdNew;
    private System.Windows.Forms.Button cmdLeft;
    private System.Windows.Forms.Button cmdTop;

    private System.ComponentModel.Container components = null;

    public Form1()
    {
      InitializeComponent();

      //All the mouse move events use the same delegate
      this.cmdNew.MouseMove  += new MouseEventHandler(this.Button_MouseMove);
      this.cmdLeft.MouseMove += new MouseEventHandler(this.Button_MouseMove);
      this.cmdTop.MouseMove  += new MouseEventHandler(this.Button_MouseMove);

      this.KeyPress += new KeyPressEventHandler(this.FormKeyPress);

      BoxFormat.Alignment = StringAlignment.Center;
      BoxFormat.LineAlignment = StringAlignment.Center;

    }
```

```csharp
protected override void Dispose( bool disposing )
{
  if( disposing )
  {
    if (components != null)
    {
      components.Dispose();
    }
  }
  ClientCursor.Dispose();
  base.Dispose( disposing );
}

#region Windows Form Designer generated code
...
...
#endregion

[STAThread]
static void Main()
{
  Application.Run(new Form1());
}

private void Form1_Load(object sender, System.EventArgs e)
{
}

protected override void OnPaint(PaintEventArgs e)
{
  Graphics G = e.Graphics;
  using(Pen P = new Pen(Brushes.Black, 1))
  {
    if ( !RectFinished )
      P.DashStyle = DashStyle.Dash;

    G.DrawRectangle(P,UserRect);
  }

  if (RectFinished && ClientCursor == Cursors.IBeam)
    G.DrawString(RectText, new Font("Arial", 16), Brushes.Black,
                                      UserRect, BoxFormat);
```

```
  base.OnPaint(e);
}

protected override void OnMouseDown(MouseEventArgs e)
{
  //If left button then start the rectangle
  if ( e.Button == MouseButtons.Left )
  {
    if (UserRect == Rectangle.Empty)
    {
      UserRect.X = e.X;
      UserRect.Y = e.Y;
      RectStarted = true;
      RectFinished = false;
    }
  }
  //If right button then start the edit
  else if ( e.Button == MouseButtons.Right )
  {
    if ( UserRect != Rectangle.Empty )
    {
      ClientCursor = Cursors.IBeam;
      this.Cursor  = ClientCursor;
      Point pos    = new Point(UserRect.X+UserRect.Width/2,
                               UserRect.Y+UserRect.Height/2);
      //Translate cursor screen position to position on form
      int Offset = this.Height-this.ClientRectangle.Height;
      pos += new Size(this.Location.X, this.Location.Y+Offset);
      Cursor.Position = pos;
      Typing        = true;
      this.KeyPreview = true;
    }
  }
  base.OnMouseDown(e);
}
protected override void OnMouseUp(MouseEventArgs e)
{
  base.OnMouseUp(e);

  // A negative rectangle is not allowed.
  // Mouse_down then Mouse_up without Mouse_move is not allowed
  if (UserRect.Width <= 0 || UserRect.Height <=0 )
    UserRect = Rectangle.Empty;
```

```
      //Rectangle has ended
      RectStarted = false;
      RectFinished = true;
      Invalidate();
    }
    protected override void OnMouseMove(MouseEventArgs e)
    {
      base.OnMove(e);

      //Let program know if cursor is inside user rectangle
      InsideRect = false;
      if (UserRect != Rectangle.Empty)
        if (UserRect.Contains(new Point(e.X, e.Y)))
          InsideRect = true;

      this.Cursor = ClientCursor;
      //Increase the size of the rectangle each time the mouse moves.
      if (RectStarted)
      {
        Size s = new Size(e.X-UserRect.X, e.Y-UserRect.Y);
        UserRect.Size=s;
        Invalidate();
      }
    }


    private void cmdNew_Click(object sender, System.EventArgs e)
    {
      if ( Typing && InsideRect )
        return;

      //Start a new blank form
      BoxFormat.Alignment = StringAlignment.Center;
      BoxFormat.Alignment = StringAlignment.Center;
      UserRect = Rectangle.Empty;
      ClientCursor = Cursors.Default;
      RectStarted = false;
      RectFinished = false;
      RectText = string.Empty;
      this.KeyPreview=false;
      Invalidate();
    }
```

```csharp
  private void Button_MouseMove(object sender, MouseEventArgs e)
  {
    this.Cursor = Cursors.Default;
  }

  void FormKeyPress(object sender, KeyPressEventArgs e)
  {
    //Handle backspace key
    if (e.KeyChar == (char)8)
    {
      if ( RectText != string.Empty )
        RectText = RectText.Remove(RectText.Length-1, 1);
    }
    else
      RectText += e.KeyChar;

    Invalidate();
  }

  private void cmdLeft_Click(object sender, System.EventArgs e)
  {
    //Change horizontal alignment and redraw
    BoxFormat.LineAlignment = StringAlignment.Center;
    BoxFormat.Alignment = StringAlignment.Near;
    Invalidate();
  }

  private void cmdTop_Click(object sender, System.EventArgs e)
  {
    //Chnage vertical alignment and redraw
    BoxFormat.Alignment = StringAlignment.Near;
    BoxFormat.LineAlignment = StringAlignment.Near;
    Invalidate();
  }
  }
}
```

Listing 7-7b. VB Code for the String Format Example

```vb
Option Strict On

Imports System.Drawing
Imports System.Drawing.Drawing2D
Imports System.Drawing.Text

Public Class Form1
  Inherits System.Windows.Forms.Form

#Region "Class Local Variables"
  Dim UserRect As Rectangle = Rectangle.Empty
  Dim RectStarted As Boolean = False
  Dim RectFinished As Boolean = False
  Dim Typing As Boolean = False
  Dim InsideRect As Boolean = False
  Dim ClientCursor As Cursor = Cursors.Default
  Dim RectText As String = String.Empty
  Dim BoxFormat As StringFormat = StringFormat.GenericDefault
#End Region

#Region " Windows Form Designer generated code "

  Public Sub New()
    MyBase.New()

    'This call is required by the Windows Form Designer.
    InitializeComponent()

    'All the mouse move events use the same delegate
    AddHandler cmdNew.MouseMove, New MouseEventHandler(AddressOf _
                                          Me.Button_MouseMove)
    AddHandler cmdLeft.MouseMove, New MouseEventHandler(AddressOf _
                                           Me.Button_MouseMove)
    AddHandler cmdTop.MouseMove, New MouseEventHandler(AddressOf _
                                          Me.Button_MouseMove)

    AddHandler Me.KeyPress, New KeyPressEventHandler(AddressOf Me.FormKeyPress)

    BoxFormat.Alignment = StringAlignment.Center
    BoxFormat.LineAlignment = StringAlignment.Center

  End Sub
```

```
'Form overrides dispose to clean up the component list.
Protected Overloads Overrides Sub Dispose(ByVal disposing As Boolean)
  If disposing Then
    If Not (components Is Nothing) Then
      components.Dispose()
    End If
  End If
  ClientCursor.Dispose()
  MyBase.Dispose(disposing)
End Sub
...

...

#End Region

  Private Sub Form1_Load(ByVal sender As System.Object, _
                      ByVal e As System.EventArgs) Handles MyBase.Load

  End Sub

  Protected Overrides Sub OnPaint(ByVal e As PaintEventArgs)
    Dim G As Graphics = e.Graphics
    Dim P As Pen = New Pen(Brushes.Black, 1)

    If Not RectFinished Then
      P.DashStyle = DashStyle.Dash
    End If

    G.DrawRectangle(P, UserRect)

    If RectFinished And ClientCursor Is Cursors.IBeam Then
      G.DrawString(RectText, New Font("Arial", 16), Brushes.Black, _
                RectangleF.op_Implicit(UserRect), BoxFormat)
    End If
    P.Dispose()

    MyBase.OnPaint(e)
  End Sub

  Private Sub FormKeyPress(ByVal sender As Object, ByVal e As KeyPressEventArgs)
    'Handle backspace key
    If e.KeyChar = vbBack Then
      If Not RectText = String.Empty Then
        RectText = RectText.Remove(RectText.Length - 1, 1)
      End If
```

```
      Else
        RectText += e.KeyChar
      End If


      Invalidate()
    End Sub



  Protected Overrides Sub OnMouseDown(ByVal e As MouseEventArgs)
    'If left button then start the rectangle
    If e.Button = MouseButtons.Left Then
      If UserRect.IsEmpty Then
        UserRect.X = e.X
        UserRect.Y = e.Y
        RectStarted = True
        RectFinished = False
      End If
    ElseIf e.Button = MouseButtons.Right Then
      'If right button then start the edit
      If Not UserRect.IsEmpty Then
        ClientCursor = Cursors.IBeam
        Me.Cursor = ClientCursor
        Dim pos As Point = New Point(UserRect.X + CInt(UserRect.Width / 2), _
                            UserRect.Y + CInt(UserRect.Height / 2))
        'Translate cursor screen position to position on form
        Dim Offset As Int32 = Me.Height - Me.ClientRectangle.Height
        pos = Point.op_Addition(pos, New Size(Me.Location.X, _
                                          Me.Location.Y + Offset))
        Cursor.Position = pos
        Typing = True
        Me.KeyPreview = True
      End If
    End If


    MyBase.OnMouseDown(e)
  End Sub

  Protected Overrides Sub OnMouseUp(ByVal e As MouseEventArgs)
    MyBase.OnMouseUp(e)

    ' A negative rectangle is not allowed.
    ' Mouse_down then Mouse_up without Mouse_move is not allowed
    If UserRect.Width <= 0 Or UserRect.Height <= 0 Then
      UserRect = Rectangle.Empty
    End If
```

```vbnet
    'Rectangle has ended
    RectStarted = False
    RectFinished = True
    Invalidate()
End Sub

Protected Overrides Sub OnMouseMove(ByVal e As MouseEventArgs)
    MyBase.OnMove(e)

    'Let program know if cursor is inside user rectangle
    InsideRect = False
    If Not UserRect.IsEmpty Then
      If UserRect.Contains(New Point(e.X, e.Y)) Then
        InsideRect = True
      End If
    End If


    Me.Cursor = ClientCursor
    'Increase the size of the rectangle each time the mouse moves.
    If RectStarted Then
      Dim s As Size = New Size(e.X - UserRect.X, e.Y - UserRect.Y)
      UserRect.Size = s
      Invalidate()
    End If
End Sub

Private Sub Button_MouseMove(ByVal sender As Object, ByVal e As MouseEventArgs)
    Me.Cursor = Cursors.Default
End Sub

Private Sub cmdNew_Click(ByVal sender As System.Object, _
                          ByVal e As System.EventArgs) Handles cmdNew.Click
    If Typing And InsideRect Then
      Return
    End If

    ' Start a new blank form
    BoxFormat.Alignment = StringAlignment.Center
    BoxFormat.Alignment = StringAlignment.Center
    UserRect = Rectangle.Empty
    ClientCursor = Cursors.Default
    RectStarted = False
    RectFinished = False
```

```
      RectText = String.Empty
      Me.KeyPreview = False
      Invalidate()
  End Sub


  Private Sub cmdLeft_Click(ByVal sender As System.Object, _
                         ByVal e As System.EventArgs) Handles cmdLeft.Click
      'Change horizontal alignment and redraw
      BoxFormat.LineAlignment = StringAlignment.Center
      BoxFormat.Alignment = StringAlignment.Near
      Invalidate()
  End Sub


  Private Sub cmdTop_Click(ByVal sender As System.Object, _
                         ByVal e As System.EventArgs) Handles cmdTop.Click
      'Change vertical alignment and redraw
      BoxFormat.Alignment = StringAlignment.Near
      BoxFormat.LineAlignment = StringAlignment.Near
      Invalidate()
  End Sub
End Class
```

Compile and run the program. It should work like this:

- Press the left mouse button down on a section of the form and drag down and left to another section. Then lift the left mouse button up.

- While drawing the rectangle, the rectangle outline is dashed.

- When the rectangle is finished, the outline turns solid

- Press the right mouse key down after drawing the rectangle and the cursor changes to an IBeam and moves to the center of the rectangle.

- Start typing. The string is built and appears as you type on the screen. The text wraps properly and is lined up in the center of the box both vertically and horizontally.

- The Backspace key works as it should.

- Clicking the Center Left Align button moves the text to the left of the rectangle.

- Clicking the Top Left Align button moves the text vertically to the top of the rectangle.

- Moving the cursor over the buttons changes it to an arrow. Moving it back to the form changes it back to what it should be.

Figure 7-9 shows the form after I've typed in some text.

Figure 7-9. Drawing text in a rectangle

Before I go into the details of the program, I would like to point out some flaws that you will undoubtedly notice.

First of all, drawing directly on the form is not the best thing to do for a couple of reasons. For one thing, it is difficult to trap all the events you may be looking for. Once you have a control on the form, the form itself can never regain focus. Only the controls on the form can have focus. For another thing, the form is a fixed size. Once you have filled it up, where do you draw? The best place to draw a box or an image is on a control. For instance, I could have handled the event much easier if I had used a panel to draw the rectangle on.

Next, I provide no text editing capability in this example other than being able to press the Backspace key. The minimum here would be a blinking cursor under the next letter placement. There is also no delete function.

Adding in all this functionality for this example would have hidden the trees for the forest.

Anyway, back to the example. Let's dissect some of it. I use the VB code to explain some points. First, the class local variables region contains some status variable that lets me know what state I am in. A more sophisticated program would use a state machine. The constructor is as follows:

```
Public Sub New()
  MyBase.New()

  'This call is required by the Windows Form Designer.
  InitializeComponent()

  'All the mouse move events use the same delegate
  AddHandler cmdNew.MouseMove, New MouseEventHandler(AddressOf _
                                           Me.Button_MouseMove)
  AddHandler cmdLeft.MouseMove, New MouseEventHandler(AddressOf _
                                           Me.Button_MouseMove)
  AddHandler cmdTop.MouseMove, New MouseEventHandler(AddressOf _
                                           Me.Button_MouseMove)

  AddHandler Me.KeyPress, New KeyPressEventHandler(AddressOf Me.FormKeyPress)

  BoxFormat.Alignment = StringAlignment.Center
  BoxFormat.LineAlignment = StringAlignment.Center

End Sub
```

I am adding the same delegate as the event handler for the mouse move event for each button. It is in this delegate that I change the cursor to the arrow. I also add a keypress handler to the form's KeyPress event. I am not overriding this event— I could have, but I decided not to. Finally, I set up the default alignment for drawing the text in the rectangle. The KeyPress event handler is as follows:

```
Private Sub FormKeyPress(ByVal sender As Object, ByVal e As KeyPressEventArgs)
  'Handle backspace key
  If e.KeyChar = vbBack Then
    If Not RectText = String.Empty Then
      RectText = RectText.Remove(RectText.Length - 1, 1)
    End If
```

```
      Else
        RectText += e.KeyChar
      End If

      Invalidate()
   End Sub
```

In here, I check for the Backspace key, and if true, I remove the last character from the string. Otherwise, I add the character to the string and invalidate the form. If I did not invalidate the form, nothing would get written to the screen.

Now, I know what some of you are thinking about how I built the string. I use the classic "do not do it this way" method. Strings in .NET are immutable. That is, once they are created, they cannot be changed. The line `RecText += e.KeyChar` does not actually add anything to the RecText string. Instead, it makes a new string and returns it. The old string is still there. Because the old string cannot be used anymore, it needs to be garbage collected. This is a very inefficient way to build a string. Perform this operation a few thousand times and the inefficiency would soon show through. Instead, you should use the StringBuilder class provided by .NET. The RectText variable should have been defined like this:

```
Dim RectText As StringBuilder = New StringBuilder()
```

Adding the keystroke to the string would then look like this:

```
RectText.Append(e.KeyChar)
```

Building a string in this manner really does add a character at a time to the same string. It is far more efficient to use the StringBuilder class in this instance. Consider the following **OnPaint** method:

```
Protected Overrides Sub OnPaint(ByVal e As PaintEventArgs)
   Dim G As Graphics = e.Graphics
   Dim P As Pen = New Pen(Brushes.Black, 1)

   If Not RectFinished Then
     P.DashStyle = DashStyle.Dash
   End If

   G.DrawRectangle(P, UserRect)

   If RectFinished And ClientCursor Is Cursors.IBeam Then
     G.DrawString(RectText, New Font("Arial", 16), Brushes.Black, _
                  RectangleF.op_Implicit(UserRect), BoxFormat)
   End If
```

```
        P.Dispose()

    MyBase.OnPaint(e)
End Sub
```

There is not really much here. All the setup has been done previous to this point. What I do in this method is use the DashStyle enumeration to define how the rectangle looks when it is being constructed. When the rectangle is finished, I use the default style, which is solid. Then, finally, before calling the base **OnPaint** method, I draw the string to the screen within the defined on-screen rectangle, using the format that I set up.

Like I said, this example might not be usable as is, but it does show quite a few concepts, such as handling key events directly on a form, drawing within a rectangle, and formatting text. These are things you need to know when you design your own rectangle editor.

Summary

In this chapter you learned how text is handled as a drawing shape. You saw shapes such as the rectangle, ellipse, line, and so forth. Now I have shown you the text shape. While it may seem strange to equate drawing text with drawing an image, they both use the same methodology. Here are some of the similarities:

- They both need a Graphics object to draw in.

- They both need a starting location. Both can use a bounding rectangle.

- They both need refreshing if the containing window is invalidated.

If you think about it, there are more similarities than differences.

This chapter included a lot of interesting examples that showed off the capabilities of GDI+ to render text. Some of the examples also included ways to enhance the text-rendering capability of .NET by using some constituent controls as containers. You can even use a memory-based bitmap as a way to display text in nonstandard ways.

Here are some of the other things this chapter covered:

- Defining a font

- Specifying font families

- Using font families

- Font metrics and other font properties

- Enumerating installed fonts

- Private font collections

- Sealed class generation with static members

- Using bitmaps to display text

- Formatting text

The next chapter is all about printing. So far, you know how to get graphics on the screen, but what about getting graphics on paper?

CHAPTER 8

Printing

It was rather dark outside—not the kind of dark that's so dark that you can't see anything at all, but only the kind of dark where you can just barely see things after you've waited to allow your eyes to adjust to the dark, which is called dark-adaptation, which you can do best if you get enough Vitamin A.

—Carol Deppe, Corvallis, Oregon

THIS CHAPTER DEALS WITH printing what you have displayed on the screen. No, pressing Alt-PrtScn is *not* an acceptable form of printing. .NET actually has quite a few classes to help when it comes to printing. Aside from using some of the namespaces you are used to, I introduce classes from the System.Drawing.Printing and System.IO namespaces in this chapter.

Along with these namespaces, you will learn about the following dialog boxes:

- PrintDialog

- PageSetupDialog

- PrintPreviewDialog

These dialog boxes are .NET-provided forms that make it easier for you to allow your users to properly set up their printing tasks.

While this chapter leads you through the basics of printing, it is by no means a complete tutorial. You will see more than enough here, though, to print the results of any example in this book . . . and then some.

One note before I start this chapter: As with all the code in this book, the examples in this chapter are available for download from the Downloads section of the Apress Web site (http://www.apress.com). You have probably noticed that as this book progresses, the complexity of the examples increases. I would be remiss if I did not try to include some of the knowledge you gained in previous chapters.

How Printing Is Handled in .NET

As you probably know, the best way to handle printing is via events. A printer is an external device that your computer needs to talk to. Fortunately, your printer does not need to talk back to you very often. Most of the time when a printer talks back to your program, it is to tell it to either send more data or shut up. The best way to handle an external device such as a printer is via events, and this is how .NET does it. You will be writing code for several events:

- BeginPrint

- PrintPage

- EndPrint

The BeginPrint and EndPrint Events

The BeginPrint event takes as an argument an instance of the PrintEventArgs class. This event is called by the system when you invoke the **Print** method. You would normally use the BeginPrint event to initialize any resources you may use for the printing process. Such resources would include the following:

- Fonts

- Streams

- Memory space

- Graphics containers

The PrintEventArgs class has only one useful property: the **Cancel** property. This property is used to tell .NET to cancel printing or to detect if printing is being canceled. The **Cancel** property is inherited from the CancelEventArgs class.

The EndPrint event also takes an instance of the PrintEventArgs class. The EndPrint event occurs when the last page of the document has been printed. Any resources that you initialized during the BeginPrint event should be released here.

Now, technically I suppose you could do away with the EndPrint event handler because the .NET garbage collector (GC) will eventually clean up after you. Also, you know when this event is going to be fired because during the PrintPage event you tell the system that there are no more pages to print. But as I have been saying all along in this book,[1] you really should clean up after yourself. While the GC is very efficient, it is most efficient if it never has to run across your errant objects to begin with.

The PagePrint Event

This event is where all the action happens. Once you have called the **Print** method and the BeginPrint event has been called and handled, this event will occur.

The PagePrint event takes as an argument an instance of the PrintPageEventArgs class. This class has the following members:

- Cancel

- MarginBounds

- PageBounds

- PageSettings

- HasMorePages

- Graphics

The **Cancel** property serves the same function as the **Cancel** property in the BeginPrint and the EndPrint events. It tells the system to stop printing.

The **MarginBounds** property returns a rectangle that bounds the print area of the page. This is in contrast to the **PageBounds** property, which gets the bounding rectangle for the whole page. Hopefully, the **MarginBounds** rectangle is smaller than the **PageBounds** rectangle.

Unless you are printing borderless photographs or something similar using a special printer, you will find that most printers are not able to handle printing within the complete **PageBounds** rectangle.

The **HasMorePages** property gets or sets an indicator to tell if another page needs to be printed. Mostly, you would set rather than get this property in the PagePrint event handler. After all, it is within the PagePrint handler that you decide if more pages need to be printed.

Setting the **HasMorePages** property to false fires the EndPrint event that I described earlier.

---

1.   I hope my examples demonstrate this as well.

Setting Up Your Page to Print

The **PageSettings** member is an instance of a class whose members define the settings for the current page. Notice that I said the *current page.* Do I mean that you need to set up each page in a large document each time it gets printed? The answer is no. There is a class that I cover soon called PrintDocument. This class has a member called **DefaultPageSettings**. It is here that you set up a document's page settings as a whole. As each page gets printed, the **DefaultPageSettings** values get transferred to the PageSettings class for the current page.

So, when would you ever change the settings in the middle of the document? Well, how about if you were printing a word processing document that had graphics on one page that needed to be printed in landscape mode while the rest of the document needed to be printed in portrait mode? During printing you would detect that a certain page needs its settings adjusted and you would change certain values in the **PageSettings** instance. When the next page came up for printing, the settings would have changed back to the default.

The PageSettings class has the following members:

- PaperSize

- Landscape

- Bounds

- Margins

- Color

- PrinterSettings

- PrinterResolution

- PaperSource

Of course, if you were to instantiate this class yourself, you would need a constructor. In the case of the PageSettings class, there are two of them. The first uses the default printer and the second takes as an argument a PrinterSettings object, which defines a specific printer.

Let me explain these settings. First of all, you have an instance of the PaperSize class. This class has a **Kind** property that is an enumerated value according to the PaperKind enumeration. Now, you are probably thinking the same thing I did when I first came across this property. This enumeration can only contain a half-dozen paper types at the most. Well, you would be wrong. There are more than 100 kinds of paper defined in this enumeration. This takes care of far more kinds of paper than I even knew existed.

The **Landscape** property is a Boolean value that determines if the current page is going to be printed in landscape mode. Now, most people think of landscape as being 90 degrees rotated from portrait. .NET allows you to define the landscape angle using the **PrinterSettings.LandscapeAngle** property. However, the angle is restricted to either 90 or 270 degrees. You can think of this as being plus or minus 90 degrees from portrait. The default value is 90 degrees. (I should note that if your printer does not handle landscape printing, then this value would be reset to 0 degrees.)

I ought to tell you right now that there is an exception that can be thrown when you set the landscape mode. If you set up the printer by using the **PrintSettings.PrinterName** property to a device that does not exist, when you set the **Landscape** property you will get an InvalidPrinterException error. Be sure you are able to handle this and tell your user in a nice way. Crashing your system is not acceptable error handling.

The **Bounds** property returns a Rectangle structure that defines the border of the paper. This rectangle is defined according to the **Landscape** property you set. So if your page were portrait, your rectangle's height would be greater than its width. If your page were landscape, your rectangle's width would be greater than its height.

By the way, the units for the rectangle are in hundredths of an inch. Remember, we are talking about paper, not the screen.

The Margins class is also calculated in hundredths of an inch. This property allows you to get or set the margins on any of the four sides of the paper. As you would expect, the members of the Margins class are Top, Bottom, Left, and Right. Use this instance of the Margins class along with the **Bounds** property to determine the actual printing area of the page.

Color is a Boolean value that determines if the printer should print in color.

PrinterSettings is a class whose members determine the type of printer and its capabilities. I explain the PrinterSettings class in more detail later in this chapter.

The PrinterResolution class has several properties that determine the output of your printer in either general or specific terms. The members **PrinterResolution.X** and **PrinterResolution.Y** hold the actual dots-per-inch resolution of the printer. The member **PrinterResolution.Kind** is an enumerated value according to the PrinterResolutionKind enumeration. This enumeration has the following members:

- Draft

- Low

- Medium

- High

- Custom

If the PrinterResolution is Custom, then you would get the actual resolution from the **PrinterResolution.X** and **PrinterResolution.Y** properties.

The PaperSource class has two members that you can use to determine where the paper for your print job is coming from. They are **Kind** and **SourceName**. The **Kind** property is an enumerated value based on the PaperSourceKind enumeration. This enumeration has the following members:

- AutomaticFeed

- ManualFeed

- TractorFeed

- Cassette

- Custom

- Envelope

- FormSource

- LargeCapacity

- SmallFormat

- LargeFormat

- Lower

- Middle

- Upper

- Manual

It seems to me that this should just about cover every printer ever invented and currently in use. The **SourceName** property is the string representation of the **Kind** enumerated value.

Okay, now what about this PrinterSettings class? The instance of this class you get from the PageSettings class contains everything you can set up for a printer. It also includes information on how a document should be printed. This class has the following members:

- CanDuplex

- Collate

- Copies

- DefaultPageSettings

- Duplex

- FromPage

- InstalledPrinters

- IsDefaultPrinter

- IsPlotter

- IsValid

- LandscapeAngle

- MaximumCopies

- MaximumPage

- MinumumPage

- PaperSizes

- PaperSources

- PrinterName

- PrinterResolution

- PrintRange

- PrintToFile

- SupportsColor

- ToPage

As you can see, there are quite a few members. Let's look at a few in detail and perhaps write a small program that would better describe some of the other members.

The **DefaultPageSettings** member returns an instance of this class that includes setup for a standard print job. Some of these settings would include the size of the margins, the size of the paper, and whether or not to print in color. In order to fully appreciate just what .NET does for you as far as default settings go, it is perhaps best to try a small example. This example will be a console application. No need for a Windows application here.

Start a new Console application in either VB or C#. Mine is called DefPrintSettings. Listing 8-1 shows the code for both the VB and C# versions. Because this isn't a Windows application, .NET won't include a reference to the System.Drawing.Dll. If you can't guess, this DLL includes all the classes in the System.Drawing namespace. Because I use the System.Drawing.Printing namespace, you'll need this DLL.

Listing 8-1a. C# Program Showing Default Printer and Page Settings

```
using System;
using System.Drawing.Printing;

namespace DefPrintSettings_c
{
  class Class1
  {
    [STAThread]
    static void Main(string[] args)
    {
      PrintDocument pd = new PrintDocument();
      PageSettings pg = pd.DefaultPageSettings;
      PrinterSettings ps = pg.PrinterSettings;
```

```
    Console.WriteLine("Printer Settings");
    Console.WriteLine("PrinterName = " + pd.PrinterSettings.PrinterName);
    Console.WriteLine("Is default Printer = " +
                      ps.IsDefaultPrinter.ToString());
    Console.WriteLine("Is plotter = " + ps.IsPlotter.ToString());
    Console.WriteLine("Is printer valid = " + ps.IsValid.ToString());
    Console.WriteLine("Can Duplex = " + ps.IsValid.ToString());
    Console.WriteLine("Num copies = " + ps.Copies.ToString());
    Console.WriteLine("Max Copies = " + ps.MaximumCopies.ToString());
    Console.WriteLine("Max Page = " + ps.MaximumPage.ToString());
    Console.WriteLine("Min Page = " + ps.MinimumPage.ToString());
    Console.WriteLine("Supports Color = " + ps.SupportsColor.ToString());
    foreach (PaperSize p in ps.PaperSizes)
      Console.WriteLine("Supports Paper Size: " + p.PaperName);
    foreach (PaperSource p in ps.PaperSources)
      Console.WriteLine("Supports Paper Source: " + p.SourceName);

    Console.WriteLine("\nPage Settings");
    Console.WriteLine("Is Color = " + pg.Color.ToString());
    Console.WriteLine("Top Bound = " + pg.Bounds.Top.ToString());
    Console.WriteLine("Bottom Bound = " + pg.Bounds.Bottom.ToString());
    Console.WriteLine("Left Bound = " + pg.Bounds.Left.ToString());
    Console.WriteLine("Right Bound = " + pg.Bounds.Right.ToString());
    Console.WriteLine("Top Margin = " + pg.Margins.Top.ToString());
    Console.WriteLine("Bottom Margin = " + pg.Margins.Bottom.ToString());
    Console.WriteLine("Left Margin = " + pg.Margins.Left.ToString());
    Console.WriteLine("Right Margin = " + pg.Margins.Right.ToString());
    Console.WriteLine("Landscape = " + pg.Landscape.ToString());
    Console.WriteLine("PaperSize = " + pg.PaperSize.PaperName);
    Console.WriteLine("PaperSource = " + pg.PaperSource.SourceName);
    Console.WriteLine("PrinterResolution = " +
                      pg.PrinterResolution.Kind.ToString());
    Console.WriteLine("PrinterResolution X = " +
                      pg.PrinterResolution.X.ToString());
    Console.WriteLine("PrinterResolution Y = " +
                      pg.PrinterResolution.Y.ToString());

    Console.ReadLine();

  }
 }
}
```

Listing 8-1b. VB Program Showing Default Printer and Page Settings

```vb
Option Strict On

Imports System
Imports System.Drawing.Printing

Module Module1

  Sub Main()
    Dim pd As PrintDocument = New PrintDocument()
    Dim pg As PageSettings = pd.DefaultPageSettings
    Dim ps As PrinterSettings = pg.PrinterSettings

    Console.WriteLine("Printer Settings")
    Console.WriteLine("PrinterName = " + pd.PrinterSettings.PrinterName)
      Console.WriteLine("Is default Printer = " + _
                        ps.IsDefaultPrinter.ToString())
    Console.WriteLine("Is plotter = " + ps.IsPlotter.ToString())
    Console.WriteLine("Is printer valid = " + ps.IsValid.ToString())
    Console.WriteLine("Can Duplex = " + ps.IsValid.ToString())
    Console.WriteLine("Num copies = " + ps.Copies.ToString())
    Console.WriteLine("Max Copies = " + ps.MaximumCopies.ToString())
    Console.WriteLine("Max Page = " + ps.MaximumPage.ToString())
    Console.WriteLine("Min Page = " + ps.MinimumPage.ToString())
    Console.WriteLine("Supports Color = " + ps.SupportsColor.ToString())
    Dim p As PaperSize
    For Each p In ps.PaperSizes
      Console.WriteLine("Supports Paper Size: " + p.PaperName)
    Next
    Dim p1 As PaperSource
    For Each p1 In ps.PaperSources
      Console.WriteLine("Supports Paper Source: " + p1.SourceName)
    Next

    Console.WriteLine("\nPage Settings")
    Console.WriteLine("Is Color = " + pg.Color.ToString())
    Console.WriteLine("Top Bound = " + pg.Bounds.Top.ToString())
    Console.WriteLine("Bottom Bound = " + pg.Bounds.Bottom.ToString())
    Console.WriteLine("Left Bound = " + pg.Bounds.Left.ToString())
    Console.WriteLine("Right Bound = " + pg.Bounds.Right.ToString())
    Console.WriteLine("Top Margin = " + pg.Margins.Top.ToString())
    Console.WriteLine("Bottom Margin = " + pg.Margins.Bottom.ToString())
    Console.WriteLine("Left Margin = " + pg.Margins.Left.ToString())
```

```
      Console.WriteLine("Right Margin = " + pg.Margins.Right.ToString())
      Console.WriteLine("Landscape = " + pg.Landscape.ToString())
      Console.WriteLine("PaperSize = " + pg.PaperSize.PaperName)
      Console.WriteLine("PaperSource = " + pg.PaperSource.SourceName)
      Console.WriteLine("PrinterResolution = " + _
                   pg.PrinterResolution.Kind.ToString())
      Console.WriteLine("PrinterResolution X = " + _
                   pg.PrinterResolution.X.ToString())
      Console.WriteLine("PrinterResolution Y = " + _
                   pg.PrinterResolution.Y.ToString())


      Console.ReadLine()

  End Sub
End Module
```

The printer I have is an older model HP LaserJet 6L. It is set up as my default printer. The following output list shows all the settings for this printer. Your printer may be different. Anyway, here are all the defaults for this simple print job defined in the first line of the Main code:

```
Printer Settings
PrinterName = HP LaserJet 6L
Is default Printer = True
Is plotter = False
Is printer valid = True
Can Duplex = True
Num copies = 1
Max Copies = 32767
Max Page = 9999
Min Page = 0
Supports Color = False
Supports Paper Size: Letter
Supports Paper Size: Legal
Supports Paper Size: Executive
Supports Paper Size: A4
Supports Paper Size: A5
Supports Paper Size: Envelope #10
Supports Paper Size: Envelope DL
Supports Paper Size: Envelope C5
Supports Paper Size: Envelope Monarch
Supports Paper Source: Automatically Select
Supports Paper Source: Paper Input Bin
Supports Paper Source: Manual Paper Feed
```

```
Page Settings
Is Color = False
Top Bound = 0
Bottom Bound = 1100
Left Bound = 0
Right Bound = 850
Top Margin = 100
Bottom Margin = 100
Left Margin = 100
Right Margin = 100
Landscape = False
PaperSize = Letter
PaperSource = Automatically Select
PrinterResolution = Custom
PrinterResolution X = 600
PrinterResolution Y = 600
```

As you can see, .NET does quite a bit for you behind the scenes to set up a simple print job to run without any additional settings by you. All I need to do is set up a stream to print and I am just about done.

Notice that in the last example everything was keyed off the PrintDocument class. This class has just one constructor that as you saw sets up a print job based on the system's default printer. The PrintDocument class has four properties that you should know. These properties are as follows:

- DefaultPageSettings

- PrinterSettings

- DocumentName

- PrintController

The **DefaultPageSettings** property you already know, along with the **PrinterSettings** property. The **DocumentName** property is the name of the document as it would appear in the print queue. Do not get this confused with the name of the file to print. The **DocumentName** property is set to the string "Document" as a default, and the name of the file you want to print is specified in the PagePrint event handler. It is nice to give a valid name to the **DocumentName** property during a print job, but it is not necessary.

The **PrintController** property is something you have not seen yet. A PrintController is a class that defines how a PrintDocument job is to be printed. What do I mean by this? Perhaps you would like to see your document before you print it. You would then use a specialized version of the PrintController class called

PrintPreviewControl. Suppose you wanted to show a dialog box to a user that tracks the document as it is being printed. You would use another specialized version of this class called PrintControllerWithStatusDialog. (That is quite a long name.)

It is amazing to me how many ways you can set up a print job and how its status can be displayed at various points during printing. Microsoft has indeed done a very good job of making this easy.

Anyway, back to the printing. Each version of the **PrintController** property has four methods:

- OnStartPrint

- OnStartPage

- OnEndPage

- OnEndPrint

Each of these methods is invoked at certain times during the print process. Knowing what is called, why, and by whom can be somewhat confusing. The following is the order of calls when the **PrintDocument.Print** method is invoked. This **Print** method starts a cascade of events that happen in this order:

1. The **PrintDocument.BeginPrint** method is called. This method is used by you to set up any printing defaults.

2. The **PrintController.OnStartPrint** method is called. This method creates a Graphics object that is sent to the printer.

3. The **PrintController.OnStartPage** method is called, which sets the Graphics object to a graphic of a single page.

4. The **PrintDocument.PrintPage** event is fired and its handler is run. It is in here that you will actually send the page to the printer.

5. The **PrintController.OnEndPage** method is called, which clears the Graphics object.

6. The **PrintDocument.EndPrint** event is fired and its handler is run. This event is fired when you set the **HasMorePages** property to false in your **PrintPage** handler.

7. The **PrintController.OnEndPrint** method is run, which deallocates the Graphics object along with any other resources the PrintController used.

I bet this is kind of confusing to you. It was to me when I first played around with it. In order to make things clearer, I wrote a small program that reads a file and prints it. I put code in my program that writes to the screen during all the important events and method calls. I show you this program next.

First of all, you will need a file to print. It also helps if you have a default printer set up for your computer. You do not actually have to be connected to the printer for this to work, but you will need to cancel the print job within Windows if it is not able to print.

Back to the file. I created a file called Test.txt. It has four pages of the word "TEXT" in it. Not very exciting, but it serves the purpose. You will find this file along with the code for this example if you downloaded it from the Downloads section of the Apress Web site (http://www.apress.com).

Start a new Windows Forms project in either C# or VB. I called mine PrintEvents. There are some things to do before you add any code:

1. Size the form to be 300×350.

2. Add a label to the form and call it lblEvents.

3. Size the label to fit most of the form. Make the border style 3D.

4. Add a button to the form just below the label. Call it cmdPrint.

5. Double-click the button to get the standard event handler.

Your form should end up looking like the one shown in Figure 8-1.

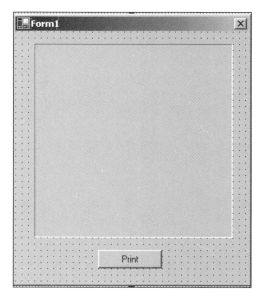

Figure 8-1. Form setup for the PrintEvents example

Now comes the tricky bit: the code. The code for this example is not quite as easy as it may first appear.

What I want to do is print a message to the label whenever any of the following methods are called:

- PrintDocument.BeginPrint

- PrintDocument.PagePrint

- PrintDocument.EndPrint

- PrintController.OnStartPrint

- PrintController.OnStartPage

- PrintController.OnEndPage

- PrintController.OnEndPrint

The PrintDocument methods are easy. You will have to write delegates for them anyway. But what about the PrintController? The PrintDocument, when created, gets a print controller by default. It is called—you guessed it—StandardPrintController. Most times you will never have to do anything with the **PrintDocument.PrintController** property. The standard one is used to good effectiveness in any print job that goes to the printer. You may, however, change this print controller for one that sends output to a preview dialog box, or you may change it for one that shows a print dialog box.

In the case of this example I need to override the methods of the print controller for the current PrintDocument. The only way to do this is to derive a new class that inherits from the StandardPrintController. Within this new class, I can override the base class' methods, insert my display code, and then call the base class' methods. Effectively, I am forcing the print controller to take a little detour through my new class.

Listing 8-2 shows the code for the standard form as well as the new class. By the way, notice that in order to print directly to the label, I pass in a reference to it during initialization. Otherwise, I would have the text to write and the ability to write the text, but nothing to write it on.

I am not going to bother showing you the Windows Form Designer generated code except for the constructor and destructor. I will not be changing any of the other wizard-generated code.

Listing 8-2a. C# Code for the Default Form

```csharp
using System;
using System.IO;
using System.Drawing;
using System.Drawing.Printing;
using System.Collections;
using System.ComponentModel;
using System.Windows.Forms;
using System.Data;

namespace PrintEvents_c
{
  public class Form1 : System.Windows.Forms.Form
  {
    private Font PrintFont;
    private StreamReader PrintStream;

    private System.Windows.Forms.Button cmdPrint;
    private System.Windows.Forms.Label lblEvents;

    private System.ComponentModel.Container components = null;

    Public Form1()
    {
      InitializeComponent();
    }

    protected override void Dispose( bool disposing )
    {
      if( disposing )
      {
        if (components != null)
        {
          components.Dispose();
        }
        PrintFont.Dispose();
      }
      base.Dispose( disposing );
    }
```

```
#region Windows Form Designer generated code

...

...

#endregion

[STAThread]
static void Main()
{
  Application.Run(new Form1());
}

private void Form1_Load(object sender, System.EventArgs e)
{
}

// Print the file.
public void Print_It()
{
  try
  {
    //Get the file to print
    PrintStream = new StreamReader ("Test.txt");
    try
    {
      PrintFont = new Font("Arial", 10);
      PrintDocument pd = new PrintDocument();

      //Assign my overloaded version of the standard print controller
      //Send it a reference to the label so it can tell us what is
      //going on.
      pd.PrintController = new MyPrintController(ref lblEvents);

      //Install event handlers
      pd.BeginPrint += new PrintEventHandler(this.pd_StartPrint);
      pd.PrintPage  += new PrintPageEventHandler(this.pd_PrintPage);
      pd.EndPrint   += new PrintEventHandler(this.pd_EndPrint);

      // Print the document.
      pd.Print();
    }
```

```csharp
        finally
        {
          PrintStream.Close();
        }
      }
    catch(Exception ex)
    {
      MessageBox.Show(ex.Message);
    }
}


private void pd_StartPrint(object sender, PrintEventArgs ev)
{
  lblEvents.Text += "PrintDocument: BeginPrint\n";
}


private void pd_EndPrint(object sender, PrintEventArgs ev)
{
  lblEvents.Text += "PrintDocument: EndPrinting\n";
}


// The PrintPage event is raised for each page to be printed.
private void pd_PrintPage(object sender, PrintPageEventArgs ev)
{
  float linesPerPage = 0;
  float yPos =  0;
  int   count = 0;
  float leftMargin = ev.MarginBounds.Left;
  float topMargin = ev.MarginBounds.Top;
  String line=null;

  lblEvents.Text += "PrintDocument:  PagePrint\n";

  // Calculate the number of lines per page.
  linesPerPage = ev.MarginBounds.Height / PrintFont.GetHeight(ev.Graphics);
```

```
      // Iterate over the file, printing each line. Use a basic StringFormat
      while (count++ < linesPerPage && ((line=PrintStream.ReadLine()) != null))
      {
        //Calculate vertical position of the line.
        yPos = topMargin + (count * PrintFont.GetHeight(ev.Graphics));
        //This is the graphics object obtained by the PrintController
        //OnStartPage method.  We are drawing to the printer!!
        ev.Graphics.DrawString (line, PrintFont, Brushes.Black,
                              leftMargin, yPos, new StringFormat());
      }

      // If more lines exist, print another page.
      if (line != null)
        ev.HasMorePages = true;
      else
        ev.HasMorePages = false;
    }

    private void cmdPrint_Click(object sender, System.EventArgs e)
    {
      Print_It();
    }
  }
}
```

Listing 8-2b. C# Code Showing the Derived Class

```
using System;
using System.Windows.Forms;
using System.Drawing;
using System.Drawing.Printing;
using System.ComponentModel;

namespace PrintEvents_c
{
  public class MyPrintController : StandardPrintController
  {
    private Label lblEvents;
    public MyPrintController(ref Label lbl): base()
    {
      lblEvents = lbl;
    }
```

```csharp
        public override void OnStartPrint(PrintDocument doc, PrintEventArgs e)
        {
          lblEvents.Text += "        PrintController: OnStartPrint\n";
          base.OnStartPrint(doc, e);
        }
        public override Graphics OnStartPage(PrintDocument doc, PrintPageEventArgs e)
        {
          lblEvents.Text += "        PrintController: OnStartPage\n";
          return( base.OnStartPage(doc, e) );
        }
        public override void OnEndPage(PrintDocument doc, PrintPageEventArgs e)
        {
          lblEvents.Text += "        PrintController: OnEndPage\n";
          base.OnEndPage(doc, e);
        }
        public override void OnEndPrint(PrintDocument doc, PrintEventArgs e)
        {
          lblEvents.Text += "        PrintController: OnEndPrint\n";
          base.OnEndPrint(doc, e);
        }
      }
    }
```

Listing 8-2c. VB Code Showing the Default Form

```vbnet
Option Strict On

Imports System
Imports System.IO
Imports System.Drawing
Imports System.Drawing.Printing

Public Class Form1
  Inherits System.Windows.Forms.Form

  Private PrintFont As Font
  Private PrintStream As StreamReader

#Region " Windows Form Designer generated code "
...
...
#End Region
```

```
' Print the file.
Public Sub Print_It()
  Try
    'Get the file to print
    PrintStream = New StreamReader("Test.txt")
    Try
      PrintFont = New Font("Arial", 10)
      Dim pd As PrintDocument = New PrintDocument()

      'Assign my overloaded version of the standard print controller
      'Send it a reference to the label so it can tell us what is
      'going on.
      pd.PrintController = New MyPrintController(lblEvents)

      'Install event handlers
      AddHandler pd.BeginPrint, _
                New PrintEventHandler(AddressOf Me.pd_StartPrint)
      AddHandler pd.PrintPage, _
                New PrintPageEventHandler(AddressOf Me.pd_PrintPage)
      AddHandler pd.EndPrint, _
                New PrintEventHandler(AddressOf Me.pd_EndPrint)

      'Print the document.
      pd.Print()
    Finally
      PrintStream.Close()
    End Try
  Catch ex As Exception
    MessageBox.Show(ex.Message)
  End Try
End Sub

Private Sub pd_StartPrint(ByVal sender As Object, ByVal ev As PrintEventArgs)
  lblEvents.Text += "PrintDocument: BeginPrint" + vbCrLf
End Sub

' The PrintPage event is raised for each page to be printed.
Private Sub pd_PrintPage(ByVal sender As Object, _
                    ByVal ev As PrintPageEventArgs)
  Dim linesPerPage As Single = 0
  Dim yPos As Single = 0
  Dim count As Int32 = 0
  Dim leftMargin As Single = ev.MarginBounds.Left
```

```vbnet
      Dim topMargin As Single = ev.MarginBounds.Top
      Dim line As String = String.Empty

      lblEvents.Text += "PrintDocument:  PagePrint" + vbCrLf

      ' Calculate the number of lines per page.
      linesPerPage = ev.MarginBounds.Height / PrintFont.GetHeight(ev.Graphics)

      ' Iterate over the file, printing each line. Use a basic StringFormat
      While count < linesPerPage
        line = PrintStream.ReadLine()
        If line Is Nothing Then
          Exit While
        End If
        'Calculate vertical position of the line.
        yPos = topMargin + count * PrintFont.GetHeight(ev.Graphics)
        'This is the graphics object obtained by the PrintController
        'OnStartPage method.  We are drawing to the printer!!
        ev.Graphics.DrawString(line, PrintFont, Brushes.Black, leftMargin, _
            yPos, New StringFormat())
        count += 1
      End While

      ' If more lines exist, print another page.
      If Not line Is Nothing Then
        ev.HasMorePages = True
      Else
        ev.HasMorePages = False
      End If

    End Sub

    Private Sub pd_EndPrint(ByVal sender As Object, ByVal ev As PrintEventArgs)
      lblEvents.Text += "PrintDocument: EndPrinting" + vbCrLf
    End Sub

    Private Sub cmdPrint_Click(ByVal sender As System.Object, _
                            ByVal e As System.EventArgs) Handles cmdPrint.Click
      Print_It()
    End Sub
End Class
```

Listing 8-2d. VB Code Showing the Derived Class

```vb
Option Strict On

Imports System
Imports System.IO
Imports System.Drawing
Imports System.Drawing.Printing

Public Class MyPrintController
  Inherits StandardPrintController

  Private lblEvents As Label

  Public Sub New(ByRef lbl As Label)
    MyBase.New()
    lblEvents = lbl
  End Sub

  Public Overrides Sub OnStartPrint(ByVal doc As PrintDocument, _
                                    ByVal e As PrintEventArgs)
    lblEvents.Text += "    PrintController: OnStartPrint" + vbCrLf
    MyBase.OnStartPrint(doc, e)
  End Sub

  Public Overrides Function OnStartPage(ByVal doc As PrintDocument, _
                                        ByVal e As PrintPageEventArgs) _
                                    As Graphics
    lblEvents.Text += "    PrintController: OnStartPage" + vbCrLf
    Return (MyBase.OnStartPage(doc, e))
  End Function

  Public Overrides Sub OnEndPage(ByVal doc As PrintDocument, _
                                 ByVal e As PrintPageEventArgs)
    lblEvents.Text += "    PrintController: OnEndPage" + vbCrLf
    MyBase.OnEndPage(doc, e)
  End Sub

  Public Overrides Sub OnEndPrint(ByVal doc As PrintDocument, _
                                  ByVal e As PrintEventArgs)
    lblEvents.Text += "    PrintController: OnEndPrint" + vbCrLf
    MyBase.OnEndPrint(doc, e)
  End Sub
End Class
```

Let's attack the derived class first. First of all, notice that the base class is the StandardPrintController.

The constructor takes a reference to the label from the form as an argument. It also makes sure to call the base class constructor.

Next, I override all the methods that get called during the printing of a document. In each of these methods, I send a line of text to the label and then call the base class method.

While the code for this is simple enough, knowing how to inherit from a base class properly requires some knowledge on your part. If this is not second nature to you, then I respectfully suggest that it needs to be.

Now on to the code for the form. Let's look at the Try block in the **Print_It** method:

```
try
{
  PrintFont = new Font("Arial", 10);
  PrintDocument pd = new PrintDocument();

  //Assign my overloaded version of the standard print controller
  //Send it a reference to the label so it can tell us what is
  //going on.
  pd.PrintController = new MyPrintController(ref lblEvents);

  //Install event handlers
  pd.BeginPrint += new PrintEventHandler(this.pd_StartPrint);
  pd.PrintPage  += new PrintPageEventHandler(this.pd_PrintPage);
  pd.EndPrint   += new PrintEventHandler(this.pd_EndPrint);

  // Print the document.
  pd.Print();
}
```

In here I create a new PrintDocument. The next thing I do is create an instance of my new PrintController and pass in a reference to the label. This new PrintController gets assigned to the PrintDocument.

I then assign delegates to handle the various printing events. The final thing I do here is call the PrintDocument's **Print** method. This is what starts the whole ball rolling.

The other major method of this form is the **pd_PrintPage** method:

```
private void pd_PrintPage(object sender, PrintPageEventArgs ev)
{
  float linesPerPage = 0;
  float yPos =  0;
  int   count = 0;
  float leftMargin = ev.MarginBounds.Left;
  float topMargin = ev.MarginBounds.Top;
  String line=null;

  lblEvents.Text += "PrintDocument:  PagePrint\n";

  // Calculate the number of lines per page.
  linesPerPage = ev.MarginBounds.Height / PrintFont.GetHeight(ev.Graphics);

  // Iterate over the file, printing each line. Use a basic StringFormat
  while (count++ < linesPerPage && ((line=PrintStream.ReadLine()) != null))
  {
    //Calculate vertical position of the line.
    yPos = topMargin + (count * PrintFont.GetHeight(ev.Graphics));
    //This is the graphics object obtained by the PrintController
    //OnStartPage method.  We are drawing to the printer!!
    ev.Graphics.DrawString (line, PrintFont, Brushes.Black,
                            leftMargin, yPos, new StringFormat());
  }

  // If more lines exist, print another page.
  if (line != null)
    ev.HasMorePages = true;
  else
    ev.HasMorePages = false;
}
```

Here I calculate the line heights while reading from the stream. I use the **Graphics.DrawString** method to draw the text on the graphics page, which gets sent to the printer. This **DrawString** method should tell you that everything gets sent to the printer as graphics.

When I come to the last line of the file, I set the **HasMorePages** property to false, which triggers the end of the print job.

NOTE *Because I am not doing a read-ahead of the lines in the file, I may not recognize when the last line occurs. If the last line occurs on the current page, another cycle of PrintPage will occur that results in a blank page being printed at the end of the document. I leave it to you to figure out how to solve this problem.*

Run the code and you should see output on your form similar to that shown in Figure 8-2.

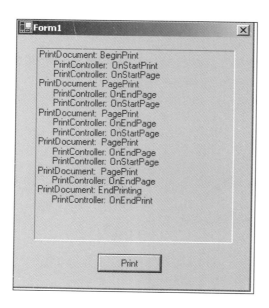

```
Form1                                          ×
PrintDocument: BeginPrint
    PrintController: OnStartPrint
    PrintController: OnStartPage
PrintDocument: PagePrint
    PrintController: OnEndPage
    PrintController: OnStartPage
PrintDocument: PagePrint
    PrintController: OnEndPage
    PrintController: OnStartPage
PrintDocument: PagePrint
    PrintController: OnEndPage
    PrintController: OnStartPage
PrintDocument: PagePrint
    PrintController: OnEndPage
PrintDocument: EndPrinting
    PrintController: OnEndPrint



              Print
```

Figure 8-2. Output of the PrintEvents example

Figure 8-2 shows you the complete sequence of events for printing any document in .NET.

Now, as I mentioned, .NET provides you with three PrintControllers:

- StandardPrintController

- PreviewPrintController

- PrintControllerWithStatusDialog

In all likelihood, these three implementations will automagically handle just about any printing need you have. So the question is, did I really need to show you this last example? The answer is not really. It is entirely possible for you to create code to print all kinds of documents without ever knowing or caring what goes on behind the scenes. .NET will happily insulate you from the details. However, is that what you really want? My feeling is that to become a true expert programmer, you should know what goes on under the covers of .NET. An example like this gives you a much better understanding of how printing really works. From this understanding, you will be able to extend the functionality to solve some problems you may encounter in the future. Okay, that's the end of my lecture for today.

Creating a Standard Print Job

Before you can start printing graphics or text to the screen, you need to learn how to create a standard print job. I already took you through a simple print job in the example for Listing 8-2. In this section I go over some more details.

As the previous example showed you, it is not necessary to provide a delegate for the **PrintDocument.BeginPrint** and **PrintDocument.EndPrint** events. All I did with these delegates was display some progress to the screen.

What else could you do with these events? Let's start with the BeginPrint event. A delegate for this event would normally handle the setup of file streams, fonts, any printer settings, and so forth. It is also a good place to set the PageSettings for the whole document.

A few things in the PageSettings class are commonly changed:

- PaperSize

- Margins

- PaperSource

- PrinterResolution

Of course, all these items are printer dependent. It would do no good to change the **PaperSize** property to A4, for instance, if your printer knows of no such paper. I suppose you could handle an error such as this by trapping the InvalidPrinterException error. As a last resort, this is what you should do, but it is better to query your printer to see what it can handle then decide from here.

The PrinterSettings class has three collections that contain the capabilities of the printer as far as paper size, paper source, and printer resolution go:

- PaperSizes

- PaperSources

- PrinterResoultions

What you can do is iterate through these collections after you have decided on the printer and then make sure that what the user chose as far as paper size, for instance, is correct. You can then fall back to the default for that printer if the selected paper is not available. You could also make a nice dialog box notifying the user that the paper is not available and present a list of paper sizes that are available for the chosen printer.

Let's expand on the example in Listing 8-2 to include some setup inside the **BeginPrint** method and also set an individual page's settings inside the **PagePrint** method. Finally, some resources will be released in the **EndPrint** method.

This next example is a Windows Forms example that lets the user choose ahead of time from a list of printers, paper sizes, and printer resolutions. The code then makes sure that these choices are valid and enables the choices if they are valid. Otherwise, the code keeps the default.

Start a new Windows Forms project in either C# or VB. Mine is called BeginPrint. Add the following controls to the form:

1. Add a label near the top of the form and set the text to "Paper Size".

2. Add a list box below this label. Call it lstPaper. Size it to hold four or five items.

3. Add another label below lstPaper and set the text to "Printer Resolution".

4. Add a list box below this label. Call it lstRes. Size it to hold four or five items.

5. Add a label below lstRes and set the text to "Installed Printers".

6. Add a button at the bottom of the form and call it cmdStartPrint. Set the text to "Start Print".

Your form should end up looking like the one shown in Figure 8-3.

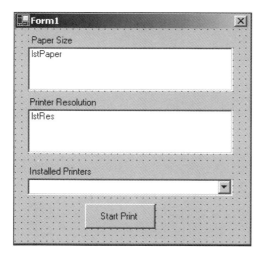

Figure 8-3. Setup of the form for the BeginPrint example

Double-click the button to get the wizard-generated event handler set up for you.

Listing 8-3 shows the code that makes all this work. As usual, I include as little of the Windows Form Designer generated code as is necessary.

Listing 8-3a. C# Code for the BeginPrint Example

```csharp
using System;
using System.Drawing;
using System.IO;
using System.Drawing.Printing;
using System.Collections;
using System.ComponentModel;
using System.Windows.Forms;
using System.Data;

namespace BeginPrint_c
{
    /// <summary>
    /// Summary description for Form1.
    /// </summary>
    public class Form1 : System.Windows.Forms.Form
    {
        #region Class Local Storage
        PrintDocument Pd;
        Font Pf;
        TextReader file;
        int Pages = 0;
        #endregion

        private System.Windows.Forms.ComboBox cmbPrinters;
        private System.Windows.Forms.Label label1;
        private System.Windows.Forms.Button cmdStartPrint;
        private System.Windows.Forms.ListBox lstPaper;
        private System.Windows.Forms.Label label2;
        private System.Windows.Forms.Label label3;
        private System.Windows.Forms.ListBox lstRes;

        private System.ComponentModel.Container components = null;
```

```csharp
public Form1()
{
  InitializeComponent();

}

protected override void Dispose( bool disposing )
{
  if( disposing )
  {
    if (components != null)
    {
      components.Dispose();
    }
  }

  base.Dispose( disposing );
}

#region Windows Form Designer generated code
…
…
…
#endregion

[STAThread]
static void Main()
{
  Application.Run(new Form1());
}

private void Form1_Load(object sender, System.EventArgs e)
{
  Init();
}

private void Init()
{
  foreach(String p in PrinterSettings.InstalledPrinters)
    cmbPrinters.Items.Add(p);

  if ( cmbPrinters.Items.Count > 0 )
    cmbPrinters.SelectedIndex = 0;
```

```csharp
    //Add a few paper sizes to the list box
    lstPaper.Items.Add(PaperKind.A4.ToString());
    lstPaper.Items.Add(PaperKind.Letter.ToString());
    lstPaper.Items.Add(PaperKind.CSheet.ToString());

    //Add all the printer resolutions to the list box
    lstRes.Items.Add(PrinterResolutionKind.Custom.ToString());
    lstRes.Items.Add(PrinterResolutionKind.Draft.ToString());
    lstRes.Items.Add(PrinterResolutionKind.High.ToString());
    lstRes.Items.Add(PrinterResolutionKind.Low.ToString());
    lstRes.Items.Add(PrinterResolutionKind.Medium.ToString());

}

private void cmdStartPrint_Click(object sender, System.EventArgs e)
{
  try
  {
    file = new StreamReader("Test.txt");
    try
    {
      //Create the document and give it a somewhat unique name
      Pd = new PrintDocument();
      Pd.DocumentName = DateTime.Now.Millisecond.ToString();

      //Install event handlers
      Pd.BeginPrint += new PrintEventHandler(this.BeginPrint);
      Pd.PrintPage  += new PrintPageEventHandler(this.PagePrint);
      Pd.EndPrint    += new PrintEventHandler(this.EndPrint);

      // Print the document.
      Pd.Print();
    }
    finally
    {
      file.Close();
      if (Pd != null)
        Pd.Dispose();
      if (Pf != null)
        Pf.Dispose();
    }
  }
```

```
      catch(Exception ex)
      {
        MessageBox.Show(ex.Message);
      }
    }

    private void BeginPrint(object sender, PrintEventArgs ev)
    {
      PageSettings Psettings = Pd.DefaultPageSettings;

      //Initialize the font
      Pf = new Font("Times New Roman", 12);

      Pd.PrinterSettings.PrinterName = cmbPrinters.SelectedItem.ToString();

      foreach (PaperSize ps in Pd.PrinterSettings.PaperSizes)
      {
        if (ps.PaperName == lstPaper.SelectedItem.ToString())
        {
          Psettings.PaperSize = ps;
          break;
        }
      }

      foreach (PrinterResolution pr in Pd.PrinterSettings.PrinterResolutions)
      {
        if (pr.Kind.ToString() == lstRes.SelectedItem.ToString())
        {
          Psettings.PrinterResolution = pr;
          break;
        }
      }

      //Make 1/4 inch margins all around
      Psettings.Margins = new Margins(25, 25, 25, 25);
      Pd.DefaultPageSettings = Psettings;
      //Reset the pages
      Pages = 0;
    }

    private void EndPrint(object sender, PrintEventArgs ev)
    {
      Pf.Dispose();
    }
```

```csharp
// The PrintPage event is raised for each page to be printed.
private void PagePrint(object sender, PrintPageEventArgs ev)
{
  float linesPerPage = 0;
  float yPos =  0;
  int   count = 0;
  float leftMargin = ev.MarginBounds.Left;
  float topMargin = ev.MarginBounds.Top;
  String line = null;

  //Keep track of pages as they are printed
  if (++Pages == 2)
  {
    try
    {
      ev.PageSettings.Landscape = true;
    }
    catch (Exception ex)
    {
      ev.PageSettings.Landscape = false;
    }
  }
  else
    ev.PageSettings.Landscape = false;

  // Calculate the number of lines per page.
  linesPerPage = ev.MarginBounds.Height / Pf.GetHeight(ev.Graphics);

  // Iterate over the file, printing each line. Use a basic StringFormat
  while (count++ < linesPerPage && ((line=file.ReadLine()) != null))
  {
    yPos = topMargin + (count * Pf.GetHeight(ev.Graphics));
    ev.Graphics.DrawString (line, Pf, Brushes.Black,
                            leftMargin, yPos, new StringFormat());
  }

  // If more lines exist, print another page.
  if (line != null)
    ev.HasMorePages = true;
  else
    ev.HasMorePages = false;

  }
 }
}
```

Listing 8-3b. VB Code for the BeginPrint Example

```vb
Option Strict On

Imports System
Imports System.IO
Imports System.Drawing
Imports System.Drawing.Printing

Public Class Form1
  Inherits System.Windows.Forms.Form

#Region "Class Local Storage"
  Private Pd As PrintDocument
  Private Pf As Font
  Private file As TextReader
  Private Pages As Int32 = 0
#End Region


#Region " Windows Form Designer generated code "
…
…
…
#End Region


  Private Sub Form1_Load(ByVal sender As System.Object, _
                       ByVal e As System.EventArgs) Handles MyBase.Load
    Init()
  End Sub

  Private Sub cmdStartPrint_Click(ByVal sender As System.Object, _
                              ByVal e As System.EventArgs) _
                              Handles cmdStartPrint.Click
    Try
      file = New StreamReader("Test.txt")
      Try
        'Create the document and give it a somewhat unique name
        Pd = New PrintDocument()
        Pd.DocumentName = DateTime.Now.Millisecond.ToString()
```

```vbnet
      'Install event handlers
      AddHandler Pd.BeginPrint, _
                New PrintEventHandler(AddressOf Me.BeginPrint)
      AddHandler Pd.PrintPage, _
                New PrintPageEventHandler(AddressOf Me.PagePrint)
      AddHandler Pd.EndPrint, _
                New PrintEventHandler(AddressOf Me.EndPrint)


      ' Print the document.
      Pd.Print()
    Finally
      file.Close()
      If Not Pd Is Nothing Then
        Pd.Dispose()
      End If
      If Not Pf Is Nothing Then
        Pf.Dispose()
      End If
    End Try
  Catch ex As Exception
    MessageBox.Show(ex.Message)
  End Try

End Sub


Private Sub Init()
  Dim p As String

  For Each p In PrinterSettings.InstalledPrinters
    cmbPrinters.Items.Add(p)
  Next

  If cmbPrinters.Items.Count > 0 Then
    cmbPrinters.SelectedIndex = 0
  End If

  'Add a few paper sizes to the list box
  lstPaper.Items.Add(PaperKind.A4.ToString())
  lstPaper.Items.Add(PaperKind.Letter.ToString())
  lstPaper.Items.Add(PaperKind.CSheet.ToString())
```

```vbnet
    'Add all the printer resolutions to the list box
    lstRes.Items.Add(PrinterResolutionKind.Custom.ToString())
    lstRes.Items.Add(PrinterResolutionKind.Draft.ToString())
    lstRes.Items.Add(PrinterResolutionKind.High.ToString())
    lstRes.Items.Add(PrinterResolutionKind.Low.ToString())
    lstRes.Items.Add(PrinterResolutionKind.Medium.ToString())
  End Sub

  Private Sub BeginPrint(ByVal sender As Object, ByVal ev As PrintEventArgs)
    Dim Psettings As PageSettings = Pd.DefaultPageSettings

    'Initialize the font
    Pf = New Font("Times New Roman", 10)

    Pd.PrinterSettings.PrinterName = cmbPrinters.SelectedItem.ToString()

    Dim ps As PaperSize
    For Each ps In Pd.PrinterSettings.PaperSizes
      If ps.PaperName = lstPaper.SelectedItem.ToString() Then
        Psettings.PaperSize = ps
        Exit For
      End If
    Next

    Dim pr As PrinterResolution
    For Each pr In Pd.PrinterSettings.PrinterResolutions
      If pr.Kind.ToString() = lstRes.SelectedItem.ToString() Then
        Psettings.PrinterResolution = pr
        Exit For
      End If
    Next

    'Make 1/4 inch margins all around
    Psettings.Margins = New Margins(25, 25, 25, 25)
    Pd.DefaultPageSettings = Psettings
    'Reset the pages
    Pages = 0
  End Sub

  Private Sub EndPrint(ByVal sender As Object, ByVal ev As PrintEventArgs)
    Pf.Dispose()
  End Sub
```

```
Private Sub PagePrint(ByVal sender As Object, ByVal ev As PrintPageEventArgs)
  Dim linesPerPage As Single = 0
  Dim yPos As Single = 0
  Dim count As Int32 = 0
  Dim leftMargin As Single = ev.MarginBounds.Left
  Dim topMargin As Single = ev.MarginBounds.Top
  Dim line As String = String.Empty

  'Keep track of pages as they are printed
  Pages += 1

  If Pages = 2 Then
    Try
      ev.PageSettings.Landscape = True
    Catch ex As Exception
      ev.PageSettings.Landscape = False
    End Try
  Else
    ev.PageSettings.Landscape = False
  End If

  ' Calculate the number of lines per page.
  linesPerPage = ev.MarginBounds.Height / Pf.GetHeight(ev.Graphics)

  ' Iterate over the file, printing each line. Use a basic StringFormat
  While count < linesPerPage
    line = file.ReadLine()
    If line Is Nothing Then
      Exit While
    End If
    'Calculate vertical position of the line.
    yPos = topMargin + count * Pf.GetHeight(ev.Graphics)
    'This is the graphics object obtained by the PrintController
    'OnStartPage method.  We are drawing to the printer!!
    ev.Graphics.DrawString(line, Pf, Brushes.Black, leftMargin, _
                           yPos, New StringFormat())
    count += 1
  End While
```

```
    ' If more lines exist, print another page.
    If Not line Is Nothing Then
      ev.HasMorePages = True
    Else
      ev.HasMorePages = False
    End If

  End Sub
End Class
```

Before you run this program, I ought to say that your output is printer dependent. If your printer does not support landscape mode, then you will not see landscape. If your printer does not support one of the resolutions, then you will see your output in the default resolution. That said, Figure 8-4 shows what my screen looks like before I click the Start Print button.

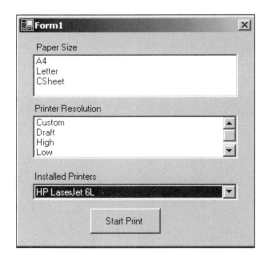

Figure 8-4. The BeginPrint example screen

I have filled the top portion with three possible paper sizes (of which only Letter is valid for my printer) and the second list box is filled with all the possible printer resolutions. I also have several installed printers that fill the combo box, but I chose the one you see here.

The code to fill these three controls is repeated here:

```
private void Init()
{
  foreach(String p in PrinterSettings.InstalledPrinters)
    cmbPrinters.Items.Add(p);

  if ( cmbPrinters.Items.Count > 0 )
    cmbPrinters.SelectedIndex = 0;

  //Add a few paper sizes to the list box
  lstPaper.Items.Add(PaperKind.A4.ToString());
  lstPaper.Items.Add(PaperKind.Letter.ToString());
  lstPaper.Items.Add(PaperKind.CSheet.ToString());

  //Add all the printer resolutions to the list box
  lstRes.Items.Add(PrinterResolutionKind.Custom.ToString());
  lstRes.Items.Add(PrinterResolutionKind.Draft.ToString());
  lstRes.Items.Add(PrinterResolutionKind.High.ToString());
  lstRes.Items.Add(PrinterResolutionKind.Low.ToString());
  lstRes.Items.Add(PrinterResolutionKind.Medium.ToString());
}
```

I use the static method **PrinterSettings.InstalledPrinters** to enumerate the printers on my machine. Remember this method—it is very handy. I fill the list boxes by choosing some kinds of paper and every resolution type.

Once I start the print job, the first event to be fired is the BeginPrint event. The delegate that handles this is as follows:

```
private void BeginPrint(object sender, PrintEventArgs ev)
{
  PageSettings Psettings = Pd.DefaultPageSettings;

  //Initialize the font
  Pf = new Font("Times New Roman", 10);

  Pd.PrinterSettings.PrinterName = cmbPrinters.SelectedItem.ToString();

  foreach (PaperSize ps in Pd.PrinterSettings.PaperSizes)
  {
    if (ps.PaperName == lstPaper.SelectedItem.ToString())
    {
      Psettings.PaperSize = ps;
      break;
    }
  }
```

```
    foreach (PrinterResolution pr in Pd.PrinterSettings.PrinterResolutions)
    {
      if (pr.Kind.ToString() == lstRes.SelectedItem.ToString())
      {
        Psettings.PrinterResolution = pr;
        break;
      }
    }

    //Make 1/4 inch margins all around
    Psettings.Margins = new Margins(25, 25, 25, 25);
    Pd.DefaultPageSettings = Psettings;
    //Reset the pages
    Pages = 0;
  }
```

This example is somewhat contrived, but it is intended to show you what to set and when. Anyway, in here I set the font and the printer name. I also check all the paper sizes allowed by my printer. If the paper size I chose in the list box is among them, I set the default paper size to this value. If it is not, the loop falls through and the default paper size is kept. I do the same thing for the printer resolution.

At the end of this method, I set the page margins and initialize a variable that I use to keep track of the number of pages being printed.

The **PagePrint** method prints the page normally except for one thing: It changes the paper orientation on the third page to be landscape mode. All other pages are in portrait mode. The code is as follows:

```
...
    //Keep track of pages as they are printed
    if (++Pages == 2)
    {
      try
      {
        ev.PageSettings.Landscape = true;
      }
      catch (Exception ex)
      {
        ev.PageSettings.Landscape = false;
      }
    }
    else
      ev.PageSettings.Landscape = false;
...
```

If the printer does not support landscape mode, then the Catch block will set it back to false.

> **NOTE**   *I am catching the most generic error here. Your professional code should catch the InvalidPrinterException before the Exception in this case.*

I have tried this small program with several printers and it works with all of them. Hopefully, it will work with yours. If it does not, as a programmer it is up to you to add extra code to make sure it does not choke on your printer.

By the way, I am sure you have noticed that there can be quite a few class-local variables that keep track of different things that go on while you are printing. This begs for a class wrapper. It would not take much for you to write a really nice printing class that encapsulates all the printing functionality you need. You could instantiate such a class and have it run in its own thread. Printing is the classic multithreaded task.

Printing Graphics

Yes, I know. This is what you have really been waiting for. Printing a text file can be pretty boring after a while. Of course, I still have not gone over the print preview or print dialog box capabilities of .NET yet. I will get to that soon. For now, let's concentrate on printing images.

On second thought, I think I will combine the PrintPreviewDialog with printing drawings and images. It makes for less paper waste if you can see the result of printing on the screen without having to actually print something.

So, all the examples in this chapter so far have centered on reading a file from disk and printing it. In fact, no user interface is needed for this at all. But what about printing something that is already on the screen and has not been persisted to disk? And, oh yeah, what about printing graphics?

I have already pointed out that printing text is a matter of using the **DrawString** method on the Graphics object that represents a hard-copy page. What do you think you would use to print a bitmap? Perhaps **DrawImage**? You would be correct in this assumption. In fact, if you wanted to draw any shape to the printer, you would use the drawing methods that are in the Graphics class. Microsoft has made it very easy to go from drawing on the screen to drawing on the printer or, for that matter, drawing on a PrintPreviewDialog screen. It is all the same.

Now, this begs the following question: Couldn't you use the same drawing method for printing as for drawing on the screen or drawing on the PrintPreviewDialog? Yes, you can and this is the preferred method. The next example uses the PrintPreviewDialog to display the contents of the basic form.

This dialog box can then be used to actually print the form. The example is not terribly difficult, but you do need to be able to follow what is going on. To this end, I have included a control on the form that tells you when the print event is being called and who is doing the calling.

Start a new Windows Forms project in either C# or VB. Mine is called PrintDialogs. You will need to do the following before adding any code:

1. Size the form to 450×400.

2. Add a label to the form and call it lblPrint.

3. Make the label size 280×135.

4. Make the label have a 3D border.

5. Put the label near the top right of the form.

6. Add a button to the form called cmdShow.

7. Set the text of the button to "Show".

Your form should look like the one shown in Figure 8-5.

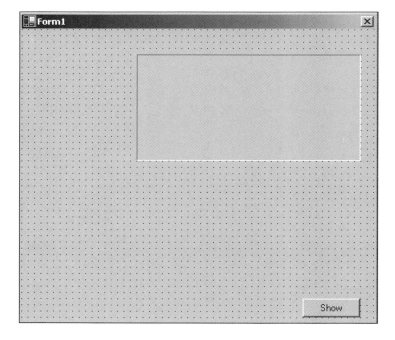

Figure 8-5. PrintDialogs form

Double-click the button to get the standard click event delegate. Listing 8-4 shows the code for this example. The Windows Form Designer generated code is not interesting for this example, so I will not show it here except for the constructor.

Listing 8-4a. C# Code for the PrintDialogs Example

```csharp
using System;
using System.Drawing;
using System.Drawing.Printing;
using System.Drawing.Drawing2D;
using System.Drawing.Imaging;
using System.Collections;
using System.ComponentModel;
using System.Windows.Forms;
using System.Data;

namespace PrintDialogs_c
{
  public class Form1 : System.Windows.Forms.Form
  {
    private Image MyImage;
    private PrintDocument pd;
    private PrintPreviewDialog Preview;

    private System.Windows.Forms.Button cmdShow;
    private System.Windows.Forms.Label lblPrint;
    private System.ComponentModel.Container components = null;

    public Form1()
    {
      InitializeComponent();

      MyImage = Bitmap.FromFile(@"d:\colorbars.jpg");
      Preview = new PrintPreviewDialog();
      Preview.UseAntiAlias = true;
    }
```

```
protected override void Dispose( bool disposing )
{
  if( disposing )
  {
    if (components != null)
    {
      components.Dispose();
    }
  }
  base.Dispose( disposing );
}

#region Windows Form Designer generated code
…
…
…
#endregion

[STAThread]
static void Main()
{
  Application.Run(new Form1());
}

private void Form1_Load(object sender, System.EventArgs e)
{
  pd = new PrintDocument();
  pd.PrintPage += new PrintPageEventHandler(this.pd_Print);

  Preview.Document = pd;
}

protected override void OnPaint(PaintEventArgs e)
{
  DrawIt(e.Graphics);
}

private void pd_Print(object sender, PrintPageEventArgs e)
{
  lblPrint.Text += "pd_Print pd= " + sender.ToString() + "\n" ;
  DrawIt(e.Graphics);
}
```

```
    private void DrawIt(Graphics G)
    {
      G.SmoothingMode=SmoothingMode.AntiAlias;
      G.DrawImage(MyImage, 10, 10);

      LinearGradientBrush B = new LinearGradientBrush(
                             new Rectangle(0, 0, 50, 10),
                             Color.Red, Color.Blue,
                             LinearGradientMode.ForwardDiagonal);
      G.FillEllipse(B, 10, 200, 200, 75);

      G.DrawString("Print Preview Test",
                 new Font("Comic Sans MS",24), B, 50, 275);
    }

    private void cmdShow_Click(object sender, System.EventArgs e)
    {
      Preview.WindowState = FormWindowState.Maximized;
      pd.DocumentName = DateTime.Now.Ticks.ToString();
      Preview.ShowDialog();
    }
  }
}
```

Listing 8-4b. VB Code for the PrintDialogs Example

```
Option Strict On
Imports System
Imports System.Drawing
Imports System.Drawing.Drawing2D
Imports System.Drawing.Text
Imports System.Drawing.Printing
Imports System.IO

Public Class Form1
  Inherits System.Windows.Forms.Form

  Private MyImage As Image
  Private pd As PrintDocument
  Private Preview As PrintPreviewDialog

#Region " Windows Form Designer generated code "
```

```vb
        Public Sub New()
          MyBase.New()

          InitializeComponent()

          MyImage = Bitmap.FromFile("d:\colorbars.jpg")
          Preview = New PrintPreviewDialog()
          Preview.UseAntiAlias = True

        End Sub
...
...
...

#End Region

    Private Sub Form1_Load(ByVal sender As System.Object, _
                            ByVal e As System.EventArgs) Handles MyBase.Load
        pd = New PrintDocument()
        AddHandler pd.PrintPage, New PrintPageEventHandler(AddressOf Me.pd_Print)

        Preview.Document = pd

    End Sub

    Protected Overrides Sub OnPaint(ByVal e As PaintEventArgs)
        DrawIt(e.Graphics)
    End Sub

    Private Sub pd_Print(ByVal sender As Object, ByVal e As PrintPageEventArgs)
        lblPrint.Text += "pd_Print pd= " + sender.ToString() + vbCrLf
        DrawIt(e.Graphics)
    End Sub

    Private Sub DrawIt(ByVal G As Graphics)
        G.SmoothingMode = SmoothingMode.AntiAlias
        G.DrawImage(MyImage, 10, 10)

        Dim B As LinearGradientBrush = New LinearGradientBrush( _
                                New Rectangle(0, 0, 50, 10), _
                                Color.Red, Color.Blue, _
                                LinearGradientMode.ForwardDiagonal)
        G.FillEllipse(B, 10, 200, 200, 75)
```

```
        G.DrawString("Print Preview Test", _
                    New Font("Comic Sans MS", 24), B, 50, 275)
    End Sub

    Private Sub cmdShow_Click(ByVal sender As System.Object, _
                            ByVal e As System.EventArgs) Handles cmdShow.Click
        Preview.WindowState = FormWindowState.Maximized
        pd.DocumentName = DateTime.Now.Ticks.ToString()
        Preview.ShowDialog()
    End Sub
End Class
```

Compile and run the program and you will get a screen similar to the one shown in Figure 8-6.

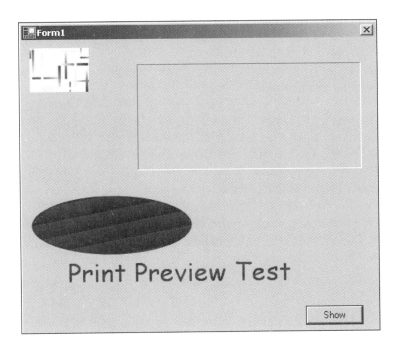

Figure 8-6. Running the PrintDialogs program

Click the Show button and you will see the print preview screen come up with a view of this page as it would be printed. Click the Print button and close the print preview screen. Your main form should now look similar to the one shown in Figure 8-7.

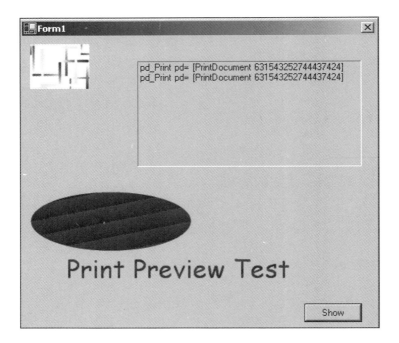

Figure 8-7. PrintDialogs screen showing print events

The label has two entries in it. The first one is from the bringing up the Print-PreviewDialog. The second is from printing the document. By the way, the number you see in this screen shot is the name I gave to the document. It is the timer tick's value at the time I create the PrintDocument.

Look at the code. The Print event delegate is as follows:

```
Private Sub pd_Print(ByVal sender As Object, ByVal e As PrintPageEventArgs)
    lblPrint.Text += "pd_Print pd= " + sender.ToString() + vbCrLf
    DrawIt(e.Graphics)
End Sub
```

The Print delegate calls the **DrawIt** method and writes to the label. Because the label is written to twice (once by print preview and once by printing), this method is called by both tasks. Interesting. What do you suppose is different that sends output to the screen in one case and to the printer in the other? Well, the Graphics object is different, for one thing.

Now notice that the **OnPaint** method also calls the **DrawIt** method. Only the Graphics object that is passed to this method is the one for the form. So what you have here is a function called **DrawIt** that renders shapes and images on a Graphics object. It is being called by three different tasks, and each time it is passed a different Graphics object.

This is how you share programming duties among several different objects.

Dialog Box–Based Printing

So far, I have done the printing tasks in what you would call the "hard way." I could have introduced you to the printing dialog boxes at the start and I would have been done with this chapter in a few short pages. However, what would you have learned? My feeling is that you can make effective use of the shortcuts only when you know what goes on behind the scenes.

 NOTE   *This chapter deals with the most common printing tasks. There is quite a bit more you can accomplish by digging through the System.IO namespace and applying the different stream classes to printer output. If you were going to create your own "better mouse-trap" word processor, I would encourage you to explore much more about printing than I have presented in this chapter.*

Several dialog boxes are available to you that give a nice presentation of printing to the user:

- PrintPreviewDialog

- PageSetupDialog

- PrintDialog

All three of these dialog boxes are available as controls that you can drop on your form. Each of these dialog controls is invisible at runtime, unless of course you invoke the particular dialog box. As you saw in the previous example, I was able to create a PrintPreview dialog box without using the control. That said, I am not sure what dropping a print dialog on your form gets you over making it yourself.

You have already learned about the PrintPreviewDialog. There are many more attributes you can set for this dialog box, some of which are as follows:

- Make it an MDI child.

- Make it an MDI container.

- Make it modal—or not.

- Add some more controls to the dialog box.

- Change the client size.

- Allow drag-and-drop capability.

There are a whole host of other things you can set to change the behavior of this dialog box.

The PageSetupDialog is pretty self-explanatory. Choose the Page Setup option in Microsoft Word and this is pretty much what you get. The PrintDialog allows you to choose the printer and also allows you to choose which pages to print, how many copies, and so forth.

Let's go through one last example showing the three main printing dialog boxes and how to use them. I don't include any error checking in this example. The code is much clearer without it.

Start a new C# or VB Windows Forms project. Mine is called UIPrint. Perform the following steps:

1. Add a button to the bottom of the form called cmdQuit. Set the text to "Quit".

2. Add a MainMenu control to the form.

3. Set the first-level menu item text to "File".

4. Set the second-level menu item text to "Page Setup". Call it mnuSetup.

5. Set the third-level menu item text to "Print Preview". Call it mnuPreview.

6. Set the fourth-level menu item text to "Print". Call it mnuPrint.

Double-click each of the menu items (except File) to get an event handler. Do this also for the Quit button. Your form should look like the one shown in Figure 8-8.

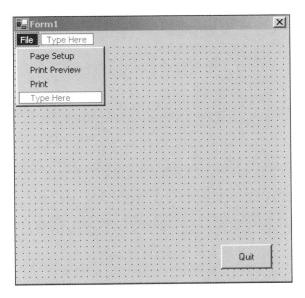

Figure 8-8. Form setup for the UIPrint example

The code in Listing 8-5 shows how this example sets up the three dialog boxes using default values for all. This code is by no means comprehensive, but it does show you how to use this functionality.

Listing 8-5a. VB Code for the UIPrint Example Using Multiple Print Dialog Boxes

```
Imports System
Imports System.Drawing
Imports System.Drawing.Drawing2D
Imports System.Drawing.Text
Imports System.Drawing.Printing

Public Class Form1
  Inherits System.Windows.Forms.Form

  Private Pv As PrintPreviewDialog
  Private Ps As PageSetupDialog
  Private Pd As PrintDocument
  Private Pr As PrintDialog
```

```
#Region " Windows Form Designer generated code "

  Public Sub New()
    MyBase.New()

    'This call is required by the Windows Form Designer.
    InitializeComponent()

    Pv = New PrintPreviewDialog()
    Ps = New PageSetupDialog()
    Pr = New PrintDialog()
    Pd = New PrintDocument()

    Pd.DocumentName = "My New Document"
    Pv.Document = Pd
    Ps.Document = Pd
    Pr.Document = Pd

  End Sub

  'Form overrides dispose to clean up the component list.
  Protected Overloads Overrides Sub Dispose(ByVal disposing As Boolean)
    If disposing Then
      If Not (components Is Nothing) Then
        components.Dispose()
      End If
    End If
    MyBase.Dispose(disposing)
  End Sub
...
...
...
#End Region

  Private Sub Form1_Load(ByVal sender As System.Object, _
                       ByVal e As System.EventArgs) Handles MyBase.Load
    AddHandler Pd.PrintPage, New PrintPageEventHandler(AddressOf Me.pd_Print)
  End Sub

  Protected Overrides Sub OnPaint(ByVal e As PaintEventArgs)
    DrawIt(e.Graphics)
  End Sub
```

```
Private Sub DrawIt(ByVal G As Graphics)
  G.SmoothingMode = SmoothingMode.AntiAlias
  Dim P1 As Pen = New Pen(Brushes.Violet, 5)

  G.DrawString("Test of Print dialog and page setup", _
               New Font("Time New Roman", 16), _
               Brushes.Blue, _
               New PointF(5, 5))
  G.DrawPie(P1, 10, 10, 150, 150, 28, 57)
  G.FillEllipse(Brushes.BurlyWood, 10, 200, Me.Width - 50, 50)
End Sub

Private Sub pd_Print(ByVal sender As Object, ByVal e As PrintPageEventArgs)
  DrawIt(e.Graphics)
End Sub

Private Sub mnuSetup_Click(ByVal sender As System.Object, _
                           ByVal e As System.EventArgs) _
                           Handles mnuSetup.Click
  Ps.ShowDialog()
  Pd.DefaultPageSettings = Ps.PageSettings
  Pd.PrinterSettings = Ps.PrinterSettings
End Sub

Private Sub mnuPreview_Click(ByVal sender As System.Object, _
                             ByVal e As System.EventArgs) _
                             Handles mnuPreview.Click
  Pv.WindowState = FormWindowState.Maximized
  Pv.ShowDialog()
End Sub


Private Sub cmdQuit_Click(ByVal sender As System.Object, _
                          ByVal e As System.EventArgs) _
                          Handles cmdQuit.Click
  Me.Dispose()
End Sub
```

```
     Private Sub mnuPrint_Click(ByVal sender As System.Object, _
                               ByVal e As System.EventArgs) _
                           Handles mnuPrint.Click
   If Pr.ShowDialog() = DialogResult.OK Then
     Pd.Print()
   End If
 End Sub
End Class
```

Listing 8-5b. C# Code for the UIPrint Example Using Multiple Print Dialog Boxes

```csharp
using System;
using System.Drawing;
using System.Drawing.Text;
using System.Drawing.Drawing2D;
using System.Drawing.Printing;
using System.Collections;
using System.ComponentModel;
using System.Windows.Forms;
using System.Data;

namespace UIPrint_c
{
  public class Form1 : System.Windows.Forms.Form
  {
    private PrintPreviewDialog Pv;
    private PageSetupDialog Ps;
    private PrintDocument Pd;
    private PrintDialog Pr;

    private System.Windows.Forms.MainMenu mainMenu1;
    private System.Windows.Forms.MenuItem mnuFile;
    private System.Windows.Forms.MenuItem mnuSetup;
    private System.Windows.Forms.MenuItem mnuPreview;
    private System.Windows.Forms.MenuItem mnuPrint;
    private System.Windows.Forms.Button cmdQuit;

    private System.ComponentModel.Container components = null;
```

```csharp
public Form1()
{
  InitializeComponent();

  Pv = new PrintPreviewDialog();
  Ps = new PageSetupDialog();
  Pr = new PrintDialog();
  Pd = new PrintDocument();

  Pd.DocumentName = "My New Document";
  Pv.Document = Pd;
  Ps.Document = Pd;
  Pr.Document = Pd;
}

protected override void Dispose( bool disposing )
{
  if( disposing )
  {
    if (components != null)
    {
      components.Dispose();
    }
  }
  base.Dispose( disposing );
}

#region Windows Form Designer generated code
...
...
...
#endregion

[STAThread]
static void Main()
{
  Application.Run(new Form1());
}

private void Form1_Load(object sender, System.EventArgs e)
{
  Pd.PrintPage += new PrintPageEventHandler(this.pd_Print);
}
```

```
protected override void OnPaint(PaintEventArgs e)
{
  DrawIt(e.Graphics);
}

private void DrawIt(Graphics G)
{
  G.SmoothingMode = SmoothingMode.AntiAlias;
  Pen P1 = new Pen(Brushes.Violet, 5);

  G.DrawString("Test of Print dialog and page setup",
               new Font("Time New Roman", 16),
               Brushes.Blue,
               new Point(5, 5));
  G.DrawPie(P1, 10, 10, 150, 150, 28, 57);
  G.FillEllipse(Brushes.BurlyWood, 10, 200, this.Width-50, 50);
}

private void pd_Print(object sender, PrintPageEventArgs e)
{
  DrawIt(e.Graphics);
}

private void mnuSetup_Click(object sender, System.EventArgs e)
{
  Ps.ShowDialog();
  Pd.DefaultPageSettings = Ps.PageSettings;
  Pd.PrinterSettings = Ps.PrinterSettings;
}

private void mnuPreview_Click(object sender, System.EventArgs e)
{
  Pv.WindowState = FormWindowState.Maximized;
  Pv.ShowDialog();
}

private void mnuPrint_Click(object sender, System.EventArgs e)
{
  if (Pr.ShowDialog() == DialogResult.OK)
    Pd.Print();
}
```

```
    private void cmdQuit_Click(object sender, System.EventArgs e)
    {
      this.Dispose();
    }
  }
}
```

Compile and run the code. Your screen should look like the one shown in Figure 8-9.

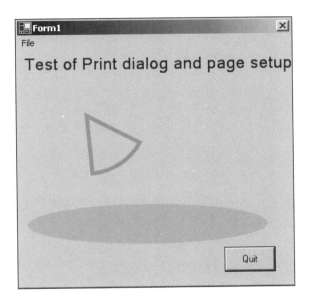

Figure 8-9. Form with graphics for the UIPrint example

Try the menu for Print Preview, Print, and Page Setup. All these forms will look familiar to you. More important, they will look familiar to the users of your software. Unless you spend a lot of time at it, you will find it much nicer to use the ones supplied by .NET than to roll your own.

If you look at the code, you will notice that I am again using a common drawing routine to write the text and shapes to whatever Graphics object is passed in.

There is quite a lot more I could do as far as setup goes, but it is all pretty basic stuff. You can handle the rest just fine.

Summary

This chapter introduced you to the printing support provided by .NET. Mainly, the classes in the System.Drawing.Printing namespace provide the printing support.

Printing is performed by writing to a Graphics object, which represents each page of a document. Because all the methods for drawing text, shapes, and images are the same for a printer as they are for the screen, you can use the same code to do both.

The main steps for setting up a print job are as follows:

1. Make a PrintDocument.

2. Extend the functionality of the PrintDocument.PrintPage event by coding your own delegate.

3. All drawing to the printer goes in the PrintPage delegate.

4. Use the BeginPrint delegate to set up any variables that may be necessary for your print job to run.

5. Use the EndPrint delegate to release any resources from your print job and to notify the user that printing is done.

In this chapter you learned the mechanics of how .NET calls different functions during printing. You also learned how to use the three different print dialog boxes to present a nice user interface.

The next two chapters deal strictly with examples using all the techniques you have learned so far in this book.

Part Two
Application Notes

TIME TO TAKE a breather. Actually, at this point you can probably put the book down and start coding. You now have enough knowledge to start a career in graphics programming. Or do you?

The first eight chapters in this book presented the theory you would find in any computer book. Although I peppered Chapters 1 through 8 with insightful examples (hopefully), they were all somewhat incomplete. As with most books, the examples I created were, for the most part, single purpose. They served to illustrate a point. They were missing context.

Now you have a decision to make. Do you go on or do you stop? Are basic theory and examples enough? That all depends on what is next.

I have created a few in-depth programs that use the features you have learned throughout this book. These are not examples—they are programs that you can use in your everyday programming life. While these programs may not be salable as is, they are full featured enough that you can extend them with a little imagination. They provide a good basis for similar professional programs.

These programs are designed to give the theory you learned in the previous eight chapters context. They provide the answer to the question "Okay, now what?"

If you are a seasoned GDI programmer who picked up this book as a reference on GDI+, I would imagine that you already have ideas on how to use what you have learned in this book. Perhaps you feel there is no need to go on from here.

If you are a new or journeyman programmer whose experience in graphics programming is light, I think the next two chapters will serve to round things out.

Whoever you are, I hope you will read on and glean what you can from the rest of the book. Whether you are a seasoned vet or just starting out, I do not think you will be disappointed with what is to come.

CHAPTER 9

GDI+ Projects

"Ace, watch your head!" hissed Wanda urgently, yet somehow provocatively,
through red, full, sensuous lips, but he couldn't you know, since nobody
can actually watch more than part of his nose or a little cheek or lips
if he really tries, but he appreciated her warning.

—Janice Estey, Aspen, Colorado (1996 Winner)

WELL, HERE WE ARE. There is nothing more to learn. If you believe that, I have a
bridge to sell you. I guess I could have gone droning on about the minutiae of
GDI+ programming for another few chapters. The book would have been heavier
that way. It would have also taken up more space on the shelf and shipping would
have cost you more. You see, I always have you, the customer, in mind.

I think I have given you enough detail to program pretty thoroughly using the
GDI+ classes. If there is anything more complicated that you need to do, look in
the .NET documentation and experiment.

This chapter is about application. I will go through a pretty complicated and
complete application using GDI+. This project not only includes what you have
learned so far, but it also includes quite a few other aspects of programming in .NET.

This project is a screen capture program . . . with a twist. It will be very interactive and, I hope, useful to you.

The Truth About GDI+

Before we start, I must confess something. I lied. Well, maybe not so much lied as
failed to tell you the complete truth. GDI+ does not do everything you might want
it to.

Throughout the book I have been consciously steering away from doing any
graphics work that did not make use of the GDI+ classes. I was successful.
I even got around the problem of the ubiquitous **BitBlt** API call.[1]

---

1. Actually, Microsoft got around this problem

One of the other major factors that would have forced me to go outside of GDI+ is the need for speed. I skirted that problem by judicious use of the **Invalidate** method as well as using the ControlStyle enumeration to provide double buffering.

So far, so good. The .NET Framework has provided enough classes and methods to program successfully in GDI+, at least up until this point.

GDI+ is comprehensive, but it is not all-encompassing. In fact, there are quite a few instances where you would need to resort to Win32 API calls to get things done. While the "meat" of the book has not really covered this, this program will. Remember, the InteropServices is your friend.

The Screen Capture Program

This project is very useful, I think. In fact, with the exception of Figure 9-4, I used a professional screen capture program to generate all the images in this book. While my version is not as feature-rich as the professional program, there were a few things missing from the professional one that I wished I had. There were also quite a few features in the professional version that I did not need. And to tell the truth, mine could use a little more polish, but then again, it is only an example.

This brings up a good point: This screen capture project is just an example. There are features missing from it and it really could use some extra pizzazz. You are more than welcome to upgrade it and use it for all your daily screen-capturing chores. I will say, though, that as an example, there is quite a bit to this program.

Designing the Program

Let's do what most programmers do and start writing code. After all, the design comes through iteration and frequent code changes, right? Wrong!

This type of programming practice has become so prevalent and is the cause of so much waste in programville. You, more often than not, end up with something completely different from what you started out programming. You also end up with code that is not well put together and therefore not easily extendable in the future. A functional specification is the minimum you should have before programming. Anyway, enough of that subject.

Here is the functional specification for this screen capture program boiled down to this small list:

- The program must be able to run at all times. Therefore, the initial screen must be small and hidden if needed.

- The program must be very easy to use, and therefore it must be graphically intuitive.

- The program must capture the whole screen.

- The user must be able to "carve out" a portion of the screen capture to save.

- The program must be able to change the screen capture resolution.

- The program must be able to add a border to the screen capture for a clean, sharp look.

- The program must be able to save the screen capture to disk in any supported format.

- The program must be able to print the screen capture. It should also be able to preview the printed output.

Okay, that is the functional specification. Now let's write a small technical specification based on the functional specification. The two combined will give you a very good basis to start programming.

The program must be able to run at all times and be unobtrusive. To this end, you will make the initial screen very small. It will have just two buttons: Capture and Quit. Instead of running in the task bar, it will reside in the system tray. When minimized, this program will only appear as an icon in the system tray. The tray icon will have a small menu and a tool tip.

The program must be easy to use. The user must be able to carve out a portion of the screen. "Easy to use" means big, fat buttons or using the mouse. You will capture the screen and layer it on top of the screen the user is viewing. It will appear to the user that he or she is still viewing the original screen. The cursor will change to a hand holding a crossbar. The user will drag a red dashed rectangle across the screen, thereby choosing the area he or she wants to capture.

The capability to add a border is something I wish I had in my professional screen capture program. There are lots of times when you only want part of a screen and the edges may not be clear. A border helps a lot in this case.

There are also times you need to change the resolution. Authoring programs often need high resolution to make crisp pictures.

Printing and print preview are also two things that this program cannot be without. You will put what you learned in Chapter 8 to good use here.

Drawing the Rectangle

Before you start on the project, you need to take a little detour. One of the project's requirements is that the user be able to use the mouse to draw a rectangle on the screen.

NOTE *I have seen a lot of grousing on user groups about the missing rubber-banding capability of GDI+. It seems that these people miss the raw GDI XOR capability that allows rubber-banding of lines. I do not see the problem at all. You can rubber-band lines and rectangles with ease in GDI+. This section will show you how.*

You probably have an idea of how to draw a rectangle on the screen using the mouse. It probably goes something like this: Just note the start location in the rectangle structure during the mouse down event. Complete the rectangle structure during the mouse move event by doing a little math to find the size of the rectangle. Once the rectangle is complete, invalidate the screen and draw the rectangle in the **OnPaint** method. Every time you get a mouse move event, you redraw the rectangle.

This works . . . sort of.

The **Graphics.DrawRectangle** method chokes big time if the rectangle is not positive. What do I mean by "positive"? The starting X and Y points must be positive numbers, and the width and height must also be positive numbers.

It is possible to create a rectangle whose width or height is negative. This means that the rectangle starts at one point and ends at a point to the left and/or above the starting point. A positive rectangle is one that ends both to the right and below the starting point.[2] This is the kind of rectangle that the **DrawRectangle** method needs. The user would create this kind of rectangle by dragging the mouse down the screen and to the right.

TIP *A rectangle whose starting point is any of its four corners can be used with the **DrawImage** method. The top left of the image always starts at the origin of the rectangle. You can use this fact to invert or mirror an image.*

The user needs to be able to start his or her rectangle at any of the four corners and drag the mouse toward the diagonal corner. This is not easy to do.

---

2. Remember, the origin is at the top left.

In this section I take you though a very small example where you can create a rubber-banded rectangle on the screen in any direction. You will then use some of the code in this example for the larger screen capture project. This small example is in C# only. When I transcribe the necessary code to the screen capture program, I transcribe it in both VB and in C#. The screen capture program will be in both languages.

Start out with a new Windows Forms program. Mine is called AllCornerRect. There are no controls on the form, so go straight to the code pane.

What you will be doing in here is making delegates for some of the mouse events and also overriding the OnPaint event. The best place to put all the code for creating a positive rectangle that starts at the proper point is in a class. This way, you can hide all the functionality and just expose a few essential properties.

Add a class to the project called RealRect. Listing 9-1 shows the code necessary for this class. Remember, there is top-secret rectangular information in here.

Listing 9-1. Class to Generate a Positive Rectangle

```
using System;
using System.Drawing;

namespace AllCornerRect
{
  public class RealRect
  {
    #region Class Local Variables

    private Point mStart;
    private Point mEnd;
    private Point mRealStart;
    private Point mRealEnd;
    private Size  mRealSize;
    private Rectangle mRect;

    #endregion


    public RealRect(int X, int Y)
    {
      mStart      = Point.Empty;
      mEnd        = Point.Empty;
      mRealStart  = Point.Empty;
      mRealEnd    = Point.Empty;
      mRealSize   = Size.Empty;
```

```csharp
    mStart.X      = X;
    mStart.Y      = Y;
    mRealStart.X  = X;
    mRealStart.Y  = Y;

    mRect = Rectangle.Empty;
}

public RealRect()
{
    mStart        = Point.Empty;
    mEnd          = Point.Empty;
    mRealStart    = Point.Empty;
    mRealEnd      = Point.Empty;
    mRealSize     = Size.Empty;

    mStart.X      = 0;
    mStart.Y      = 0;
    mRealStart.X  = 0;
    mRealStart.Y  = 0;

    mRect = Rectangle.Empty;
}

/// <summary>
/// Ending X Value of rectangle
/// </summary>
public int EndX
{
    set{ mEnd.X = value; }
}

/// <summary>
/// Ending Y Value of rectangle
/// </summary>
public int EndY
{
    set{ mEnd.Y = value; }
}
```

```
/// <summary>
/// Get the corrected rectangle
/// </summary>
public Rectangle Rect
{
  get
  {
    MakeReal();
    mRect.Location = mRealStart;
    mRect.Size = mRealSize;
    return mRect;
  }
}

private void MakeReal()
{
  //Started top left, ended bottom right
  if (mEnd.X > mStart.X && mEnd.Y > mStart.Y)
  {
    mRealStart = mStart;
    mRealEnd = mEnd;
    mRealSize = new Size(mRealEnd.X-mRealStart.X, mRealEnd.Y-mRealStart.Y);
    return;
  }

  //Started bottom right, ended top left
  if (mEnd.X < mStart.X && mEnd.Y < mStart.Y)
  {
    mRealEnd = mStart;
    mRealStart = mEnd;
    mRealSize = new Size(mRealEnd.X-mRealStart.X, mRealEnd.Y-mRealStart.Y);
    return;
  }

  //Started top right, ended bottom left
  if (mEnd.X < mStart.X && mEnd.Y > mStart.Y)
  {
    mRealStart.X = mEnd.X;
    mRealStart.Y = mStart.Y;
    mRealEnd.X   = mStart.X;
    mRealEnd.Y   = mEnd.Y;
    mRealSize = new Size(mRealEnd.X-mRealStart.X, mRealEnd.Y-mRealStart.Y);
    return;
  }
```

```
        //Started bottom left, ended top right
        if (mEnd.X > mStart.X && mEnd.Y < mStart.Y)
        {
          mRealStart.X = mStart.X;
          mRealStart.Y = mEnd.Y;
          mRealEnd.X   = mEnd.X;
          mRealEnd.Y   = mStart.Y;
          mRealSize = new Size(mRealEnd.X-mRealStart.X, mRealEnd.Y-mRealStart.Y);
          return;
        }
      }
    }
}
```

What I have here are two constructors and three properties. The first constructor assumes that the starting point is at the origin. The second constructor takes as arguments the X and Y values of the starting point for the rectangle. The **EndX** and **EndY** properties save the end points of the rectangle.

Each time the **Rect** property is called, the object rearranges the values to come up with a positive rectangle that starts at the proper place. This rearranging of values takes place in the private **MakeReal** method. Look it over carefully and see what I am doing. It will probably help if you have a piece of graph paper and a pencil handy to draw out the possible rectangles. You should understand why I am flipping the X and Y values around like I am.

Now for the code that uses this class. Listing 9-2 shows the code for the form.

Listing 9-2. Code for the Form That Draws a Rectangle on the Screen

```
using System;
using System.Drawing;
using System.Drawing.Drawing2D;
using System.Collections;
using System.ComponentModel;
using System.Windows.Forms;
using System.Data;

namespace AllCornerRect
{
  public class Form1 : System.Windows.Forms.Form
  {

    #region Class Local Variables
```

```csharp
RealRect MyRect;

#endregion

private System.ComponentModel.Container components = null;

public Form1()
{
  InitializeComponent();

  this.SetStyle( ControlStyles.AllPaintingInWmPaint, true);
  this.SetStyle( ControlStyles.DoubleBuffer, true);

  this.MouseDown  += new MouseEventHandler(this.M_down);
  this.MouseUp    += new MouseEventHandler(this.M_up);
  this.MouseMove  += new MouseEventHandler(this.M_move);

  MyRect = new RealRect();
}

protected override void Dispose( bool disposing )
{
  if( disposing )
  {
    if (components != null)
    {
      components.Dispose();
    }
  }
  base.Dispose( disposing );
}

#region Windows Form Designer generated code
#endregion

[STAThread]
static void Main()
{
  Application.Run(new Form1());
}

private void Form1_Load(object sender, System.EventArgs e)
{
}
```

```
protected override void OnPaint(PaintEventArgs e)
{
  base.OnPaint(e);

  Graphics G = e.Graphics;

  G.DrawRectangle(Pens.Red, MyRect.Rect);
}

#region Squeek

private void M_up(object sender, MouseEventArgs e)
{
  Invalidate();
}

private void M_down(object sender, MouseEventArgs e)
{
  if (e.Button != MouseButtons.Left)
    return;

  MyRect = new RealRect(e.X, e.Y);
}

private void M_move(object sender, MouseEventArgs e)
{
  if (e.Button != MouseButtons.Left)
    return;

  MyRect.EndX = e.X;
  MyRect.EndY = e.Y;
  Invalidate();
}

#endregion
  }
}
```

What you do here is add delegates to the mouse events. Within the mouse down event you store the start values of the rectangle. During the mouse move event you store the current mouse values as the rectangle's end values.

In the **OnPaint** method you get the corrected rectangle from the new class and use it to draw the red rectangle.

Compile and run this code. Use the mouse to drag a rectangle around the screen. Start at any point and end at any point. It all works as it should. You are now ready to tackle the screen capture.

Start the Project

Okay, now you have a good idea of what you need in a screen capture program. It is time to start the project.

Open up a new VB or C# Windows Forms project. Mine is called Clipper. I thought about calling it Clippy, but I still have nightmares about being attacked by a giant talking paper clip.

This project will have four forms and two classes. Let's start by adding the forms and classes. You will fill the code in later. Do the following:

1. In the Solution Explorer window, rename the default form to "Main.cs".

2. Add a form called frmSave.

3. Add a form called dtBitmap.

4. Add a form called Attributes.

5. Add a class called DeskTop.cs.

6. Add a class called Corectangle.cs.

That's it for objects.

The default form, now called Main, is required to be small and unobtrusive. This form needs the following attributes:

1. Size the form to be 230×100.

2. Make the StartPosition be center screen.

3. Make the FormBorderStyle fixed single.

4. Add a button to the form called cmdCatch. Change the text to "Screen Capture".

5. Add a button to the form called cmdQuit. Change the text to "Quit".

That's it for the appearance of this form. It should look like the one shown in Figure 9-1.

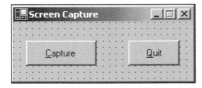

Figure 9-1. Main screen

The next form to add controls to is frmSave. Make the following changes to this form:

1. Size the form to be 800×600 and make it start in the center of the screen.

2. Change the text to "Save Image".

3. Add a panel to the form and call it P1. Size the panel to fit most of the form.

4. Add a menu to the form. Keep the default name of mainMenu1.

Table 9-1 shows the menu hierarchy for the menu on this form.

Table 9-1. Menu Hierarchy for frmSave Form

Menu Name	Method Name
File	mnuFile
Save	mnuSave
Close	mnuClose
Attributes	NoMenu
Resolution	mnuAttr
Border	mnuBorder

Table 9-1. Menu Hierarchy for frmSave Form (Continued)

Menu Name	Method Name
Print	mnuPrint
Preview	mnuPrintPreview
Print	mnuPrintNow

This is all that is needed for controls and setup for this form. The form should look like the one shown in Figure 9-2.

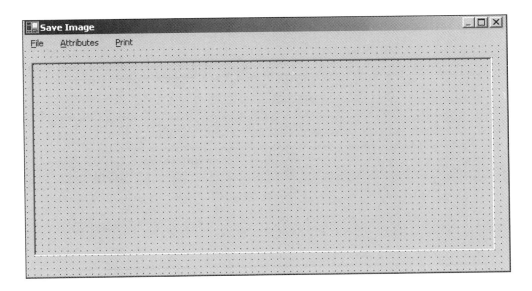

Figure 9-2. Form to view and save screen captures

The third form to set up is the Attributes form. This form is used to change the resolution of the screen capture. The resolution is defined as the number of dots per inch (dpi) of the image. Make the following changes to this form:

1. Size the form to be 300×230.

2. Make the form start up in the center of the screen.

3. Make the FormBorderStyle fixed single.

4. Remove the Maximize and Minimize buttons.

5. Add a label to the form and change the text to "Current Resolution".

6. Add a label to the form below the Current Resolution label and call it lblRes. Make this label's border Fixed3D.

7. Add a label next to the Current Resolution label. Change the text to "Size".

8. Add a label below the Size label and call it lblSize. Make this label's border Fixed3D.

9. Add a GroupBox below the labels. Change the text to "Save Resolution".

10. Add a radio button inside the group box. Call it optCurrent. Change the text to "Current".

11. Add a radio button inside the group box. Call it opt120. Change the text to "120 DPI".

12. Add a radio button inside the group box. Call it opt150. Change the text to "150 DPI".

13. Add a radio button inside the group box. Call it opt300. Change the text to "300 DPI".

14. Add a button to the lower right of the form. Call it cmdOK and change the text to "OK".

This form is shown in Figure 9-3.

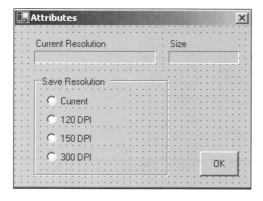

Figure 9-3. Attributes form

Changing the Resolution

While you are here at this Attributes form, you might as well add the code necessary for the form. There is not much code here. Listing 9-3 shows the code for this form. The C# code will not show the "Windows Forms Designer generated code" section. The VB code will show the constructor only.

Listing 9-3a. C# Code for the Attributes Form

```
using System;
using System.Drawing;
using System.Collections;
using System.ComponentModel;
using System.Windows.Forms;

namespace Clipper_c
{
  public class Attributes : System.Windows.Forms.Form
  {
    private float m_Res;

    private System.Windows.Forms.Label lblCurrentRes;
    private System.Windows.Forms.Label lblRes;
    private System.Windows.Forms.Button cmdOK;
    private System.Windows.Forms.GroupBox groupBox1;
    private System.Windows.Forms.RadioButton optCurrent;
    private System.Windows.Forms.RadioButton opt120;
    private System.Windows.Forms.RadioButton opt150;
    private System.Windows.Forms.RadioButton opt300;
    private System.Windows.Forms.Label lblSize;
    private System.Windows.Forms.Label lblSizeVal;

    private System.ComponentModel.Container components = null;

    public Attributes(float CurrentResolution, Size sz)
    {
      InitializeComponent();

      m_Res = CurrentResolution;
      lblRes.Text = m_Res.ToString() + " DPI";
      lblSizeVal.Text = sz.Width.ToString() + "w X " + sz.Height.ToString() +
                                        "h";
```

```
          optCurrent.Checked = true;
          this.Opacity = 1.0;
        }

        protected override void Dispose( bool disposing )
        {
          if( disposing )
          {
            if(components != null)
            {
              components.Dispose();
            }
          }
          base.Dispose( disposing );
        }

        #region Windows Form Designer generated code
...

...

...

        #endregion

        private void Attributes_Load(object sender, System.EventArgs e)
        {
        }

        public float SaveRes { get{return m_Res;} }

        private void cmdOK_Click(object sender, System.EventArgs e)
        {
          if (opt120.Checked)
            m_Res = 120f;

          if (opt150.Checked)
            m_Res = 150f;

          if (opt300.Checked)
            m_Res = 300f;

          this.Close();
        }
      }
    }
```

Listing 9-3b. VB Code for the Attributes Form

```vb
Option Strict On

Imports System
Imports System.Drawing

Public Class Attributes
  Inherits System.Windows.Forms.Form

  Private m_Res As Single

#Region " Windows Form Designer generated code "

  Public Sub New(ByVal CurrentResolution As Single, ByVal sz As Size)
    MyBase.New()

    'This call is required by the Windows Form Designer.
    InitializeComponent()

    m_Res = CurrentResolution
    lblRes.Text = m_Res.ToString() + " DPI"
    lblSizeVal.Text = sz.Width.ToString() + "w X " + sz.Height.ToString() + "h"
    optCurrent.Checked = True
    Me.Opacity = 1.0

  End Sub

#End Region

  Private Sub Attributes_Load(ByVal sender As System.Object, _
                              ByVal e As System.EventArgs) Handles MyBase.Load

  End Sub

  Public ReadOnly Property SaveRes() As Single
    Get
      Return m_Res
    End Get
  End Property
```

```
        Private Sub cmdOK_Click(ByVal sender As System.Object, _
                            ByVal e As System.EventArgs) Handles cmdOK.Click
      If opt120.Checked Then
        m_Res = 120.0F
      End If

      If opt150.Checked Then
        m_Res = 150.0F
      End If

      If opt300.Checked Then
        m_Res = 300.0F
      End If

      Me.Close()
    End Sub
End Class
```

The last form in this example is the dtBitmap form. It is a blank form with no changed attributes. This form is used for displaying the captured bitmap of the screen. All form attributes will be changed in the code.

Whew! That is quite a bit of setup for what will appear to be a simple program. You haven't even written any code yet!

Once you have all your forms and classes made, try compiling the program. You should certainly get no errors. Your Solution Explorer window should look like the one shown in Figure 9-4.

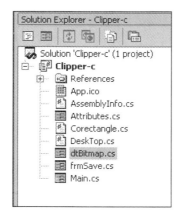

Figure 9-4. Solution Explorer for the Clipper project

By the way, notice the nice border around Figure 9-4? This screen capture was taken with the program you are writing right now.

Entering Code for the Main Screen

It is time to program the main screen. First, double-click both buttons to get the default event handlers for these buttons. At this point, you will enter in all the code for this form except for the code for **cmdCatch_Click**. This method does some sneaky stuff and it also calls another form. I explain this code a little later.

Without the **cmdCatch_Click** method, this form does the following:

- Shows the form in a semitransparent state

- Sets its icon in the system tray

- Minimizes itself with no screen presence

- Reappears using the tray icon menu choice

- Becomes the topmost form via the tray icon menu choice

- Closes using the Quit button or the tray icon menu choice

Just this bit of manipulation with no screen capture takes a little doing. All of this satisfies the first object of the functional specification: Be unobtrusive, but also be available when needed. Listing 9-4 shows the code for the Main form sans the **cmd_Click** code. As far as the Windows Form Designer generated code goes, I only show the constructor and **Dispose** methods.

NOTE *If you download the book's code from the Downloads section of the Apress Web site (*http://www.apress.com*), you will also get the icons and cursors I use for this project. If you choose not to download the code, use your own icons and cursors.*

Listing 9-4a. C# Code for the Main Form

```csharp
using System;
using System.Drawing;
using System.Drawing.Drawing2D;
using System.Drawing.Imaging;
using System.Drawing.Text;
using System.Collections;
using System.ComponentModel;
using System.Windows.Forms;
using System.Data;

namespace Clipper_c
{
  /// <summary>
  /// Copyright Nicholas Symmonds 2002
  /// This software is for instructional purposes only.
  /// It may not be sold as is.
  /// </summary>
  public class Form1 : System.Windows.Forms.Form
  {

    #region Class Local Storage
    Bitmap bmp;
    NotifyIcon trayIcon       = new  NotifyIcon();
    ContextMenu trayIconMenu = new ContextMenu();
    #endregion

    private System.Windows.Forms.Button cmdCatch;
    private System.Windows.Forms.Button cmdQuit;
    /// <summary>
    /// Required designer variable.
    /// </summary>
    private System.ComponentModel.Container components = null;

    public Form1()
    {
      InitializeComponent();

      this.Icon = new Icon("icon.ico");
      this.BackColor         = Color.BlanchedAlmond;
      this.TransparencyKey   = this.BackColor;
      this.cmdCatch.BackColor = Color.Tomato;
      this.cmdQuit.BackColor  = Color.Tomato;
```

```
    trayIconMenu.MenuItems.Add("Catch",
                            new EventHandler(this.cmdCatch_Click));
    trayIconMenu.MenuItems.Add("Always On Top",
                            new EventHandler(this.ClipperOnTop));
    trayIconMenu.MenuItems.Add("Show",
                            new EventHandler(this.Show_Main));
    trayIconMenu.MenuItems.Add("Quit",
                            new EventHandler(this.cmdQuit_Click));

    trayIcon.Icon = new Icon("icon.ico");
    trayIcon.Text = "Clipper - Screen Capture";
    trayIcon.ContextMenu = trayIconMenu;
    trayIcon.Visible = true;

    this.ShowInTaskbar = false;

}

protected override void Dispose( bool disposing )
{
  if( disposing )
  {
    if (components != null)
    {
      components.Dispose();
    }

    if (bmp != null)
      bmp.Dispose();

    trayIcon.Dispose();
  }
  base.Dispose( disposing );
}

#region Windows Form Designer generated code
...
...
...
#endregion
```

```csharp
[STAThread]
static void Main()
{
  Application.Run(new Form1());
}

private void Form1_Load(object sender, System.EventArgs e)
{
}

protected override void OnResize(EventArgs e)
{
  base.OnResize(e);

  if (this.WindowState == FormWindowState.Minimized)
    this.Opacity = 0;
  else
    this.Opacity = 1;
}

/// <summary>
/// The desktop capture method makes this form invisible before
/// snapping the picture. Once the Save form has run this form becomes
/// visible. Making this form invisible is done via the form's opacity.
/// </summary>
private void cmdCatch_Click(object sender, System.EventArgs e)
{
}

private void cmdQuit_Click(object sender, System.EventArgs e)
{
  trayIcon.Visible = false;
  this.Close();
}

private void Show_Main(object sender, System.EventArgs e)
{
  this.Visible = true;
  this.WindowState = FormWindowState.Normal;
}

private void ClipperOnTop(object sender, System.EventArgs e)
{
  if ( trayIconMenu.MenuItems[1].Checked )
```

```
        {
          trayIconMenu.MenuItems[1].Checked = false;
          this.TopMost = false;
        }
        else
        {
          trayIconMenu.MenuItems[1].Checked = true;
          this.TopMost = true;
        }
      }
    }
}
```

Listing 9-4b. VB Code for the Main Form

```vb
Option Strict On

Imports System
Imports System.Drawing
Imports System.Drawing.Drawing2D

Public Class Form1
  Inherits System.Windows.Forms.Form

#Region "Class Local Storage"
  Dim bmp As Bitmap
  Dim trayIcon As NotifyIcon = New NotifyIcon()
  Dim trayIconMenu As ContextMenu = New ContextMenu()
#End Region

#Region " Windows Form Designer generated code "

  Public Sub New()
    MyBase.New()

    'This call is required by the Windows Form Designer.
    InitializeComponent()

    Me.Icon = New Icon("icon.ico")
    Me.BackColor = Color.BlanchedAlmond
    Me.TransparencyKey = Me.BackColor
    Me.cmdCatch.BackColor = Color.Tomato
    Me.cmdQuit.BackColor = Color.Tomato
```

```
            trayIconMenu.MenuItems.Add("Catch", _
                              New EventHandler(AddressOf Me.cmdCatch_Click))
            trayIconMenu.MenuItems.Add("Always On Top", _
                              New EventHandler(AddressOf Me.ClipperOnTop))
            trayIconMenu.MenuItems.Add("Show", _
                              New EventHandler(AddressOf Me.Show_Main))
            trayIconMenu.MenuItems.Add("Quit", _
                              New EventHandler(AddressOf Me.cmdQuit_Click))


            trayIcon.Icon = New Icon("icon.ico")
            trayIcon.Text = "Clipper - Screen Capture"
            trayIcon.ContextMenu = trayIconMenu
            trayIcon.Visible = True


            Me.ShowInTaskbar = False

        End Sub


        'Form overrides dispose to clean up the component list.
        Protected Overloads Overrides Sub Dispose(ByVal disposing As Boolean)
          If disposing Then
            If Not (components Is Nothing) Then
              components.Dispose()
            End If
          End If
          If Not bmp Is Nothing Then
            bmp.Dispose()
          End If

          trayIcon.Dispose()
          MyBase.Dispose(disposing)
        End Sub

...
...


#End Region

    Private Sub Form1_Load(ByVal sender As System.Object, _
                      ByVal e As System.EventArgs) Handles MyBase.Load

      End Sub
```

```
Protected Overrides Sub OnResize(ByVal e As EventArgs)
  MyBase.OnResize(e)
  If Me.WindowState = FormWindowState.Minimized Then
    Me.Opacity = 0
  Else
    Me.Opacity = 1
  End If
End Sub


Private Sub cmdCatch_Click(ByVal sender As System.Object, _
                           ByVal e As System.EventArgs) Handles cmdCatch.Click


End Sub

Private Sub cmdQuit_Click(ByVal sender As System.Object, _
                          ByVal e As System.EventArgs) Handles cmdQuit.Click
  Me.Close()
End Sub

Private Sub Show_Main(ByVal sender As Object, ByVal e As EventArgs)
  Me.Visible = True
  Me.WindowState = FormWindowState.Normal
End Sub

Private Sub ClipperOnTop(ByVal sender As Object, ByVal e As EventArgs)
  If trayIconMenu.MenuItems(1).Checked Then
    trayIconMenu.MenuItems(1).Checked = False
    Me.TopMost = False
  Else
    trayIconMenu.MenuItems(1).Checked = True
    Me.TopMost = True
  End If
End Sub
End Class
```

Compile and run the code. You'll see a small screen whose background is transparent and whose buttons are a nice tomato color.[3] You'll also notice that the background isn't just transparent in color, but it's also transparent to your mouse. Move the screen over some icon on your desktop and click the icon though this screen. Pretty cool, huh? I have yet to find a really effective use for this feature . . . but whatever.

---

3. I could not resist playing with this.

Try out the tray icon menu items. Except for Capture, they should all work. Try minimizing the form. You should not see it at all except for the tray icon.

Getting the Desktop Image

Unfortunately, GDI+ has no mechanism for obtaining the handle to the desktop window. You will need this handle so you can use the **Image.FromHbitmap** method to take a snapshot of the screen. You must resort to the API using the InteropServices.

Using the PInvoke capability of .NET means that you are essentially going outside of the protection of .NET into the unmanaged world of API calls. You must be careful. Always be mindful that if you create a resource, you must manually delete it. If you do not, you will have memory leaks.

The best way to handle common API calls is to provide a class wrapper for them. This provides one central point for all API calls and this one class can be tested thoroughly. I use such a class to get the bitmap of the whole desktop. This is the DeskTop class that you created at the beginning of this project.

Listing 9-5 shows the code necessary for this class. It is quite effective in that all the necessary API calls are wrapped up in one method. Notice that this class cannot be inherited from, and its single method is static.

Listing 9-5a. C# Code for the DeskTop Class

```
using System;
using System.Drawing;
using System.Runtime.InteropServices;

namespace Clipper_c
{
    /// <summary>
    /// Copyright Nicholas Symmonds 2002
    /// This software is for instructional purposes only.
    /// It may not be sold as is.
    ///
    /// This class encapsulates the API functions necessary to get the
    /// desktop image and form a bitmap from it.
    /// Not everything can be done in GDI+ :)
    /// </summary>

    public sealed class DeskTop
    {
```

```
[DllImport("user32.dll")]
internal extern static IntPtr GetDesktopWindow();
[DllImport("user32.dll")]
internal extern static IntPtr GetDC( IntPtr windowHandle );
[DllImport("gdi32.dll")]
internal extern static IntPtr GetCurrentObject( IntPtr hdc,
                                                ushort objectType );
[DllImport("user32.dll")]
internal extern static void ReleaseDC( IntPtr hdc );
[DllImport("user32.dll")]
internal extern static void UpdateWindow( IntPtr hwnd );


public static Bitmap Capture()
  {
  //Get a pointer to the desktop window
  IntPtr desktopWindow = GetDesktopWindow();
  //Get a device context from the desktop window
  IntPtr desktopDC = GetDC( desktopWindow );
  //Get a GDI handle to the image
  IntPtr desktopBitmap = GetCurrentObject( desktopDC, 7 );
  //This call takes as an argument the handle to a GDI image
  Bitmap desktopImage = Image.FromHbitmap( desktopBitmap );


  //Do not create any memory leaks
  ReleaseDC( desktopDC );


  return desktopImage;
  }
}
}
```

Listing 9-5b. VB Code for the DeskTop Class

```
Option Strict On

Imports System
Imports System.Drawing
Imports System.Drawing.Imaging
Imports System.Runtime.InteropServices


Public NotInheritable Class DeskTop
```

```
'/// <summary>
'/// Copyright Nicholas Symmonds 2002
'/// This software is for instructional purposes only.
'/// It may not be sold as is.
'///
'/// This class encapsulates the API functions necessary to get the
'/// desktop image and form a bitmap from it.
'/// Not everything can be done in GDI+ :)
'/// </summary>

Declare Function GetDesktopWindow Lib "user32.dll" () As IntPtr
Declare Function GetDC Lib "user32.dll" (ByVal windowHandle As IntPtr) _
                                         As IntPtr
Declare Function GetCurrentObject Lib "gdi32.dll" (ByVal hdc As IntPtr, _
                                        ByVal objectType As Short) As IntPtr
Declare Sub ReleaseDC Lib "user32.dll" (ByVal hdc As IntPtr)
Declare Sub UpdateWindow Lib "user32.dll" (ByVal hwnd As IntPtr)

Public Shared Function Capture() As Bitmap
  'Get a pointer to the desktop window
  Dim desktopWindow As IntPtr = GetDesktopWindow()
  'Get a device context from the desktop window
  Dim desktopDC As IntPtr = GetDC(desktopWindow)
  'Get a GDI handle to the image
  Dim desktopBitmap As IntPtr = GetCurrentObject(desktopDC, 7)
  'This call takes as an argument the handle to a GDI image
  Dim desktopImage As Bitmap = Image.FromHbitmap(desktopBitmap)

  'Do not create any memory leaks
  ReleaseDC(desktopDC)

  Return desktopImage
End Function
End Class
```

This class is actually very simple. Once you have this class set up, it is time to wire it up to the Main form. If you recall, I did not have you put any code in the **cmdCatch_Click** method of the Main form. Make your **cmdCatch_Click** method look like this:

C#

```
private void cmdCatch_Click(object sender, System.EventArgs e)
{
  bmp = DeskTop.Capture();
}
```

VB

```
Private Sub cmdCatch_Click(ByVal sender As System.Object, _
                          ByVal e As System.EventArgs) Handles cmdCatch.Click
  bmp = DeskTop.Capture()

End Sub
```

Because the method is static, there's no need to construct an object out of this DeskTop class. Make sure your program still runs. You won't be able to see anything of any consequence yet, but that comes next.

TIP *Make good use of breakpoints and trace the code. Make sure you know how things work.*

Showing the DeskTop Image

So now you need to show this snapshot of the desktop that you just took. Not only that, but you also need to provide a way for the user to carve out the portion of the image they are interested in.

The "carving out" bit is the code from the first example in this chapter. In order for the form to work properly, the user needs to be able to start his or her rectangle anywhere on the screen and end the rectangle anywhere on the screen. This is not so easy to do, which is why I spent time up front coming up with a class to do it for you.

The Corectangle class that I had you add to this project is where this code will reside. Listing 9-6 shows the code for this class.

Listing 9-6a. C# Code for the Corrected Rectangle Class

```csharp
using System;
using System.Drawing;

namespace Clipper_c
{
  /// <summary>
  /// This class takes any starting point and any ending point
  /// structures and makes a rectangle.  Using this class you can use the mouse
  /// to draw a rectangle on the screen from any starting point to any ending
  /// point.  You cannot do this with a regular rectangle.
  /// </summary>
  public class Corectangle
  {

    #region Class Local Variables

    private Point mStart;
    private Point mEnd;
    private Point mRealStart;
    private Point mRealEnd;
    private Size  mRealSize;
    private Rectangle mRect;

    #endregion


    public Corectangle(int X, int Y)
    {
      mStart         = Point.Empty;
      mEnd           = Point.Empty;
      mRealStart     = Point.Empty;
      mRealEnd       = Point.Empty;
      mRealSize      = Size.Empty;

      mStart.X       = X;
      mStart.Y       = Y;
      mRealStart.X   = X;
      mRealStart.Y   = Y;

      mRect = Rectangle.Empty;
    }
```

```csharp
public Corectangle()
{
  mStart          = Point.Empty;
  mEnd            = Point.Empty;
  mRealStart      = Point.Empty;
  mRealEnd        = Point.Empty;
  mRealSize       = Size.Empty;

  mStart.X        = 0;
  mStart.Y        = 0;
  mRealStart.X    = 0;
  mRealStart.Y    = 0;

  mRect = Rectangle.Empty;
}

/// <summary>
/// Ending X Value of rectangle
/// </summary>
public int EndX
{
  set{ mEnd.X = value; }
}

/// <summary>
/// Ending Y Value of rectangle
/// </summary>
public int EndY
{
  set{ mEnd.Y = value; }
}

/// <summary>
/// Get the corrected rectangle
/// </summary>
public Rectangle Rect
{
  get
  {
    MakeReal();
    mRect.Location = mRealStart;
    mRect.Size = mRealSize;
    return mRect;
  }
}
```

```
private void MakeReal()
{
  //Started top left, ended bottom right
  if (mEnd.X > mStart.X && mEnd.Y > mStart.Y)
  {
    mRealStart = mStart;
    mRealEnd = mEnd;
    mRealSize = new Size(mRealEnd.X-mRealStart.X, mRealEnd.Y-mRealStart.Y);
    return;
  }

  //Started bottom right, ended top left
  if (mEnd.X < mStart.X && mEnd.Y < mStart.Y)
  {
    mRealEnd = mStart;
    mRealStart = mEnd;
    mRealSize = new Size(mRealEnd.X-mRealStart.X, mRealEnd.Y-mRealStart.Y);
    return;
  }

  //Started top right, ended bottom left
  if (mEnd.X < mStart.X && mEnd.Y > mStart.Y)
  {
    mRealStart.X = mEnd.X;
    mRealStart.Y = mStart.Y;
    mRealEnd.X   = mStart.X;
    mRealEnd.Y   = mEnd.Y;
    mRealSize = new Size(mRealEnd.X-mRealStart.X, mRealEnd.Y-mRealStart.Y);
    return;
  }

  //Started bottom left, ended top right
  if (mEnd.X > mStart.X && mEnd.Y < mStart.Y)
  {
    mRealStart.X = mStart.X;
    mRealStart.Y = mEnd.Y;
    mRealEnd.X   = mEnd.X;
    mRealEnd.Y   = mStart.Y;
    mRealSize = new Size(mRealEnd.X-mRealStart.X, mRealEnd.Y-mRealStart.Y);
    return;
  }
  }
 }
}
```

Listing 9-6b. VB Code for the Corrected Rectangle Class

```vb
Option Strict On

Imports System

Public Class Corectangle

   ' /// <summary>
   '/// This class takes any starting point and any ending point
   '/// structures and makes a rectangle.  Using this class you can use the mouse
   '/// to draw a rectangle on the screen from any starting point to any ending
   '/// point.  You cannot do this with a regular rectangle.
   '/// </summary>

#Region "Class Local Variables"

   Private mStart As Point
   Private mEnd As Point
   Private mRealStart As Point
   Private mRealEnd As Point
   Private mRealSize As Size
   Private mRect As Rectangle

#End Region

   Public Sub New()
     mStart = Point.Empty
     mEnd = Point.Empty
     mRealStart = Point.Empty
     mRealEnd = Point.Empty
     mRealSize = Size.Empty

     mStart.X = 0
     mStart.Y = 0
     mRealStart.X = 0
     mRealStart.Y = 0

     mRect = Rectangle.Empty
   End Sub
```

```
Public Sub New(ByVal X As Int32, ByVal Y As Int32)
  mStart = Point.Empty
  mEnd = Point.Empty
  mRealStart = Point.Empty
  mRealEnd = Point.Empty
  mRealSize = Size.Empty

  mStart.X = X
  mStart.Y = Y
  mRealStart.X = X
  mRealStart.Y = Y

  mRect = Rectangle.Empty
End Sub

Public WriteOnly Property EndX() As Int32
  Set(ByVal Value As Int32)
    mEnd.X = Value
  End Set
End Property

Public WriteOnly Property EndY() As Int32
  Set(ByVal Value As Int32)
    mEnd.Y = Value
  End Set
End Property

Public ReadOnly Property Rect() As Rectangle
  Get
    MakeReal()
    mRect.Location = mRealStart
    mRect.Size = mRealSize
    Return mRect
  End Get
End Property

Private Sub MakeReal()
  'Started top left, ended bottom right
  If mEnd.X > mStart.X And mEnd.Y > mStart.Y Then
    mRealStart = mStart
    mRealEnd = mEnd
    mRealSize = New Size(mRealEnd.X - mRealStart.X, mRealEnd.Y - mRealStart.Y)
    Return
  End If
```

```
    'Started bottom right, ended top left
    If mEnd.X < mStart.X And mEnd.Y < mStart.Y Then
      mRealEnd = mStart
      mRealStart = mEnd
      mRealSize = New Size(mRealEnd.X - mRealStart.X, mRealEnd.Y - mRealStart.Y)
      Return
    End If

    'Started top right, ended bottom left
    If mEnd.X < mStart.X And mEnd.Y > mStart.Y Then
      mRealStart.X = mEnd.X
      mRealStart.Y = mStart.Y
      mRealEnd.X = mStart.X
      mRealEnd.Y = mEnd.Y
      mRealSize = New Size(mRealEnd.X - mRealStart.X, mRealEnd.Y - mRealStart.Y)
      Return
    End If

    'Started bottom left, ended top right
    If mEnd.X > mStart.X And mEnd.Y < mStart.Y Then
      mRealStart.X = mStart.X
      mRealStart.Y = mEnd.Y
      mRealEnd.X = mEnd.X
      mRealEnd.Y = mStart.Y
      mRealSize = New Size(mRealEnd.X - mRealStart.X, mRealEnd.Y - mRealStart.Y)
      Return
    End If
  End Sub
End Class
```

You already know this code, so I will not go over it again here. Now it is time to put this class to use.

I had you add a form called dtBitmap. This form will be what the user sees when he or she chooses which part of the image to save.

This form's constructor takes the desktop image as an argument and sizes the form to be equal to the image size. Because the image is of the desktop, the form is also the size of the desktop. I also remove any border from the form. Doing this makes it seem to the user as if he or she is still looking at a live version of his or her computer screen. In order to let the user know that he or she must use the mouse to choose which part of the screen to save, I change the cursor to a hand holding a crossbar.

The image is placed as the background image on the form. This way I do not have to explicitly paint it whenever the screen changes. Listing 9-7 shows the code for the dtBitmap form.

> **NOTE** *When I made the C# version of this form, it was originally a class. I then made the class inherit from the form class. This is why it has no "Windows Form Designer generated code" section. The VB version of this form started out life as a form.*

Listing 9-7a. C# Code for the dtBitmap Form

```csharp
using System;
using System.Drawing;
using System.Drawing.Drawing2D;
using System.Drawing.Imaging;
using System.Drawing.Text;
using System.Collections;
using System.ComponentModel;
using System.Windows.Forms;
using System.Data;

namespace Clipper_c
{
  public class dtBitmap : Form
  {

    #region Class local storage

    private Bitmap bmp;
    private Rectangle InvalidRect = Rectangle.Empty;
    private Pen mRectPen;
    private Corectangle mbmpRect;

    #endregion

    public dtBitmap(Bitmap b)
    {
      mbmpRect = new  Corectangle();
      mRectPen = new Pen(Brushes.Red, 1);
      mRectPen.DashStyle = DashStyle.DashDot;
      bmp = b.Clone(new RectangleF(0, 0, b.Width, b.Height), b.PixelFormat);
```

```
  this.SetStyle(ControlStyles.AllPaintingInWmPaint,true);
  this.SetStyle(ControlStyles.DoubleBuffer,true);
  this.Size = bmp.Size;
  this.FormBorderStyle = FormBorderStyle.None;
  this.MaximizeBox = false;
  this.MinimizeBox = false;
  this.Cursor = new Cursor("hcross.cur");
  this.BackgroundImage = bmp;

  //Show as modal
  this.ShowDialog();
}

private void InitializeComponent()
{
  //
  // dtBitmap
  //
  this.AutoScaleBaseSize = new System.Drawing.Size(5, 13);
  this.ClientSize = new System.Drawing.Size(292, 273);
  this.Name = "dtBitmap";
  this.Load += new System.EventHandler(this.dtBitmap_Load);
}


protected override void Dispose( bool disposing )
{
  if( disposing )
  {
    if (bmp != null)
      bmp.Dispose();
  }
  base.Dispose( disposing );
}

public Bitmap GetBitmap
{
  get{return bmp;}
}
```

```
private void dtBitmap_Load(object sender, System.EventArgs e)
{
}
protected override void OnPaint(PaintEventArgs e)
{
  base.OnPaint(e);
  e.Graphics.DrawRectangle(mRectPen, mbmpRect.Rect);
}


#region Squeek
protected override void OnMouseDown(MouseEventArgs e)
{
  base.OnMouseDown(e);

  if (e.Button != MouseButtons.Left)
    return;

  mbmpRect = new  Corectangle(e.X, e.Y);
}

protected override void OnMouseUp(MouseEventArgs e)
{
  base.OnMouseUp(e);

  Invalidate();
  bmp = bmp.Clone(mbmpRect.Rect, bmp.PixelFormat);
  this.Close();
}

protected override void OnMouseMove(MouseEventArgs e)
{
  base.OnMouseMove(e);

  if (e.Button != MouseButtons.Left)
    return;

  mbmpRect.EndX = e.X;
  mbmpRect.EndY = e.Y;
  Invalidate();
}

#endregion
  }
}
```

Listing 9-7b. VB Code for the dtBitmap Form

```vb
Option Strict On

Imports System
Imports System.Drawing
Imports System.Drawing.Drawing2D
Imports System.Drawing.Imaging

Public Class dtBitmap
  Inherits System.Windows.Forms.Form

    '/// This form is the one that holds the complete bitmap of the screen.
    '/// The border is set to nothing and the form is maximized.  The cursor
    '/// is also changed to tell the user (s)he can now drag a line and make
    '/// a capture box. When the screen is captured this form shows up almost
    '/// immediately.
    '/// </summary>

#Region "Class local storage"

  Private bmp As Bitmap
  Private InvalidRect As Rectangle = Rectangle.Empty
  Private mRectPen As Pen
  Private mbmpRect As Corectangle

#End Region

#Region " Windows Form Designer generated code "

  Public Sub New(ByVal b As Bitmap)
    MyBase.New()

    'This call is required by the Windows Form Designer.
    InitializeComponent()

    mbmpRect = New Corectangle()
    mRectPen = New Pen(Brushes.Red, 1)
    mRectPen.DashStyle = DashStyle.DashDot
    bmp = b.Clone(New RectangleF(0, 0, b.Width, b.Height), b.PixelFormat)

    Me.SetStyle(ControlStyles.AllPaintingInWmPaint, True)
    Me.SetStyle(ControlStyles.DoubleBuffer, True)
    Me.Size = bmp.Size
```

```
            Me.FormBorderStyle = FormBorderStyle.None
            Me.MaximizeBox = False
            Me.MinimizeBox = False
            Me.Cursor = New Cursor("hcross.cur")
            Me.BackgroundImage = bmp

            'Show as modal
            Me.ShowDialog()

        End Sub


        'Form overrides dispose to clean up the component list.
        Protected Overloads Overrides Sub Dispose(ByVal disposing As Boolean)
            If disposing Then
                If Not (components Is Nothing) Then
                    components.Dispose()
                End If
            End If
            If Not bmp Is Nothing Then
                bmp.Dispose()
            End If
            MyBase.Dispose(disposing)
        End Sub

    …
    …
    …
#End Region

        Private Sub dtBitmap_Load(ByVal sender As System.Object, _
                                  ByVal e As System.EventArgs) Handles MyBase.Load

        End Sub

        Protected Overrides Sub OnPaint(ByVal e As PaintEventArgs)
            MyBase.OnPaint(e)
            e.Graphics.DrawRectangle(mRectPen, mbmpRect.Rect)
        End Sub

        Public ReadOnly Property GetBitmap() As Bitmap
            Get
                Return bmp
            End Get
        End Property
```

```
#Region "Squeek"
  Protected Overrides Sub OnMouseDown(ByVal e As MouseEventArgs)
    MyBase.OnMouseDown(e)

    If e.Button <> MouseButtons.Left Then
      Return
    End If

    mbmpRect = New Corectangle(e.X, e.Y)
  End Sub

  Protected Overrides Sub OnMouseUp(ByVal e As MouseEventArgs)
    MyBase.OnMouseUp(e)

    Invalidate()
    bmp = bmp.Clone(mbmpRect.Rect, bmp.PixelFormat)
    Me.Close()
  End Sub

  Protected Overrides Sub OnMouseMove(ByVal e As MouseEventArgs)
    MyBase.OnMouseMove(e)

    If e.Button <> MouseButtons.Left Then
      Return
    End If

    mbmpRect.EndX = e.X
    mbmpRect.EndY = e.Y
    Invalidate()
  End Sub

#End Region
End Class
```

Compile your code and make sure that it still runs. If you run the program, you will not see much because you have yet to wire this dtBitmap form up to your main code.

Again, you do this via the **cmdCatch_Click** method in the Main form. Add code to your **cmdCatch_Click** method to make it look like this:

VB

```
Private Sub cmdCatch_Click(ByVal sender As System.Object, _
                         ByVal e As System.EventArgs) Handles cmdCatch.Click
  bmp = DeskTop.Capture()

  Dim bmpShow As dtBitmap = New dtBitmap(bmp)
  bmp = bmpShow.GetBitmap
End Sub
```

C#

```
private void cmdCatch_Click(object sender, System.EventArgs e)
{
  bmp = DeskTop.Capture();

  dtBitmap bmpShow = new dtBitmap(bmp);
  bmp = bmpShow.GetBitmap;
}
```

You have added just two more lines from the last time you added code to this method. You can now compile and run the program. You should see something happen.

What you should see is that when you click the Capture button on the Main form, the screen's cursor changes to the hand holding a crossbar. Press the mouse down and drag a rectangle across the screen. The cursor will return to its normal state and the main screen will reappear. Believe it or not, you have actually accomplished the most difficult tasks.

Of course, it would be nice to see the resulting image that you carved out. It would also be nice to print or save this image. This is where the frmSave form comes up.

Functionally, the nature of this form is obvious from the menu it contains. It does just a few things. However, the code behind the scenes is not so obvious. This form, more so than all the others, includes aspects of all the chapters in this book, except maybe for writing text on the form. I suppose I could have included that as well, but it seemed unnecessary.

 NOTE *You need some kind of printer installed on your machine for the printing code in here not to fail. Even if the printer does not exist, you should install something.*

The code for this form is in Listing 9-8. This is the last form or class in this project. Once you have finished entering this code, you are done with the project.

Listing 9-8a. C# Code for the frmSave Form

```csharp
using System;
using System.Drawing;
using System.Drawing.Printing;
using System.Drawing.Drawing2D;
using System.Drawing.Imaging;
using System.Collections;
using System.ComponentModel;
using System.Windows.Forms;

namespace Clipper_c
{
  /// <summary>
  /// Copyright Nicholas Symmonds 2002
  /// This software is for instructional purposes only.
  /// It may not be sold as is.
  ///
  /// Allow the user to select a frame for the image before saving it.
  /// </summary>
  public class frmSave : System.Windows.Forms.Form
  {

    #region Class Local Storage

    private PictureBox          m_Pic;
    private Bitmap              m_bmp;
    private Bitmap              m_OriginalBmp;
    private PrintPreviewDialog  Pv;
    private PageSetupDialog     Ps;
    private PrintDocument       Pd;
    private PrintDialog         Pr;
    private Font                FooterFont = new Font("Arial", 8);
    private int                 PrintCount = 0;

    #endregion
```

```
private System.Windows.Forms.Panel P1;
private System.Windows.Forms.MainMenu mainMenu1;
private System.Windows.Forms.MenuItem mnuFile;
private System.Windows.Forms.MenuItem mnuSave;
private System.Windows.Forms.MenuItem mnuPrint;
private System.Windows.Forms.MenuItem mnuClose;
private System.Windows.Forms.MenuItem mnuPrintPreview;
private System.Windows.Forms.MenuItem mnuPrintNow;
private System.Windows.Forms.MenuItem NoMenu;
private System.Windows.Forms.MenuItem mnuAttr;
private System.Windows.Forms.MenuItem mnuBorder;

private System.ComponentModel.Container components = null;

public frmSave(Bitmap bmp)
{
  InitializeComponent();

  m_bmp = (Bitmap)bmp.Clone();
  m_OriginalBmp = (Bitmap)bmp.Clone();
  P1.BackgroundImage = GetPanelImage();
  P1.Dock = DockStyle.Fill;

  m_Pic = new PictureBox();
  m_Pic.BorderStyle = BorderStyle.None;
  m_Pic.SizeMode = PictureBoxSizeMode.AutoSize;
  m_Pic.Image = m_bmp;
  P1.Controls.Add(m_Pic);
  P1.Controls[0].Location = new Point(1, 1);

  //Set up the prnting
  Pv = new PrintPreviewDialog();
  Ps = new PageSetupDialog();
  Pr = new PrintDialog();
  Pd = new PrintDocument();

  Pd.DocumentName = "ScreenShot";
  Pv.Document = Pd;
  Ps.Document = Pd;
  Pr.Document = Pd;

  Pd.BeginPrint += new PrintEventHandler(this.pd_BeginPrint);
  Pd.PrintPage += new PrintPageEventHandler(this.pd_Print);

}
```

```
protected override void Dispose( bool disposing )
{
  if( disposing )
  {
    if(components != null)
    {
      components.Dispose();
    }
    P1.Dispose();
  }
  base.Dispose( disposing );
}


#region Windows Form Designer generated code
…
…
…

#endregion

private void frmSave_Load(object sender, System.EventArgs e)
{
}


/// <summary>
/// This routine makes a blank image and colors it with a hatch brush
/// This image is handed back to the caller who then uses this image as
/// the background image for the panel.  The panel will tile this image
/// for as many times as it takes to fill the panel.
/// </summary>
private Image GetPanelImage()
{
  Image i = new Bitmap(50, 50);
  using(Graphics G = Graphics.FromImage(i))
  {
    //No need for high quality here.  We need Speed!!!
    G.SmoothingMode = SmoothingMode.HighSpeed;
    Brush B = new HatchBrush(HatchStyle.Cross, Color.Cyan, Color.LightCyan);
    G.FillRectangle(B, 0, 0, i.Width, i.Height);
  }
  return i;
}
```

```
private void mnuAttr_Click(object sender, System.EventArgs e)
{
  Attributes frm = new Attributes(m_bmp.HorizontalResolution, m_bmp.Size);
  frm.ShowDialog();
  m_bmp.SetResolution(frm.SaveRes, frm.SaveRes);
}

private void mnuClose_Click(object sender, System.EventArgs e)
{
  this.Close();
}

private void mnuSave_Click(object sender, System.EventArgs e)
{
  SaveFileDialog sd = new SaveFileDialog();

  sd.Filter = "Bitmap (*.bmp)|*.bmp|" +
              "JPEG (*.jpg)|*.jpg|" +
              "GIF (*.Gif)|*.gif|"  +
              "TIFF (*.tif)|*.tif|"  +
              "PNG (*.png)|*.png|"  +
              "EMF (*.emf)|*.emf"  ;
  sd.FilterIndex = 1 ;
  sd.RestoreDirectory = true ;
  sd.AddExtension = true;

  if(sd.ShowDialog() == DialogResult.OK)
  {
    if (sd.FileName.Length != 0)
    {
      switch(sd.FilterIndex)
      {
        case 1:
          //Save as bitmap
          m_bmp.Save(sd.FileName, ImageFormat.Bmp);
          break;
        case 2:
          //Save as JPEG
          m_bmp.Save(sd.FileName, ImageFormat.Jpeg);
          break;
        case 3:
          //Save as GIF
          m_bmp.Save(sd.FileName, ImageFormat.Gif);
          break;
```

```
      case 4:
        //Save as TIFF
        m_bmp.Save(sd.FileName, ImageFormat.Tiff);
        break;
      case 5:
        //Save as PNG
        m_bmp.Save(sd.FileName, ImageFormat.Png);
        break;
      case 6:
        //Save as EMF
        m_bmp.Save(sd.FileName, ImageFormat.Emf);
        break;
      default:
        break;
    }
  }
 }
}

#region Printer routines

private void pd_BeginPrint ( object sender, PrintEventArgs e)
{
  Pd.DocumentName = "ScreenShot " + (++PrintCount).ToString();
}
private void pd_Print(object sender, PrintPageEventArgs e)
{
  Graphics G = e.Graphics;
  float LeftMargin = e.MarginBounds.Left;
  float TopMargin = e.MarginBounds.Top;
  float BottomMargin = e.MarginBounds.Bottom;

  StringFormat sf = new StringFormat();
  sf.Alignment = StringAlignment.Far;
  sf.LineAlignment = StringAlignment.Center;

  Rectangle Border = e.MarginBounds;
  Border.Inflate(1, 1);
  RectangleF Footer = new Rectangle(e.MarginBounds.Left,
                                    e.MarginBounds.Bottom,
                                    e.MarginBounds.Width,
                                    e.PageBounds.Bottom -
                                    e.MarginBounds.Bottom);
```

```csharp
        //Type in the footer
        G.DrawString(Pd.DocumentName, FooterFont, Brushes.Black, Footer, sf);
        sf.Alignment = StringAlignment.Near;
        G.DrawString(DateTime.Now.ToLongDateString(), FooterFont,
                     Brushes.Black,
                     Footer, sf);

        //Draw the rectangle and the image.  Image is stretched to fit!!!
        G.DrawRectangle(Pens.Black, Border);
        G.DrawImage(m_bmp, e.MarginBounds);

        sf.Dispose();

}


private void mnuPrintPreview_Click(object sender, System.EventArgs e)
{
    Pv.WindowState = FormWindowState.Maximized;
        Pv.ShowDialog();
}


private void mnuPrintNow_Click(object sender, System.EventArgs e)
{
    if (Pr.ShowDialog() == DialogResult.OK)
      Pd.Print();
}


#endregion

private void mnuBorder_Click(object sender, System.EventArgs e)
{
    if (!mnuBorder.Checked)
    {
      using (Graphics G = Graphics.FromImage(m_bmp))
      {
        using (Pen P = new Pen(Brushes.Black, 2))
        {
          G.DrawRectangle(P, new Rectangle(0, 0, m_bmp.Size.Width,
                          m_bmp.Size.Height));
          m_Pic.Image = m_bmp;
          mnuBorder.Checked = true;
        }
      }
    }
```

```
      else
      {
        m_bmp = (Bitmap)m_OriginalBmp.Clone();
        m_Pic.Image = m_bmp;
        mnuBorder.Checked = false;
      }
    }
  }
}
```

Listing 9-8b. VB Code for the frmSave Form

```
Option Strict On

Imports System
Imports System.Drawing
Imports System.Drawing.Drawing2D
Imports System.Drawing.Imaging
Imports System.Drawing.Printing

Public Class frmSave
  Inherits System.Windows.Forms.Form

  ' /// <summary>
  ' /// Copyright Nicholas Symmonds 2002
  ' /// This software is for instructional purposes only.
  ' /// It may not be sold as is.
  ' ///
  ' /// Allow the user to select a frame for the image before saving it.
  '/// </summary>

#Region "Class Local Storage"

  Private m_Pic As PictureBox
  Private m_bmp As Bitmap
  Private m_OriginalBmp As Bitmap
  Private Pv As PrintPreviewDialog
  Private Ps As PageSetupDialog
  Private Pd As PrintDocument
  Private Pr As PrintDialog
  Private FooterFont As Font = New Font("Arial", 8)
  Private PrintCount As Int32 = 0

#End Region
```

```vbnet
#Region " Windows Form Designer generated code "

  Public Sub New(ByVal bmp As Bitmap)
    MyBase.New()

    'This call is required by the Windows Form Designer.
    InitializeComponent()

    m_bmp = CType(bmp.Clone(), Bitmap)
    m_OriginalBmp = CType(bmp.Clone(), Bitmap)
    P1.BackgroundImage = GetPanelImage()
    P1.Dock = DockStyle.Fill

    m_Pic = New PictureBox()
    m_Pic.BorderStyle = BorderStyle.None
    m_Pic.SizeMode = PictureBoxSizeMode.AutoSize
    m_Pic.Image = m_bmp
    P1.Controls.Add(m_Pic)
    P1.Controls(0).Location = New Point(1, 1)

    'Set up the prnting
    Pv = New PrintPreviewDialog()
    Ps = New PageSetupDialog()
    Pr = New PrintDialog()
    Pd = New PrintDocument()

    Pd.DocumentName = "ScreenShot"
    Pv.Document = Pd
    Ps.Document = Pd
    Pr.Document = Pd

    AddHandler Pd.BeginPrint, New PrintEventHandler(AddressOf Me.pd_BeginPrint)
    AddHandler Pd.PrintPage, New PrintPageEventHandler(AddressOf Me.pd_Print)

  End Sub

  'Form overrides dispose to clean up the component list.
  Protected Overloads Overrides Sub Dispose(ByVal disposing As Boolean)
    If disposing Then
      If Not (components Is Nothing) Then
        components.Dispose()
      End If
    End If
```

```vb
    P1.Dispose()
    MyBase.Dispose(disposing)
  End Sub


…

…

…

#End Region

  Private Sub frmSave_Load(ByVal sender As System.Object, _
                          ByVal e As System.EventArgs) Handles MyBase.Load

  End Sub

  Private Function GetPanelImage() As Image
    Dim i As Image = New Bitmap(50, 50)
    Dim G As Graphics = Graphics.FromImage(i)

    Try
      'No need for high quality here.  We need Speed!!!
      G.SmoothingMode = SmoothingMode.HighSpeed
      Dim B As Brush = New HatchBrush(HatchStyle.Cross, _
                                    Color.Cyan, Color.LightCyan)
      G.FillRectangle(B, 0, 0, i.Width, i.Height)
    Finally
      G.Dispose()
    End Try

    Return i
  End Function

#Region "Printer routines"

  Private Sub pd_BeginPrint(ByVal sender As Object, ByVal e As PrintEventArgs)
    Pd.DocumentName = "ScreenShot " + (++PrintCount).ToString()
  End Sub

  Private Sub pd_Print(ByVal sender As Object, ByVal e As PrintPageEventArgs)
    Dim G As Graphics = e.Graphics
    Dim LeftMargin As Single = e.MarginBounds.Left
    Dim TopMargin As Single = e.MarginBounds.Top
    Dim BottomMargin As Single = e.MarginBounds.Bottom
```

```vbnet
        Dim sf As StringFormat = New StringFormat()
        sf.Alignment = StringAlignment.Far
        sf.LineAlignment = StringAlignment.Center

        Dim Border As Rectangle = e.MarginBounds
        Border.Inflate(1, 1)
        Dim Footer As RectangleF = New RectangleF(e.MarginBounds.Left, _
                                   e.MarginBounds.Bottom, _
                                   e.MarginBounds.Width, _
                                   e.PageBounds.Bottom - e.MarginBounds.Bottom)

        'Type in the footer
        G.DrawString(Pd.DocumentName, FooterFont, Brushes.Black, Footer, sf)
        sf.Alignment = StringAlignment.Near
        G.DrawString(DateTime.Now.ToLongDateString(), FooterFont, _
                    Brushes.Black, Footer, sf)

        'Draw the rectangle and the image.  Image is stretched to fit!!!
        G.DrawRectangle(Pens.Black, Border)
        G.DrawImage(m_bmp, e.MarginBounds)

        sf.Dispose()

    End Sub

    Private Sub mnuPrintPreview_Click(ByVal sender As Object, _
                        ByVal e As System.EventArgs)
      Pv.WindowState = FormWindowState.Maximized
      Pv.ShowDialog()
    End Sub

    Private Sub mnuPrintNow_Click(ByVal sender As Object, _
                        ByVal e As System.EventArgs)
      If Pr.ShowDialog() = DialogResult.OK Then
        Pd.Print()
      End If
    End Sub

#End Region

    Private Sub mnuSave_Click(ByVal sender As System.Object, _
                            ByVal e As System.EventArgs) Handles mnuSave.Click
        Dim sd As SaveFileDialog = New SaveFileDialog()
```

```vb
        sd.Filter = "Bitmap (*.bmp)|*.bmp|" + _
                    "JPEG (*.jpg)|*.jpg|" + _
                    "GIF (*.Gif)|*.gif|" + _
                    "TIFF (*.tif)|*.tif|" + _
                    "PNG (*.png)|*.png|" + _
                    "EMF (*.emf)|*.emf"
        sd.FilterIndex = 1
        sd.RestoreDirectory = True
        sd.AddExtension = True

        If sd.ShowDialog() = DialogResult.OK Then
          If sd.FileName.Length <> 0 Then
            Select Case (sd.FilterIndex)
              Case 1
                'Save as bitmap
                m_bmp.Save(sd.FileName, ImageFormat.Bmp)
              Case 2
                'Save as JPEG
                m_bmp.Save(sd.FileName, ImageFormat.Jpeg)
              Case 3
                'Save as GIF
                m_bmp.Save(sd.FileName, ImageFormat.Gif)
              Case 4
                'Save as TIFF
                m_bmp.Save(sd.FileName, ImageFormat.Tiff)
              Case 5
                'Save as PNG
                m_bmp.Save(sd.FileName, ImageFormat.Png)
              Case 6
                'Save as EMF
                m_bmp.Save(sd.FileName, ImageFormat.Emf)
            End Select
          End If
        End If

End Sub


Private Sub mnuClose_Click(ByVal sender As System.Object, _
                        ByVal e As System.EventArgs) Handles mnuClose.Click

  Me.Close()
End Sub
```

```vb
Private Sub mnuAttr_Click(ByVal sender As System.Object, _
                          ByVal e As System.EventArgs) _
                          Handles mnuAttr.Click
  Dim frm As Attributes = New Attributes(m_bmp.HorizontalResolution, _
                                  m_bmp.Size)
  frm.ShowDialog()
  m_bmp.SetResolution(frm.SaveRes, frm.SaveRes)
End Sub


Private Sub mnuBorder_Click(ByVal sender As System.Object, _
                            ByVal e As System.EventArgs) _
                            Handles mnuBorder.Click
  If mnuBorder.Checked = False Then
    Dim G As Graphics = Graphics.FromImage(m_bmp)
    Dim P As Pen = New Pen(Brushes.Black, 2)
    Try
      G.DrawRectangle(P, New Rectangle(0, 0, m_bmp.Size.Width, _
                                  m_bmp.Size.Height))
      m_Pic.Image = m_bmp
      mnuBorder.Checked = True
    Finally
      G.Dispose()
      P.Dispose()
    End Try
  Else
    m_bmp = CType(m_OriginalBmp.Clone(), Bitmap)
    m_Pic.Image = m_bmp
    mnuBorder.Checked = False
  End If

End Sub


Private Sub mnuPrintPreview_Click_1(ByVal sender As System.Object, _
                                ByVal e As System.EventArgs) _
                                Handles mnuPrintPreview.Click
  Pv.WindowState = FormWindowState.Maximized
  Pv.ShowDialog()
End Sub
```

```
      Private Sub mnuPrintNow_Click_1(ByVal sender As System.Object, _
                                      ByVal e As System.EventArgs) _
                                      Handles mnuPrintNow.Click

        If Pr.ShowDialog() = DialogResult.OK Then
          Pd.Print()
        End If
      End Sub
    End Class
```

Compile your code and make sure that it still runs. If you run the program, you will not see much because you have yet to wire this frmSave form up to your main code.

Again, you do this via the **cmdCatch_Click** method in the Main form. Add code to your **cmdCatch_Click** method to make it look like this:

VB

```
    Private Sub cmdCatch_Click(ByVal sender As System.Object, _
                               ByVal e As System.EventArgs) Handles cmdCatch.Click

      bmp = DeskTop.Capture()

      'Make the form invisible
      Me.Opacity = 0
      Dim bmpShow As dtBitmap = New dtBitmap(bmp)
      bmp = bmpShow.GetBitmap

      If Not bmp Is Nothing Then
        Dim frm As frmSave = New frmSave(bmp)
        frm.ShowDialog()
      End If
      Me.Opacity = 1

    End Sub
```

C#

```
      private void cmdCatch_Click(object sender, System.EventArgs e)
      {
        bmp = DeskTop.Capture();

        //Make the form invisible
        this.Opacity = 0;
        dtBitmap bmpShow = new dtBitmap(bmp);
        bmp = bmpShow.GetBitmap;
```

```
    if (bmp != null)
    {
      frmSave frm = new frmSave(bmp);
      frm.ShowDialog();
    }
    this.Opacity = 1;
}
```

You have added just a few more lines from the last time you added code to this method. You can now compile and run the program. You will see the Save form come up.

Once you capture the screen and choose the portion of the screen you want saved, the Save form comes up. This form puts the image into a PictureBox that resides inside a panel that is on the form. This may sound complicated, but it allows an image that is much bigger than the form to be displayed correctly using scroll bars to maneuver around the image.

Granted, the printing could use some work. For instance, the preview shows the image as it fits on a single page. If the image is smaller than a page, it is stretched, and if it is bigger, it is squashed. Feel free to add some aspect ratio code to this section of the program.

There is, of course, something else that could use some work: error checking and recovery. I intentionally did not put any major error checking in this code because it would have muddied the waters somewhat. If you are going to use this program yourself, I suggest you make it a little more robust.

Summary

This chapter showed you a pretty involved project that uses everything you have learned so far. But have you learned anything new? (Besides the API calls, that is.)

Remember back in high school when you were learning geometry and algebra? If you were like me, you probably wondered how you were ever going to apply this stuff. Well, as far as GDI+ programming goes, that is what this chapter was for. You went through all the theory and examples in the previous chapters. Hopefully, you learned in this chapter just how you can apply them.

Reflecting back on this screen capture program, I can come up with some aspects from just about every chapter in the book. These points are in no particular order:

- Using the Color enumeration

- Using standard Pens and Brushes

- Making your own Pens and Brushes

- Setting up and using delegates

- Overriding protected base class methods

- Using the Image base class

- Using the Bitmap class

- Using existing Graphics objects

- Creating your own Graphics objects

- Creating a sealed class with static methods

- Drawing directly on a bitmap

- Saving images in various formats

- Using .NET standard controls to display images

- Rubber-banding rectangles using the mouse

- Speeding up drawing

- Using the Graphics drawing methods

- Using Point, Size, and Rectangle structures

- Printing a bitmap

- Setting up a print preview

- And so on

That last point is actually *not* a feature of GDI+. Anyway, I could probably double this list if I scoured the code.

So, not only did you use in this chapter all that you have learned so far in this book, but also I think this project is actually useful. It was to me.

CHAPTER 10

GDI+ with Forms

The sun oozed over the horizon, shoved aside darkness, crept along the green sward, and, with sickly fingers, pushed through the castle window, revealing the pillaged princess, hand at throat, crown asunder, gaping in frenzied horror at the sated, sodden amphibian lying beside her, disbelieving the magnitude of the frog's deception, screaming madly, "You lied!"

—Barbara C. Kroll, Kennett Square, Pennsylvania

WELL, HERE WE ARE: the last chapter. Like Chapter 9, this chapter takes you through a somewhat complex project using quite a few features of GDI+.

The project in this chapter, however, is a little different from the one in Chapter 9. The project in Chapter 9 was designed to have as minimal a user interface (UI) as possible. It was designed to be unobtrusive. This project has a fairly complex UI.

This chapter's project is a custom form designer. Sounds pretty cool, huh? I bet you are wondering just what a custom form designer does.

Most of the windows you see on your desktop are rectangular. Windows XP rounds the corners a little, but they are still basically rectangular. Have you ever seen a user interface in which the windows were not rectangular? There is one I can think of whose shape is that of a shield. Naturally, a program like that defends your computer from viruses.

.NET allows you to define the shape of a window by defining its visible region. The project for this chapter makes it easy for the user to create windows with a different shape.

NOTE *As with all the examples in this book, you can download the code for this project from the Downloads section of the Apress Web site (http://www.apress.com). This project includes a few cursors and icons. If you decide to download this project, you will get the cursors and icons as well. If you do not download the project, you will need to supply your own cursors and icons.*

What's the Point?

Okay, generating a funny window shape may be theoretically interesting, but what are you going to use it for? Right now, I can't think of anything useful. However, the point of this example is not so much the end result, but the process of how you achieve the end result.

The point of this project is to demonstrate the interaction of the GDI+ drawing capability along with using the provided .NET controls. A combination of these two things allows you to create a really good UI.

To my mind, the blending of GDI+ and controls is what making a truly graphical UI is really all about.

The Project Design

So, what will this project do to make it easy for someone to generate a custom window shape? I've listed a few things here that I think are necessary. I left some things out, such as a toolbar, that I would use in a professional product. However, if I put everything including the kitchen sink into this project, it would soon take on a life of its own.

Here's what this project does:

- It has three sections. Each section provides different information.

- It uses splitter bars to allow the user to resize any section within the program.

- It has a drawing surface that allows the user to draw a shape using a mouse.

- It allows the user to save a window shape.

- It has a TreeView control that shows a list of previously saved window shapes.

- It allows the user to drag and drop a shape from the tree view onto the drawing surface.

- It has a debug window that provides a textual representation of what is happening in the program.

- It has a function to smooth the original shape and shows it overlaid on the drawing surface with the original shape.

- It has a menu.

- It allows the user to spawn a form using the original shape or the smoothed shape.

Come to think of it, this project does quite a bit.

The Main Screen's Layout

When I thought of this project, I looked at several other programs' user interfaces. I looked at programs I thought were easy to use, and I looked at programs that were a jumble of screens. I came up with a design for the GUI that I think provides a lot of power with a minimum of user fuss. Figure 10-1 shows the screen that I ended up with.

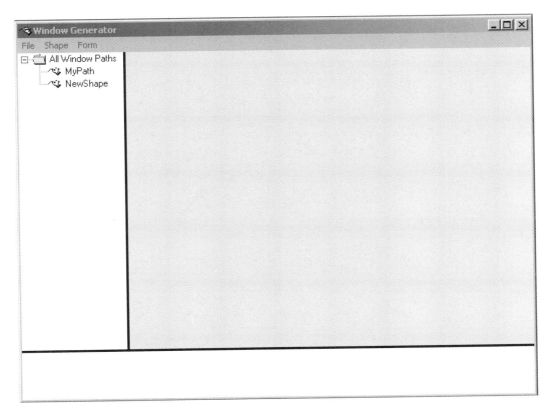

Figure 10-1. User interface for Window Generator

As you can see, the screen has three sections. The section on the left is a tree view of all the shapes that I have stored for this program. This is a TreeView control.

The bottom section is a rich text box that is used to display debug information. Personally, I think it is a good idea to have some kind of debug output available to you. Of course, in a professional program you would turn this off for normal operation and turn it back on again only when necessary.

The top right panel is the drawing surface. I talk about this later.

The three sections are divided by splitter bars. Just like any other program that uses splitter bars, you can drag these bars around the screen and thereby resize each section to your liking.

So how do you set up this layout? It is not so easy unless you know the trick. What you see are five controls on the screen:

- A Panel

- A TreeView

- A RichTextBox

- Two splitter bars

Take a minute and make a small side project. Add these five items to the form and try to rearrange them in this configuration. The program, when running, must allow you to resize each section using the splitter bars.

Give up? Can't do it, can you? Believe it or not, this wasn't wasted effort. It's sometimes more instructive to know what can't be done before you find out how to do it. Once I show you how it is done, you'll have a better understanding of how to do similar things in the future.[1]

Start the Project

Start a new project in either VB or C#. Mine is called CustomWindow.

 NOTE *There is certain syntax in C# that is not available in VB and vice versa. I try to take advantage of the best syntax that each language has to offer. Because of this, you will find some functions in the VB version will be coded differently than their C# counterparts. I think this is interesting because you get a real sense of the difference between the two. I hear all the time that VB is just C# without semicolons. Anyone who has programmed in both knows this is a gross simplification.*

---

1. I would have said the answer is at the bottom of the page and upside down, but then the rest of the chapter would have been upside down.

The first thing to do is size the form to be about 500×400. You will resize it via code later. Also, make the form start up in the center of the screen. The title bar for this form should read "Window Generator". You should include the following namespaces in this form:

- System.Drawing

- System.Drawing.Drawing2D

- System.Drawing.Imaging

- System.IO

The first control on this form is the MainMenu. The following list shows the menu hierarchy. The text in bold is the text property of the menu item.

File. Do not name this menu item.

Exit. Place this menu below the File menu item. Name it mnuExit.

Shape. Do not name this menu item. Place it next to the File menu item.

Create. Place this under the Shape menu item. Name it mnuCreate.

Smooth. Place this under the Shape menu item. Name it mnuSmooth.

---. Place this under the Shape menu item. Use a dash for the name.

SaveShape. Place this under the Shape menu item. Name it mnuSaveShape.

Form. Do not name this menu item. Place it next to the Shape menu item.

Spawn. Do not name this menu item. Place it under the Shape menu item.

Original. Place this under the Spawn menu item. Name it mnuSpawnForm.

Smooth. Place this under the Spawn menu item. Name it mnuSpawnSmooth.

Figure 10-2 shows the Form menu and its submenu. Yours should look similar.

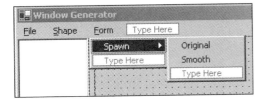

Figure 10-2. The Form menu and submenu

Once you have the menu set up, it is time to add the controls necessary to create the three-section form. The order in which you add the controls is important.

1. Add a RichTextBox to the form. Call it DebugWindow. Set its Dock property to Bottom.

2. Add a splitter to the form. Call it PanelSplitter. Set its Dock property to Bottom.

3. Add a Panel to the form just above the splitter. Call it BasePanel. Set its Dock property to Fill. You should now see a text box at the bottom of the form. A splitter is on top of the text box and a panel is on top of the splitter.

4. Add a TreeView control to the BasePanel panel. Call it PathTree. Set its Dock property to Left.

5. Add a splitter to the BasePanel panel. Call it TreeSplitter. Set its Dock property to Left. The BasePanel panel now contains a tree view and a splitter, with both docked to the left side.

6. Add a Panel to the BasePanel panel. Call it P1. Set its Dock property to Fill.

You now have all the controls on the form and they are in the correct order. Compile and run the program and try out the splitter bars. They should both work as expected.

As you saw, the trick to laying out this form was using the BasePanel panel as the container for the tree, the splitter, and the drawing panel.

Drawing the Shape

The first and main thing that this program needs to do is use the mouse to render a shape on the screen. You have done this many times in past examples. The difference here is that the shape that can be drawn on the screen will be free-form. So far, you have used the mouse to draw rectangles of various sizes and shapes. It is not a big stretch to draw free-form.

The device you will be drawing on is the P1 panel. This is the topmost panel on the screen. Here are some requirements for drawing on the screen:

- Drawing can only be started by choosing Create from the menu.

- The cursor should change while the mouse is over the drawing surface. This tells the user that drawing should start.

- Drawing starts when user presses down on the left mouse button.

- Drawing ends when user releases the left mouse button.

Double-click each of the following menu items. You should get the default delegate for each one.

- Exit

- Create

- Smooth

- Save Shape

- Original

- Smooth

No need for any code connected to the other menu items. They are just navigational stops in the menu hierarchy.

Open up the code pane to the main form. Listing 10-1 shows some of the code for this form. It shows the form setup, menu delegates, and some functions necessary to draw. As you progress in this chapter, you will add code to this form to fill out some of the other functionality.

This C# code will not show any Windows Form Designer generated code. The VB code will only show the constructor and **Dispose** methods of the Windows Form Designer generated code.

Listing 10-1a. C# Code for the CustomWindow Main Form

```
using System;
using System.IO;
using System.Drawing;
using System.Drawing.Drawing2D;
using System.Drawing.Imaging;
using System.Collections;
using System.ComponentModel;
using System.Windows.Forms;
using System.Data;
```

```csharp
namespace CustomWindow
{
  public class Form1 : System.Windows.Forms.Form
  {
    #region Class Local Storage

    private const int CLOSEDICON    = 0;
    private const int OPENICON      = 1;
    private const int DRAWICON      = 2;
    private const int DRAGICON      = 3;

    private ImageList      mImageList;
    private GraphicsPath   mOriginalPath;
    private GraphicsPath   mSmoothPath;
    private Point          mStartPoint;
    private Point          mLastPoint;
    private Rectangle      mInvalidRect;
    private Cursor         mDrawCursor;
    private Cursor         mDragCursor;
    private Icon           mDrawIcon;
    private string         mRecallFileName;

    private bool           mAllowDrawing;
    private bool           mDrawing;
    private bool           mDraging;

    #endregion

    private System.Windows.Forms.MainMenu mainMenu1;
    private System.Windows.Forms.MenuItem menuItem1;
    private System.Windows.Forms.MenuItem mnuExit;
    private System.Windows.Forms.MenuItem menuItem3;
    private System.Windows.Forms.MenuItem menuItem2;
    private System.Windows.Forms.MenuItem menuItem7;
    private System.Windows.Forms.RichTextBox DebugWindow;
    private System.Windows.Forms.MenuItem mnuCreate;
    private System.Windows.Forms.MenuItem mnuSmooth;
    private System.Windows.Forms.MenuItem mnuSaveShape;
    private System.Windows.Forms.MenuItem None;
    private System.Windows.Forms.MenuItem mnuSpawnForm;
    private System.Windows.Forms.MenuItem mnuSpawnSmooth;
    private System.Windows.Forms.Splitter PanelSplitter;
    private System.Windows.Forms.Panel BasePanel;
    private System.Windows.Forms.Panel P1;
```

```
private System.Windows.Forms.TreeView PathTree;
private System.Windows.Forms.Splitter TreeSplitter;

private System.ComponentModel.Container components = null;

public Form1()
{
  InitializeComponent();

  //Initialize class variables
  mDrawIcon     = new Icon("draw.ico");
  mDrawCursor   = new Cursor("Pen.cur");
  mDragCursor   = new Cursor("drag.cur");
  mImageList    = new ImageList();
  mOriginalPath = new GraphicsPath();
  mSmoothPath   = new GraphicsPath();
  mDrawing      = false;
  mInvalidRect  = Rectangle.Empty;

  //Set the screen
  this.Icon = mDrawIcon;
  this.Size = new Size(800, 600);
  this.SetStyle(ControlStyles.AllPaintingInWmPaint,true);
  this.SetStyle(ControlStyles.DoubleBuffer,true);

  //Set up the image list
  mImageList.Images.Add(new Icon("closed.ico"));
  mImageList.Images.Add(new Icon("open.ico"));
  mImageList.Images.Add(mDrawIcon);
  mImageList.Images.Add(new Icon("drag.ico"));

  //Set RichTextBox properties
  DebugWindow.ReadOnly = true;
  DebugWindow.Height   = this.Height /8;
  DebugWindow.Text     = "";

  //Set up the splitters
  PanelSplitter.Height    = 3;
  PanelSplitter.BackColor = Color.Blue;
  TreeSplitter.BackColor  = Color.Blue;
  TreeSplitter.Location   = new Point(PathTree.Width, 0);
  TreeSplitter.Size       = new Size(3, this.Height);
```

```
                    // Set properties of TreeView control.
                    PathTree.Width          = this.ClientSize.Width / 6;
                    PathTree.TabIndex       = 0;
                    PathTree.ImageList      = mImageList;

                    //Set Drawing Panel Properties
                    P1.BackColor    = Color.Bisque;
                    P1.Paint        += new PaintEventHandler(this.PanelPaint);
                    P1.MouseDown    += new MouseEventHandler(this.M_Down);
                    P1.MouseUp      += new MouseEventHandler(this.M_Up);
                    P1.MouseMove    += new MouseEventHandler(this.M_Move);

                    //Set all the border styles to none.
                    BasePanel.BorderStyle   = BorderStyle.None;
                    P1.BorderStyle          = BorderStyle.None;
                    PathTree.BorderStyle    = BorderStyle.None;
                    DebugWindow.BorderStyle = BorderStyle.None;

                    //Disable some menu selections
                    mnuSpawnForm.Enabled    = false;
                    mnuSpawnSmooth.Enabled  = false;
                }

                protected override void Dispose( bool disposing )
                {
                    if( disposing )
                    {
                        if (components != null)
                        {
                            components.Dispose();
                        }
                    }
                    mOriginalPath.Dispose();
                    mSmoothPath.Dispose();
                    base.Dispose( disposing );
                }

                #region Windows Form Designer generated code
...
...

                #endregion
```

```csharp
#region Main Entry Point
/// <summary>
/// The main entry point for the application.
/// </summary>
[STAThread]
static void Main()
{
  Application.Run(new Form1());
}
#endregion

private void Form1_Load(object sender, System.EventArgs e)
{
}

private void PanelPaint(object sender, PaintEventArgs e)
{
  PaintMe(e.Graphics);
}

private void PaintMe(Graphics G)
{
  G.SmoothingMode = SmoothingMode.HighSpeed;

  if (mOriginalPath.PointCount > 0)
    G.DrawPath(Pens.Black, mOriginalPath);

  if (mSmoothPath.PointCount > 0)
  {
    G.SmoothingMode = SmoothingMode.HighQuality;
    G.DrawPath(Pens.Red, mSmoothPath);
  }
}

#region Squeek events for Panel

private void M_Down(object sender, MouseEventArgs m)
{
  if (mAllowDrawing && m.Button == MouseButtons.Left)
  {
    mStartPoint  = new Point(m.X, m.Y);
    mLastPoint   = mStartPoint;
    mOriginalPath = new GraphicsPath();
    mDrawing     = true;
```

```
      DebugWindow.AppendText("Starting Path\n");
      DebugWindow.ScrollToCaret();
      P1.Invalidate();
    }
  }

  private void M_Up(object sender, MouseEventArgs m)
  {
    if (mDrawing)
    {
      mOriginalPath.CloseFigure();
      mDrawing      = false;
      mAllowDrawing = false;
      P1.Cursor     = Cursors.Default;
      if (mOriginalPath.PointCount > 2)
      {
        mnuSpawnForm.Enabled = true;
        DebugWindow.AppendText("Path Points: " +
                             mOriginalPath.PointCount.ToString() + "\n");
        DebugWindow.AppendText("Path Ended\n");
      }
      else
      {
        mnuSpawnForm.Enabled   = false;
        mnuSpawnSmooth.Enabled = false;
        DebugWindow.SelectionColor = Color.Red;
        DebugWindow.AppendText("!!!INVALID PATH!!!\n");
        DebugWindow.SelectionColor = Color.Black;
        DebugWindow.AppendText("Path Ended\n");
      }
      DebugWindow.ScrollToCaret();

      //Draw the paths and make a window.
      P1.Invalidate();
    }
  }

  private void M_Move(object sender, MouseEventArgs m)
  {
    if(mDrawing && m.Button == MouseButtons.Left)
    {
      mOriginalPath.AddLine(mLastPoint.X, mLastPoint.Y, m.X, m.Y);
      mLastPoint.X = m.X;
      mLastPoint.Y = m.Y;
```

```
      mInvalidRect = Rectangle.Truncate(mOriginalPath.GetBounds());
      mInvalidRect.Inflate( new Size(2, 2) );
      P1.Invalidate(mInvalidRect);
   }
}


#endregion


#region Menu functions

private void mnuExit_Click(object sender, System.EventArgs e)
{
  this.Close();
}

private void mnuSmooth_Click(object sender, System.EventArgs e)
{
}

private void mnuSpawnForm_Click(object sender, System.EventArgs e)
{
}

private void mnuSpawnSmooth_Click(object sender, System.EventArgs e)
{
}

private void mnuCreate_Click(object sender, System.EventArgs e)
{
  P1.Cursor = mDrawCursor;
  mSmoothPath.Reset();
  mOriginalPath.Reset();

  mnuSpawnForm.Enabled = false;
  mnuSpawnSmooth.Enabled = false;
  mAllowDrawing = true;
  P1.Invalidate();
}

private void mnuSaveShape_Click(object sender, System.EventArgs e)
{
}
```

```
        #endregion
    }
}
```

Listing 10-1b. VB Code for the CustomWindow Main Form

```vb
Option Strict On

Imports System
Imports System.IO
Imports System.Drawing
Imports System.Drawing.Drawing2D

Public Class Form1
    Inherits System.Windows.Forms.Form

#Region "Class Local Storage"

    Private Const CLOSED_ICON As Int32 = 0
    Private Const OPEN_ICON As Int32 = 1
    Private Const DRAW_ICON As Int32 = 2
    Private Const DRAG_ICON As Int32 = 3

    Private mImageList As ImageList
    Private mOriginalPath As GraphicsPath
    Private mSmoothPath As GraphicsPath
    Private m_StartPoint As Point
    Private m_LastPoint As Point
    Private mInvalidRect As Rectangle
    Private mDrawCursor As Cursor
    Private mDragCursor As Cursor
    Private mDrawIcon As Icon
    Private mRecallFileName As String

    Private mAllowDrawing As Boolean
    Private m_Drawing As Boolean
    Private mDraging As Boolean

#End Region

#Region " Windows Form Designer generated code "
```

```
Public Sub New()
  MyBase.New()

  'This call is required by the Windows Form Designer.
  InitializeComponent()

  'Initialize class variables
  mDrawIcon = New Icon("draw.ico")
  mDrawCursor = New Cursor("Pen.cur")
  mDragCursor = New Cursor("drag.cur")
  mImageList = New ImageList()
  mOriginalPath = New GraphicsPath()
  mSmoothPath = New GraphicsPath()
  m_Drawing = False
  mInvalidRect = Rectangle.Empty

  'Set the screen
  Me.Icon = mDrawIcon
  Me.Size = New Size(800, 600)
  Me.SetStyle(ControlStyles.AllPaintingInWmPaint, True)
  Me.SetStyle(ControlStyles.DoubleBuffer, True)

  'Set up the image list
  mImageList.Images.Add(New Icon("closed.ico"))
  mImageList.Images.Add(New Icon("open.ico"))
  mImageList.Images.Add(mDrawIcon)
  mImageList.Images.Add(New Icon("drag.ico"))

  'Set RichTextBox properties
  DebugWindow.ReadOnly = True
  DebugWindow.Height = CInt(Me.Height / 8)
  DebugWindow.Text = ""

  'Set up the splitters
  PanelSplitter.Height = 3
  PanelSplitter.BackColor = Color.Blue
  TreeSplitter.BackColor = Color.Blue
  TreeSplitter.Location = New Point(PathTree.Width, 0)
  TreeSplitter.Size = New Size(3, Me.Height)

  ' Set properties of TreeView control.
  PathTree.Width = CInt(Me.ClientSize.Width / 6)
  PathTree.TabIndex = 0
  PathTree.ImageList = mImageList
```

```
            'Set Drawing Panel Properties
            P1.BackColor = Color.Bisque
            AddHandler P1.Paint, New PaintEventHandler(AddressOf Me.PanelPaint)
            AddHandler P1.MouseDown, New MouseEventHandler(AddressOf Me.M_Down)
            AddHandler P1.MouseUp, New MouseEventHandler(AddressOf Me.M_Up)
            AddHandler P1.MouseMove, New MouseEventHandler(AddressOf Me.M_Move)

            'Set all the border styles to none.
            BasePanel.BorderStyle = BorderStyle.None
            P1.BorderStyle = BorderStyle.None
            PathTree.BorderStyle = BorderStyle.None
            DebugWindow.BorderStyle = BorderStyle.None

            'Disable some menu selections
            mnuSpawnForm.Enabled = False
            mnuSpawnSmooth.Enabled = False

        End Sub

        'Form overrides dispose to clean up the component list.
        Protected Overloads Overrides Sub Dispose(ByVal disposing As Boolean)
            If disposing Then
                If Not (components Is Nothing) Then
                    components.Dispose()
                End If
            End If
            mOriginalPath.Dispose()
            mSmoothPath.Dispose()
            MyBase.Dispose(disposing)
        End Sub
    …
    …
    …

#End Region

    Private Sub Form1_Load(ByVal sender As System.Object, _
                           ByVal e As System.EventArgs) Handles MyBase.Load
        'FillTree()
    End Sub

    Private Sub PanelPaint(ByVal sender As Object, ByVal e As PaintEventArgs)
        PaintMe(e.Graphics)
    End Sub
```

```vbnet
  Private Sub PaintMe(ByVal G As Graphics)
    G.SmoothingMode = SmoothingMode.HighSpeed

    If mOriginalPath.PointCount > 0 Then
      G.DrawPath(Pens.Black, mOriginalPath)
    End If

    If mSmoothPath.PointCount > 0 Then
      G.SmoothingMode = SmoothingMode.HighQuality
      G.DrawPath(Pens.Red, mSmoothPath)
    End If
  End Sub

#Region "Squeek events for Panel"

  Private Sub M_Down(ByVal sender As Object, ByVal m As MouseEventArgs)
    If mAllowDrawing And m.Button = MouseButtons.Left Then
      m_StartPoint = New Point(m.X, m.Y)
      m_LastPoint = m_StartPoint
      mOriginalPath = New GraphicsPath()
      m_Drawing = True
      DebugWindow.AppendText("Starting Path\n")
      DebugWindow.ScrollToCaret()
      P1.Invalidate()
    End If
  End Sub

  Private Sub M_Up(ByVal sender As Object, ByVal m As MouseEventArgs)
    If m_Drawing Then
      mOriginalPath.CloseFigure()
      m_Drawing = False
      mAllowDrawing = False
      P1.Cursor = Cursors.Default
      If mOriginalPath.PointCount > 2 Then
        mnuSpawnForm.Enabled = True
        DebugWindow.AppendText("Path Points: " + _
                               mOriginalPath.PointCount.ToString() + _
                               vbCrLf)
        DebugWindow.AppendText("Path Ended" + vbCrLf)
      Else
        mnuSpawnForm.Enabled = False
        mnuSpawnSmooth.Enabled = False
        DebugWindow.SelectionColor = Color.Red
        DebugWindow.AppendText("!!!INVALID PATH!!!" + vbCrLf)
```

```
            DebugWindow.SelectionColor = Color.Black
            DebugWindow.AppendText("Path Ended" + vbCrLf)
         End If


        'Draw the paths and make a window.
        P1.Invalidate()
      End If
    End Sub


  Private Sub M_Move(ByVal sender As Object, ByVal m As MouseEventArgs)
     If m_Drawing And m.Button = MouseButtons.Left Then
        mOriginalPath.AddLine(m_LastPoint.X, m_LastPoint.Y, m.X, m.Y)
        m_LastPoint.X = m.X
        m_LastPoint.Y = m.Y

        mInvalidRect = Rectangle.Truncate(mOriginalPath.GetBounds())
        mInvalidRect.Inflate(New Size(2, 2))
        P1.Invalidate(mInvalidRect)
     End If
   End Sub


#End Region


#Region "Menu functions"

  Private Sub mnuExit_Click(ByVal sender As System.Object, _
                            ByVal e As System.EventArgs) _
                            Handles mnuExit.Click
    Me.Close()
  End Sub


  Private Sub mnuCreate_Click(ByVal sender As System.Object, _
                              ByVal e As System.EventArgs) _
                              Handles mnuCreate.Click
    P1.Cursor = mDrawCursor
    mSmoothPath.Reset()
    mOriginalPath.Reset()

    mnuSpawnForm.Enabled = False
    mnuSpawnSmooth.Enabled = False
    mAllowDrawing = True
    P1.Invalidate()
  End Sub
```

```
  Private Sub mnuSmooth_Click(ByVal sender As System.Object, _
                              ByVal e As System.EventArgs) _
                          Handles mnuSmooth.Click
  End Sub

  Private Sub mnuSaveShape_Click(ByVal sender As System.Object, _
                                 ByVal e As System.EventArgs) _
                             Handles mnuSaveShape.Click
    'Dim frm As SaveMe = New SaveMe(mOriginalPath)
    'frm.ShowDialog()
    'FillTree()
  End Sub

  Private Sub mnuSpawnForm_Click(ByVal sender As System.Object, _
                                 ByVal e As System.EventArgs) _
                             Handles mnuSpawnForm.Click
  End Sub

  Private Sub mnuSpawnSmooth_Click(ByVal sender As System.Object, _
                                   ByVal e As System.EventArgs) _
                               Handles mnuSpawnSmooth.Click
  End Sub

#End Region
End Class
```

Compile the program. You should not get any errors.

If you run the program, you will see that you have functionality for the Exit menu and the Create menu, and the ability to draw on the panel.

Click the Create menu item and move your cursor over the drawing panel. Your cursor should change to a pen. This indicates you can now draw. Press the left button of the mouse down and drag/draw a shape with the mouse on the panel. When you have finished, release the left mouse button.

The figure you are drawing is actually a GraphicsPath. Each time the mouse is moved and drawing is legal, I update the mOriginalPath variable with a new line. This new line consists of the endpoint of the last mouse move event and the current point of the current mouse move event.

The mouse up event handler for the panel does several things:

- It resets some variables to stop drawing.

- It resets the panel cursor back to the default.

- It closes the figure you just made.

- It decides if the figure is big enough to draw.

- It sends some output to the debug window.

If I did not close the path, you would not get a complete figure. You do not have to finish drawing the figure by trying to mate the last point with the first. Closing the path does this for you.

Smoothing the Path

Now you have undoubtedly seen some code in here that refers to a smooth path. In fact, there is a variable called mSmoothPath. Look at the shape you made. If your hand is as unsteady as mine, your shape looks a little jagged. Most times this would not be an acceptable shape for anything. It would be nice to smooth it out.

So, how would you smooth out a figure of undetermined shape and size? There are a few things you can do, one of which I do in this program:

- Look at the shape algorithmically and replace any curvy bits with actual curves.

- Allow the user to pick points on the shape and create a new shape using Bézier splines. Allow the use of movable control points.

- Look at all the points in the shape and try to reduce the number of lines they represent.

I do not do any reshaping via curves or splines in this section. This kind of algorithm and drawing code would take up a whole chapter. Also, how would you save the shape?

The smoothing algorithm I use is reducing the number of straight lines in the shape. This would probably be the first smoothing algorithm in a smoothing set anyway, and it also provides the most bang for your buck, so to speak.

It should be noted that this is actually more of a data-reduction algorithm. In some cases, it may grossly distort the original shape. But then again, this is an example, and this simple algorithm is meant to show what you *can* do, not necessarily what you *should* do.

It is time to add some more code to the form. I created a region at the bottom of the code called Helper Functions. This is where the smoothing function will go. Listing 10-2 shows the Smooth menu delegate filled in as well as the new **SmootherPath** function.

Listing 10-2a. C# Code for a Smoother Path

```csharp
private void mnuSmooth_Click(object sender, System.EventArgs e)
{
  //Smooth out the path by reducing lines that make up path
  mSmoothPath = SmootherPath(mOriginalPath);

  //Translate a little to the side and below
  Matrix Q = new Matrix();
  Q.Translate(5, 5);
  mSmoothPath.Transform(Q);

  //Enable the ability to create smooth forms
  mnuSpawnSmooth.Enabled = true;

  P1.Invalidate();
  DebugWindow.AppendText("Original Path Points: " +
                        mOriginalPath.PointCount.ToString() + "\n");
  DebugWindow.SelectionColor = Color.Red;
  DebugWindow.AppendText("Smooth Path Points: " +
                        mSmoothPath.PointCount.ToString() + "\n");
  DebugWindow.SelectionColor = Color.Black;
}

#region Helper Functions

/// <doc>
/// Start first with reducing the number of lines in this graphics path
/// 1. read first point
/// 2. if x value of next point = x value of last point then skip
/// 3. if x value of next point != value of last point then...
/// 3a. make line based on these two points
/// 3b. add line to new path
/// 3c. first point = next point
/// 4. repeat 1-3c
/// 5. Repeat 1-4 for both X and Y
/// </doc>
private GraphicsPath SmootherPath(GraphicsPath gp)
{
  PathData pd = gp.PathData;
  PointF pt1 = new Point(-1, -1);
```

```
      //First do all values in the X range
      GraphicsPath FixedPath_X = new GraphicsPath();
      foreach (PointF p in pd.Points)
      {
        if (pt1.X == -1)
        {
          pt1 = p;
          continue;
        }
        // If I introduced an error factor here I could smooth it out even more
        if (p.X != pt1.X)
        {
          FixedPath_X.AddLine(pt1, p);
          pt1 = p;
        }
      }
      FixedPath_X.CloseFigure();

      //Second do all values in the Y range
      pd = FixedPath_X.PathData;
      pt1 = new Point(-1, -1);
      GraphicsPath FixedPath_Y = new GraphicsPath();
      foreach (PointF p in pd.Points)
      {
        if (pt1.Y == -1)
        {
          pt1 = p;
          continue;
        }
        // If I introduced an error factor here I could smooth it out even more
        if (p.Y != pt1.Y)
        {
          FixedPath_Y.AddLine(pt1, p);
          pt1 = p;
        }
      }
      FixedPath_Y.CloseFigure();

      return FixedPath_Y;
    }

    #endregion
```

Listing 10-2b. VB Code for a Smoother Path

```vb
Private Sub mnuSmooth_Click(ByVal sender As System.Object, _
                            ByVal e As System.EventArgs) _
                            Handles mnuSmooth.Click
    'Smooth out the path by reducing lines that make up path
    mSmoothPath = SmootherPath(mOriginalPath)

    'Translate a little to the side and below
    Dim Q As Matrix = New Matrix()
    Q.Translate(5, 5)
    mSmoothPath.Transform(Q)

    'Enable the ability to create smooth forms
    mnuSpawnSmooth.Enabled = True

    P1.Invalidate()
    DebugWindow.AppendText("Original Path Points: " + _
                        mOriginalPath.PointCount.ToString() + vbCrLf)
    DebugWindow.SelectionColor = Color.Red
    DebugWindow.AppendText("Smooth Path Points: " + _
                        mSmoothPath.PointCount.ToString() + vbCrLf)
    DebugWindow.SelectionColor = Color.Black
End Sub

#Region "Helper Functions"

    '/// <doc>
    '/// Start first with reducing the number of lines in this graphics path
    '/// 1. read first point
    '/// 2. if x value of next point = x value of last point then skip
    '/// 3. if x value of next point != value of last point then...
    '/// 3a. make line based on these two points
    '/// 3b. add line to new path
    '/// 3c. first point = next point
    '/// 4. repeat 1-3c
    '/// 5. Repeat 1-4 for both X and Y
    '/// </doc>
    Private Function SmootherPath(ByVal gp As GraphicsPath) As GraphicsPath
        Dim pd As PathData = gp.PathData
        Dim pt1 As PointF = New PointF(-1, -1)
```

```
      'First do all values in the X range
    Dim FixedPath_X As GraphicsPath = New GraphicsPath()
    Dim p As PointF
    For Each p In pd.Points
      If pt1.X = -1 Then
        pt1 = p
      Else
        ' If I introduced an error factor here I could smooth it out even more
        If p.X <> pt1.X Then
          FixedPath_X.AddLine(pt1, p)
          pt1 = p
        End If
      End If
    Next
    FixedPath_X.CloseFigure()

      'Second do all values in the Y range
    pd = FixedPath_X.PathData
    pt1 = New PointF(-1, -1)
    Dim FixedPath_Y As GraphicsPath = New GraphicsPath()
    For Each p In pd.Points
      If pt1.Y = -1 Then
        pt1 = p
      Else
        ' If I introduced an error factor here I could smooth it out even more
        If p.Y <> pt1.Y Then
          FixedPath_Y.AddLine(pt1, p)
          pt1 = p
        End If
      End If
    Next
    FixedPath_Y.CloseFigure()

    Return FixedPath_Y
  End Function

#End Region
```

Figure 10-3 shows the screen after I drew a shape and smoothed it out.

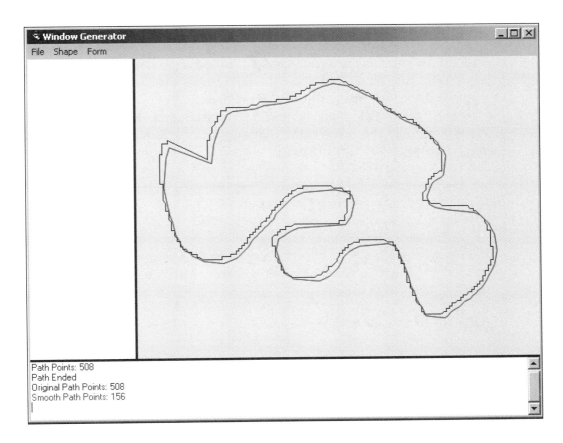

Figure 10-3. Drawing the panel after smoothing a shape

Notice that the smoothing algorithm does a really nice job of smoothing out the figure. Look inside the **mnuSmooth_Click** method. You will see that after I create the smooth shape, I translate it down and over to the right 5 pixels. This is the effect you see on the screen of the smooth figure not totally overlaying the original one. It lets the user see things more easily.

Have you looked at the debug window yet? There is a secondary reason for using this piecewise linear algorithm. You get far fewer points in the final GraphicsPath. This reduces the file space necessary to store the shape. This algorithm gives more than a 3:1 reduction in the number of points for essentially the same curve. It is a kind of lossy compression algorithm. Of course, the point reduction you get will be different for every shape you make.

If you like, you can add a smoothing factor to this algorithm. I look for sets of points that make one continuous, straight line. If I took into consideration sets of points that made an *almost* straight line, I would be able to reduce the number of points even more. However, this would result in a less curvy shape.

Generating the Custom Form

You now have the ability to create a unique shape and generate a smoothed-out version of it. Now what? The end result of this exercise is to create a new form with a unique shape that you can use in other programs.

I have to say at this point that the form I create is rather useless as is. It is more of a demonstration form. I create the form and destroy it within the same method. You get to see the form and move it around, but other than that it does not do much. However, it is not the form that needs saving.

You have seen some code already that turns on and off the menu choices for making a form from the original path or from the smoothed path. You will now add code to realize those menu choices.

Listing 10-3 shows the code necessary for the **mnuSpawnForm_Click** and **mnuSpawnSmooth_Click** methods. It also shows the code for the **MakeWindow** method that actually generates the form. I keep the **MakeWindow** method within the Helper Functions region.

Listing 10-3a. C# Code to Allow Generation of a Custom Form

```
private void mnuSpawnForm_Click(object sender, System.EventArgs e)
{
  DebugWindow.AppendText("Spawning Window based on original path\n");
  MakeWindow(mOriginalPath);
}

private void mnuSpawnSmooth_Click(object sender, System.EventArgs e)
{
  DebugWindow.AppendText("Spawning Window based on smoothed path\n");
  MakeWindow(mSmoothPath);
}

private void MakeWindow(GraphicsPath ArgPath)
{
  Form frm = new Form();
  GraphicsPath path = (GraphicsPath)ArgPath.Clone();
  Matrix Xlate = new Matrix();

  //Find the lowest Y value and normalize all Y values to zero
  //Find the lowest X value and normalize all X values to zero
  //Doing this always gives me some part of a title bar
  PointF[] p = path.PathPoints;
  int Xoffset = 9999;
  int Yoffset = 9999;
```

```
  foreach (PointF p2 in p)
  {
    if (p2.X < Xoffset)
      Xoffset = (int)p2.X;
    if (p2.Y < Yoffset)
      Yoffset = (int)p2.Y;
  }
  Xlate.Translate(-Xoffset, -Yoffset);
  path.Transform(Xlate);

  // Set the paractical viewing region of the form
  frm.Region = new Region(path);

  //Set the size of the form
  Rectangle frmRect = Rectangle.Truncate(path.GetBounds());
  frm.Size = frmRect.Size;

  //Set some other parameters
  frm.StartPosition = FormStartPosition.CenterParent;
  frm.FormBorderStyle = FormBorderStyle.FixedSingle;

  //Show as modal because the form will be disposed of
  //This is, after all, just an example
  frm.ShowDialog();

  frm.Dispose();
  Xlate.Dispose();
}
```

Listing 10-3b. VB Code to Allow Generation of a Custom Form

```
Private Sub mnuSpawnForm_Click(ByVal sender As System.Object, _
                               ByVal e As System.EventArgs) _
                               Handles mnuSpawnForm.Click
  DebugWindow.AppendText("Spawning Window based on original path" + vbCrLf)
  MakeWindow(mOriginalPath)
End Sub

Private Sub mnuSpawnSmooth_Click(ByVal sender As System.Object, _
                                 ByVal e As System.EventArgs) _
                                 Handles mnuSpawnSmooth.Click
  DebugWindow.AppendText("Spawning Window based on smoothed path" + vbCrLf)
  MakeWindow(mSmoothPath)
End Sub
```

```vbnet
Private Sub MakeWindow(ByVal ArgPath As GraphicsPath)
  Dim frm As Form = New Form()
  Dim path As GraphicsPath = CType(ArgPath.Clone(), GraphicsPath)
  Dim Xlate As Matrix = New Matrix()

  'Find the lowest Y value and normalize all Y values to zero
  'Find the lowest X value and normalize all X values to zero
  'Doing this always gives me some part of a title bar
  Dim p() As PointF = path.PathPoints
  Dim Xoffset As Int32 = 9999
  Dim Yoffset As Int32 = 9999
  Dim p2 As PointF
  For Each p2 In p
    If p2.X < Xoffset Then
      Xoffset = CInt(p2.X)
    End If
    If p2.Y < Yoffset Then
      Yoffset = CInt(p2.Y)
    End If
  Next
  Xlate.Translate(-Xoffset, -Yoffset)
  path.Transform(Xlate)

  ' Set the paractical viewing region of the form
  frm.Region = New Region(path)

  'Set the size of the form
  Dim frmRect As Rectangle = Rectangle.Truncate(path.GetBounds())
  frm.Size = frmRect.Size

  'Set some other parameters
  frm.StartPosition = FormStartPosition.CenterParent
  frm.FormBorderStyle = FormBorderStyle.FixedSingle
```

```
'Show as modal because the form will be disposed of
'This is, after all, just an example
frm.ShowDialog()

frm.Dispose()
Xlate.Dispose()
End Sub
```

Now try to compile and run the program. Make a shape, smooth it, and generate a form using the Form ➤ Spawn ➤ Original or Form ➤ Spawn ➤ Smooth menu choices.

Once you spawn a form, it is modal and must be deleted before you can do anything else in the program. There are some other things to note about the **MakeWindow** method:

- I find the smallest X and Y values for all the points and translate the path by those values.

- I make the size of the form equal to the bounding rectangle of the path.

- I make the form a FixedSingle style and center it on the screen at start-up.

Translating all the points by the lowest X and Y values normalizes the path to the top left of a form. What this does is guarantee at least some small part of the title bar in the form. You will need the title bar to move the form around and to cancel it as well.

 TIP *You should know that you can cancel a form by right-clicking its title bar. You should also know that to move a form around the screen, you need to grab the title bar.*

At the end of this chapter I show you a way to move a form that has no title bar.

Figure 10-4 shows the Window Generator after I make a shape and spawn a smooth form.

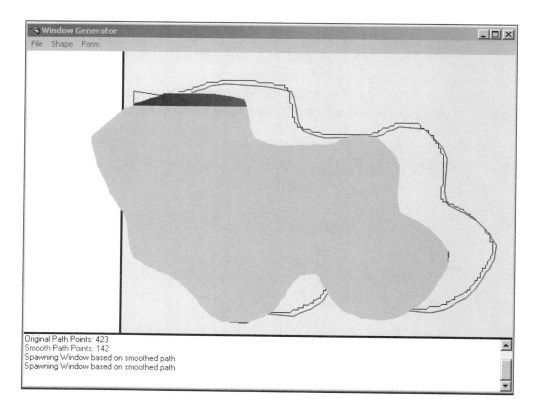

Figure 10-4. Custom form made from a smooth shape

I think this is pretty cool, and I actually have a few uses in mind now, as I am sure you do.

Okay, this works for as long as you have the shape on the screen. What about if you want to save the shape and recall it? Saving the shape of the form allows you to reconstruct the form in a real program.

Saving and recalling the form are repetitive tasks that are best left up to a class. In fact, I think they are such a repetitive tasks that the class and its methods should all be static (shared in VB). This makes the class methods look like simple function calls to any code that uses them.

First things first, though. You need to ask for a name of the shape you want to save. You do this with a small form, as shown in Figure 10-5.

Figure 10-5. The Save form

This form is so simple I will let you glean all the information necessary to make it from the code in Listing 10-4.

Listing 10-4a. C# Code for the Save Form

```csharp
using System;
using System.Drawing;
using System.Drawing.Drawing2D;
using System.Collections;
using System.ComponentModel;
using System.Windows.Forms;

namespace CustomWindow
{
  public class SaveMe : System.Windows.Forms.Form
  {
    private GraphicsPath mPath;

    private System.Windows.Forms.Button cmdSave;
    private System.Windows.Forms.TextBox txtSave;
    private System.ComponentModel.Container components = null;

    public SaveMe(GraphicsPath p)
    {
      InitializeComponent();

      mPath = p;
      this.txtSave.TabIndex = 0;
      this.cmdSave.TabIndex = 1;
    }
```

```csharp
        protected override void Dispose( bool disposing )
        {
          if( disposing )
          {
            if(components != null)
            {
              components.Dispose();
            }
          }
          base.Dispose( disposing );
        }

        #region Windows Form Designer generated code
...
...
...

        #endregion

        private void SaveMe_Load(object sender, System.EventArgs e)
        {
        }

        private void cmdSave_Click(object sender, System.EventArgs e)
        {
          if (txtSave.Text != string.Empty && mPath.PointCount !=0)
            WindowPath.SavePath(txtSave.Text + ".pth", mPath);

          this.Close();
        }
      }
}
```

Listing 10-4b. VB Code for the Save Form

```vb
Option Strict On

Imports System
Imports System.Drawing
Imports System.Drawing.Drawing2D

Public Class SaveMe
  Inherits System.Windows.Forms.Form
```

```vb
    Private mPath As GraphicsPath

#Region " Windows Form Designer generated code "

  Public Sub New(ByVal p As GraphicsPath)
    MyBase.New()

    'This call is required by the Windows Form Designer.
    InitializeComponent()

    mPath = p
    Me.txtSave.TabIndex = 0
    Me.cmdSave.TabIndex = 1
  End Sub

  'Form overrides dispose to clean up the component list.
  Protected Overloads Overrides Sub Dispose(ByVal disposing As Boolean)
    If disposing Then
      If Not (components Is Nothing) Then
        components.Dispose()
      End If
    End If
    MyBase.Dispose(disposing)
  End Sub
   …
   …
   …
#End Region

  Private Sub SaveMe_Load(ByVal sender As System.Object, _
                          ByVal e As System.EventArgs) Handles MyBase.Load

  End Sub

  Private Sub cmdSave_Click(ByVal sender As System.Object, _
                            ByVal e As System.EventArgs) Handles cmdSave.Click
    If txtSave.Text <> String.Empty And mPath.PointCount <> 0 Then
      WindowPath.SavePath(txtSave.Text + ".pth", mPath)
    End If

    Me.Close()
  End Sub
End Class
```

Notice that the form takes a path as an argument. It also calls a method of that static class I mentioned.

Add a class to your project called WindowPath. This class has several methods and properties:

- GetPath

- SavePath

- LastError

- GraphicsPathFileNames

All these methods are single purpose and are therefore good candidates for being static/shared.

The **LastError** method gets a string that contains any error messages that were encountered during the **GetPathFileNames** method. This error string is empty if there were no errors. Now obviously if this were a professional program, I would have quite bit more error checking in these methods. I would also use the **LastError** method to report on any errors found during saving the **SavePath** or **GetPath** methods. However, I leave that up to you. Listing 10-5 shows the code for this class.

Listing 10-5a. C# Code for the WindowPath Static Class

```
using System;
using System.Collections;
using System.Drawing;
using System.Drawing.Drawing2D;
using System.IO;

namespace CustomWindow
{
  public sealed class WindowPath
  {
    private static GraphicsPath mP;
    private static string[] mFileNames;
    private static string mIOerror;

    /// <summary>
    /// Gets GraphicsPath stored in file
    /// </summary>
    /// <param name="fname"></param>
    /// <returns GraphicsPath></returns>
```

```
public static GraphicsPath GetPath(string fname)
{
  Point BeginP = Point.Empty;
  Point EndP   = Point.Empty;
  Point P      = Point.Empty;
  string s;
  string[] x;
  mP = new  GraphicsPath();

  StreamReader sr = new StreamReader(fname);
  sr.BaseStream.Seek(0, SeekOrigin.Begin);
  while (sr.Peek() > -1)
  {
    s = sr.ReadLine();
    x = s.Split(new Char[] {','});
    P.X = Convert.ToInt32(x[0]);
    P.Y = Convert.ToInt32(x[1]);

    if (BeginP == Point.Empty)
    {
      BeginP = P;
      continue;
    }

    EndP = P;
    mP.AddLine( BeginP, EndP);
    BeginP = EndP;
  }
  mP.CloseFigure();

  return mP;
}

public static void SavePath(string fname, GraphicsPath P)
{
  FileStream fs = new FileStream(fname, FileMode.Create);
  StreamWriter sw = new StreamWriter(fs);
  foreach (PointF p in P.PathPoints)
  {
    sw.Write(p.X.ToString() + "," + p.Y.ToString() + "\n");
  }
  sw.Close();
  GetFileNames();
}
```

```
public static string[] GraphicsPathFileNames
{
  get
  {
    GetFileNames();
    return mFileNames;
  }
}

public static string LastError
{
  get {return mIOerror;}
}

private static void GetFileNames()
{
  ArrayList a = new  ArrayList();
  mIOerror = "";
  try
  {
    mFileNames = Directory.GetFiles(Directory.GetCurrentDirectory());

    //We are only interested in the graphics path filenames that end in .pth
    for (int k=0; k<mFileNames.Length; k++)
    {
      if ( Path.GetExtension(mFileNames[k].ToLower()) == ".pth" )
        a.Add(Path.GetFileName(mFileNames[k]));
    }

    //Convert the explicit array to implicit array so I can return string[]
    a.TrimToSize();
    mFileNames = new string[a.Count];
    for (int k=0; k<a.Count; k++)
      mFileNames[k] = (string)a[k];

  }
  catch (ArgumentNullException)
  {
    mIOerror = "Path is a null reference.";
  }
```

```
    catch (System.Security.SecurityException)
    {
      mIOerror = "The caller does not have the " +
        "required permission.";
    }
    catch (ArgumentException)
    {
      mIOerror = "Path is an empty string, " +
        "contains only white spaces, " +
        "or contains invalid characters.";
    }
    catch (System.IO.DirectoryNotFoundException)
    {
      mIOerror = "The path encapsulated in the " +
        "Directory object does not exist.";
    }
   }
  }
}
```

Listing 10-5b. VB Code for the WindowPath Static Class

```
Option Strict On

Imports System
Imports System.IO
Imports System.Drawing
Imports System.Drawing.Drawing2D

Public NotInheritable Class WindowPath

  Private Shared mP As GraphicsPath
  Private Shared mFileNames() As String
  Private Shared mIOerror As String

  Public Shared Function GetPath(ByVal fname As String) As GraphicsPath
    Dim BeginP As Point = Point.Empty
    Dim EndP As Point = Point.Empty
    Dim P As Point = Point.Empty
    Dim s As String
    Dim x() As String
    mP = New GraphicsPath()
```

```vbnet
        Dim sr As StreamReader = New StreamReader(fname)
        sr.BaseStream.Seek(0, SeekOrigin.Begin)
        While (sr.Peek() > -1)
          s = sr.ReadLine()
          x = s.Split(New Char() {CType(",", Char)})
          P.X = Convert.ToInt32(x(0))
          P.Y = Convert.ToInt32(x(1))

          If Point.op_Equality(BeginP, Point.Empty) Then
            BeginP = P
          Else
            EndP = P
            mP.AddLine(BeginP, EndP)
            BeginP = EndP
          End If
        End While
        mP.CloseFigure()

      Return mP
    End Function


    Public Shared Sub SavePath(ByVal fname As String, ByVal P As GraphicsPath)
      Dim fs As FileStream = New FileStream(fname, FileMode.Create)
      Dim sw As StreamWriter = New StreamWriter(fs)
      Dim p2 As PointF
      For Each p2 In P.PathPoints
        sw.Write(p2.X.ToString() + "," + p2.Y.ToString() + vbCrLf)
      Next
      sw.Close()
      GetFileNames()
    End Sub


    Public Shared ReadOnly Property GraphicsPathFileNames() As String()
      Get
        GetFileNames()
        Return mFileNames
      End Get
    End Property


    Public Shared ReadOnly Property LastError() As String
      Get
        Return mIOerror
      End Get
    End Property
```

```
Private Shared Sub GetFileNames()
  Dim a As ArrayList = New ArrayList()
  Dim k As Int32

  mIOerror = ""
  Try
    mFileNames = Directory.GetFiles(Directory.GetCurrentDirectory())

    'We are only interested in the graphics path filenames that end in .pth
    For k = 0 To mFileNames.Length - 1
      If Path.GetExtension(mFileNames(k).ToLower()) = ".pth" Then
        a.Add(Path.GetFileName(mFileNames(k)))
      End If
    Next

    'Convert the explicit array to implicit array so I can return string[]
    a.TrimToSize()
    If a.Count > 0 Then
      ReDim mFileNames(a.Count - 1)
      For k = 0 To a.Count - 1
        mFileNames(k) = CType(a(k), String)
      Next
    Else
      ReDim mFileNames(0)
      mFileNames(0) = String.Empty
    End If

  Catch ex As ArgumentNullException
    mIOerror = "Path is a null reference."
  Catch ex As System.Security.SecurityException
    mIOerror = "The caller does not have the required permission."
  Catch ex As ArgumentException
    mIOerror = "Path is an empty string, contains only white spaces, " + _
               "or contains invalid characters."
  Catch ex As System.IO.DirectoryNotFoundException
    mIOerror = "The path encapsulated in the Directory object does not exist."
  End Try
End Sub
End Class
```

Let's take a closer look at some of the methods in this class.

The **SavePath** method takes each point in the path and saves it to a file in the current directory. It delimits X and Y values with a comma and Points with a carriage return/line feed combination.

The following is a section of the **GetFileNames** method:

```
ArrayList a = new  ArrayList();
mIOerror = "";
try
  {
    mFileNames = Directory.GetFiles(Directory.GetCurrentDirectory());

    //We are only interested in the graphics path filenames that end in .pth
    for (int k=0; k<mFileNames.Length; k++)
    {
      if ( Path.GetExtension(mFileNames[k].ToLower()) == ".pth" )
        a.Add(Path.GetFileName(mFileNames[k]));
    }

    //Convert the explicit array to implicit array so I can return string[]
    a.TrimToSize();
    mFileNames = new string[a.Count];
    for (int k=0; k<a.Count; k++)
      mFileNames[k] = (string)a[k];
  }
```

What I want to do is return an array of strings. However, this is not as easy as it seems in C#. VB has the **ReDim** statement that lets you resize an array at any time. C# has no such mechanism that I am aware of.

In C# there are implicit arrays such as int[3] or string[5]. There are also several types of explicit arrays whose base object is Array. These explicit arrays allow quite a bit of manipulation. However, they are not the same as implicit arrays.[2]

An object whose type is Array can start out as one length and be added to so it ends up as another length. Implicit arrays cannot do this. Before you use an implicit array such as string[], you need to define its length somehow and this length cannot change.

Because I need to return an implicit array of strings that represent the list of shape files in the current directory, I need to start out using an Array. After the array is filled, I trim it to size and manually transfer the data over to the implicit array.

Of course I could have returned a type of Array and been done with it. But where's the fun in that?

---

2. Implicit and explicit arrays are not actually Microsoft terms. These terms help me keep identify array types in my own mind.

NOTE *I have to say that working with the System.IO namespace classes is a delight. File I/O has never been easier. Neither has path manipulation.*

Now that you have added the Save form and the WindowPath class, it is time to connect everything together.

The main form has a method called **mnuSaveShape_Click**. Add code to this method so it looks like the following:

C#

```
private void mnuSaveShape_Click(object sender, System.EventArgs e)
{
   SaveMe frm = new SaveMe(mOriginalPath);
   frm.ShowDialog();
}
```

VB

```
Private Sub mnuSaveShape_Click(ByVal sender As System.Object, _
                        ByVal e As System.EventArgs) _
                     Handles mnuSaveShape.Click
   Dim frm As SaveMe = New SaveMe(mOriginalPath)
   frm.ShowDialog()
End Sub
```

All this code does is instantiate the save form, which in turn saves the shape. By the way, I save the original shape. I know that I said the smooth path has fewer points and therefore takes up less space. However, if I save the smooth path, I can never re-create the original one. If this were a professional program, I would give the user the option of which one to save.

Compile and run the program. Save a shape and look in the current directory to see if the file is there. If it is, then move on to the next step.

Adding a Tree View of the Saved Paths

You can create a shape, smooth it, generate a form that looks like either shape, and save the original shape. This is a lot already. However, it would not be much of a user interface if you could not retrieve the shapes and re-create the forms.

The last control on this form that is not doing anything right now is the TreeView control called PathTree. This is where the user will view all his or her saved paths.

You need to write a helper function that gets the list of saved path file names and displays them in the tree. This function is called **FillTree**. Listing 10-6 shows the code for the **FillTree** method.

Listing 10-6a. C# Code for the FillTree Method

```csharp
private void FillTree()
{
  TreeNode BaseNode;
  TreeNode NodeX;
  string[] AllFileNames = WindowPath.GraphicsPathFileNames;

  PathTree.Nodes.Clear();

  //Create the base node
  BaseNode = new TreeNode("All Window Paths");
  BaseNode.ImageIndex = OPENICON;
  BaseNode.SelectedImageIndex = BaseNode.ImageIndex;
  BaseNode.ExpandAll();
  BaseNode.Tag = string.Empty;

  //Create each node in the tree under the base node
  foreach (string s in AllFileNames)
  {
    NodeX = new TreeNode();
    NodeX.ImageIndex = DRAWICON;
    NodeX.SelectedImageIndex = NodeX.ImageIndex;
    NodeX.Text = Path.GetFileNameWithoutExtension(s);
    NodeX.Tag  = s;
    BaseNode.Nodes.Add(NodeX);
  }

  PathTree.Nodes.Add(BaseNode);
}
```

Listing 10-6b. VB Code for the FillTree Method

```
Private Sub FillTree()
  Dim BaseNode As TreeNode
  Dim NodeX As TreeNode
  Dim AllFileNames() As String = WindowPath.GraphicsPathFileNames

  PathTree.Nodes.Clear()

  'Create the base node
  BaseNode = New TreeNode("All Window Paths")
  BaseNode.ImageIndex = OPEN_ICON
  BaseNode.SelectedImageIndex = BaseNode.ImageIndex
  BaseNode.ExpandAll()
  BaseNode.Tag = String.Empty

  'Create each node in the tree under the base node
  Dim s As String
  For Each s In AllFileNames
    If s <> String.Empty Then
      NodeX = New TreeNode()
      NodeX.ImageIndex = DRAW_ICON
      NodeX.SelectedImageIndex = NodeX.ImageIndex
      NodeX.Text = Path.GetFileNameWithoutExtension(s)
      NodeX.Tag = s
      BaseNode.Nodes.Add(NodeX)
    End If
  Next

  PathTree.Nodes.Add(BaseNode)
End Sub
```

I am a big fan of tree views. So much information can be shown in such a small space and so efficiently.

As you can see here, I use the **WindowPath.GraphicsPathFileNames** method to get a list of files that hold saved shapes. I then build the tree view, adding visually descriptive icons along the way. This is why I used the ImageList in the constructor.

Add one line of code to the Form_Load event handler.

C#

```csharp
private void Form1_Load(object sender, System.EventArgs e)
{
    FillTree();
}
```

VB

```vb
Private Sub Form1_Load(ByVal sender As System.Object, _
                        ByVal e As System.EventArgs) Handles MyBase.Load
    FillTree()
End Sub
```

Now compile and run the code. If you have been saving shapes, you should see them pop up in this TreeView control. Figure 10-6 shows my form with the TreeView control activated.

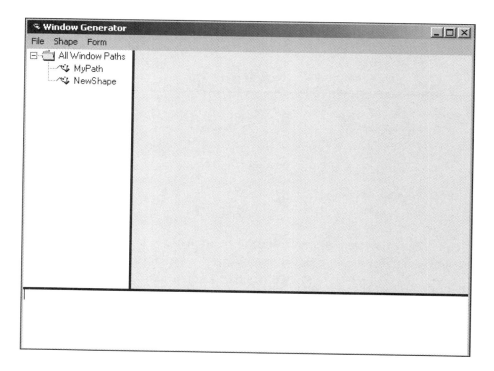

Figure 10-6. Window with the TreeView control activated

There is one other place that you need to call **FillTree** from. If you save a shape, it should immediately come up in the tree view. Your **mnuSaveShape_Click** method should now look like this:

C#

```
private void mnuSaveShape_Click(object sender, System.EventArgs e)
{
  SaveMe frm = new SaveMe(mOriginalPath);
  frm.ShowDialog();
  FillTree();
}
```

VB

```
Private Sub mnuSaveShape_Click(ByVal sender As System.Object, _
                        ByVal e As System.EventArgs) _
                    Handles mnuSaveShape.Click
  Dim frm As SaveMe = New SaveMe(mOriginalPath)
  frm.ShowDialog()
  FillTree()
End Sub
```

Run the code and save a shape. The shape's name should appear in the tree view. This program is getting a little more polished now. However, there is one last major thing to do here: Allow the user to retrieve the shape and re-create the form.

Before you look ahead, how would you do this? Perhaps another dialog box that the user could type a name into? That is so 1990s.

This program will allow the user to drag the name of the shape from the tree view over to the drawing panel and drop it there. Through the magic of what was originally called DDE, the original shape will appear on the screen. The following section details how to do this.

Dropping Names

There is some setup to do with both the TreeView control and the drawing panel. The TreeView needs to be set up to be the source of the drag operation and the Panel needs to be set up to be the destination.

Essentially, the drag and drop for this program works like this:

1. The user presses the left mouse button, which fires the MouseDown event for the TreeView.

2. The user moves the mouse, which fires the MouseMove event for the TreeView.

3. The user drags an object into view of the Panel. This fires the DragEnter event for the Panel.

4. The user lifts up on the mouse while in the Panel. This fires the DragDrop event for the Panel.

There are actually quite a few other events you can attach to while doing a drag-and-drop procedure. These are the basic ones, though.

I created a region in the main form's code called "Drag-n-Drop events for TreeView and Panel." Within this region are all the delegates to handle drag and drop. The code is shown in Listing 10-7.

Listing 10-7a. C# Code for the Drag-and-Drop Region

```
#region Drag-n-Drop events for TreeView and Panel

private void TreeMouseDown(object sender, MouseEventArgs m)
{
  if (m.Button == MouseButtons.Left)
    mDraging = true;
}

private void TreeMouseMove(object sender, MouseEventArgs m)
{
  if (!mDraging)
    return;

  if (m.Button != MouseButtons.Left)
    return;

  //Initial condition
  if (PathTree.SelectedNode == null)
    return;

  mRecallFileName = (string)PathTree.SelectedNode.Tag;

  //Make sure that there is a filename associated with this node
  if (mRecallFileName == string.Empty)
  {
    mDraging = false;
    return;
  }
```

```
      DebugWindow.AppendText("Dragging File: " + mRecallFileName + "\n");
      PathTree.DoDragDrop(mRecallFileName ,
                          DragDropEffects.Copy | DragDropEffects.Move );
    }

    private void PanelDragEnter(object sender, DragEventArgs e)
    {
      if (e.Data.GetDataPresent(DataFormats.Text))
        e.Effect = DragDropEffects.Copy;
      else
        e.Effect = DragDropEffects.None;
    }

    private void PanelDragDrop(object sender, DragEventArgs e)
    {
      mDraging = false;

      mOriginalPath = WindowPath.GetPath(mRecallFileName);
      mSmoothPath.Reset();
      P1.Invalidate();

      mnuSpawnSmooth.Enabled = false;
      if (mOriginalPath.PointCount == 0)
        DebugWindow.AppendText("Empty Path File: " + mRecallFileName + "\n");
      else
      {
        mnuSpawnForm.Enabled = true;
        DebugWindow.AppendText("Path Complete\n");
      }
    }

    #endregion
```

Listing 10-7b. VB Code for the Drag-and-Drop Region

```
#Region "Drag-n-Drop events for TreeView and Panel"

  Private Sub TreeMouseDown(ByVal sender As Object, ByVal m As MouseEventArgs)
    If m.Button = MouseButtons.Left Then
      mDraging = True
    End If
  End Sub
```

```vb
Private Sub TreeMouseMove(ByVal sender As Object, ByVal m As MouseEventArgs)
  If Not mDraging Then
    Return
  End If

  If m.Button <> MouseButtons.Left Then
    Return
  End If

  'Initial condition
  If PathTree.SelectedNode Is Nothing Then
    Return
  End If

  mRecallFileName = CType(PathTree.SelectedNode.Tag, String)

  'Make sure that there is a filename associated with this node
  If mRecallFileName = String.Empty Then
    mDraging = False
    Return
  End If
  DebugWindow.AppendText("Dragging File: " + mRecallFileName + vbCrLf)
  PathTree.DoDragDrop(mRecallFileName, _
                      DragDropEffects.Copy Or DragDropEffects.Move)
End Sub

Private Sub PanelDragEnter(ByVal sender As Object, ByVal e As DragEventArgs)
  If e.Data.GetDataPresent(DataFormats.Text) Then
    e.Effect = DragDropEffects.Copy
  Else
    e.Effect = DragDropEffects.None
  End If
End Sub

Private Sub PanelDragDrop(ByVal sender As Object, ByVal e As DragEventArgs)
  mDraging = False

  mOriginalPath = WindowPath.GetPath(mRecallFileName)
  mSmoothPath.Reset()
  P1.Invalidate()

  mnuSpawnSmooth.Enabled = False
```

```
    If mOriginalPath.PointCount = 0 Then
      DebugWindow.AppendText("Empty Path File: " + mRecallFileName + vbCrLf)
    Else
      mnuSpawnForm.Enabled = True
      DebugWindow.AppendText("Path Complete" + vbCrLf)
    End If
  End Sub

#End Region
```

None of this will work, of course, until these delegates are all wired up. This is done in the constructor. Listing 10-8 shows the complete code for the constructor, including all the delegate wiring.

Listing 10-8a. C# Code for the Complete Constructor

```csharp
public Form1()
{
  InitializeComponent();

  //Initialize class variables
  mDrawIcon     = new Icon("draw.ico");
  mDrawCursor   = new Cursor("Pen.cur");
  mDragCursor   = new Cursor("drag.cur");
  mImageList    = new ImageList();
  mOriginalPath = new GraphicsPath();
  mSmoothPath   = new GraphicsPath();
  mDrawing      = false;
  mInvalidRect  = Rectangle.Empty;

  //Set the screen
  this.Icon   = mDrawIcon;
  this.Size = new Size(800, 600);
  this.SetStyle(ControlStyles.AllPaintingInWmPaint,true);
  this.SetStyle(ControlStyles.DoubleBuffer,true);

  //Set up the image list
  mImageList.Images.Add(new Icon("closed.ico"));
  mImageList.Images.Add(new Icon("open.ico"));
  mImageList.Images.Add(mDrawIcon);
  mImageList.Images.Add(new Icon("drag.ico"));
```

```
        //Set RichTextBox properties
        DebugWindow.ReadOnly   = true;
        DebugWindow.Height     = this.Height /8;
        DebugWindow.Text       = "";

        //Set up the splitters
        PanelSplitter.Height    = 3;
        PanelSplitter.BackColor = Color.Blue;
        TreeSplitter.BackColor  = Color.Blue;
        TreeSplitter.Location   = new Point(PathTree.Width, 0);
        TreeSplitter.Size       = new Size(3, this.Height);

        // Set properties of TreeView control.
        PathTree.Width          = this.ClientSize.Width / 6;
        PathTree.TabIndex       = 0;
        PathTree.ImageList      = mImageList;
        PathTree.MouseDown      += new MouseEventHandler(this.TreeMouseDown);
        PathTree.MouseMove      += new MouseEventHandler(this.TreeMouseMove);

        //Set Drawing Panel Properties
        P1.BackColor    = Color.Bisque;
        P1.AllowDrop    = true;
        P1.DragEnter    += new DragEventHandler(this.PanelDragEnter);
        P1.DragDrop     += new DragEventHandler(this.PanelDragDrop);
        P1.Paint        += new PaintEventHandler(this.PanelPaint);
        P1.MouseDown    += new MouseEventHandler(this.M_Down);
        P1.MouseUp      += new MouseEventHandler(this.M_Up);
        P1.MouseMove    += new MouseEventHandler(this.M_Move);

        //Set all the border styles to none.
        BasePanel.BorderStyle   = BorderStyle.None;
        P1.BorderStyle          = BorderStyle.None;
        PathTree.BorderStyle    = BorderStyle.None;
        DebugWindow.BorderStyle = BorderStyle.None;

        //Disable some menu selections
        mnuSpawnForm.Enabled    = false;
        mnuSpawnSmooth.Enabled  = false;
    }
```

Listing 10-8b. VB Code for the Complete Constructor

```vb
Public Sub New()
  MyBase.New()

  'This call is required by the Windows Form Designer.
  InitializeComponent()

  'Initialize class variables
  mDrawIcon = New Icon("draw.ico")
  mDrawCursor = New Cursor("Pen.cur")
  mDragCursor = New Cursor("drag.cur")
  mImageList = New ImageList()
  mOriginalPath = New GraphicsPath()
  mSmoothPath = New GraphicsPath()
  m_Drawing = False
  mInvalidRect = Rectangle.Empty

  'Set the screen
  Me.Icon = mDrawIcon
  Me.Size = New Size(800, 600)
  Me.SetStyle(ControlStyles.AllPaintingInWmPaint, True)
  Me.SetStyle(ControlStyles.DoubleBuffer, True)

  'Set up the image list
  mImageList.Images.Add(New Icon("closed.ico"))
  mImageList.Images.Add(New Icon("open.ico"))
  mImageList.Images.Add(mDrawIcon)
  mImageList.Images.Add(New Icon("drag.ico"))

  'Set RichTextBox properties
  DebugWindow.ReadOnly = True
  DebugWindow.Height = CInt(Me.Height / 8)
  DebugWindow.Text = ""

  'Set up the splitters
  PanelSplitter.Height = 3
  PanelSplitter.BackColor = Color.Blue
  TreeSplitter.BackColor = Color.Blue
  TreeSplitter.Location = New Point(PathTree.Width, 0)
  TreeSplitter.Size = New Size(3, Me.Height)
```

```
        ' Set properties of TreeView control.
        PathTree.Width = CInt(Me.ClientSize.Width / 6)
        PathTree.TabIndex = 0
        PathTree.ImageList = mImageList
        AddHandler PathTree.MouseDown, New MouseEventHandler( _
                                    AddressOf Me.TreeMouseDown)
        AddHandler PathTree.MouseMove, New MouseEventHandler( _
                                    AddressOf Me.TreeMouseMove)


        'Set Drawing Panel Properties
        P1.BackColor = Color.Bisque
        P1.AllowDrop = True
        AddHandler P1.DragEnter, New DragEventHandler(AddressOf Me.PanelDragEnter)
        AddHandler P1.DragDrop, New DragEventHandler(AddressOf Me.PanelDragDrop)
        AddHandler P1.Paint, New PaintEventHandler(AddressOf Me.PanelPaint)
        AddHandler P1.MouseDown, New MouseEventHandler(AddressOf Me.M_Down)
        AddHandler P1.MouseUp, New MouseEventHandler(AddressOf Me.M_Up)
        AddHandler P1.MouseMove, New MouseEventHandler(AddressOf Me.M_Move)


        'Set all the border styles to none.
        BasePanel.BorderStyle = BorderStyle.None
        P1.BorderStyle = BorderStyle.None
        PathTree.BorderStyle = BorderStyle.None
        DebugWindow.BorderStyle = BorderStyle.None


        'Disable some menu selections
        mnuSpawnForm.Enabled = False
        mnuSpawnSmooth.Enabled = False

    End Sub
```

You now have a complete working program. Run it and try dragging a name from the tree view on the left and dropping it in the panel on the right. If all is well you should immediately see the shape appear. Look Ma, no keystrokes!

One Last Thing

When I wrote this program I spent a lot of time playing around. I was trying to find the balance between features and time. I could have added quite a few more features to this program, but to what end?

There was one feature I thought needed adding, though. When a tree view is collapsed, I like to see a closed folder appear. When it is expanded, I like to see an open folder appear. These are just visual cues.

Add another delegate to the "Drag-n-Drop events for TreeView and Panel" region. The code is as follows:

C#

```csharp
private void TreeExpandCollapse(object sender, TreeViewEventArgs e)
{
  //No need to detect which node this is since only the base node can be
  //expanded or contracted
  if (e.Action == TreeViewAction.Collapse)
    PathTree.Nodes[0].SelectedImageIndex = CLOSEDICON;
  else
    PathTree.Nodes[0].SelectedImageIndex = OPENICON;
}
```

VB

```vb
Private Sub TreeExpandCollapse(ByVal sender As Object, _
                               ByVal e As TreeViewEventArgs)
  'No need to detect which node this is since only the base node can be
  'expanded or contracted
  If e.Action = TreeViewAction.Collapse Then
    PathTree.Nodes(0).SelectedImageIndex = CLOSED_ICON
  Else
    PathTree.Nodes(0).SelectedImageIndex = OPEN_ICON
  End If
End Sub
```

Now wire it up in the constructor. Add the following lines of code in the constructor below the PathTree setup section:

C#

```csharp
PathTree.AfterCollapse  += new  TreeViewEventHandler(
                               this.TreeExpandCollapse);
PathTree.AfterExpand    += new  TreeViewEventHandler(
                               this.TreeExpandCollapse);
```

VB

```
AddHandler PathTree.AfterCollapse, New TreeViewEventHandler( _
                          AddressOf Me.TreeExpandCollapse)
AddHandler PathTree.AfterExpand, New TreeViewEventHandler( _
                          AddressOf Me.TreeExpandCollapse)
```

Compile and run the code. If you collapse the tree view, the icon will change to a closed folder. If you expand the tree view, the icon will change to an open folder.

The Final Part

Well, you have now completed the custom Window Generator. There are quite a few tasks being performed in this program to insulate the user from a difficult interface.

In the beginning of this chapter, I promised to show you a way to move a form that has no title bar. While this tidbit is not a part of this project, it is very useful for other projects you may have. I have used this technique many times.

Most methods I see concerning moving a form while the mouse is not on the title bar use brute force. You can detect where the mouse is and capture the mouse move event. When you capture this event, just move the form using the location property according to haw far the mouse has moved. This method is very problematic and results in a tremendous amount of jitter.

The better way is to fool the form into thinking that you have actually grabbed the title bar and are moving it that way. This is done through two Windows API calls:

- ReleaseCapture

- SendMessageA

Both API calls are in the user32.dll file.

Make a new Windows Forms project. Go into the code pane and enter the code shown in Listing 10-9.

Listing 10-9. Code to Move a Form via Windows API Calls

```
using System;
using System.Drawing;
using System.Collections;
using System.ComponentModel;
using System.Windows.Forms;
using System.Data;
using System.Runtime.InteropServices;
```

```
namespace moveme
{
  public class Form1 : System.Windows.Forms.Form
  {
    private const int WM_NCLBUTTONDOWN = 0xA1;

    [DllImport("user32.dll")]
    internal extern static int ReleaseCapture();
    [DllImport("user32.dll")]
    internal extern static int SendMessageA( IntPtr windowHandle, int wMsg,
                                             int wPAram, int lParam );

    private System.ComponentModel.Container components = null;

    public Form1()
    {
      InitializeComponent();

      this.MouseMove += new MouseEventHandler(this.MyMouseMove);
    }

    protected override void Dispose( bool disposing )
    {
      if( disposing )
      {
        if (components != null)
        {
          components.Dispose();
        }
      }
      base.Dispose( disposing );
    }

    #region Windows Form Designer generated code
...
...
...
    #endregion

    [STAThread]
    static void Main()
    {
      Application.Run(new Form1());
    }
```

```
    private void Form1_Load(object sender, System.EventArgs e)
    {
    }

    private void MyMouseMove(object sender, MouseEventArgs e)
    {
      if (e.Button==MouseButtons.Left)
      {
        ReleaseCapture();
        SendMessageA( this.Handle, WM_NCLBUTTONDOWN, 2, 0);
      }
    }
  }
}
```

Run the form and drag it using the mouse anywhere on the form. It works just as if you were dragging it via the title bar.

I chose not to add this code to the main project because I wanted you to see how easy it is to accomplish. Your homework—should you decide to accept it—is to make the funny-shaped form a class. This way, you can add this small amount of code, remove the form's title bar, and allow the user to move the form by dragging it around. You certainly have the knowledge to do this.

Summary

This was the last chapter in your journey through the world of graphics programming using GDI+. Like the previous chapter, this one was all about application. Chapters 1 through 8 gave you the theory, and Chapters 9 and 10 provided the applications.

This chapter covered the following:

- Using TreeView controls

- Using the file I/O capability of .NET

- Drawing on a Panel control

- Drawing free-form shapes

- Changing cursors

- Using static methods to persist and retrieve shapes

- Using a RichTextBox

- Multipane forms

- Using splitters to section and automatically size controls on a form

- Using a Path as the region to a new form

- Launching a new custom form

- Using the menu

This project was fun to build. It could definitely use some enhancements, but I leave that to you.

APPENDIX

The Enumerations

I USED QUITE A FEW enumerations throughout this book. Some I only used once or twice, and others I used multiple times. Often when I read a computer book I like to see some of the more common enumerations and constants in a handy place. This appendix is where I put all my handy stuff.

One thing to note before I go on: VB seems to have a friendlier IntelliSense capability than C#. For instance, if I am setting a value that is of type Color, the VB IntelliSense will give me the Color enumeration when I press the equal sign (=). C# does not do this. Because I wrote nearly everything in this book in both VB and C#, I find this annoying. Enumerations are automatically given to you in VB, but in C# you need to know where to get them. Anyway, I digress.

The KnownColor enumeration is the most commonly used enumeration in this book. I used it extensively in every chapter. These colors are all system-defined colors.

ActiveBorder	BlueViolet	Cornsilk
ActiveCaption	Brown	Crimson
ActiveCaptionText	BurlyWood	Cyan
AliceBlue	CadetBlue	DarkBlue
AntiqueWhite	Chartreuse	DarkCyan
AppWorkspace	Chocolate	DarkGoldenrod
Aqua	Control	DarkGray
Aquamarine	ControlDark	DarkGreen
Azure	ControlDarkDark	DarkKhaki
Beige	ControlLight	DarkMagenta
Bisque	ControlLightLight	DarkOliveGreen
Black	ControlText	DarkOrange
BlanchedAlmond	Coral	DarkOrchid
Blue	CornflowerBlue	DarkRed

DarkSalmon	InactiveCaptionText	MediumBlue
DarkSeaGreen	IndianRed	MediumOrchid
DarkSlateBlue	Indigo	MediumPurple
DarkSlateGray	Info	MediumSeaGreen
DarkTurquoise	InfoText	MediumSlateBlue
DarkViolet	Ivory	MediumSpringGreen
DeepPink	Khaki	MediumTurquoise
DeepSkyBlue	Lavender	MediumVioletRed
Desktop	LavenderBlush	Menu
DimGray	LawnGreen	MenuText
DodgerBlue	LemonChiffon	MidnightBlue
Firebrick	LightBlue	MintCream
FloralWhite	LightCoral	MistyRose
ForestGreen	LightCyan	Moccasin
Fuchsia	LightGoldenrodYellow	NavajoWhite
Gainsboro	LightGray	Navy
GhostWhite	LightGreen	OldLace
Gold	LightPink	Olive
Goldenrod	LightSalmon	OliveDrab
Gray	LightSeaGreen	Orange
GrayText	LightSkyBlue	OrangeRed
Green	LightSlateGray	Orchid
GreenYellow	LightSteelBlue	PaleGoldenrod
Highlight	LightYellow	PaleGreen
HighlightText	Lime	PaleTurquoise
Honeydew	LimeGreen	PaleVioletRed
HotPink	Linen	PapayaWhip
HotTrack	Magenta	PeachPuff
InactiveBorder	Maroon	Peru
InactiveCaption	MediumAquamarine	Pink

Plum	Sienna	Transparent
PowderBlue	Silver	Turquoise
Purple	SkyBlue	Violet
Red	SlateBlue	Wheat
RosyBrown	SlateGray	White
RoyalBlue	Snow	WhiteSmoke
SaddleBrown	SpringGreen	Window
Salmon	SteelBlue	WindowFrame
SandyBrown	Tan	WindowText
ScrollBar	Teal	Yellow
SeaGreen	Thistle	YellowGreen
SeaShell	Tomato	

Table A-1 shows the PaperKind enumeration. This is a common enumeration used in setting up print jobs. As I mentioned in Chapter 8, I never knew there were so many kinds of paper.

Table A-1. PaperKind Enumeration

Member Name	Description
A2	A2 paper (420 mm by 594 mm).
A3	A3 paper (297 mm by 420 mm).
A3Extra	A3 extra paper (322 mm by 445 mm).
A3ExtraTransverse	A3 extra transverse paper (322 mm by 445 mm).
A3Rotated	A3 rotated paper (420 mm by 297 mm).
A3Transverse	A3 transverse paper (297 mm by 420 mm).
A4	A4 paper (210 mm by 297 mm).
A4Extra	A4 extra paper (236 mm by 322 mm). This value is specific to the PostScript driver and is used only by Linotronic printers to help save paper.
A4Plus	A4 plus paper (210 mm by 330 mm).

Table A-1. PaperKind Enumeration (Continued)

Member Name	Description
A4Rotated	A4 rotated paper (297 mm by 210 mm). Requires Windows 98, Windows NT 4.0, or later.
A4Small	A4 small paper (210 mm by 297 mm).
A4Transverse	A4 transverse paper (210 mm by 297 mm).
A5	A5 paper (148 mm by 210 mm).
A5Extra	A5 extra paper (174 mm by 235 mm).
A5Rotated	A5 rotated paper (210 mm by 148 mm). Requires Windows 98, Windows NT 4.0, or later.
A5Transverse	A5 transverse paper (148 mm by 210 mm).
A6	A6 paper (105 mm by 148 mm). Requires Windows 98, Windows NT 4.0, or later.
A6Rotated	A6 rotated paper (148 mm by 105 mm). Requires Windows 98, Windows NT 4.0, or later.
APlus	SuperA/SuperA/A4 paper (227 mm by 356 mm).
B4	B4 paper (250 mm by 353 mm).
B4Envelope	B4 envelope (250 mm by 353 mm).
B4JisRotated	JIS B4 rotated paper (364 mm by 257 mm). Requires Windows 98, Windows NT 4.0, or later.
B5	B5 paper (176 mm by 250 mm).
B5Envelope	B5 envelope (176 mm by 250 mm).
B5Extra	ISO B5 extra paper (201 mm by 276 mm).
B5JisRotated	JIS B5 rotated paper (257 mm by 182 mm). Requires Windows 98, Windows NT 4.0, or later.
B5Transverse	JIS B5 transverse paper (182 mm by 257 mm).
B6Envelope	B6 envelope (176 mm by 125 mm).
B6Jis	JIS B6 paper (128 mm by 182 mm). Requires Windows 98, Windows NT 4.0, or later.
B6JisRotated	JIS B6 rotated paper (182 mm by 128 mm). Requires Windows 98, Windows NT 4.0, or later.
BPlus	SuperB/SuperB/A3 paper (305 mm by 487 mm).

Table A-1. PaperKind Enumeration (Continued)

Member Name	Description
C3Envelope	C3 envelope (324 mm by 458 mm).
C4Envelope	C4 envelope (229 mm by 324 mm).
C5Envelope	C5 envelope (162 mm by 229 mm).
C65Envelope	C65 envelope (114 mm by 229 mm).
C6Envelope	C6 envelope (114 mm by 162 mm).
CSheet	C paper (17 in. by 22 in.).
Custom	The paper size is defined by the user.
DLEnvelope	DL envelope (110 mm by 220 mm).
DSheet	D paper (22 in. by 34 in.).
ESheet	E paper (34 in. by 44 in.).
Executive	Executive paper (7.25 in. by 10.5 in.).
Folio	Folio paper (8.5 in. by 13 in.).
GermanLegalFanfold	German legal fanfold (8.5 in. by 13 in.).
GermanStandardFanfold	German standard fanfold (8.5 in. by 12 in.).
InviteEnvelope	Invite envelope (220 mm by 220 mm).
IsoB4	ISO B4 (250 mm by 353 mm).
ItalyEnvelope	Italy envelope (110 mm by 230 mm).
JapaneseDoublePostcard	Japanese double postcard (200 mm by 148 mm). Requires Windows 98, Windows NT 4.0, or later.
JapaneseDoublePostcardRotated	Japanese rotated double postcard (148 mm by 200 mm). Requires Windows 98, Windows NT 4.0, or later.
JapaneseEnvelopeChouNumber3	Japanese Chou #3 envelope. Requires Windows 98, Windows NT 4.0, or later.
JapaneseEnvelopeChouNumber3Rotated	Japanese rotated Chou #3 envelope. Requires Windows 98, Windows NT 4.0, or later.
JapaneseEnvelopeChouNumber4	Japanese Chou #4 envelope. Requires Windows 98, Windows NT 4.0, or later.
JapaneseEnvelopeChouNumber4Rotated	Japanese rotated Chou #4 envelope. Requires Windows 98, Windows NT 4.0, or later.

Table A-1. PaperKind Enumeration (Continued)

Member Name	Description
JapaneseEnvelopeKakuNumber2	Japanese Kaku #2 envelope. Requires Windows 98, Windows NT 4.0, or later.
JapaneseEnvelopeKakuNumber2Rotated	Japanese rotated Kaku #2 envelope. Requires Windows 98, Windows NT 4.0, or later.
JapaneseEnvelopeKakuNumber3	Japanese Kaku #3 envelope. Requires Windows 98, Windows NT 4.0, or later.
JapaneseEnvelopeKakuNumber3Rotated	Japanese rotated Kaku #3 envelope. Requires Windows 98, Windows NT 4.0, or later.
JapaneseEnvelopeYouNumber4	Japanese You #4 envelope. Requires Windows 98, Windows NT 4.0, or later.
JapaneseEnvelopeYouNumber4Rotated	Japanese You #4 rotated envelope. Requires Windows 98, Windows NT 4.0, or later.
JapanesePostcard	Japanese postcard (100 mm by 148 mm).
JapanesePostcardRotated	Japanese rotated postcard (148 mm by 100 mm). Requires Windows 98, Windows NT 4.0, or later.
Ledger	Ledger paper (17 in. by 11 in.).
Legal	Legal paper (8.5 in. by 14 in.).
LegalExtra	Legal extra paper (9.275 in. by 15 in.). This value is specific to the PostScript driver and is used only by Linotronic printers in order to conserve paper.
Letter	Letter paper (8.5 in. by 11 in.).
LetterExtra	Letter extra paper (9.275 in. by 12 in.). This value is specific to the PostScript driver and is used only by Linotronic printers in order to conserve paper.
LetterExtraTransverse	Letter extra transverse paper (9.275 in. by 12 in.).
LetterPlus	Letter plus paper (8.5 in. by 12.69 in.).
LetterRotated	Letter rotated paper (11 in. by 8.5 in.).
LetterSmall	Letter small paper (8.5 in. by 11 in.).
LetterTransverse	Letter transverse paper (8.275 in. by 11 in.).
MonarchEnvelope	Monarch envelope (3.875 in. by 7.5 in.).
Note	Note paper (8.5 in. by 11 in.).

Table A-1. PaperKind Enumeration (Continued)

Member Name	Description
Number10Envelope	#10 envelope (4.125 in. by 9.5 in.).
Number11Envelope	#11 envelope (4.5 in. by 10.375 in.).
Number12Envelope	#12 envelope (4.75 in. by 11 in.).
Number14Envelope	#14 envelope (5 in. by 11.5 in.).
Number9Envelope	#9 envelope (3.875 in. by 8.875 in.).
PersonalEnvelope	6 3/4 envelope (3.625 in. by 6.5 in.).
Prc16K	People's Republic of China 16K paper (146 mm by 215 mm). Requires Windows 98, Windows NT 4.0, or later.
Prc16KRotated	People's Republic of China 16K rotated paper (146 mm by 215 mm). Requires Windows 98, Windows NT 4.0, or later.
Prc32K	People's Republic of China 32K paper (97 mm by 151 mm). Requires Windows 98, Windows NT 4.0, or later.
Prc32KBig	People's Republic of China 32K big paper (97 mm by 151 mm). Requires Windows 98, Windows NT 4.0, or later.
Prc32KBigRotated	People's Republic of China 32K big rotated paper (97 mm by 151 mm). Requires Windows 98, Windows NT 4.0, or later.
Prc32KRotated	People's Republic of China 32K rotated paper (97 mm by 151 mm). Requires Windows 98, Windows NT 4.0, or later.
PrcEnvelopeNumber1	People's Republic of China #1 envelope (102 mm by 165 mm). Requires Windows 98, Windows NT 4.0, or later.
PrcEnvelopeNumber10	People's Republic of China #10 envelope (324 mm by 458 mm). Requires Windows 98, Windows NT 4.0, or later.
PrcEnvelopeNumber10Rotated	People's Republic of China #10 rotated envelope (458 mm by 324 mm). Requires Windows 98, Windows NT 4.0, or later.
PrcEnvelopeNumber1Rotated	People's Republic of China #1 rotated envelope (165 mm by 102 mm). Requires Windows 98, Windows NT 4.0, or later.

Table A-1. PaperKind Enumeration (Continued)

Member Name	Description
PrcEnvelopeNumber2	People's Republic of China #2 envelope (102 mm by 176 mm). Requires Windows 98, Windows NT 4.0, or later.
PrcEnvelopeNumber2Rotated	People's Republic of China #2 rotated envelope (176 mm by 102 mm). Requires Windows 98, Windows NT 4.0, or later.
PrcEnvelopeNumber3	People's Republic of China #3 envelope (125 mm by 176 mm). Requires Windows 98, Windows NT 4.0, or later.
PrcEnvelopeNumber3Rotated	People's Republic of China #3 rotated envelope (176 mm by 125 mm). Requires Windows 98, Windows NT 4.0, or later.
PrcEnvelopeNumber4	People's Republic of China #4 envelope (110 mm by 208 mm). Requires Windows 98, Windows NT 4.0, or later.
PrcEnvelopeNumber4Rotated	People's Republic of China #4 rotated envelope (208 mm by 110 mm). Requires Windows 98, Windows NT 4.0, or later.
PrcEnvelopeNumber5	People's Republic of China #5 envelope (110 mm by 220 mm). Requires Windows 98, Windows NT 4.0, or later.
PrcEnvelopeNumber5Rotated	People's Republic of China Envelope #5 rotated envelope (220 mm by 110 mm). Requires Windows 98, Windows NT 4.0, or later.
PrcEnvelopeNumber6	People's Republic of China #6 envelope (120 mm by 230 mm). Requires Windows 98, Windows NT 4.0, or later.
PrcEnvelopeNumber6Rotated	People's Republic of China #6 rotated envelope (230 mm by 120 mm). Requires Windows 98, Windows NT 4.0, or later.
PrcEnvelopeNumber7	People's Republic of China #7 envelope (160 mm by 230 mm). Requires Windows 98, Windows NT 4.0, or later.
PrcEnvelopeNumber7Rotated	People's Republic of China #7 rotated envelope (230 mm by 160 mm). Requires Windows 98, Windows NT 4.0, or later.

Table A-1. PaperKind Enumeration (Continued)

Member Name	Description
PrcEnvelopeNumber8	People's Republic of China #8 envelope (120 mm by 309 mm). Requires Windows 98, Windows NT 4.0, or later.
PrcEnvelopeNumber8Rotated	People's Republic of China #8 rotated envelope (309 mm by 120 mm). Requires Windows 98, Windows NT 4.0, or later.
PrcEnvelopeNumber9	People's Republic of China #9 envelope (229 mm by 324 mm). Requires Windows 98, Windows NT 4.0, or later.
PrcEnvelopeNumber9Rotated	People's Republic of China #9 rotated envelope (324 mm by 229 mm). Requires Windows 98, Windows NT 4.0, or later.
Quarto	Quarto paper (215 mm by 275 mm).
Standard10×11	Standard paper (10 in. by 11 in.).
Standard10×14	Standard paper (10 in. by 14 in.).
Standard11×17	Standard paper (11 in. by 17 in.).
Standard12×11	Standard paper (12 in. by 11 in.). Requires Windows 98, Windows NT 4.0, or later.
Standard15×11	Standard paper (15 in. by 11 in.).
Standard9×11	Standard paper (9 in. by 11 in.).
Statement	Statement paper (5.5 in. by 8.5 in.).
Tabloid	Tabloid paper (11 in. by 17 in.).
TabloidExtra	Tabloid extra paper (11.69 in. by 18 in.). This value is specific to the PostScript driver and is used only by Linotronic printers in order to conserve paper.
USStandardFanfold	US standard fanfold (14.875 in. by 11 in.).

Table A-2 shows the different hatch styles available to you. You use these hatch styles when making a HatchBrush. Chapters 4 and 5 used HatchBrushes for different effects.

Table A-2. HatchBrush HatchStyle Enumeration

Member Name	Description
BackwardDiagonal	A pattern of lines on a diagonal from upper right to lower left.
Cross	Specifies horizontal and vertical lines that cross.
DarkDownwardDiagonal	Specifies diagonal lines that slant to the right from top points to bottom points, are spaced 50 percent closer together than and are twice the width of ForwardDiagonal. This hatch pattern is not antialiased.
DarkHorizontal	Specifies horizontal lines that are spaced 50 percent closer together than Horizontal and are twice the width of HatchStyleHorizontal.
DarkUpwardDiagonal	Specifies diagonal lines that slant to the left from top points to bottom points, are spaced 50 percent closer together than BackwardDiagonal and are twice its width, but the lines are not antialiased.
DarkVertical	Specifies vertical lines that are spaced 50 percent closer together than Vertical and are twice its width.
DashedDownwardDiagonal	Specifies dashed diagonal lines that slant to the right from top points to bottom points.
DashedHorizontal	Specifies dashed horizontal lines.
DashedUpwardDiagonal	Specifies dashed diagonal lines that slant to the left from top points to bottom points.
DashedVertical	Specifies dashed vertical lines.
DiagonalBrick	Specifies a hatch that has the appearance of layered bricks that slant to the left from top points to bottom points.
DiagonalCross	Specifies forward diagonal and backward diagonal lines that cross. The lines are antialiased.
Divot	Specifies a hatch that has the appearance of divots.
DottedDiamond	Specifies forward diagonal and backward diagonal lines, each of which is composed of dots, that cross.

Table A-2. HatchBrush HatchStyle Enumeration (Continued)

Member Name	Description
DottedGrid	Specifies horizontal and vertical lines, each of which is composed of dots, that cross.
ForwardDiagonal	A pattern of lines on a diagonal from upper left to lower right.
Horizontal	A pattern of horizontal lines.
HorizontalBrick	Specifies a hatch that has the appearance of horizontally layered bricks.
LargeCheckerBoard	Specifies a hatch that has the appearance of a checkerboard with squares that are twice the size of SmallCheckerBoard.
LargeConfetti	Specifies a hatch that has the appearance of confetti and is composed of larger pieces than SmallConfetti.
LargeGrid	Specifies the hatch style Cross.
LightDownwardDiagonal	
LightHorizontal	Specifies horizontal lines that are spaced 50 percent closer together than Horizontal.
LightUpwardDiagonal	Specifies diagonal lines that slant to the left from top points to bottom points and are spaced 50 percent closer together than BackwardDiagonal, but they are not antialiased.
LightVertical	Specifies vertical lines that are spaced 50 percent closer together than Vertical.
Max	Specifies the hatch style SolidDiamond.
Min	Specifies the hatch style Horizontal.
NarrowHorizontal	Specifies horizontal lines that are spaced 75 percent closer together than the hatch style Horizontal (or 25 percent closer together than LightHorizontal).
NarrowVertical	Specifies vertical lines that are spaced 75 percent closer together than the hatch style Vertical (or 25 percent closer together than LightVertical).
OutlinedDiamond	Specifies forward diagonal and backward diagonal lines that cross but are not antialiased.

Table A-2. HatchBrush HatchStyle Enumeration (Continued)

Member Name	Description
Percent05	Specifies a 5 percent hatch. The ratio of foreground color to background color is 5:100.
Percent10	Specifies a 10 percent hatch. The ratio of foreground color to background color is 10:100.
Percent20	Specifies a 20 percent hatch. The ratio of foreground color to background color is 20:100.
Percent25	Specifies a 25 percent hatch. The ratio of foreground color to background color is 25:100.
Percent30	Specifies a 30 percent hatch. The ratio of foreground color to background color is 30:100.
Percent40	Specifies a 40 percent hatch. The ratio of foreground color to background color is 40:100.
Percent50	Specifies a 50 percent hatch. The ratio of foreground color to background color is 50:100.
Percent60	Specifies a 60 percent hatch. The ratio of foreground color to background color is 60:100.
Percent70	Specifies a 70 percent hatch. The ratio of foreground color to background color is 70:100.
Percent75	Specifies a 75 percent hatch. The ratio of foreground color to background color is 75:100.
Percent80	Specifies an 80 percent hatch. The ratio of foreground color to background color is 80:100.
Percent90	Specifies a 90 percent hatch. The ratio of foreground color to background color is 90:100.
Plaid	Specifies a hatch that has the appearance of a plaid material.
Shingle	Specifies a hatch that has the appearance of diagonally layered shingles that slant to the right from top points to bottom points.

Table A-2. HatchBrush HatchStyle Enumeration (Continued)

Member Name	Description
SmallCheckerBoard	Specifies a hatch that has the appearance of a checkerboard.
SmallConfetti	Specifies a hatch that has the appearance of confetti.
SmallGrid	Specifies horizontal and vertical lines that cross and are spaced 50 percent closer together than the hatch style Cross.
SolidDiamond	Specifies a hatch that has the appearance of a checkerboard placed diagonally.
Sphere	Specifies a hatch that has the appearance of spheres laid adjacent to one another.
Trellis	Specifies a hatch that has the appearance of a trellis.
Vertical	A pattern of vertical lines.
Wave	Specifies horizontal lines that are composed of tildes.
Weave	Specifies a hatch that has the appearance of a woven material.
WideDownwardDiagonal	Specifies diagonal lines that slant to the right from top points to bottom points, have the same spacing as the hatch style ForwardDiagonal and are triple its width, but are not antialiased.
WideUpwardDiagonal	Specifies diagonal lines that slant to the left from top points to bottom points, have the same spacing as the hatch style BackwardDiagonal and are triple its width, but are not antialiased.
ZigZag	Specifies horizontal lines that are composed of zigzags.

The enumeration in Table A-3 specifies the format flags for the StringFormatFlags. These members can be bitwise combined to provide an unnamed combination attribute. Chapter 7 was all about drawing text on the screen. I used this enumeration in a few examples in Chapter 7.

Table A-3. StringFormatFlags Enumeration

Member Name	Description
DirectionRightToLeft	Specifies that text is right to left.
DirectionVertical	Specifies that text is vertical.
DisplayFormatControl	Causes control characters, such as the left-to-right mark, to be shown in the output with a representative glyph.
FitBlackBox	Specifies that no part of any glyph overhangs the bounding rectangle. By default, some glyphs overhang the rectangle slightly where necessary to appear at the edge visually. For example, when an italic lowercase letter *f* in a font such as Garamond is aligned at the far left of a rectangle, the lower part of the *f* will reach slightly further left than the left edge of the rectangle. Setting this flag will ensure no painting outside the rectangle but will cause the aligned edges of adjacent lines of text to appear uneven.
LineLimit	Only entire lines are laid out in the formatting rectangle. By default, layout continues until the end of the text or until no more lines are visible as a result of clipping—whichever comes first. Note that the default settings allow the last line to be partially obscured by a formatting rectangle that is not a whole multiple of the line height. To ensure that only whole lines are seen, specify this value and be careful to provide a formatting rectangle at least as tall as the height of one line.
MeasureTrailingSpaces	By default, the boundary rectangle returned by the **MeasureString** method excludes the space at the end of each line. Set this flag to include that space in measurement.
NoClip	Overhanging parts of glyphs and unwrapped text reaching outside the formatting rectangle are allowed to show. By default, all text and glyph parts reaching outside the formatting rectangle are clipped.
NoFontFallback	Disables fallback to alternate fonts for characters not supported in the requested font. Any missing characters are displayed with the font's missing glyph (usually an open square).

Table A-3. StringFormatFlags Enumeration (Continued)

Member Name	Description
NoWrap	Disables wrapping of text between lines when formatting within a rectangle. This flag is implied when a point is passed instead of a rectangle or when the specified rectangle has a zero line length.

The enumerations in Tables A-4 through A-6 deal with fonts. You will find the following three enumerations handy pretty much anytime you want to print something to the screen: FontStyle (Table A-4), TextRenderingHint (Table A-5), and GenericFontFamilies (Table A-6).

Table A-4. FontStyle Enumeration

Member Name	Description
Bold	Bold text
Italic	Italic text
Regular	Normal text
Strikeout	Text with a line through the middle
Underline	Underlined text

Table A-5. TextRenderingHint Enumeration

Member Name	Description
AntiAlias	Specifies that each character is drawn using its antialiased glyph bitmap without hinting. Better quality due to antialiasing. Stem width differences may be noticeable because hinting is turned off.
AntiAliasGridFit	Specifies that each character is drawn using its antialiased glyph bitmap with hinting. Much better quality due to antialiasing, but at a higher performance cost.
ClearTypeGridFit	Specifies that each character is drawn using its glyph CT bitmap with hinting. The highest quality setting. Used to take advantage of ClearType font features.

Table A-5. TextRenderingHint Enumeration (Continued)

Member Name	Description
SingleBitPerPixel	Specifies that each character is drawn using its glyph bitmap. Hinting is not used.
SingleBitPerPixelGridFit	Specifies that each character is drawn using its glyph bitmap. Hinting is used to improve character appearance on stems and curvature.
SystemDefault	Specifies that each character is drawn using its glyph bitmap, with the system default rendering hint. The text will be drawn using whatever font smoothing settings the user has selected for the system.

Table A-6. GenericFontFamilies Enumeration

Member Name	Description
Monospace	A generic Monospace FontFamily object
SansSerif	A generic Sans Serif FontFamily object
Serif	A generic Serif FontFamily object

Index

Symbols and Numbers

A

B

Apress Titles

ISBN	PRICE	AUTHOR	TITLE
1-893115-73-9	$34.95	Abbott	Voice Enabling Web Applications: VoiceXML and Beyond
1-893115-01-1	$39.95	Appleman	Dan Appleman's Win32 API Puzzle Book and Tutorial for Visual Basic Programmers
1-893115-23-2	$29.95	Appleman	How Computer Programming Works
1-893115-97-6	$39.95	Appleman	Moving to VB .NET: Strategies, Concepts, and Code
1-59059-023-6	$39.95	Baker	Adobe Acrobat 5: The Professional User's Guide
1-59059-039-2	$49.95	Barnaby	Distributed .NET Programming
1-893115-09-7	$29.95	Baum	Dave Baum's Definitive Guide to LEGO MINDSTORMS
1-893115-84-4	$29.95	Baum, Gasperi, Hempel, and Villa	Extreme MINDSTORMS: An Advanced Guide to LEGO MINDSTORMS
1-893115-82-8	$59.95	Ben-Gan/Moreau	Advanced Transact-SQL for SQL Server 2000
1-893115-91-7	$39.95	Birmingham/Perry	Software Development on a Leash
1-893115-48-8	$29.95	Bischof	The .NET Languages: A Quick Translation Guide
1-59059-041-4	$49.95	Bock	CIL Programming: Under the Hood of .NET
1-893115-67-4	$49.95	Borge	Managing Enterprise Systems with the Windows Script Host
1-59059-019-8	$49.95	Cagle	SVG Programming: The Graphical Web
1-893115-28-3	$44.95	Challa/Laksberg	Essential Guide to Managed Extensions for C++
1-893115-39-9	$44.95	Chand	A Programmer's Guide to ADO.NET in C#
1-893115-44-5	$29.95	Cook	Robot Building for Beginners
1-893115-99-2	$39.95	Cornell/Morrison	Programming VB .NET: A Guide for Experienced Programmers
1-893115-72-0	$39.95	Curtin	Developing Trust: Online Privacy and Security
1-59059-014-7	$44.95	Drol	Object-Oriented Macromedia Flash MX
1-59059-008-2	$29.95	Duncan	The Career Programmer: Guerilla Tactics for an Imperfect World
1-893115-71-2	$39.95	Ferguson	Mobile .NET
1-893115-90-9	$49.95	Finsel	The Handbook for Reluctant Database Administrators
1-59059-024-4	$49.95	Fraser	Real World ASP.NET: Building a Content Management System
1-893115-42-9	$44.95	Foo/Lee	XML Programming Using the Microsoft XML Parser
1-893115-55-0	$34.95	Frenz	Visual Basic and Visual Basic .NET for Scientists and Engineers
1-893115-85-2	$34.95	Gilmore	A Programmer's Introduction to PHP 4.0
1-893115-36-4	$34.95	Goodwill	Apache Jakarta-Tomcat
1-893115-17-8	$59.95	Gross	A Programmer's Introduction to Windows DNA
1-893115-62-3	$39.95	Gunnerson	A Programmer's Introduction to C#, Second Edition
1-59059-009-0	$49.95	Harris/Macdonald	Moving to ASP.NET: Web Development with VB .NET
1-893115-30-5	$49.95	Harkins/Reid	SQL: Access to SQL Server
1-893115-10-0	$34.95	Holub	Taming Java Threads
1-893115-04-6	$34.95	Hyman/Vaddadi	Mike and Phani's Essential C++ Techniques
1-893115-96-8	$59.95	Jorelid	J2EE FrontEnd Technologies: A Programmer's Guide to Servlets, JavaServer Pages, and Enterprise JavaBeans
1-893115-49-6	$39.95	Kilburn	Palm Programming in Basic
1-893115-50-X	$34.95	Knudsen	Wireless Java: Developing with Java 2, Micro Edition
1-893115-79-8	$49.95	Kofler	Definitive Guide to Excel VBA
1-893115-57-7	$39.95	Kofler	MySQL
1-893115-87-9	$39.95	Kurata	Doing Web Development: Client-Side Techniques

ISBN	PRICE	AUTHOR	TITLE
1-893115-75-5	$44.95	Kurniawan	Internet Programming with VB
1-893115-38-0	$24.95	Lafler	Power AOL: A Survival Guide
1-893115-46-1	$36.95	Lathrop	Linux in Small Business: A Practical User's Guide
1-893115-19-4	$49.95	Macdonald	Serious ADO: Universal Data Access with Visual Basic
1-59059-044-9	$49.95	MacDonald	User Interfaces in VB .NET: Windows Forms and Custom Controls
1-893115-06-2	$39.95	Marquis/Smith	A Visual Basic 6.0 Programmer's Toolkit
1-893115-22-4	$27.95	McCarter	David McCarter's VB Tips and Techniques
1-59059-021-X	$34.95	Moore	Karl Moore's Visual Basic .NET: The Tutorials
1-893115-76-3	$49.95	Morrison	C++ For VB Programmers
1-59059-003-1	$39.95	Nakhimovsky/Meyers	XML Programming: Web Applications and Web Services with JSP and ASP
1-893115-80-1	$39.95	Newmarch	A Programmer's Guide to Jini Technology
1-893115-58-5	$49.95	Oellermann	Architecting Web Services
1-59059-020-1	$44.95	Patzer	JSP Examples and Best Practices
1-893115-81-X	$39.95	Pike	SQL Server: Common Problems, Tested Solutions
1-59059-017-1	$34.95	Rainwater	Herding Cats: A Primer for Programmers Who Lead Programmers
1-59059-025-2	$49.95	Rammer	Advanced .NET Remoting
1-893115-20-8	$34.95	Rischpater	Wireless Web Development
1-893115-93-3	$34.95	Rischpater	Wireless Web Development with PHP and WAP
1-893115-89-5	$59.95	Shemitz	Kylix: The Professional Developer's Guide and Reference
1-893115-40-2	$39.95	Sill	The qmail Handbook
1-893115-24-0	$49.95	Sinclair	From Access to SQL Server
1-893115-94-1	$29.95	Spolsky	User Interface Design for Programmers
1-893115-53-4	$44.95	Sweeney	Visual Basic for Testers
1-59059-002-3	$44.95	Symmonds	Internationalization and Localization Using Microsoft .NET
1-59059-010-4	$54.95	Thomsen	Database Programming with C#
1-893115-29-1	$44.95	Thomsen	Database Programming with Visual Basic .NET
1-893115-65-8	$39.95	Tiffany	Pocket PC Database Development with eMbedded Visual Basic
1-893115-59-3	$59.95	Troelsen	C# and the .NET Platform
1-59059-011-2	$59.95	Troelsen	COM and .NET Interoperability
1-893115-26-7	$59.95	Troelsen	Visual Basic .NET and the .NET Platform
1-893115-54-2	$49.95	Trueblood/Lovett	Data Mining and Statistical Analysis Using SQL
1-893115-68-2	$54.95	Vaughn	ADO.NET and ADO Examples and Best Practices for VB Programmers, Second Edition
1-59059-012-0	$49.95	Vaughn/Blackburn	ADO.NET Examples and Best Practices for C# Programmers
1-893115-83-6	$44.95	Wells	Code Centric: T-SQL Programming with Stored Procedures and Triggers
1-893115-95-X	$49.95	Welschenbach	Cryptography in C and C++
1-893115-05-4	$39.95	Williamson	Writing Cross-Browser Dynamic HTML
1-893115-78-X	$49.95	Zukowski	Definitive Guide to Swing for Java 2, Second Edition
1-893115-92-5	$49.95	Zukowski	Java Collections
1-893115-98-4	$54.95	Zukowski	Learn Java with JBuilder 6

Available at bookstores nationwide or from Springer Verlag New York, Inc. at 1-800-777-4643; fax 1-212-533-3503. Contact us for more information at sales@apress.com.

Apress Titles Publishing SOON!

ISBN	AUTHOR	TITLE
1-59059-022-8	Alapati	Expert Oracle 9i Database Administration
1-59059-053-8	Bock/Stromquist/ Fischer/Smith	.NET Security
1-59059-015-5	Clark	An Introduction to Object Oriented Programming with Visual Basic .NET
1-59059-000-7	Cornell	Programming C#
1-59059-056-2	Cornell	Programming VB .NET, Second Edition
1-59059-043-0	Ezzio	Using and Understanding Java Data Objects
1-59059-033-3	Fraser	Managed C++ and .NET Development
1-59059-038-4	Gibbons	.NET Development for Java Programmers
1-59059-030-9	Habibi/Camerlengo/ Patterson	The Sun Certified Java Developer Exam with J2SE 1.4
1-59059-006-6	Hetland	Instant Python with Ten Instant Projects
1-59059-029-5	Kampa/Bell	Unix Storage Management
1-59059-049-X	Lakshman	Oracle 9i PL/SQL Application Development
1-59059-045-7	MacDonald	User Interfaces in C#: Windows Forms and Custom Controls
1-893115-27-5	Morrill	Tuning and Customizing a Linux System
1-59059-050-3	Pearce	Debugging VB .NET Development
1-59059-028-7	Rischpater	Wireless Web Development, Second Edition
1-59059-026-0	Smith	Writing Add-Ins for Visual Studio.NET
1-893115-43-7	Stephenson	Standard VB: An Enterprise Developer's Reference for VB 6 and VB .NET
1-59059-035-X	Symmonds	GDI+ Programming in C# and VB .NET
1-59059-032-5	Thomsen	Database Programming with Visual Basic .NET, Second Edition
1-59059-007-4	Thomsen/Dunn	Building Web Services with VB .NET
1-59059-042-2	Thomsen/Hansen	Enterprise Development with Visual Studio .NET, UML and MSF
1-59059-027-9	Torkelson/Petersen/ Torkelson	Programming the Web with Visual Basic .NET
1-59059-018-X	Tregar	Writing Perl Modules for CPAN
1-59059-055-4	Troelsen	C# and the .NET Platform, Second Edition
1-59059-047-3	Zukowski	Definitive Guide to Swing for Java 2, Third Edition

Available at bookstores nationwide or from Springer Verlag New York, Inc. at 1-800-777-4643; fax 1-212-533-3503. Contact us for more information at sales@apress.com.

books for professionals by professionals™

About Apress

Apress, located in Berkeley, CA, is a fast-growing, innovative publishing company devoted to meeting the needs of existing and potential programming professionals. Simply put, the "A" in Apress stands for *"The Author's Press*™*"* and its books have *"The Expert's Voice*™*."* Apress' unique approach to publishing grew out of conversations between its founders Gary Cornell and Dan Appleman, authors of numerous best-selling, highly regarded books for programming professionals. In 1998 they set out to create a publishing company that emphasized quality above all else. Gary and Dan's vision has resulted in the publication of over 50 titles by leading software professionals, all of which have *The Expert's Voice*™.

Do You Have What It Takes to Write for Apress?

Apress is rapidly expanding its publishing program. If you can write and refuse to compromise on the quality of your work, if you believe in doing more than rehashing existing documentation, and if you're looking for opportunities and rewards that go far beyond those offered by traditional publishing houses, we want to hear from you!

Consider these innovations that we offer all of our authors:

- **Top royalties with _no_ hidden switch statements**
  Authors typically only receive half of their normal royalty rate on foreign sales. In contrast, Apress' royalty rate remains the same for both foreign and domestic sales.

- **A mechanism for authors to obtain equity in Apress**
  Unlike the software industry, where stock options are essential to motivate and retain software professionals, the publishing industry has adhered to an outdated compensation model based on royalties alone. In the spirit of most software companies, Apress reserves a significant portion of its equity for authors.

- **Serious treatment of the technical review process**
  Each Apress book has a technical reviewing team whose remuneration depends in part on the success of the book since they too receive royalties.

Moreover, through a partnership with Springer-Verlag, New York, Inc., one of the world's major publishing houses, Apress has significant venture capital behind it. Thus, we have the resources to produce the highest quality books *and* market them aggressively.

If you fit the model of the Apress author who can write a book that gives the "professional what he or she needs to know™," then please contact one of our Editorial Directors, Gary Cornell (gary_cornell@apress.com), Dan Appleman (dan_appleman@apress.com), Peter Blackburn (peter_blackburn@apress.com), Jason Gilmore (jason_gilmore@apress.com), Karen Watterson (karen_watterson@apress.com), or John Zukowski (john_zukowski@apress.com) for more information.